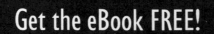

Get the eBook FREE!

(PDF, ePub, Kindle, and liveBook all included)

We believe that once you buy a book from us, you should be able to read it in any format we have available. To get electronic versions of this book at no additional cost to you, purchase and then register this book at the Manning website.

Go to https://www.manning.com/freebook and follow the instructions to complete your pBook registration.

That's it!
Thanks from Manning!

Svelte and Sapper in Action

Svelte and Sapper
in Action

R. MARK VOLKMANN

MANNING

SHELTER ISLAND

For online information and ordering of this and other Manning books, please visit www.manning.com. The publisher offers discounts on this book when ordered in quantity. For more information, please contact

Special Sales Department
Manning Publications Co.
20 Baldwin Road
PO Box 761
Shelter Island, NY 11964
Email: orders@manning.com

Manning Publications Co.
20 Baldwin Road
PO Box 761
Shelter Island, NY 11964

Development editor:	Jenny Stout
Technical development editor:	Alain Couniot
Review editor:	Mihaela Batinic
Production editor:	Lori Weidert
Copy editor:	Andy Carroll
Proofreader:	Keri Hales
Technical proofreader:	Erik Vullings
Typesetter:	Dennis Dalinnik
Cover designer:	Marija Tudor

ISBN: 9781617297946
Printed in the United States of America

brief contents

PART 1 GETTING STARTED 1

    1 ▪ Meet the players   3

    2 ▪ Your first Svelte app   19

PART 2 DEEPER INTO SVELTE 41

    3 ▪ Creating components   43

    4 ▪ Block structures   64

    5 ▪ Component communication   82

    6 ▪ Stores   106

    7 ▪ DOM interactions   124

    8 ▪ Lifecycle functions   141

    9 ▪ Client-side routing   152

    10 ▪ Animation   170

    11 ▪ Debugging   190

    12 ▪ Testing   198

    13 ▪ Deploying   235

    14 ▪ Advanced Svelte   242

PART 3   DEEPER INTO SAPPER 261

           15 ▪ Your first Sapper app   263
           16 ▪ Sapper applications   271
           17 ▪ Sapper server routes   289
           18 ▪ Exporting static sites with Sapper   307
           19 ▪ Sapper offline support   321

PART 4   BEYOND SVELTE AND SAPPER 341

           20 ▪ Preprocessors   343
           21 ▪ Svelte Native   356

  appendix A ▪ Resources   391
  appendix B ▪ Calling REST services   397
  appendix C ▪ MongoDB   400
  appendix D ▪ ESLint for Svelte   407
  appendix E ▪ Prettier for Svelte   409
  appendix F ▪ VS Code   411
  appendix G ▪ Snowpack   415

contents

preface xv
acknowledgments xvi
about this book xviii
about the author xxiii
about the cover illustration xxiv

PART 1 GETTING STARTED 1

1 Meet the players 3

1.1 Introducing Svelte 4

*Why Svelte? 4 ▪ Rethinking reactivity 9 ▪ Current issues in
Svelte 11 ▪ How does Svelte work? 11 ▪ Does Svelte
disappear? 13*

1.2 Introducing Sapper 13

*Why consider Sapper? 14 ▪ How does Sapper work? 15 ▪ When
should Sapper be used? 16 ▪ When should Sapper not be used? 16*

1.3 Introducing Svelte Native 16

1.4 How does Svelte compare with other web
frameworks? 17

Angular 17 ▪ React 17 ▪ Vue 17

1.5 What tools are needed to get started? 18

2 *Your first Svelte app*   *19*

2.1 The Svelte REPL   20

*Using the Svelte REPL   20 ▪ Your first REPL app   22
Saving REPL apps   26 ▪ Sharing REPL apps   28
REPL URLs   28 ▪ Exporting REPL apps   29 ▪ Using npm
packages   29 ▪ REPL limitations   30 ▪ CodeSandbox   30*

2.2 Working outside the REPL   31

*Starting with npx degit   31 ▪ Provided package.json   33
Important files   33 ▪ Your first non-REPL app   35*

2.3 Bonus app   37

PART 2 DEEPER INTO SVELTE 41

3 *Creating components*   *43*

3.1 Content of .svelte files   44

3.2 Component markup   45

3.3 Component names   47

3.4 Component styles   48

3.5 CSS specificity   49

3.6 Scoped vs. global styles   50

3.7 Using CSS preprocessors   53

3.8 Component logic   53

3.9 Component state   54

3.10 Reactive statements   55

3.11 Module context   57

3.12 Building a custom component   59

3.13 Building the Travel Packing app   60

4 *Block structures*   *64*

4.1 Conditional logic with {#if}   65

4.2 Iteration with {#each}   66

4.3 Promises with {#await}   67

4.4 Building the Travel Packing app   70

*Item component   71 ▪ Utility functions   73 ▪ Category
component   73 ▪ Checklist component   76 ▪ App
component   79 ▪ Try it   80*

5   *Component communication   82*

   5.1   Component communication options   83
   5.2   Props   83

        *Props go in with export   84 ▪ Reacting to prop changes   86
        Prop types   86 ▪ Directives   87 ▪ The bind directive on form
        elements   88 ▪ bind:this   90 ▪ Props go out with bind   92*

   5.3   Slots   96
   5.4   Events   97

        *Event dispatching   97 ▪ Event forwarding   99 ▪ Event
        modifiers   99*

   5.5   Context   100
   5.6   Building the Travel Packing app   101

6   *Stores   106*

   6.1   Writable stores   107
   6.2   Readable stores   108
   6.3   Where to define stores   109
   6.4   Using stores   109
   6.5   Derived stores   116
   6.6   Custom stores   117
   6.7   Using stores with classes   118
   6.8   Persisting stores   122
   6.9   Building the Travel Packing app   123

7   *DOM interactions   124*

   7.1   Inserting HTML   125
   7.2   Actions   128
   7.3   The tick function   129
   7.4   Implementing a dialog component   132
   7.5   Drag and drop   135
   7.6   Building the Travel Packing app   137

8   *Lifecycle functions   141*

   8.1   Setup   142
   8.2   The onMount lifecycle function   143

        Moving focus   143 ▪ Retrieving data from an API service   144

8.3   The onDestroy lifecycle function   145

8.4   The beforeUpdate lifecycle function   146

8.5   The afterUpdate lifecycle function   147

8.6   Using helper functions   148

8.7   Building the Travel Packing app   150

9   Client-side routing   152

9.1   Manual routing   153

9.2   Hash routing   160

9.3   Using the page.js library   162

9.4   Using path and query parameters with page.js   164

9.5   Building the Travel Packing app   167

10   Animation   170

10.1   Easing functions   171

10.2   The svelte/animate package   172

10.3   The svelte/motion package   174

10.4   The svelte/transition package   177

10.5   The fade transition and flip animation   179

10.6   The crossfade transition   181

10.7   The draw transition   183

10.8   Custom transitions   184

10.9   The transition vs. in and out props   186

10.10   Transition events   186

10.11   Building the Travel Packing app   187

11   Debugging   190

11.1   The @debug tag   191

11.2   Reactive statements   193

11.3   Svelte Devtools   194

12   Testing   198

12.1   Unit tests with Jest   199

Unit tests for the Todo app   201 ▪ Unit tests for the Travel Packing app   203

12.2 End-to-end tests with Cypress 208

End-to-end tests for the Todo app 210 ▪ End-to-end tests for the Travel Packing app 211

12.3 Accessibility tests 216

Svelte compiler 217 ▪ Lighthouse 217 ▪ axe 220 WAVE 223

12.4 Component demos and debugging with Storybook 225

Storybook for Travel Packing app 227

13 **Deploying 235**

13.1 Deploying to any HTTP server 236

13.2 Using Netlify 236

Netlify from the website 237 ▪ Netlify from the command line 238 ▪ Netlify plans 239

13.3 Using Vercel 239

Vercel from the website 240 ▪ Vercel from the command line 240 Vercel tiers 241

13.4 Using Docker 241

14 **Advanced Svelte 242**

14.1 Form validation 243

14.2 Using CSS libraries 247

14.3 Special elements 250

14.4 Importing JSON files 254

14.5 Creating component libraries 254

14.6 Web components 256

PART 3 DEEPER INTO SAPPER 261

15 **Your first Sapper app 263**

15.1 Creating a new Sapper app 265

15.2 Recreating the shopping app with Sapper 266

16 **Sapper applications 271**

16.1 Sapper file structure 272

16.2 Page routes 275

16.3   Page layouts   276
16.4   Handling errors   279
16.5   Running on both server and client   279
16.6   Fetch API wrapper   280
16.7   Preloading   280
16.8   Prefetching   282
16.9   Code splitting   284
16.10   Building the Travel Packing app   285

17 Sapper server routes   289
17.1   Server route source files   290
17.2   Server route functions   291
17.3   A create/retrieve/update/delete (CRUD) example   292
17.4   Switching to Express   299
17.5   Building the Travel Packing app   300

18 Exporting static sites with Sapper   307
18.1   Sapper details   308
18.2   When to export   308
18.3   Example app   309

19 Sapper offline support   321
19.1   Service worker overview   322
19.2   Caching strategies   323
19.3   Sapper service worker configuration   326
19.4   Service worker events   327
19.5   Managing service workers in Chrome   328
19.6   Enabling the use of HTTPS in the Sapper server   332
19.7   Verifying offline behavior   334
19.8   Building the Travel Packing app   335

PART 4 BEYOND SVELTE AND SAPPER 341

20 Preprocessors 343

20.1 Custom preprocessing 344

Using Webpack 345

20.2 The svelte-preprocess package 346

Auto-preprocessing mode 347 ▪ External files 347 ▪ Global styles 349 ▪ Using Sass 349 ▪ Using TypeScript 350 A VS Code tip 352

20.3 Using Markdown 352

20.4 Using multiple preprocessors 354

20.5 Image compression 354

21 Svelte Native 356

21.1 Provided components 357

Display components 357 ▪ Form components 358 Action components 358 ▪ Dialog components 359 Layout components 359 ▪ Navigation components 363

21.2 Getting started with Svelte Native 363

21.3 Developing Svelte Native apps locally 364

21.4 NativeScript styling 365

21.5 Predefined NativeScript CSS classes 366

21.6 NativeScript themes 368

21.7 Comprehensive example 368

21.8 NativeScript UI component library 385

21.9 Svelte Native issues 390

appendix A Resources 391
appendix B Calling REST services 397
appendix C MongoDB 400
appendix D ESLint for Svelte 407
appendix E Prettier for Svelte 409
appendix F VS Code 411
appendix G Snowpack 415

index 419

preface

I have been a professional software developer for 37 years and a web developer for around 10 years. My projects have used many technologies and frameworks, including raw DOM manipulation, jQuery, Ruby, Angular 1, React, Polymer, Angular 2+, Vue, Svelte, and probably some I have forgotten.

I place a high value on developer productivity. Unnecessary complexity really works against this. While I find many things to love about Svelte and Sapper, the main driver for me is their simplicity compared to other web development approaches. I know from my experience of using other frameworks that I am far more productive when using Svelte and Sapper.

My first exposure to Svelte came from watching a talk titled "Rethinking Reactivity" by the creator of Svelte, Rich Harris. It is a very compelling talk and definitely appealed to my desire to reduce the complexity of web development. That led me to dig in further, write a long article about Svelte, give talks at user groups, and expand to giving talks at conferences. The next logical step was to write this book!

The book covers nearly every topic related to Svelte and Sapper, and some that are only tangentially related. After reading this, you should be well-poised to use these tools in your next web development project.

acknowledgments

Many authors thank their spouses for the patience they showed during the writing process. The experience of writing this book has made clear to me the sacrifices involved. My wife Tami generously gave me lots of encouragement and time to complete this project. Thank you so much Tami for helping me to achieve the goal of finally writing a book!

Thanks to my Manning development editor, Jennifer Stout, who provided just the right amount of corrections, suggestions, encouragement, and compliments to keep me going. Seeing comments like "I love this!" mixed in with comments like "You need to explain why someone would want to do this" made the writing process so much more bearable.

Thanks to Manning technical editor Alain Couniot who continually pointed out when I wasn't being clear or was short on providing compelling examples. He also made sure I mentioned TypeScript wherever possible. The book is much better because of his feedback!

Thanks to Manning technical reviewer Erik Vullings. He tried many things in the example code that never crossed my mind to try and suggested many improvements in the text. His thoroughness was greatly appreciated!

Thanks to Peer Reynders, a volunteer MEAP reviewer who went through all the code examples with a fine-tooth comb and pointed out many ways I could improve it.

Thanks to reviewers who added their own takes on ways to improve the book: Adail Retamal, Amit Lamba, Clive Harber, Damian Esteban, David Cabrero Souto, David Paccoud, Dennis Reil, Gerd Klevesaat, Gustavo Filipe Ramos Gomes, Jonathan Cook,

Kelum Senanayake, Konstantinos Leimonis, Matteo Gildone, Potito Coluccelli, Robert Walsh, Rodney Weis, Sander Zegveld, Sergio Arbeo, and Tanya Wilke. More eyes and more opinions definitely helped!

Thanks to Charles Sharp of Object Computing, Inc. He has been the most frequent editor of all my previous writings. Charles donated large amounts of time over past 10 plus years to making me a better writer . . . Oxford comma and all!

Thanks to Eldon Ahrold of Object Computing, Inc. for reviewing the chapter on Svelte Native. Eldon is a very experienced mobile and web developer, and I'm lucky to be able to bounce ideas off of him.

Finally, thanks to Dr. Ebrahim Moshiri who hired me into Object Computing, Inc. 24 years ago. He provided me with an environment that encourages continual learning and I've never stopped. I most likely would not have been in a position to write this book if it wasn't for the career he gave me.

about this book

Who should read this book

Svelte and Sapper in Action is for web developers who want to increase their productivity. Maybe you have a nagging suspicion that there must be an easier way to develop web applications. Good news—there is, and you will learn about it here!

Through numerous code examples, you will learn how to use Svelte and Sapper to implement many common features of web applications.

The book assumes that readers have a basic familiarity with HTML, CSS, and JavaScript:

- On the topic of HTML, readers should be familiar with elements like html, head, link, style, script, body, div, span, p, ol, ul, li, input, textarea, and select.
- On the topic of CSS, readers should understand the syntax of CSS rules, the CSS meaning of "cascade," basic CSS selectors (including element names, class names, ids, descendants, and children), commonly used CSS properties (including color, font-family, font-size, font-style, and font-weight), and the CSS box model (content, padding, border, and margin).
- On the topic of JavaScript, readers should know about variables, strings, arrays, objects, functions, classes, Promises, destructuring, the spread operator, exports, and imports.

I am easy to find online, should you have questions about anything in the book. My hope is that by the time you make it through this book, you will be convinced that there is something special about Svelte and Sapper. These are technologies that deserve a shot at being used in your next project.

How this book is organized: A roadmap

This book is divided into 4 parts containing a total of 21 chapters.

Part 1 introduces Svelte and Sapper.

- Chapter 1 explains why these approaches to web development deserve your attention. It concludes with a brief introduction to Svelte Native, a comparison of Svelte to other popular web frameworks, and a description of the tools you will need to get started.
- Chapter 2 walks you through building your first Svelte applications using an online tool (called the "REPL"). Apps built this way can be saved, shared with others, and exported to continue development locally. Then the steps for developing Svelte apps locally are described.

Part 2 dives deep into Svelte, providing thorough coverage along with lots of example code.

- Chapter 3 teaches you how to build Svelte components. This includes the logic, markup, and styling. Then it covers managing component state, using reactive statements, and using module context. Finally, an example of developing and using a custom component is presented.
- Chapter 4 covers Svelte block structures that wrap conditional logic, iteration, and promise handling around markup, which is typically HTML. Conditional logic is implemented using {#if}, iteration is implemented using {#each}, and promise handling is implemented using {#await}.
- Chapter 5 explores several options for communicating between components. These include using props, two-way binding, slots, events, and context.
- Chapter 6 describes the use of stores to share state between components. There are four kinds of stores: writable, readable, derived, and custom. Then techniques for using stores with JavaScript classes and persisting store data are described.
- Chapter 7 shows various approaches to interacting with the DOM in Svelte components. This includes inserting HTML, using "actions" to gain access to DOM elements, and using the tick function to manually modify the DOM after Svelte updates it. Finally, approaches to implementing dialog boxes and drag-and-drop are presented.
- Chapter 8 reviews the provided lifecycle functions that enable registering functions to be called at key points in the lifecycle of components. These include onMount, beforeUpdate, afterUpdate, and onDestroy. Finally, an approach to implementing custom lifecycle functions based on the provided lifecycle functions is presented.

- Chapter 9 demonstrates three approaches to adding page routing in Svelte applications: manual routing, hash routing, and using the page.js library. A shopping app is developed to demonstrate each of these options. Another popular approach is to use Sapper. Sapper routing is discussed in chapter 16.

- Chapter 10 explores the extensive support for animation that is built into Svelte. The packages svelte/animate, svelte/motion, and svelte/transition are described in detail. Two approaches to animating moving items between two lists are presented. One uses a combination of the `fade` transition and the `flip` animation. Another uses the `crossfade` transition. Finally, the creation of custom animations and using transition events is discussed.

- Chapter 11 shows several approaches to debugging issues in Svelte applications. These include using the `@debug` tag, reactive statements with `console` methods, and the svelte-devtools browser extension.

- Chapter 12 demonstrates various approaches to testing Svelte applications. Unit tests are implemented with Jest and svelte-testing-library. End-to-end tests are implemented with Cypress. Some accessibility checking is provided by the Svelte compiler. Additional accessibility testing is performed with Lighthouse, axe, and WAVE. Finally, Storybook is used to demonstrate and manually test components.

- Chapter 13 explores a few options for deploying Svelte applications. These include manual deployment to an HTTP server, using Netlify, using Vercel Now, and using Docker.

- Chapter 14 covers additional topics related to Svelte. These include form validation, using CSS libraries, using "special elements," creating Svelte component libraries, and generating web components from Svelte components.

Part 3 explores Sapper in depth. Sapper builds on Svelte to add many features.

- Chapter 15 walks through building your first Sapper application. The shopping app developed in chapter 9 is recreated using Sapper.

- Chapter 16 explores many aspects of Sapper. First, the default file structure of Sapper applications is explained. Then several Sapper features are described, including page routes, page layouts, preloading, prefetching, and code splitting.

- Chapter 17 explores Sapper server routes. These enable implementing API services in the same project as the client side of a web app. An example of implementing create, retrieve, update, delete (CRUD) services is presented.

- Chapter 18 shows how Sapper apps can be "exported" to generate static sites. This can be desirable for apps where it is possible to generate the HTML for every page at build time. An example of such an app is implemented, containing pages related to the rock/paper/scissors game, and dogs in my family.

- Chapter 19 describes how Sapper apps support offline operation using a service worker. Many caching strategies are described. Details about the default Sapper service worker are provided, as are descriptions of the service worker events install, `activate`, and `fetch`. An approach to enabling the use of HTTPS in the Sapper server is presented. Finally, techniques to verify the offline behavior of a Sapper app are shared.

Part 4 goes beyond Svelte and Sapper.

- Chapter 20 explores preprocessing source files to add support for alternative syntaxes. Popular options include Sass, TypeScript, and Markdown. Examples of using each of these are provided.
- Chapter 21 provides an introduction to Svelte Native. This combines Svelte and NativeScript to build mobile applications for Android and iOS. Two online REPL apps will get you started building Svelte Native apps without installing any software on your computer. The provided components for display, forms, actions, dialogs, layout, and navigation are described, and details about styling Svelte Native components are provided. An example app that demonstrates most of these is implemented. Finally, the NativeScript UI add-on library is described, and an example app using one of its components, `RadSideDrawer`, is presented.

The learning doesn't stop after the last chapter! The seven appendixes contain important information.

- Appendix A provides links to many resources related to Svelte, Sapper, Svelte Native, and more.
- Appendix B describes how to use the Fetch API to invoke REST services.
- Appendix C describes the basics of using the MongoDB database, which is used in chapter 17.
- Appendix D describes how to configure and use ESLint to check for issues in your Svelte and Sapper apps.
- Appendix E describes how to configure and use Prettier to format the code in Svelte and Sapper apps.
- Appendix F describes how to use several VS Code extensions when editing Svelte and Sapper apps with VS Code.
- Appendix G describes how to use Snowpack to build Svelte applications. Snowpack implements a more efficient way to build web applications than the approach typically used by module bundlers such as Webpack, Rollup, and Parcel.

Throughout the book we'll develop a Travel Packing application. Most chapters add features to the app based on the topics they cover.

Readers who are new to Svelte should read chapters 1 through 8 before skipping to any of the later chapters. These cover the core principles of Svelte. Readers with previous Svelte experience can skip to chapters of interest.

About the code

Much of the code in the book can be found in the author's GitHub repositories at https://github.com/mvolkmann. In particular, see https://github.com/mvolkmann/svelte-and-sapper-in-action and https://github.com/mvolkmann/svelte-native-components.

To run the code, you will need to install a recent version of Node.js. If you do not already have this installed, browse to https://nodejs.org/ and click either the LTS or Current button to download it.

This book contains many examples of source code both in numbered listings and in line with normal text. In both cases, source code is formatted in a `fixed-width font like this` to separate it from ordinary text. Sometimes code is also in **bold** to highlight code that has changed from previous steps in the chapter, such as when a new feature adds to an existing line of code.

In many cases, the original source code has been reformatted; we've added line breaks and reworked indentation to accommodate the available page space in the book. In rare cases, even this was not enough, and listings include line-continuation markers (➡). Additionally, comments in the source code have often been removed from the listings when the code is described in the text. Code annotations accompany many of the listings, highlighting important concepts.

liveBook discussion forum

Purchase of *Svelte and Sapper in Action* includes free access to a private web forum run by Manning Publications where you can make comments about the book, ask technical questions, and receive help from the author and from other users. To access the forum, go to https://livebook.manning.com/#!/book/svelte-and-sapper-in-action/discussion. You can also learn more about Manning's forums and the rules of conduct at https://livebook.manning.com/#!/discussion.

Manning's commitment to our readers is to provide a venue where a meaningful dialogue between individual readers and between readers and the author can take place. It is not a commitment to any specific amount of participation on the part of the author, whose contribution to the forum remains voluntary (and unpaid). We suggest you try asking the author some challenging questions lest his interest stray! The forum and the archives of previous discussions will be accessible from the publisher's website as long as the book is in print.

Other online resources

Appendix A lists a large number of online resources. Most of these are directly related to Svelte and Sapper, but some cover topics applicable to all varieties of web development.

about the author

 **R. Mark Volkmann** is a partner at Object Computing, Inc. (OCI) in St. Louis, where he has provided software consulting and training since 1996. As a consultant, Mark has assisted many companies with JavaScript, Node.js, Svelte, React, Vue, Angular, and more. Mark has created and taught many courses on topics including React, Vue, AngularJS, Node.js, jQuery, JavaScript, HTML5, CSS3, Ruby, Java, and XML. He is a frequent presenter at St. Louis-area user groups. He has presented at many conferences, including Nordic.js, Jfokus, NDC Oslo, Strange Loop, MidwestJS, No Fluff Just Stuff, and XML DevCon. Mark frequently writes articles on various software development topics. These can be found at https://objectcomputing.com/resources/publications/mark-volkmann.

In his spare time, Mark likes to run. To date he has run 49 marathons in 39 states.

about the cover illustration

The figure on the cover of *Svelte and Sapper in Action* is captioned "femme Corfiote," or a woman from the island of Corfu, in Greece. The illustration is taken from a collection of dress costumes from various countries by Jacques Grasset de Saint-Sauveur (1757–1810), titled *Costumes de Différents Pays*, published in France in 1797. Each illustration is finely drawn and colored by hand. The rich variety of Grasset de Saint-Sauveur's collection reminds us vividly of how culturally apart the world's towns and regions were just 200 years ago. Isolated from each other, people spoke different dialects and languages. In the streets or in the countryside, it was easy to identify where they lived and what their trade or station in life was just by their dress.

The way we dress has changed since then and the diversity by region, so rich at the time, has faded away. It is now hard to tell apart the inhabitants of different continents, let alone different towns, regions, or countries. Perhaps we have traded cultural diversity for a more varied personal life—certainly for a more varied and fast-paced technological life.

At a time when it is hard to tell one computer book from another, Manning celebrates the inventiveness and initiative of the computer business with book covers based on the rich diversity of regional life of two centuries ago, brought back to life by Grasset de Saint-Sauveur's pictures.

Part 1

Getting Started

Welcome to *Svelte and Sapper in Action*! We'll start here by learning why these approaches to web development deserve your attention, then we'll learn about Svelte Native, compare Svelte to other popular web frameworks, and delve into the tools you'll need to get started. We're also going to build our first Svelte application with an online tool called the REPL. Apps built this way can be saved, shared with others, and exported to continue development locally.

Meet the players

1

This chapter covers

- Svelte
- Sapper
- Svelte Native

Svelte (https://svelte.dev/) is a tool for building JavaScript-based web applications. It is an alternative to web frameworks like React, Vue, and Angular. Like them, Svelte focuses on defining user-interface (UI) components and their interactions. Each UI component is an independent, potentially reusable part of a larger user interface that can be independently designed and implemented.

Svelte has many benefits over other web frameworks:

- Apps produced using Svelte require less code than most frameworks to implement the equivalent functionality.
- Svelte produces smaller bundle sizes, which results in decreased browser load times.
- Svelte greatly simplifies state management, both within and across components. (State management includes organizing the data that drives an app and responding to changes in the data.)

Sapper (https://sapper.svelte.dev/) is a framework built on top of Svelte for creating more advanced web applications. It adds many features over Svelte, including page routing, server-side rendering, code splitting, and static site generation. But web applications that do not need these features, or that wish to implement them in a different way, can opt to use Svelte by itself.

Svelte Native (https://svelte-native.technology/) also builds on Svelte. It integrates the use of NativeScript for building Android and iOS mobile applications.

> **NOTE** Throughout this book when referring to various options for creating web applications, I will refer to them as "frameworks," even though some use the term "library."

1.1 Introducing Svelte

Do we really need another tool for building web applications?

Putting in the effort to learn yet another approach is only worthwhile if it brings significant benefits. Perhaps it could require writing less code to achieve the same outcome. Maybe it could do less actual work at runtime to accomplish the same result. Or perhaps it could result in fewer total bytes needing to be downloaded to browsers.

Check, check, and check! Svelte delivers on all of these goals and more.

Like other frameworks, Svelte can be used to build entire web applications. Svelte components can be used in a single application or can be defined in a library that is shared by multiple applications. It can also be used to create custom elements (web components) that are usable in web apps implemented with other frameworks or with no framework at all.

Rich Harris, who formerly worked at *The Guardian* and is currently at *The New York Times*, developed Svelte starting in 2016. He previously created the Ractive web framework (https://ractive.js.org/), which is used at *The Guardian* and inspired parts of Vue. He also created the Rollup module bundler, which is an alternative to Webpack and Parcel.

The word *svelte* means slender, which describes both the syntax of Svelte and the bundle sizes it produces.

1.1.1 Why Svelte?

Svelte has many advantages over existing web frameworks. The most significant of these are summarized in the following sections.

SVELTE IS A COMPILER

Other popular web frameworks include large runtime libraries to support all their features. But Svelte is not a runtime library. It is a web application compiler implemented in TypeScript.

> **NOTE** A compiler is software that translates code in one programming language to another. Typically this is from a high-level language (such as Go or Java) to a lower-level language (such as machine code or bytecode).

NOTE TypeScript is an open source programming language that is a superset of JavaScript; its programs are compiled to JavaScript. TypeScript adds many features above JavaScript, the most significant of which is the ability to define the types of variables and functions. TypeScript is developed and maintained by Microsoft.

Svelte UI components are defined in `.svelte` files. These can contain a combination of JavaScript, CSS, and HTML. For example, a component could contain HTML elements for a login form, CSS to style it, and JavaScript to pass the data entered to an authentication service when the Login button is clicked.

The Svelte compiler compiles `.svelte` files to JavaScript and CSS. This has many benefits, one being that new features can be added to Svelte without bloating the bundle size of deployed applications. The compiler only includes code for the features of Svelte that are actually used.

SVELTE PRODUCES SMALL BUNDLES

Svelte apps have significantly smaller bundle sizes than equivalent apps created with other web frameworks. This means that Svelte apps can be downloaded to browsers more quickly.

NOTE In the context of web applications, *bundles* are JavaScript files that are created by combining, optimizing, and minimizing all the JavaScript code needed by an application.

In large part, Svelte achieves smaller bundle sizes by including only the required framework code instead of an entire framework library. For example, the Todo app presented in chapter 2 has a bundle size that is 13% of the size of an equivalent React app. Links to Svelte, React, and Vue versions of this app can be found in chapter 2.

NOTE All of these web frameworks incorporate some amount of "tree shaking" to eliminate unused code. But Svelte retains far less framework code. For example, React apps must ship code that produces virtual DOM representations and finds differences between them. The use of virtual DOMs is described later.

FreeCodeCamp's comparison of frameworks, "A RealWorld Comparison of Front-End Frameworks with Benchmarks (2019 update)," catalogs statistics on building a real world web application using many web frameworks (http://mng.bz/8pxz). In this case, the app used in the comparison is a social blogging site called "Conduit," similar to Medium.com.

The reported gzipped app size for some popular framework choices include

- Angular + ngrx: 134 KB
- React + Redux: 193 KB
- Vue: 41.8 KB
- Svelte: 9.7 KB

Clearly Svelte shines on this metric.

SVELTE REQUIRES LESS CODE

Svelte requires less code to implement the same functionality. The reported number of lines of code from these same benchmarks are

- Angular + ngrx: 4,210
- React + Redux: 2,050
- Vue: 2,076
- Svelte: 1,116

This is significant for multiple reasons. Having less code to read means there is less code to understand. It also means there are fewer places for bugs to hide.

SVELTE PROVIDES REACTIVITY WITHOUT USING A VIRTUAL DOM

Some web frameworks, including React and Vue, use a virtual Document Object Model (DOM) to optimize updating the real DOM in response to data changes. When component state changes, the framework builds a new version of the DOM in memory and then compares it to the previous version. Only the differences are applied to the real DOM. Although this is faster than updating everything in the real DOM, it does take time to build a virtual DOM and compare it to the previous one.

Reactivity is the ability to update the DOM in response to application and component state changes. Svelte provides reactivity by tracking changes to top-level component variables (not scoped inside functions) that affect what components render. It updates only the affected parts of the DOM rather than re-rendering the entire component. This allows Svelte to do less work than many frameworks to keep the DOM in sync with application state.

SVELTE IS FAST

Check out Stefan Krause's benchmarks at https://krausest.github.io/js-framework-benchmark/current.html. The app used in these tests renders a table with 4 columns and 1,000 rows. On this page you can select the frameworks to be compared and see side-by-side statistics. For example, select "angular-v8.0.1-keyed," "react-v16.8.6-keyed," "svelte-v3.5.1-keyed," and "vue-v2.6.2-keyed." This returns the results for application startup time shown in figure 1.1. These results demonstrate that Svelte is quite fast compared to other options.

> **NOTE**   The term *keyed* in these selections means the code creates an association between data and DOM elements. When the data changes, the associated DOM element is updated. Adding and removing array elements causes DOM elements to be added and removed. The test results in figure 1.1 are from "keyed" implementations because that is more representative of what apps typically use to make updating of existing DOM elements more efficient.

Name	svelte-v3.5.1-keyed	vue-v2.6.2-keyed	react-v16.8.6-keyed	angular-v8.0.1-keyed
Script bootup time The total ms required to parse/compile/evaluate all the page's scripts	19.5 ±2.4 (1.00)	59.6 ±28.6 (3.06)	55.6 ±45.2 (2.85)	159.8 ±8.8 (8.21)
Total kilobyte weight Network transfer cost (post-compression) of all the resources loaded into the page	145.7 ±0.0 (1.00)	211.2 ±0.0 (1.45)	260.8 ±0.0 (1.79)	295.5 ±0.0 (2.03)

Figure 1.1   **Benchmark boot-up time and download time**

SVELTE REQUIRES LESS MEMORY

Using less memory is a significant benefit when web applications are run on older computers or mobile devices, which tend to have less available memory for running applications.

The benchmark site used in the previous section reports the comparison for memory usage shown in figure 1.2. These results demonstrate that Svelte apps typically use less memory than other options.

SVELTE COMPONENTS DO NOT USE A JAVASCRIPT CONTAINER

`.svelte` files do not define any kind of JavaScript container for the component. Instead, a component is defined by a combination of a `script` element, HTML to render, and a `style` element.

This approach is simpler than that used by most other web frameworks. Fewer lines of code are required to define a component, and there are fewer JavaScript concepts to think about. For example, Angular components are defined by a class, React components are defined by a function or a class, Vue 2 components are defined by an object literal, and Vue 3 components are defined by functions.

SVELTE STYLING IS SCOPED

By default, the CSS specified in each Svelte component only applies to that component. This means that CSS rules defined in a `.svelte` file do not accidentally "leak out" and affect the styling of other components.

Styles are treated differently in other frameworks. In Angular, styles specified in the `styles` property of a component are also scoped to the component by default. In Vue, styles are only scoped to components if they are specified inside a `style` element with the `scoped` attribute. React does not provide support for scoping styles to components, which is one reason why CSS-in-JS solutions are popular in React applications. There is little appeal for these CSS-in-JS solutions in Svelte.

Name	svelte-v3.5.1-keyed	vue-v2.6.2-keyed	react-v16.8.6-keyed	angular-v8.0.1-keyed
Ready memory Memory usage after page load	1.9 ±0.0 (1.00)	2.1 ±0.0 (1.13)	2.3 ±0.0 (1.23)	4.8 ±0.0 (2.54)
Run memory Memory usage after adding 1000 rows	3.9 ±0.0 (1.00)	7.1 ±0.0 (1.81)	6.9 ±0.0 (1.76)	9.1 ±0.0 (2.34)
Update each 10th row for 1k rows (5 cycles) Memory usage after clicking update every 10th row 5 times	4.3 ±0.0 (1.00)	7.5 ±0.0 (1.76)	8.0 ±0.0 (1.89)	9.5 ±0.0 (2.23)
Repace 1k rows (5 cycles) Memory usage after clicking create 1000 rows 5 times	4.5 ±0.0 (1.00)	7.7 ±0.0 (1.71)	8.9 ±0.0 (1.98)	9.9 ±0.1 (2.20)
Creating/clearing 1k rows (5 cycles) Memory usage after creating and clearing 1000 rows 5 times	3.2 ±0.0 (1.00)	3.8 ±0.0 (1.20)	4.7 ±0.1 (1.48)	6.6 ±0.0 (2.07)

Figure 1.2   Benchmark memory utilization in MBs

SVELTE PROVIDES A PLACE FOR GLOBAL STYLES

Svelte provides a clear place to specify global styles that can affect any component. This is in the file public/global.css.

SVELTE SIMPLIFIES STATE MANAGEMENT

Management of application and component state is much easier in Svelte compared to other frameworks. Contributing features include context, stores, and module context, each of which will be covered in detail later.

SVELTE SUPPORTS TWO-WAY DATA BINDINGS

Svelte makes it easy to bind the value of a form control to a component variable. Form controls include input, textarea, and select elements. Top-level variables in .svelte files represent the state of a component.

When the value of a bound variable changes, the values of associated form controls are automatically updated. When the user changes the value of a bound form control, the value of the associated variable is automatically updated.

SVELTE MAKES ANIMATION EASY

Svelte has built-in support for a variety of animations. Adding animation to an application is surprisingly simple. This encourages the use of more animation, which can result in a better user experience.

Examples of such animations in a Todo app include causing new todo items to fade into view and deleted todo items to fade out of view. If todo items are maintained in categorized lists, animation can be used to smoothly move an item out of its current category and into a new category.

SVELTE ENCOURAGES ACCESSIBILITY

Svelte provides runtime warnings for accessibility issues. For example, `img` elements that have no `alt` attribute are flagged. This makes it more likely that Svelte applications will be usable by users that require special ways of interacting with web browsers.

1.1.2 Rethinking reactivity

In the context of web applications, *reactivity* is the ability of the DOM to be updated automatically in response to changes in data (a.k.a. state). This can be compared to spreadsheets. A change to the value of one cell can cause the values displayed in other cells to change. This happens when a cell's value is based on the values of other cells using a formula.

Svelte makes implementing reactivity easier than other frameworks. It supports a unique way of managing the state of a component that relies on watching top-level variables (explained in section 3.9). It also simplifies the ways in which state can be shared across components.

HTML DOM

The HTML DOM provides an in-memory representation of a web page. It is composed of a tree of JavaScript objects that represent nodes. There is a JavaScript object that represents the entire `Document`, and it has references to other DOM objects that represent elements on the page. DOM objects have methods that can be called to get information about a node, add child nodes, register event listeners, and more. Modifying the DOM changes what the browser displays.

Here is a sample HTML document:

```
<!DOCTYPE html>
<html>
  <head>
    <title>My Page</title>
  </head>
  <script>
    // For exploring the DOM from the DevTools console ...
    window.onload = () => console.dir(document);
  </script>
  <body>
    <h1>My Page</h1>
```

(continued)

```
   <p>I like these colors:</p>
   <ul>
     <li>yellow</li>
     <li>orange</li>
   </ul>
 </body>
</html>
```

The following figure illustrates the DOM nodes created by a web browser that represent the HTML document in memory.

DOM nodes

The "Rethinking Reactivity" conference talk given by Rich Harris on multiple occasions clearly describes the concerns that motivated the creation of Svelte (www.youtube .com/watch?v=gJ2P6hGwcgo). The top 10 points in this talk all correlate to features implemented in Svelte:

1 Implement real "reactive programming" as seen in spreadsheets. When a value changes, other values can update in response.

2 Avoid use of a virtual DOM. Rich says, "As engineers we should be offended by all that inefficiency."

3 Write less code. It's better for developers and better for performance. Rich says, "There's only one reliable way to speed up your code, and that is to get rid of it."

4 Provide warnings for accessibility issues.

5 Scope styles to components so they don't leak out and affect each other.

6 Identify unused CSS rules so they can be removed.

7 Make it easy to add transitions and animations, using CSS for performance.

8 Allow framework features to be added without bloating the bundle size of apps that don't use them.

9 Use Sapper (a wrapper around Svelte) to add page routing, code splitting, server-side rendering, and more.

10 Use Svelte Native for mobile apps. This is an alternative to React Native.

1.1.3 Current issues in Svelte

Using Svelte is appropriate for nearly any web application. However, there are issues you should consider that may cause some developers to prefer other frameworks.

Svelte is implemented in TypeScript, but it does not support using TypeScript to define components out of the box. However, with a little configuration and added tooling, TypeScript can be used with Svelte now. Work to improve TypeScript support in Svelte is ongoing.

> **NOTE** Chapter 20 discusses using svelte-preprocessor to support using Type-Script in .svelte files. It also touches on using the command-line tool svelte-check to check for errors in .svelte files, including TypeScript errors. Appendix F discusses using the VS Code extension Svelte for VS Code, which uses the Svelte Language Server to report errors in opened .svelte files, including TypeScript errors.

Svelte is not a particularly good option for web applications that must run in Internet Explorer. Polyfills are required to run Svelte apps in Internet Explorer 11 (see https://github.com/sveltejs/svelte/issues/2621 and https://mvolkmann.github.io/blog/topics/#/blog/svelte/supporting-ie11/). Svelte apps are unlikely to run in versions of Internet Explorer before version 11. Fortunately, it is no longer a requirement for most web applications to run in Internet Explorer.

Some web frameworks (such as React and Vue) make it easy to generate the content for different parts of a component in separate functions within a component definition. Contrast this with the approach used by Svelte, where all the HTML for a component is specified outside its JavaScript code. A downside of the Svelte approach is that dividing the HTML to be rendered into separately managed chunks requires defining additional components in separate .svelte files. However, since these files contain almost no boilerplate code, creating a new component is easy.

Web frameworks that predate Svelte have had many years for their supporting libraries to be created. One example is collections of pre-built components. Fewer of these libraries currently exist for Svelte, but the number is growing.

Consider whether the benefits of Svelte outweigh the limitations described here. I'm confident that after a little experience with Svelte, you will conclude, as I have, that they do!

1.1.4 How does Svelte work?

Figure 1.3 shows the role of the Svelte compiler. User-interface (UI) components are implemented in .svelte files. These can contain JavaScript code (in a script element), CSS (in a style element), and HTML to be rendered.

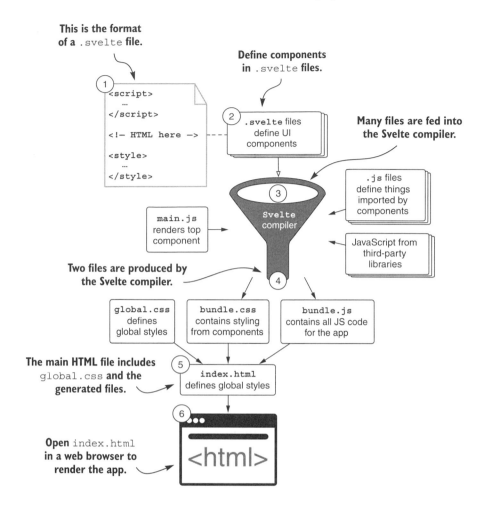

Figure 1.3   Flow of files into and out of the Svelte compiler

.svelte files can import other .svelte files to use as child components. For example, a TodoList component that represents an entire Todo application can import and use a Todo component that represents a single todo item, perhaps with a checkbox, the text of the item, and a Delete button.

.svelte files can also import things such as functions from .js files and from third-party libraries (typically obtained from npm). For example, functions from the popular Lodash library can be imported and used in a Svelte app.

The Svelte compiler compiles all of this into a single bundle.js file and a single bundle.css file. These contain only the JavaScript code and CSS rules that are used in the application. Only the parts of the Svelte library that are needed are included in bundle.js.

Styling that can affect any component is placed in the `global.css` file. The main HTML file, `index.html`, includes `global.css` and the bundle files produced by the Svelte compiler. This HTML file is loaded into a web browser to run the application.

The Svelte compiler also generates `bundle.css.map` and `bundle.js.map` files, which support mapping from the generated code to original source lines. These are used by debuggers, such as those built into browsers.

1.1.5   Does Svelte disappear?

In most web frameworks, the code that is delivered to web browsers to run an application includes code written by the developers and a framework library. If the framework implements a large number of features, the code to support those features is often delivered even if only a subset of the features is actually used.

Some say that Svelte "disappears" once an app is built. This refers to not including a Svelte library in the bundle produced by the Svelte compiler. But some Svelte library code is included.

The Svelte library is mostly defined by JavaScript files in the `node_modules/svelte` directory. The main functions are defined in `internal.js`, which is currently around 1,400 lines of code. Other library files are used for specific features, including `easing.js`, `motion.js`, `register.js`, `store.js`, and `transition.js`.

As you will see later, Svelte applications are compiled by running the `npm run dev` or `npm run build` commands. These produce files in the `public` directory, including `bundle.js` and `bundle.css`. Svelte library functions that are used by the app are copied to the top of `bundle.js`. For small to medium size apps (such as a Todo app), this amounts to around 500 lines of code.

The Svelte library code doesn't disappear, but it is very small compared to other web frameworks.

1.2   Introducing Sapper

Sapper is a framework that builds on Svelte. It includes all of Svelte and adds many features that are not included in Svelte by default. These features can be added to Svelte applications, but it is easier to use Sapper and automatically gain them.

The name *Sapper* has two meanings. First, it is a contraction of "Svelte app maker." Second, the English word *sapper* is defined as "a soldier responsible for tasks such as building and repairing roads and bridges, laying and clearing mines, etc." In a sense, this is what Sapper does for Svelte.

Like Svelte, Sapper was created and is maintained by Rich Harris along with many other contributors.

1.2.1 Why consider Sapper?

Each of the following features are added by Sapper. We'll look at them in detail in later chapters.

- *Sapper provides page routing.* Page routing associates URLs with "pages" in an app and defines how navigation between pages is described in markup. Sapper page routing is entirely defined by directory and file naming conventions. This makes it easier to understand and implement than approaches that require calling library functions to configure routing.
- *Sapper supports page layouts.* Page layouts define a common layout for sets of pages within an app. For example, many pages might contain common `header`, `footer`, and `nav` sections. Page layouts remove the need to repeat these common sections on each page that requires them.
- *Sapper provides server-side rendering (SSR), which generates the HTML for visited pages on the server instead of in the browser.* This can provide a better user experience, because the JavaScript for the page does not have to be downloaded before the page is rendered. It can also result in better search engine optimization (SEO). Sapper SSR does this automatically for the first page visited within a session.
- *Sapper supports server routes.* Server routes provide an easy way to implement Node-based API services in the same project as the client-side web application. This is convenient for developers who wish to work on the full stack of an application rather than only the frontend. Using this feature is optional. The API/REST services used by Svelte and Sapper apps can be implemented with any technology stack.

REST

REST stands for *representational state transfer*, and it is described in Roy Fielding's PhD dissertation from 2000. It is an architectural style, not a standard or API.

These are the main ideas behind REST:

1. A software component requests a "resource" from a service by supplying a resource identifier and a desired media type. A resource identifier can be a URL, and a request can be made using Ajax (https://developer.mozilla.org/en-US/docs/Web/Guide/AJAX).
2. A "representation" of the resource is returned. This is a sequence of bytes, and metadata to describe it. For example, it can be JSON, name/value pairs in HTTP headers, an image, etc. A representation can contain identifiers of other resources.
3. Obtaining this representation causes the software component to "transfer" to a new "state."

In common usage, REST uses HTTP requests and responses. The HTTP verbs POST, GET, PUT, and DELETE are mapped to the "CRUD" operations *create*, *retrieve*, *update*, and *delete* respectively.

- *Sapper supports code splitting.* Code splitting allows the JavaScript required for each page of the application to be downloaded only when a page is visited for the first time. This is much more efficient than downloading all the code for the entire application when the first page is visited.
- *Sapper supports prefetching.* Prefetching provides faster page loads by anticipating the next page a user will visit based on mouse hovers. This can be configured on each page link. The first time a user hovers over such a page link, Sapper will begin downloading the JavaScript required by the page. It can also initiate calls to API services that gather data required by the page.
- *Sapper supports static site generation.* Static site generation (or exporting) crawls a Svelte web application at build time and generates the HTML that each page renders. This results in highly efficient websites because each page is, in a sense, prerendered.

Sites created this way are not required to be entirely static. They can still include Java-Script code and take advantage of Svelte reactivity for updating the DOM.

- *Sapper supports offline usage.* Sapper web applications use a service worker in order to remain usable, perhaps in a limited sense, when network connectivity is lost. This is done by caching certain files and responses so that cached versions are used when there is no connection to the internet.
- *Sapper supports end-to-end testing.* Sapper apps come with support for using Cypress to implement tests that walk through an application in the way a user would, performing tasks like logging in, navigating to various pages, entering text, and clicking buttons.

1.2.2 How does Sapper work?

The "pages" of a Sapper app are defined in `.svelte` files that reside in the `src/routes` directory. The components used by these pages are defined in `.svelte` files that reside in the `src/components` directory. Navigation between pages is implemented with plain HTML anchor elements (`<a>`) that specify a page name in their `href` attribute.

By default, Sapper apps are served by the Polka server library. This is a Node-based library that has nearly the same API as Express, but Polka is more efficient in terms of performance and size. If desired, Sapper apps can easily be modified to use Express instead.

As you saw earlier, the Svelte compiler generates `bundle.js` and `bundle.css` files that contain all the JavaScript and CSS for the entire application. Sapper is different. It generates separate `.js` and `.css` files for each page of the application. These are placed in the `__sapper__/build/client` directory. On each page load, only the Java-Script and CSS needed for that page are downloaded.

1.2.3   *When should Sapper be used?*

Using Sapper instead of straight Svelte is as easy as creating a project with a different initial set of directories and files. These sets of files can be created with the npx command, as you will see later.

All of the features described in the previous section are available by default in Sapper applications. No additional libraries are required.

Using Sapper instead of Svelte is recommended any time an app needs one or more of the features provided by Sapper, and when developers approve of the way Sapper has implemented them. For example, developers who prefer an alternative way of describing page routes might opt to use Svelte, where they can choose a routing strategy. For most apps, the approaches used by Sapper are acceptable.

1.2.4   *When should Sapper not be used?*

At the time of writing, Sapper had not yet reached version 1.0.0. This means that its features are still subject to breaking changes. Developers who are concerned about this may want to wait until Sapper is more mature before using it in production applications.

However, the features provided by Sapper are so valuable and well-implemented that it may be better to use it in its current state than attempt to duplicate these features in a Svelte app. After all, it is likely that you already use many npm packages that are not yet tagged as version 1 or above.

1.3   *Introducing Svelte Native*

NativeScript (https://nativescript.org/) is a framework for creating mobile applications that run on Android and iOS devices. It was created and is maintained by Telerik, which was acquired by Progress Software in 2014.

NativeScript applications are built using XML syntax (with custom elements), CSS, and JavaScript. They can be written without using any web framework, or they can use Angular, React, Svelte, or Vue.

NativeScript applications use native components rather than web views. In this sense, NativeScript is similar to React Native. Plugins allow access to all native device APIs.

Svelte Native (https://svelte-native.technology/) builds on top of NativeScript to enable developers to build mobile applications using Svelte. It provides a thin layer over the NativeScript API, which will make it easy to ensure compatibility with future NativeScript versions.

Chapter 21 will provide an introduction to writing Svelte Native applications.

1.4 How does Svelte compare with other web frameworks?

Svelte differs from other currently popular web frameworks in several ways. Let's examine some of them.

1.4.1 Angular

Angular apps require developers to write more code to accomplish the same tasks. Svelte code is more, well, ... svelte.

Angular concepts appeal to Java and C# developers who are accustomed to writing lots of classes and using dependency injection.

Angular apps typically use "effects" and libraries like RxJS and ngrx/store. These increase the time required to become proficient in Angular.

1.4.2 React

React components use JSX (short for JavaScript XML) to describe what should be rendered. JSX is an extension to JavaScript syntax that looks like HTML. React converts this to function calls that produce DOM nodes. Although JSX is very similar to HTML, there are differences. Some developers dislike JSX because they do not like mixing it into their JavaScript code. While Svelte components define their JavaScript, CSS, and HTML in the same file, they are specified in distinct sections of the file.

React uses a virtual DOM. Issues with this were described earlier.

The number of concepts that must be grasped to be proficient in React continues to grow. For example, hooks are a big topic, and there are many others to learn. There are multiple ways to deal with state, including `this.setState`, the `useState` hook, Redux, and many more. On the horizon we have Suspense and Concurrent Mode. Svelte is much easier to learn.

1.4.3 Vue

Vue 2 components are described with object literals. These describe many things about a component, including the props it accepts, computed properties (based on others), data used (component state), watch functions (to react to state changes), and methods (such as event handling). Code in Vue 2 components make frequent use of the `this` keyword, and some developers feel this makes the code more difficult to understand. It also makes the code more verbose. Vue 3 components are described with functions. In addition, Vue uses a virtual DOM, and the issues with this were described earlier.

But with Svelte components, all of these things are defined using plain JavaScript variables and functions with the help of reactive statements (described in the next chapter).

1.5   *What tools are needed to get started?*

This book assumes that you understand the fundamentals of using HTML, CSS, and JavaScript in the context of implementing web applications. You should be familiar with basic HTML (including form elements), CSS syntax (including the box model), and JavaScript syntax (including some features added in ECMAScript 2015 and beyond).

Getting started with Svelte and Sapper only requires that you have a recent version of Node.js installed. An installer can be downloaded from https://nodejs.org/.

> **NOTE**   As it states on the main Node.js website (https://nodejs.org/), "Node.js is a JavaScript runtime built on Chrome's V8 JavaScript engine." Node.js enables you to build many kinds of applications using JavaScript. These include network applications such as HTTP servers and tooling such as code linters, code formatters, and even the Svelte compiler.

Installing Node.js provides the commands node, npm, and npx:

- The node command is used to start the local servers that are needed to test an app and to run other development tasks, such as linting, code formatting, and running tests.
- The npm command is used to install the libraries used by a project.
- The npx command is used to create new Svelte and Sapper projects.

> **NOTE**   Although it's not yet ready for production use, another Svelte-related tool to consider is svelte-gl (https://github.com/sveltejs/gl). This library is similar to three.js (https://threejs.org/), but it's tailored for use in Svelte. It takes as input a 3D scene graph description and outputs WebGL code to render it. You can see a demo at http://mng.bz/lG02.

Prepare to be amazed at how easy web development can be, compared to the approaches you currently use!

Summary

- Svelte is a tool for building web applications that is an alternative to currently popular web frameworks like React, Vue, and Angular.
- Svelte is a web application compiler, not a library.
- Svelte has many features that make it an attractive option, such as writing less code, producing smaller bundles (which improves startup times), and simplifying state management.
- Sapper builds on Svelte, adding more features like page routing, server-side rendering, code splitting, and static site generation.
- Svelte Native uses the features of Svelte to provide an alternative to React Native for building Android and iOS mobile applications.

Your first Svelte app 2

This chapter covers

- Using the Svelte REPL
- Developing a Svelte app outside the REPL
- Developing a simple Todo app

In this chapter, you will learn everything you need to know to experiment with Svelte without having to download or install anything. This will be accomplished using a web-based REPL tool.

REPL stands for *read, evaluate, print, loop.* A REPL *reads* the code you enter, *evaluates* it (possibly compiling and reporting errors), *prints* the result of the code, and *loops* to allow for repeating this process. There are REPLs for many programming languages and web frameworks.

The REPL is a perfect gateway to developing larger apps locally, outside of the REPL, using common programming editors such as VS Code. This chapter will cover how to download REPL apps for further local development and how to create an app from scratch without using the REPL.

By the end of the chapter, you will be ready to start developing your own Svelte applications.

2.1 *The Svelte REPL*

Svelte provides a browser-based REPL that supports defining Svelte components, seeing their rendered output, and more. Using the REPL is the easiest way to experiment with Svelte. Your first Svelte application is just a click away!

To get started, browse to the main Svelte website at https://svelte.dev/. Then click the REPL link near the upper-right corner of the page.

Code for a Hello World app is provided by default, as shown in figure 2.1. You can modify this code to experiment with the various features of Svelte.

Figure 2.1   The initial REPL screen

Experimenting is just one use of the REPL. Another is creating an ever-growing collection of examples you can draw from as you learn about Svelte. I highly encourage you to take advantage of this feature.

2.1.1 *Using the Svelte REPL*

Initially, the only file provided in the REPL is App.svelte. This file can import other files defined in additional tabs within the REPL (not in separate browser tabs).

To add more .svelte or .js files, click the plus button (+) to the right of the existing file tabs, and give the new file a name. By default, newly created files have a .svelte extension, but this can be changed to .js by typing .js at the end of the filename.

> **NOTE**   The REPL error "Failed to construct 'URL': Invalid base URL" typically means that a file created in the REPL is missing its file extension and couldn't be imported.

To delete a file, click its tab and then click the "X" that appears to the right of the filename.

The right side of the REPL page contains three tabs:

- *Result*—The Result tab shows the rendered output of `App.svelte`. When this tab is selected, the lower-right corner of the REPL shows output from calls to `console` methods, such as `console.log`.
- *JS Output*—The JS Output tab shows the JavaScript code generated for the app by the Svelte compiler.
- *CSS Output*—The CSS Output tab shows the minimized CSS generated for the app by the Svelte compiler. Unused CSS selectors are not included. All selectors include generated CSS class names that scope the CSS to the component. We will discuss how these names are generated later.

The top bar in the REPL (see figure 2.2) contains links to many Svelte resources including a tutorial, the API docs, examples, the Svelte blog, the Svelte FAQ, the main page for Sapper, the Discord chat, and the Svelte GitHub repo.

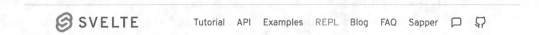

Figure 2.2   The Svelte website header

To hide this bar and gain more editing room, click the full-screen editor icon, which looks like a dashed square (see figure 2.3).

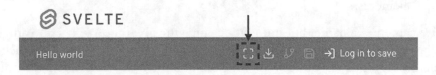

Figure 2.3   The REPL full screen button

After you click it, this icon will change to an "X" (see figure 2.4). Click it to restore the top bar.

Figure 2.4   The REPL exit full screen button

There is currently no option in the REPL to format `.svelte` files. Perhaps an option to do this using Prettier will be added in the future.

> **NOTE** Prettier (https://prettier.io) is a very popular tool for formatting code from many languages, including JavaScript, HTML, CSS, and more.

To reset the REPL to its starting point, which is a basic Hello World app, click the REPL link in the header (see figure 2.5).

Figure 2.5   The REPL reset button

2.1.2   *Your first REPL app*

Using only what you have learned so far, let's create a simple app and begin learning about some features of Svelte.

The provided Hello World app always says hello to "world." Let's change this so it can say hello to anybody. Add the following HTML before the h1 element:

```
<label for="name">Name</label>
<input id="name" value={name}>
```

> **NOTE** The input HTML element is an example of an *empty element*, which means it cannot have child nodes. When empty elements are used in Svelte components, they do not need to be terminated with />. However, if Prettier is used to format the code, it will change empty elements so they're terminated this way. This is why some code examples in this book show terminated empty elements.

Now we can enter a name, but it doesn't change the greeting. We need to add event handling so the value of the name variable is updated when the user types in the input. We can do this using an inline arrow function or a reference to a function defined in the script element. Change the input to the following:

```
<input
  id="name"
  on:input={event => name = event.target.value}
  value={name}
>
```

This works, but it's a bit verbose. We can do better using the Svelte bind directive. You will see many uses of the bind directive later, but one use is to bind the value of a form element to a variable. This causes the form element to display the current value of the variable. If a user changes the value of the form element, the variable will be updated to match.

Change the `input` element to match the following:

```
<input id="name" bind:value={name}>
```

Oh my, that's nice! And if the variable name is `value` instead of `name`, it can be shortened as follows:

```
<input id="name" bind:value>
```

This isn't very stylish, though. Let's add styling to change the color of the greeting. Add the following at the bottom of the file, after the HTML.

```
<style>
  h1 {
    color: red;
  }
</style>
```

Great! Now the greeting is red.

Let's allow the user to select a color. We will do this by adding an `input` element with a `type` of `color`. This uses the native color picker to select a color. It appears as a rectangle containing a horizontal line in figure 2.6. Clicking it opens a Color Picker dialog.

Top-level variables in the `script` element of a component define the state of the component. For example, the state of the component below includes the `color` and `name` variables.

Here is the full code for this version of `App.svelte`.

Figure 2.6   A REPL app with color input

Listing 2.1   A REPL app with color input

```
<script>
  let color = 'red';
  let name = 'world';
</script>

<label for="name">Name</label>
<input id="name" bind:value={name}>

<label for="color">Color</label>
<input id="color" type="color" bind:value={color}>
<div style="background-color: {color}" class="swatch" />

<h1 style="color: {color}">Hello {name}!</h1>

<style>
  .swatch {
    display: inline-block;
    height: 20px;
    width: 20px;
  }
</style>
```

Let's allow the user to toggle a checkbox to change the case of the greeting. Add the following inside the `script` element, at the bottom:

```
let upper = false;
$: greeting = `Hello ${name}!`;
$: casedGreeting = upper ? greeting.toUpperCase() : greeting;
```

What does `$:` mean? It's called a *reactive statement*. Reactive statements are re-executed any time the value of a variable they reference changes. Reactive statements that assign a value to a variable are also called *reactive declarations*. They are covered in more detail in chapter 3.

In the preceding code above we calculate a new value for `greeting` any time the value of `name` changes. Then we calculate a new value for `casedGreeting` any time the value of `upper` or `greeting` changes. This is incredibly convenient!

Now we just need a way to change the value of `upper` when a checkbox is toggled, and to render the value of `casedGreeting`. Add the following code before the `h1` element to render the checkbox, as shown in figure 2.7.

```
<label>
  <input type="checkbox" bind:checked={upper}>
  Uppercase
</label>
```

Figure 2.7   A REPL app with an Uppercase checkbox

Change the `h1` element to the following:

```
<h1 style="color: {color}">{casedGreeting}</h1>
```

So far we have implemented everything in a single `.svelte` file named `App.svelte`. Let's move beyond this by defining a second component.

Click the plus button (+) to the right of the `App` `.svelte` tab in the REPL. Enter `Clock` for the name of the component, as shown in figure 2.8. Component names and their source file names should use camel case, starting with an uppercase letter.

We want this component to display the current time in `hh:mm:ss` format.

Start by adding only the following in `Clock.svelte`:

Figure 2.8   REPL app with Clock tab

```
<div>
  I will be a clock.
</div>
```

Back in `App.svelte`, add the following inside the `script` element, at the top:

```
import Clock from './Clock.svelte';
```

Add the following at the bottom of the HTML in `App.svelte`:

```
<Clock />
```

> **NOTE** The space before the slash in `<Clock />` is not required, but many developers, and the Prettier code formatter, prefer to include it.

You will now see "I will be a clock." at the bottom of the rendered output (see figure 2.9).

Props allow data to be passed into components (they will be discussed in detail in chapter 5). Svelte uses the `export` keyword to define a prop that a component accepts. In a `.js` file, `export` makes a value visible outside that file and able to be imported. When you use `export` in a component, other components that use this component can pass in a value.

Change `Clock.svelte` so it contains the following. In this component, `color` is a prop with a default value.

```
<script>
  export let color = 'blue';        ⟵  This defines the
  let hhmmss = '';                       color prop.
  setInterval(() => {
    hhmmss = new Date().toLocaleTimeString();   ⟵  This is executed
  }, 1000);                                          once every second.
</script>

<span style="color: {color}">{hhmmss}</span>
```

Modify `App.svelte` to pass a `color` prop to the `Clock` component. The following line demonstrates a shorthand syntax that is equivalent to `<Clock color={color} />`.

```
<Clock {color} />
```

We now have a functioning clock component, as shown in figure 2.10.

This gives you a taste of some of what you can do in Svelte. We will dive deeper in the chapters that follow.

If you are familiar with other web frameworks, now is a good time to pause and think about what code you would need to write to implement this in those frameworks. Is it longer? Is it more complicated?

Name
world

Color

☐ Uppercase

Hello world!

I will be a clock.

Figure 2.9   A REPL app with "I will be a clock."

Name
world

Color

☐ Uppercase

Hello world!

4:22:09 PM

Figure 2.10   A REPL app with a clock

Figure 2.11   The REPL Log In to Save button

2.1.3   *Saving REPL apps*

To save apps created in the REPL so they can be recalled in the future, click the Log In to Save button in the upper right (see figure 2.11). This will open the browser window shown in figure 2.12.

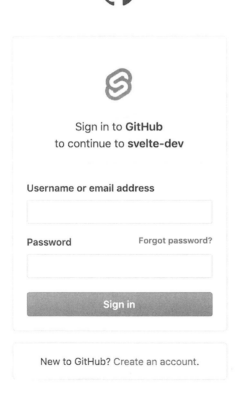

Figure 2.12   The GitHub Sign In page

Enter your GitHub username and password, and click the Sign In button.

If you do not already have a GitHub account, browse to https://github.com/ and click the large, green Sign Up for GitHub button (see figure 2.13). After signing into GitHub, you will be returned to the REPL.

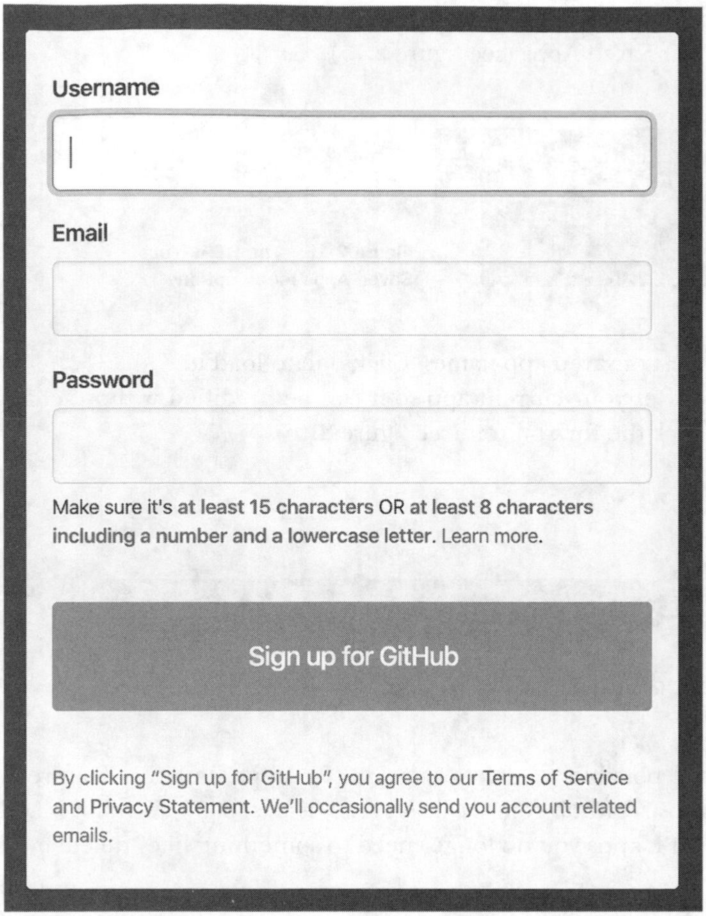
Username
Email
Password
Make sure it's at least 15 characters OR at least 8 characters including a number and a lowercase letter. Learn more.
Sign up for GitHub
By clicking "Sign up for GitHub", you agree to our Terms of Service and Privacy Statement. We'll occasionally send you account related emails.

Figure 2.13 The GitHub Sign Up page

To save your current app, enter a name for it on the left side of the gray bar at the top, and click the floppy disk icon (see figure 2.14). Pressing Ctrl-S (or Cmd-S on macOS) also saves the app.

SVELTE
Hello world
Log in to save

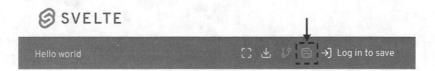

Figure 2.14 The REPL save button

To load a previously saved app, hover over your username at the upper-right of the page, and click Your Saved Apps (see figure 2.15).

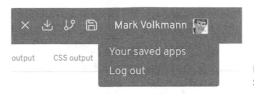

Figure 2.15   The REPL Your Saved Apps menu option

This will display a list of saved app names. Click one to load it.

To make a copy of your current app so it can be modified without changing the current version, click the fork button (see figure 2.16).

Figure 2.16   The REPL fork button

Currently it is not possible to delete saved REPL apps, but this feature has been requested (see https://github.com/sveltejs/svelte/issues/3457). Until it is added, consider renaming REPL apps you no longer need to something like "delete me."

2.1.4   *Sharing REPL apps*

To share a REPL app with other developers, copy its URL from the browser address bar. Then provide it to others via chat, text message, or email. They will be able to modify the REPL app and save the changes as their own app, but they cannot modify your version of the app.

Sharing REPL apps is great for asking questions in the Svelte Discord chat. Post a question along with a REPL URL that demonstrates something you would like to share.

2.1.5   *REPL URLs*

The URL of every REPL app ends with a query parameter named `version` that specifies the version of Svelte being used. It defaults to the newest version, but you can change this to test the REPL app with a different version of Svelte.

This is particularly useful if you suspect a bug has been introduced in Svelte. You can try the REPL app in several versions and determine if its behavior changes.

2.1.6 Exporting REPL apps

At some point in the development of an app in the REPL, you may want to break out of the REPL. There are many reasons to do this:

- To avoid the limitations of the REPL described in the next section
- To manage the app in a source control system such as Git
- To use a build system (such as npm scripts) for tasks such as building the app for deployment and running unit or end-to-end tests
- To get automatic code formatting, perhaps with Prettier
- To get code completion (a.k.a. IntelliSense), perhaps with VS Code

To download the current app so you can continue developing it locally, click the download button (see figure 2.17). This downloads a zip file whose name defaults to svelte-app.zip.

Figure 2.17   The REPL download button

Follow these steps to run the app locally:

1 If Node.js is not already installed, install it from https://nodejs.org. This installs the node, npm, and npx commands.
2 Unzip the downloaded zip file.
3 cd to the directory it creates.
4 Enter npm install.
5 Enter npm run dev to run the app in development mode.

Running Svelte apps outside of the REPL in this way will be covered in more detail later.

2.1.7 Using npm packages

REPL apps can import functions and other values from npm packages. For example, to use the capitalize function from the lodash package, first import it:

```
import capitalize from 'lodash/capitalize';
```

You can then call this function with capitalize(*someString*).

Alternatively, the entire library can be imported.

```
import _ from 'lodash';
```

> **NOTE** An underscore is a valid variable name in JavaScript. It is commonly used as the name of the variable that holds the Lodash library because an underscore looks like a "low dash."

With this kind of import, you can call the `capitalize` function with `_.capitalize (someString)`.

The REPL obtains npm package code from https://unpkg.com, which is a content delivery network (CDN) for all the packages in npm. To import a specific version of an npm package, follow the name with @ followed by the version. For example,

```
import _ from 'lodash@4.16.6'
```

2.1.8   *REPL limitations*

The Svelte REPL is great, but it does have some limitations. It cannot do these things:

- Delete a selected saved project.
- Sort saved projects by name or date.
- Filter the list of saved projects based on text in a project name or text found in one of the files.
- Edit the provided files `src/main.js` and `public/global.css`. Global styles can be defined in a REPL app by defining them in the `style` element within `App.svelte`, enclosing them in the syntax `:global(body) { … }`. This syntax is described in chapter 3.

2.1.9   *CodeSandbox*

CodeSandbox provides an alternative to the Svelte REPL for building Svelte applications without downloading or installing anything. This is an online version of the VS Code editor.

To use it, browse to https://codesandbox.io. No signup is required. To save your work, sign in with your GitHub account.

To create a Svelte project, click the + Create Sandbox button. Under Official Templates, select Svelte.

To enable Vim keybindings, select File > Preferences > CodeSandbox Settings > Editor and toggle Enable VIM Extension to on.

Apps developed in CodeSandbox can be deployed to Vercel Now or Netlify by clicking the left navigation button containing a rocket icon, and then clicking the Deploy to Vercel or the Deploy to Netlify button. This will take a couple of minutes to complete. For Vercel Now, click the supplied link to visit the new app. For Netlify, click the Visit button to visit the new app, and click the Claim button to add the app to your Netlify dashboard.

> **NOTE** Deploying Svelte apps using Netlify and Vercel Now is covered in more detail in chapter 13. The ZEIT company was renamed to Vercel in April 2020.

CodeSandbox supports a Live mode where you can live-edit the files of an application collaboratively with others.

2.2 Working outside the REPL

There are two common ways to create a Svelte application that can be developed and run outside the REPL.

You have already seen the first option. An app created in the REPL can be downloaded as a zip file, and unzipping this provides all the files you need to get started. It is not necessary to enter any code in the REPL. It is sufficient to download the example Hello World app that the REPL provides, and modify the code from that starting point.

The second option is to use the npx tool that is installed with Node.js to execute the degit command. Rich Harris, the creator of Svelte, created degit to simplify project scaffolding. Think of the "de" prefix in the name as meaning "out of." It simply downloads a Git repository that contains a predefined directory structure, including starting files. By default, it downloads the master branch.

It is helpful to use a powerful code editor when working outside the REPL. Although any code editor or IDE can be used, VS Code is recommended. Details on using VS Code to develop Svelte and Sapper apps, including the use of specific extensions, is provided in appendix F.

2.2.1 Starting with npx degit

Let's walk through the steps for creating and running a Svelte application using the degit command.

1 Enter npx degit sveltejs/template *app-name*.

In this case, sveltejs is the organization, and template is the name of a repository owned by that organization.

The second argument is the name of the subdirectory to create, and it is also the name of the application.

This repository uses the Rollup module bundler (https://rollupjs.org). The provided rollup.config.js file uses rollup-plugin-terser which uses the terser library. This minimizes the resulting JavaScript bundle when building for production using npm run build.

Webpack (https://webpack.js.org/) is a module bundler that is an alternative to Rollup. If there are specific Webpack plugins you would like to use, enter the following to create a Svelte project that uses Webpack for module bundling instead of Rollup: npx degit sveltejs/template-webpack app-name

Parcel (https://parceljs.org/) is another module bundler that is an alternative to Rollup. Currently there is no official support for Parcel in Svelte, but unofficial support is available at https://github.com/DeMoorJasper/parcel-plugin-svelte.

2 Enter cd *app-name*.

3 Enter npm install to install all the required dependencies from npm.

4 Enter npm run dev to run the app in development mode.

This starts a local HTTP server. It also provides live reload, which rebuilds the app and refreshes it in the browser if any source files used by the app are modified using any editor.

An alternative way to run the app is to enter npm run build followed by npm start. This omits live reload. The build step is required to create the bundle files that npm start expects to exist in the public directory.

5 Browse to localhost:5000, which renders the page shown in figure 2.18.

Note that the default Webpack configuration uses port 8080 instead of 5000.

HELLO WORLD!

Visit the Svelte tutorial to learn how to build Svelte apps.

Figure 2.18   The sveltejs/ template Hello World app

Module bundlers

A JavaScript module bundler combines the JavaScript code (and sometimes other assets) needed by an application into a single JavaScript file. This includes JavaScript library dependencies such as those from npm (https://npmjs.com). It can also remove code that is not used and minimize the remaining code. All of this reduces the time required to download a JavaScript-based app to a web browser.

There are several popular JavaScript module bundlers, the most popular of which are Webpack, Rollup, and Parcel. Rollup was created by Rich Harris, the creator of Svelte.

Regardless of whether the app is built by entering npm run dev or npm run build, the following files will be created in the public directory:

- bundle.css
- bundle.css.map
- bundle.js
- bundle.js.map

The .map files support debugging the app. They map the generated code to the code you wrote so you can view and step through the code in a debugger.

Now you are ready to start modifying the app. If the browser doesn't render the expected output after you save your changes, check for compilation errors in the terminal window where the server is running. The Svelte compiler is unable to parse some syntax errors (such as unbalanced braces) and a message describing the issue may appear there. These error messages cannot be displayed in the browser because Svelte doesn't produce a new version of the app if there are syntax errors. For this reason, it is recommended that you keep the window where npm run dev is running in view.

TIP Sometimes npm run dev is able to start the server despite warning messages being output. These may scroll off the screen, but you can scroll backwards in the window where npm run dev is running to see them.

TIP If you are not seeing the results of your latest code changes, it could be because you ran npm start instead of npm run dev. The former command runs the code that was compiled the last time you ran npm run build or npm run dev. It's easy to make this mistake because in many other web frameworks npm start is the command that runs the app locally in dev mode with live reload.

2.2.2 Provided package.json

A peek at the package.json file reveals two things.

The first is that Svelte uses Rollup by default for module bundling, as seen in all the references to rollup in the devDependencies. If desired, you can change this to use Webpack or Parcel.

The second is that Svelte apps have only one required runtime dependency, sirv-cli, which provides the local HTTP server used by the npm start command. To see this, look at the values of dependencies and devDependencies in package.json. No other runtime dependencies are required because all the code needed by Svelte apps is included in the bundle.js file that the Svelte compiler produces.

2.2.3 Important files

The most important starting files in a Svelte app are public/index.html, src/main.js, and src/App.svelte. All of these can be modified to suit the needs of the application being developed.

These files use tabs for indentation, but feel free to change these to spaces if tabs aren't your cup of tea. As you will see later, Prettier can do this for you, changing all indentation to use either spaces or tabs.

The public/index.html file contains the following:

Listing 2.2 The public/index.html file

```
<!DOCTYPE html>
<html lang="en">
  <head>
    <meta charset="utf8" />
    <meta name="viewport" content="width=device-width,initial-scale=1" />
    <title>Svelte app</title>
    <link rel="icon" type="image/png" href="/favicon.png" />
```

```
    <link rel="stylesheet" href="/global.css" />
    <link rel="stylesheet" href="/build/bundle.css" />

    <script defer src="/build/bundle.js"></script>
  </head>
  <body>
  </body>
</html>
```

Note that this includes two CSS files and one JavaScript file. The global.css file holds CSS that can affect any component. The bundle.css file is generated from the CSS in each component .svelte file. The bundle.js file is generated from the JavaScript and HTML in each component .svelte file and any other JavaScript code the components use.

The src/main.js file contains the following:

Listing 2.3   The `src/main.js` file

```
import App from './App.svelte';

const app = new App({
  target: document.body,
  props: {
    name: 'world'
  }
});

export default app;
```

This renders the App component. The target property specifies where the component should be rendered. For most apps this is the body of the document.

This code passes the name prop to the App component. Typically the topmost component does not need props, and the props property seen here can be deleted. This is because any data that is hardcoded in main.js can alternatively be hardcoded in App.svelte instead of passing it in through props.

The src/main.js file is expected to make the instance of the topmost component, App in this case, be the default export.

The src/App.svelte file contains the following:

Listing 2.4   The `src/App.svelte` file

```
<script>
  export let name;
</script>

<main>
  <h1>Hello {name}!</h1>
  <p>
    Visit the <a href="https://svelte.dev/tutorial">Svelte tutorial</a>
    to learn how to build Svelte apps.
```

```
    </p>
</main>

<style>
  main {
    text-align: center;
    padding: 1em;
    max-width: 240px;
    margin: 0 auto;
  }

  h1 {
    color: #ff3e00;
    text-transform: uppercase;
    font-size: 4em;
    font-weight: 100;
  }

  @media (min-width: 640px) {
    main {
      max-width: none;
    }
  }
</style>
```

All `.svelte` files can contain a `script` element, arbitrary HTML, and a `style` element. Each section is optional. The order of these sections is not important, but the most common order is `script` first, HTML second, and `style` last. This places the parts that interact next to each other. Variables and functions in the `script` element are typically used by the HTML, and the HTML is styled by the CSS, but the `style` element is rarely affected by code in the `script` element.

The `export` keyword before the `name` variable at the top of the `script` element indicates it is a prop. Prop values can be set in other components that use this component. This is a case where the Svelte compiler treats valid JavaScript syntax (the `export` keyword) in a special way. Another such case is the syntax `$:` for reactive statements, which you learned about earlier.

Curly braces are used to output or render the value of a JavaScript expression, in this case just the variable `name`. This is referred to as *interpolation*. As you will see later, curly braces are also used for dynamic attribute values.

At this point you are free to modify the provided files and add more, just like we did earlier in the REPL.

2.2.4 *Your first non-REPL app*

Let's build a Svelte app that calculates monthly loan payments given a loan amount, annual interest rate, and number of years. Users should be able to change any of the inputs and see the newly calculated monthly payment. We can build this in just 28 lines of code. The details of the calculation are not important. Focus on the layout of the code and the use of reactive declarations.

Follow along with these steps:

1 Enter npx degit sveltejs/template loan.
2 Enter cd loan.
3 Enter npm install.
4 Edit src/App.svelte and change it to match the code in listing 2.4.
5 Enter npm run dev.
6 Browse to localhost:5000.
7 Try changing any of the inputs and verify that the monthly payment is updated.

Listing 2.5   Loan calculator app in `src/App.svelte`

```
<script>
  let interestRate = 3;
  let loanAmount = 200000;
  let years = 30;
  const MONTHS_PER_YEAR = 12;

  $: months = years * MONTHS_PER_YEAR;
  $: monthlyInterestRate = interestRate / 100 / MONTHS_PER_YEAR;
  $: numerator = loanAmount * monthlyInterestRate;
  $: denominator = 1 - (1 + monthlyInterestRate) ** -months;
  $: payment =
    !loanAmount || !years ? 0 :
    interestRate ? numerator / denominator :
    loanAmount / months;
</script>

<label for="loan">Loan Amount</label>
<input id="loan" type="number" bind:value={loanAmount}>

<label for="interest">Interest Rate</label>
<input id="interest" type="number" bind:value={interestRate}>

<label for="years">Years</label>
<input id="years" type="number" bind:value={years}>

<div>
  Monthly Payment: ${payment.toFixed(2)}
</div>
```

> **When an input type is "number," bind coerces the value of the variable, in this case loanAmount, to a number.**

Note the use of reactive declarations in the preceding code. When the value of interestRate, loanAmount, or years changes, the value of payment is recomputed and displayed in the div element at the bottom.

It's not fancy. There is no styling. But it works and dcmonstrates the ease with which useful web apps can be created with Svelte.

2.3   *Bonus app*

Let's implement the famous Todo app in Svelte, as shown in figure 2.19. I have implemented this app in Svelte, React, and Vue, and you can find my implementations here:

- https://github.com/mvolkmann/svelte-todo
- https://github.com/mvolkmann/react-todo
- https://github.com/mvolkmann/vue-todo

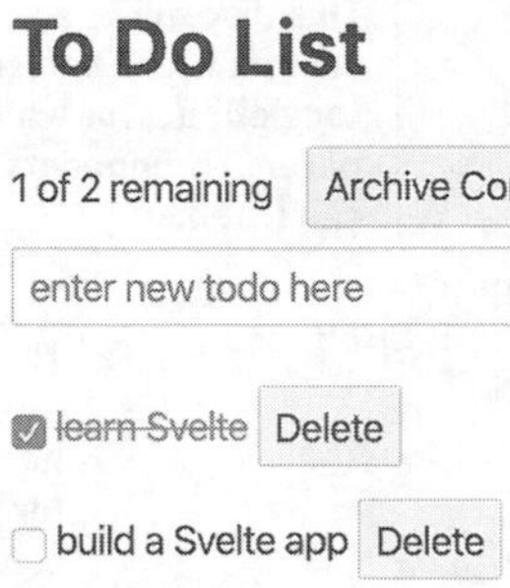

To Do List

1 of 2 remaining   Archive Completed

enter new todo here   Add

☑ ~~learn Svelte~~ Delete

☐ build a Svelte app Delete

Figure 2.19   Todo app

With this app, users can

- Add todos
- Check todos to mark them as completed
- Uncheck todos to mark them as not completed
- Archive the completed todos
- Delete todos
- See the number of todos that have been completed and the total number of todos

We will implement this with two Svelte components named Todo and TodoList.

To create your own version of this app, begin by entering npx degit sveltejs/ template todo.

The Todo component renders a list item (<li>) for a single todo item. It contains a checkbox, the text of the todo, and a Delete button. This component doesn't know what to do when the checkbox is toggled. It also doesn't know what to do when the Delete button is clicked. It just dispatches events that are received by the TodoList component.

The TodoListcomponent is the topmost component in the app. It renders a list of todos inside an unordered list (<ul>). It also listens for events from the Todo component and takes the appropriate actions.

This simple implementation does not actually persist todos to a storage location such as a database when they are archived. It just deletes them.

Listing 2.6 shows the code for the Todo component. We will cover event dispatching in more detail in chapter 5. When todos are added or deleted, the built-in fade transition is used so they gradually appear and disappear.

Listing 2.6   Todo component in `src/Todo.svelte`

```
<script>
  import {createEventDispatcher} from 'svelte';
  import {fade} from 'svelte/transition';
  const dispatch = createEventDispatcher();

  export let todo;
</script>

<li transition:fade>
  <input
    type="checkbox"
    checked={todo.done}
    on:change={() => dispatch('toggleDone')} />
  <span class={'done-' + todo.done}>{todo.text}</span>
  <button on:click={() => dispatch('delete')}>Delete</button>
</li>

<style>
  .done-true {
    color: gray;
    text-decoration: line-through;
  }

  li {
    margin-top: 5px;
  }
</style>
```

This creates a dispatch function that is used to dispatch an event.

TodoList passes an object describing a todo as a prop.

This dispatches a custom event named toggleDone, for which parent components can listen.

This dispatches a custom event named delete, for which parent components can listen.

The todo text will have a CSS class of done-true or done-false. We do not need any special styling for done-false.

Next is the code for the TodoList component.

Listing 2.7   TodoList component in `src/TodoList.svelte`

```
<script>
  import Todo from './Todo.svelte';

  let lastId = 0;

  const createTodo = (text, done = false) => ({id: ++lastId, text, done});

  let todoText = '';

  let todos = [
    createTodo('learn Svelte', true),
    createTodo('build a Svelte app')
  ];

  $: uncompletedCount = todos.filter(t => !t.done).length;

  $: status = `${uncompletedCount} of ${todos.length} remaining`;

  function addTodo() {
    todos = todos.concat(createTodo(todoText));
```

This is a function that creates a todo object.

The app starts with two todos already created.

This is recomputed when the todos array changes.

This is recomputed when the todos array or uncompletedCount changes.

```
    todoText = ''; // clears the input
  }

  function archiveCompleted() {
    todos = todos.filter(t => !t.done);
  }

  function deleteTodo(todoId) {
    todos = todos.filter(t => t.id !== todoId);
  }

  function toggleDone(todo) {
    const {id} = todo;
    todos = todos.map(t => (t.id === id ? {...t, done: !t.done} : t));
  }
</script>

<div>
  <h1>To Do List</h1>
  <div>
    {status}
    <button on:click={archiveCompleted}>Archive Completed</button>
  </div>
  <form on:submit|preventDefault>
    <input
      size="30"
      placeholder="enter new todo here"
      bind:value={todoText} />
    <button disabled={!todoText} on:click={addTodo}>Add</button>
  </form>
  <ul>
    {#each todos as todo}
      <Todo
        {todo}
        on:delete={() => deleteTodo(todo.id)}
        on:toggleDone={() => toggleDone(todo)} />
    {/each}
  </ul>
</div>

<style>
  button {
    margin-left: 10px;
  }

  ul {
    list-style: none; /* removes bullets */
    margin-left: 0;
    padding-left: 0;
  }
</style>
```

This keeps only the todos that are not done.

This deletes the todo with a given ID.

When we use a form, pressing the return key while focus is in the input activates the Add button, calling the addTodo function. But we don't want to POST the form data. The preventDefault modifier prevents that.

This is the Svelte syntax for iterating over an array.

We listen for delete and toggleDone events here.

The Add button is disabled if no text has been entered in the input.

The main.js file is modified to render a TodoList component instead of the default App component.

Listing 2.8   Todo app `src/main.js` file

```
import TodoList from './TodoList.svelte';

const app = new TodoList({target: document.body});

export default app;
```

The following steps will build and run this app:

1 Enter npm install.
2 Enter npm run dev.
3 Browse to localhost:5000.

That's it! We now have a functioning Todo app implemented with a very small amount of code. It demonstrates many of the Svelte concepts we have covered up to this point.

Hopefully what you have seen so far is enough to convince you that there is something special about Svelte. It has a minimal syntax that makes implementing web applications very easy compared to the alternatives.

Svelte has many more features that we will cover in the following chapters. Along the way we will build a web application that serves as a travel-packing checklist. In the next chapter we will dive deeper into defining Svelte components.

Summary

- Svelte provides an online REPL that makes it easy to experiment with Svelte without downloading or installing anything. It can even save apps so they can be recalled later for further study, or it can download them so development can continue outside of the REPL.
- Svelte components are described by files with a .svelte extension that can contain JavaScript, HTML, and CSS.
- Svelte provides a template for generating a starting point for new apps that run outside the REPL.
- Creating a Svelte application outside the REPL only requires a few extra steps.

Part 2

Deeper into Svelte

This part of the book dives deep into Svelte, providing thorough coverage along with lots of example code as we build and manage Svelte components. We'll cover Svelte block structures that wrap conditional logic, iteration, and promise handling around markup, component communication, the use of "stores" to share state between components, lifecycle functions, page routing, animation, debugging, and testing. This part of the book will close out with some options for deploying Svelte applications and additional Svelte-related topics, such as form validation, libraries, and "special elements."

Creating components 3

This chapter covers
- Creating Svelte components
- Styling Svelte components
- Implementing logic in Svelte components
- Defining and updating state in Svelte components

In this chapter we will delve deeper into defining components by creating `.svelte`-files. These files specify the JavaScript that implements state and logic, the HTML to be rendered, and the CSS that will style them.

Components are the fundamental building blocks of web applications in most frameworks. Components are composed of closely related portions of a user interface. They can encapsulate data that is specific to their part of the UI, often referred as *state*. They split a UI into potentially reusable parts.

Some components represent entire pages while others are used within pages. For example, a page that displays a shopping list can be implemented by a `ShoppingList` component, and it can render each item in the list using an `Item` component.

Components accept data passed to them from other components using *props*. These have a syntax similar to HTML attributes, but their values can be any Java-Script type.

The state of a component is the data that is unique to each component instance. The logic of a component is defined by a set of functions that specify its behavior and include event handling.

Styling can be global, potentially affecting all components. More often it is scoped, so it only affects the component in which it is defined. CSS preprocessors such as Sass can be used to gain additional styling functionality.

Reactive statements allow code to be re-executed any time the value of a variable they use changes. Often these statements change the value of a state variable, which causes parts of the component UI to be updated.

Module context can be used to define things that are shared between all instances of a component. For example, it can define variables that hold data to be shared.

By the end of the chapter, you'll be able to create components that can be used in any Svelte app.

3.1   *Content of .svelte files*

Svelte components are defined by the content of a file, not by a JavaScript container in the file, such as a class, function, or object literal. Creating a Svelte component is as easy as creating a file with a .svelte extension that follows some basic rules. These files belong in or below the src directory of an app.

.svelte files can contain at most one <script context="module"> element, one script element, one style element, and any number of HTML elements that can appear in a body element. Each of these are optional, and these elements can appear in any order. This means that something as simple as the following is a valid Svelte component:

```
<div>Hello Svelte!</div>
```

Other currently popular web frameworks require more code than this to define a component.

Most .svelte files have the following structure:

```
<script>
  // Scoped JavaScript goes here.
</script>

<!-- HTML to render goes here. -->

<style>
  /* Scoped CSS rules go here. */
</style>
```

Note the different forms of comment syntax that can be used in each section.

JavaScript constructs defined in the script element are scoped to this component, meaning they are not visible in other components. Likewise, the CSS rules defined in the style element are scoped to this component. In both cases, the benefit is that code in one component cannot accidentally affect other components, which simplifies debugging.

3.2 *Component markup*

As you saw in the previous chapter, the syntax used to refer to and render a Svelte component matches the syntax of HTML elements. For example, a `Hello` component can be used like this:

```
<Hello name="World" />
```

Instances of Svelte components can be passed props and children. The preceding example has a `name` prop, but no children. Props are used to pass data to components. Children provide content to components. Components can then decide when and where to render the children. The children can be text, HTML elements, and other Svelte components.

> **NOTE** In terms of syntax, *props* look just like HTML attributes, but there is a difference. Attributes are specified on HTML elements, whereas props become the properties on JavaScript objects that represent DOM elements, which are in-memory representations of HTML elements.

A prop value can be a literal value of any type (Boolean, number, string, object, array, or function) or the value of a JavaScript expression. When the value is a string, it is enclosed in single or double quotes. Otherwise the value is enclosed in curly braces. These curly braces can optionally be surrounded by quotes to satisfy syntax highlighters.

Here are some examples of props on a Svelte component named `Person`:

```
<Person
  fullName="Jane Programmer"
  developer={true}
  ball={{name: 'baseball', grams: 149, new: false}}
  favoriteColors={['yellow', 'orange']}
  age={calculateAge(person)}
  onBirthday={celebrate}      ⟵——— celebrate is a function.
/>
```

When the value of a prop on an HTML element is `null` or `undefined`, it is not added to the DOM. For example, in `<img alt={description} src={imageUrl}>` if the `description` variable is `null` or `undefined`, the `img` element will not have an `alt` attribute.

We can define this component in a file named `src/Person.svelte` as follows:

```
<script>
  export let age;
  export let ball;
  export let developer;
  export let favoriteColors;
  export let fullName;
  export let onBirthday;
</script>
```

```
<div>
  {fullName} is {age} years old and
  {developer ? 'is' : 'is not'} a developer.
</div>
<div>
  They like the colors {favoriteColors.join(' and ')}.
</div>
<div>
  They like to throw {ball.new ? 'a new' : 'an old'} {ball.name}
  that weighs {ball.grams} grams.
</div>
<button on:click={onBirthday}>It's my birthday!</button>
```

String values can use interpolation to compute values based on JavaScript expressions. Expressions in a string surrounded by curly braces are replaced by their corresponding values. For example,

```
<Person fullName="{lastName}, {firstName} {middleName[0]}." />
```

A shorthand syntax can be used when a prop value is held in a variable with the same name as the prop. For example, if there is a variable named `fullName`, the following are equivalent:

```
<Person fullName={fullName} />
<Person {fullName} />
```

The JavaScript spread operator (. . .) can be used to insert multiple props if they are in an object where the keys are prop names and the values are the prop values. For example, suppose we want to render an `input` element that allows the user to enter a number from 0 to 10. If we have some of the needed `input` attributes in a JavaScript object, we can spread the properties of the object into an HTML `input` element as follows:

```
<script>
  let score = 0;
  const scoreAttrs = {
    type: 'number',
    max: 10,
    min: 0
  };
</script>

<input {...scoreAttrs} bind:value={score}>
```

This uses the bind directive you saw in chapter 2. Recall that this binds the value of a form element to a variable.

If we didn't use the spread operator, we would have to write one of the following:

```
<input type="number" min="0" max="10" bind:value={score}>

<input
  type={scoreAttrs.type}
  min={scoreAttrs.min}
  max={scoreAttrs.max}
  bind:value={score}>
```

DOM properties

Some DOM properties get their initial value from an HTML attribute. Some of these DOM properties can be modified, but their corresponding attribute value never changes. For example, consider the following HTML, which uses JavaScript but not Svelte. The initial value displayed in the input is "initial". If a user changes the value to "new" by typing in the input and clicks the Log button, this will write values from the input to the DevTools console. The DOM property value will be "new", but the HTML attribute value will still be "initial".

```html
<html>
  <head>
    <script>
      function log() {
        const input = document.querySelector('input');
        console.log('DOM prop value =', input.value);
        console.log('HTML attr value =',
          input.getAttribute('value'));
      }
    </script>
  </head>
  <body>
    <label>
      Name
      <input value="initial">
    </label>
    <button onclick="log()">Log</button>
  </body>
</html>
```

Some HTML attributes do not have a corresponding DOM property. An example is the HTML attribute colspan used on td elements in a table.

Some DOM properties do not have a corresponding HTML attribute, such as the DOM property textContent.

All these technicalities aside, we never speak of Svelte components as having *attributes*. They have *props*.

3.3 Component names

Svelte component definitions do not specify a component name. There is no class name, function name, or property value that specifies the name of the component like in other frameworks. Instead, a name is associated when a .svelte file is imported.

Components can import other components inside their script element:

```
import Other from './Other.svelte';
```

Imported components can be used in the HTML section of the component that imports them:

```
<Other />
```

Component names must start with an uppercase letter, and names consisting of multiple words are in typically camel cased. Lowercase names are reserved for predefined elements like those provided by HTML and SVG.

It is common for component names to match the name of their source file, but this is not required. For example,

```
import AnyNameIWant from './some-name.svelte';    ⟵    Somewhat confusing and
                                                        doesn't follow conventions

import SameName from './SameName.svelte';    ⟵    Very clear
```

3.4   *Component styles*

One way to apply styling to an HTML element of a component is to add a `class` attribute for which a CSS rule has been defined inside the `style` element of a component.

Any number of CSS classes can be associated with an HTML element. Suppose we want to use the classes `holiday` and `sale`. Here is one approach:

```
<div class="holiday sale">large red wagon</div>
```

A CSS class can be conditionally added to an HTML element in several ways, each allowing the associated styling to only be applied when a certain condition is met.

The following example renders a message that always has the CSS class `error` if the value of the `status` variable is greater than or equal to 400.

```
<script>
  let status = 200;
  let message = 'This is a message.';
</script>

<label>
  Status                                            This allows the user to
  <input type="number" bind:value={status}>    ⟵   change the value of status.
</label>
<div class:error={status >= 400}>{message}</div>    ⟵    This
                                                          conditionally
<style>                                                   adds the
  .error {    ⟵   Conditionally used                      "error" CSS
    color: red;                                           class.
    font-weight: bold;
  }
</style>
```

An alternative way to conditionally apply the `error` class is as follows:

```
<div class={status >= 400 ? 'error' : ''}>{message}</div>    ⟵

                    The empty string used for the class name when the status is less
                    than 400 can, of course, be replaced by some other CSS class name.
```

Another approach is to use a Boolean variable with the same name. We can set it by adding the following reactive declaration to the previous `script` element:

```
$: error = status >= 400;
```

The syntax `$:`, as seen in chapter 2, marks a *reactive statement*. The important thing to know about reactive statements now is that they are re-executed when the value of any variable they reference changes. In this case, any time the value of `status` changes, the value of `error` will be recomputed. More detail on reactive statements is provided in section 3.10.

With the value of `error` in place, the `div` that uses it can be changed to the following:

```
<div class:error>{message}</div>
```

Svelte automatically excludes unused CSS rules from the generated CSS. These are rules that do not match any HTML element that can be rendered by the component. The Svelte compiler outputs warning messages that identify unused CSS rules.

3.5 CSS specificity

CSS specificity determines the precedence of conflicting CSS rules. This concept is not unique to Svelte, but understanding it will be important in the section that follows.

For example, consider the following HTML:

```
<div class="parent">
  I am the parent.
  <div id="me" class="child" style="color: red">
    I am the child.
  </div>
</div>
```

The following CSS rules set the color of the text "I am the child." to different values. The color used depends on the specificity of the selectors. Scores represented by a list of four numbers are explained after this example.

```
#me {                    ⟵  score is 0,1,0,0.
  color: orange;
}
.parent > .child {       ⟵  score is 0,0,2,0.
  color: yellow;
}
.parent .child {         ⟵  This has the same specificity as the
  color: green;              rule before: 0,0,2,0. The last one wins.
}
.child {          ⟵  score is 0,0,1,0.
  color: blue;
}
.parent {         ⟵  This has the same specificity as the rule before: 0,0,1,0. It applies the
  color: purple;       color purple to the element with the class "parent", but the previous
}                      rule applies the color blue to the element with the class "child".
```

The precedence order of these rules happens to be the order in which they are listed here. Using a `style` attribute on the inner `div` has the highest specificity.

There is a formula for computing the specificity score of any CSS rule that results in a list of four numbers. Considering the four numbers from left to right,

- The first is 1 for inline styles and 0 otherwise.
- The second is the number of `id` values in the selector.
- The third is the number of class names in the selector.
- The fourth is the number of element name references in the selector.

The selector with the highest combined number, obtained by removing the commas and treating it as a single 4-digit number, wins. For example, treat a score of 1,2,3,4 as 1234.

This means that inline styling specified with a `style` attribute on an HTML element always wins. After this, `id` attributes are more important than class names, which are more important than element names.

It also means that the order in which `id` values, class names, and element names appear in a selector does not affect its specificity calculation.

Here are some examples of applying this scoring:

- The CSS selector `.parent > #me` has a score of 0,1,1,0.
- The CSS selector `.parent #me` has the same score.
- The CSS selector `.parent .child` has a score of 0,0,2,0 and so has a lower score than selectors that use an `id`.

For more details on CSS specificity, see "Specifics on CSS Specificity" on the CSS-Tricks site: https://css-tricks.com/specifics-on-css-specificity/.

3.6   *Scoped vs. global styles*

Global styles are desirable when consistent styling needs to be applied across all components in an app. For example, all buttons can be styled to have a blue background with white text, no border, and rounded corners.

Scoped styles are desirable for styling the elements within a component and not affecting elements in other components. For example, a `table` element rendered by a component can be styled so rows are separated by a gray border line, but columns have no border line between them. If this styling is scoped, `table` elements rendered by other components can choose to use different borders.

As mentioned earlier, the CSS rules specified in a Svelte component `style` element are automatically scoped to the component and do not affect other components.

Style scoping is achieved by adding the same generated CSS class name, `svelte-hash`, to each rendered element of the component that is potentially affected by these CSS rules. The hash is generated from the content of the `style` element. The same value is used for all generated CSS rules of the component.

For example, suppose we define the following component in the `src/Pony.svelte` file:

```
<h1>Pony for sale</h1>
<p class="description">2 year old Shetland pony</p>

<style>
  h1 {
    color: pink;
  }
  .description {
    font-style: italic;
  }
</style>
```

The generated `public/build/bundle.css` file will contain CSS rules like the following, but all on the same line:

```
h1.svelte-uq2khz{color:pink}
.description.svelte-uq2khz{font-style:italic}
```

Note how the CSS selectors for `h1` and `.description` both specify an additional CSS class whose name starts with `svelte-` and ends with the same hash value.

It would be rare for multiple components to have the same set of CSS rules in the same order in their `style` elements. If this occurs, those components will use the same hash value. This is not an issue, but it does result in duplicate CSS rules inside the combined `build/bundle.css` file produced by the Svelte compiler.

There are two ways to specify global styles. One way is to define them in the `public/global.css` file. This file is included by `public/index.html` by default. Another way is to use the `:global(selector)` modifier inside the `style` element of a component. This syntax is borrowed from that of CSS Modules (https://github.com/css-modules/css-modules).

An advantage of placing global styles in the `public/global.css` file instead of scattering them across component source files using the `:global(selector)` syntax is that it gives developers a single place to go to discover the global styles.

CSS properties specified in global styles only take effect in a component if that component does not also specify values for the same CSS properties in its `style` element.

For example, suppose we want all `h1` elements to be red unless this is overridden in specific components. We can add the following in `public/global.css`:

```
h1 {
  color: red;
}
```

We can also specify this in the `style` element of any component with the following:

```
:global(h1) {
  color: red;
}
```

If we also use `h1` as a CSS selector inside a component, it will compile to a selector with a scoping class that has the syntax `h1.svelte-hash`. The `:global(h1)` selector compiles to the selector h1 with no scoping. So the :global modifier just prevents the addition of a scoping CSS class.

CSS properties specified using the :global modifier override those for the same CSS selector in public/global.css.

The :global modifier can also be used to override styles in descendant components. This relies on creating CSS rules with selectors that have higher specificity than rules in descendant components.

For example, suppose we have the following component that sets the color of h1 elements to red.

Listing 3.1   A child component defined in `src/Child.svelte`

```
<h1>Hello from Child</h1>

<style>
  h1 {
    color: red;
  }
</style>
```

Listing 3.2 shows a component that uses the Child component. It overrides the CSS color property for h1 elements inside any element with a CSS class of override.

Listing 3.2   A parent component defined in `src/Parent.svelte`

```
<script>
  import Child from './Child.svelte';
</script>

<div class='override'>
  <Child />
</div>

<style>
  .override :global(h1) {
    color: blue;
  }
</style>
```

The CSS generated from Child.svelte is

```
h1.svelte-bt9zrl{color:red}
```

The CSS generated from Parent.svelte is

```
.override.svelte-ul8eid h1{color:blue}
```

This CSS selector takes precedence because it has higher specificity than the CSS selector from Child.svelte. The h1 color becomes blue instead of red.

When `:global` is used, it must appear at the beginning or end of a CSS selector list, not in the middle. For example, the following is not allowed:

```
.user :global(.address) .city { ... }
```

Typically `:global` is used at the end of a selector list to override styling in an ancestor component rather than at the beginning to specify truly global styling.

A list of CSS selectors can be passed to `:global`:

```
.user :global(.address .city) { ... }
```

3.7 *Using CSS preprocessors*

The module bundler used by Svelte can be configured to support using a CSS preprocessor. A CSS preprocessor reads custom styling syntax that supports features not found in standard CSS and converts it to standard CSS. Chapter 20 provides details on configuring these.

One popular CSS preprocessor is Sass (https://sass-lang.com/), which is discussed in more detail in chapter 20. It enables the use of variables, nested rules, mixins, and Sass functions. Once Sass is configured, components can opt into using Sass by adding a `lang` attribute to their `style` element as follows:

```
<style lang="scss">
```

3.8 *Component logic*

The logic of components is defined in two ways. The first is with plain JavaScript functions defined inside their `script` element. The second is using block structures in the component HTML. These block structures are covered in chapter 4.

Many developers find using plain functions easier to understand than using methods of a class or object. Plain functions remove the need to understand the meaning of the JavaScript `this` variable.

As an example of using a plain function in a Svelte component, the following component re-implements the loan-payment calculator shown in section 2.2.4 to perform the calculation in the function `calculatePayment`. It also adds a Reset button that resets the values of all the inputs using the `reset` function.

Listing 3.3   Loan payment calculator

```
<script>
  const MONTHS_PER_YEAR = 12;
  let interestRate, loanAmount, years;

  function calculatePayment(loanAmount, interestRate, years) {
    if (!loanAmount || !years) return 0;
    const months = years * MONTHS_PER_YEAR;
    if (!interestRate) return loanAmount / months;
    const monthlyInterestRate = interestRate / 100 / MONTHS_PER_YEAR;
    const numerator = loanAmount * monthlyInterestRate;
```

```
    const denominator = 1 - (1 + monthlyInterestRate) ** -months;
    return numerator / denominator;
  }

  function reset() {
    interestRate = 3;
    loanAmount = 200000;
    years = 30;
  }

  reset();

  $: payment = calculatePayment(loanAmount, interestRate, years);
</script>

<label for="loan">Loan Amount</label>
<input id="loan" type="number" bind:value={loanAmount}>

<label for="interest">Interest Rate</label>
<input id="interest" type="number" bind:value={interestRate}>

<label for="years">Years</label>
<input id="years" type="number" bind:value={years}>

<div>
  Monthly Payment: ${payment.toFixed(2)}
</div>

<button on:click={reset}>Reset</button>
```

> **This recalculates the payment if any of the arguments to calculatePayment change.**

You may be wondering why we need to pass the arguments `loanAmount`, `interestRate`, and `years` to the `calculatePayment` function. These are also the names of variables that are in the scope of the `calculatePayment` function. Passing the values as arguments lets Svelte know that it needs to call the function again any time those values change.

If we merely used the following, Svelte would never recalculate the `payment` value.

```
$: payment = calculatePayment();
```

3.9   *Component state*

Top-level variables declared in the `script` element of a component are treated as the *state* of the component if they are referenced in HTML interpolations. They are top-level in the sense that they are not local to any function. Recall that these are JavaScript expressions inside curly braces.

Changes to these variables cause interpolations that use them to be reevaluated. If their values change, the associated parts of the DOM are updated.

```
<script>
  let count = 0;
  const increment = () => count++;
</script>
```

```
<div>count = {count}</div>
<button on:click={increment}>+</button>
```

Clicking the "+" button causes the `increment` function to be called. That updates the value of the top-level variable `count`. Because `count` is used in an interpolation inside the `div` element, that part of the DOM is updated.

A new value must be assigned with = to trigger this behavior (or alternative operators such as += and ++). Pushing new elements onto an array does not create a new array and doesn't assign a new value to the variable. The following approaches for updating an array do work:

```
myArr = myArr.concat(newValue);

myArr = [...myArr, newValue];

myArr.push(newValue);
myArr = myArr;
```

The last approach shows that Svelte looks for the assignment of a new value, even if it is just assigning the variable to itself.

From a performance perspective, using `push` is preferred because, unlike using the `concat` method or the spread operator, it does not create a new array.

3.10   *Reactive statements*

Beginning a JavaScript statement with a name followed by a colon creates a *labeled statement*. Labeled statements can be used as targets of `break` and `continue` statements, which can break out of a loop and resume execution at a specified statement. Labeled statements are a feature of JavaScript that is almost never used in practice.

When a label is added to a top-level statement (not nested inside a function or block) and the name is a dollar sign, Svelte treats it as a *reactive statement*.

Interestingly it is not an error in JavaScript to use the same label name for more than one statement in the same scope. This means that we can have more than one reactive statement using the label name $.

This is another example of the Svelte compiler treating valid JavaScript syntax in a special way. Earlier you saw that Svelte treats the `export` keyword specially to define the props that a component accepts.

Reactive statements are repeated when the value of any variable referenced by the statement changes. This is somewhat like "computed properties" in the Vue framework.

When a reactive statement is an assignment, it is called a *reactive declaration*. In the following examples, the first is a reactive declaration and the second is a reactive statement.

```
$: average = total / count;
```
← **The value of average is computed initially and recomputed if the value of total or count changes.**

```
$: console.log('count =', count);
```
← **The value of count is output in the DevTools console when this statement is first executed and again every time it changes. This is great for debugging!**

When `$:` precedes an assignment to an undeclared variable, as in the previous assignment to average, Svelte inserts a `let` for the variable ahead of the reactive statement. It doesn't allow the `let` keyword to be added after `$:` because doing that is not valid in JavaScript. For example, this is not valid:

```
$: let average = total / count;
```

`$:` can also be applied to a block in order to re-execute all the statements in the block when any variables they reference change.

Consider a set of reactive declarations such as the following:

```
$: isTeen = 13 <= age && age < 20;
$: upperName = name.toUpperCase();
```

These can be replaced by a reactive block, but the code becomes more verbose due to the need to declare all the variables outside the block.

```
let isTeen, upperName;
$: {
  isTeen = 13 <= age && age < 20;
  upperName = name.toUpperCase();
}
```

`$:` can also be applied to multiline statements such as `if` statements.

```
$: if (someCondition) {
  // body statements
}
```

The preceding example executes if any variables referenced in the condition or the body change. If the condition includes calls to functions, they will be called if any references in the body have changed. Of course, the body only executes if the condition evaluates to true.

Reactive declarations are executed in topological order. This means evaluations of variables that are used in the calculations of other reactive declarations are executed first. For example, in the app shown in figure 3.1 and listing 3.4, the reactive declarations are executed in the reverse order in which they are listed.

Cylinder Calculations

Diameter 6

Height 5

Radius: 3
Area: 28.27
Volume: 141.37

Figure 3.1   Cylinder volume calculator

Listing 3.4   Cylinder volume calculator

```
<script>
  let diameter = 1;
  let height = 1;

  $: volume = area * height;
```

This expression depends on the values of area and height.

```
$: area = Math.PI * radius ** 2;
$: radius = diameter / 2;
</script>

<h1>Cylinder Calculations</h1>
<label>
  Diameter
  <input type="number" bind:value={diameter}>
</label>
<label>
  Height
  <input type="number" bind:value={height}>
</label>
<label>Radius: {radius}</label>
<label>Area: {area.toFixed(2)}</label>
<label>Volume: {volume.toFixed(2)}</label>

<style>
  input {
    width: 50px;
  }
</style>
```

This expression depends on the value of radius.

This expression depends on the value of diameter.

Dependencies between the variables in listing 3.4 are shown in figure 3.2.

Consider ordering reactive declarations in the order in which they will be executed to make reading and understanding the code a bit easier. In this case, the order would be radius, area, and volume. The opposite order was used in listing 3.4 to emphasize that Svelte handles these correctly regardless of their order.

Svelte is able to detect reactive declarations that are circular in nature and flag them as an error. For example, the following code will trigger the error "Cyclical dependency detected."

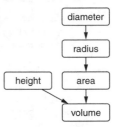

Figure 3.2 Dependencies between variables

```
$: a = b + 1;
$: b = a + 1;
```

3.11 *Module context*

Svelte supports a custom `script` element attribute that indicates the code it contains is in the *module context*. Think of this as like the distinction between instance and class (static) variables and methods in a JavaScript class.

```
<script context="module">
  ...
</script>
```

When a `script` element doesn't specify its context, it is *instance context*. One of each kind of `script` element, module and instance context, can appear in a component source file.

The module context can declare variables and define functions that are accessible in the instance context of all instances of the component. This allows the sharing of data between all instances. However, module context variables are *not reactive*, so components will not update when their values change. Instance context variables and functions are not accessible in the module context.

To run JavaScript code in a component source file only once instead of once for each component instance created, include the code in module context.

Note that it is not necessary to move functions that don't access component state to the module context because (from the Svelte API docs) "Svelte will hoist any functions that don't depend on local state out of the component definition."

However, one reason to put functions in module context is so they can be exported and called from outside the source file. Note that .svelte files cannot specify a default export—they always define a component, and that component automatically becomes the default export.

The following listing shows an example of a component definition that also exports a function from its module context.

Listing 3.5   Component code layout

```
<script context="module">
  export function add(n1, n2) {
    return n1 + n2;
  }
</script>

<script>
  <!-- Component JavaScript goes here. -->
</script>

<!-- Component HTML goes here. -->

<style>
  /* Component CSS goes here. */
</style>
```

Another component can use the exported add function as follows.

Listing 3.6   Using an exported function

```
<script>
  import {add} from './Demo.svelte';

  onMount(() => {
    const sum = add(1, 3);
    console.log('home.svelte onMount: sum =', sum);
  });
</script>
```

Although this works, it is more common to define and export utility functions like this in a .js file instead of a .svelte file.

Perhaps the most common use of module context is to define `preload` functions that are used to load data needed by a component in a Sapper app. You will learn about these in chapter 16.

3.12 *Building a custom component*

Many web apps use `select` elements to allow a user to select from a set of options. The options are specified using nested `option` elements. Each option can specify the text to display, and optionally the value to use if a user selects it. When no value is specified, the text becomes the value.

We can create a custom Svelte component that simplifies using `select` elements. Like the Todo component in chapter 2, this `Select` component dispatches a custom event named `select` for which parent components can listen. It does this by calling the `dispatch` function, which is obtained by calling the provided `createEvent-Dispatcher` function.

Listing 3.7 `Select` **component in** `src/Select.svelte`

```
<script>
  import {createEventDispatcher} from 'svelte';
  const dispatch = createEventDispatcher();
  export let options;

  const getLabel = option =>
    typeof option === 'object' ? option.label : option;

  const getValue = option =>
    typeof option === 'object' ?
      option.value || option.label :
      option;
</script>

<select on:change={event => dispatch('select', event.target.value)}>
  {#each options as option}
    <option value={getValue(option)}>{getLabel(option)}</option>
  {/each}
</select>
```

Options are passed in through this prop. They are represented by an array of strings or objects. When objects are used, they can have label and value properties. If no value is provided, the label is used for the value.

When an option is selected, a "select" event is dispatched with the selected value as the value of the event.

This is Svelte syntax for iterating over an array.

The following listing shows a component that uses the `Select` component.

Listing 3.8 **App that uses** `Select` **component in** `src/App.svelte`

```
<script>
  import Select from './Select.svelte';

  const options = [
    '',
    'Red',
    {label: 'Green'},
    {label: 'Blue', value: 'b'}
  ];
```

This represents nothing being selected.

Options can be just strings.

When the value is an object, having a value property is optional.

This object value specifies both a label and a value for the option.

```
  let selected;

  const handleSelect = event => selected = event.detail;
</script>

<Select options={options} on:select={handleSelect} />

{#if selected}
  <div>You selected {selected}.</div>
{/if}
```

The second argument to the dispatch function in Select.svelte is the value of the selected option, which is available here as event.detail.

3.13   *Building the Travel Packing app*

Let's use what we have learned so far to begin building the Travel Packing app described earlier. The finished code can be found at http://mng.bz/wBdO.

In the end, we want to allow users to do the following:

- Create an account (though we won't really implement this)
- Log in and log out
- Create, edit, and delete categories for checklist items
- Create, edit, and delete checklist items
- Check and uncheck items
- See all checklist items, only checked items, and only unchecked items
- See a progress bar that shows the percentage packed in each category
- Clear all checked items in preparation for the next trip

To create the starting files for the app, cd to the directory where you would like to create the app and enter npx degit sveltejs/template travel-packing.

Next, create the src/Login.svelte file. The Login component will consist of an input for username, an input for password, a Login button, and a Sign Up button. The buttons won't do anything yet. We're just focusing on the presentation aspects.

The CSS for the Login component uses flexbox for layout. If you are new to flexbox, check out "Flexbox Froggy" (https://flexboxfroggy.com) or the free video course from Wes Bos (https://flexbox.io/).

Here is the code for the Login component.

Listing 3.9   Login component in src/Login.svelte

```
<script>
  let password = '';
  let username = '';

  const login = () => alert('You pressed Login.');
  const signup = () => alert('You pressed Signup.');
</script>

<section>
  <form on:submit|preventDefault={login}>
    <label>
      Username
```

The preventDefault modifier prevents form submission.

```
      <input required bind:value={username}>
    </label>
    <label>
      Password
      <input type="password" required bind:value={password}>
    </label>
    <div class="buttons">
      <button>Login</button>
      <button type="button" on:click={signup}>Sign Up</button>    ⟵
    </div>
  </form>
</section>
```

The default type of button element is "submit". We only want the form to have one submit button, so this button is explicitly given a type of "button".

```
<style>
  .buttons {
    display: flex;
    justify-content: space-between;

    font-size: 1.5rem;
    margin-top: 1rem;
  }

  form {
    display: inline-block;
  }

  input {
    display: block;
    margin-top: 0.3rem;
  }

  label {
    color: white;
    display: block;
    font-size: 1.5rem;
    margin-top: 0.5rem;
  }
</style>
```

Note that the Login button does not have an on:click attribute. Clicking the button or pressing the Enter key while focus is in either input triggers a call to the login function because that is specified in the on:submit prop of the form element, and the Login button has a default type of submit.

Import the Login component in src/App.svelte by replacing the content of its script element with the following:

```
import Login from './Login.svelte';
```

Render the Login component in App.svelte by replacing the content of its main element with the following:

```
<h1 class="hero">Travel Packing Checklist</h1>
  <Login />
```

The CSS for the App component uses CSS variables and flexbox. If you are new to CSS variables, check out the "Using CSS custom properties (variables)" page on Mozilla Developer Network (MDN) at http://mng.bz/qM8A.

Replace the style element in App.svelte with the following.

Listing 3.10   The style element in App.svelte

```
<style>
  :global(body) {
    background-color: cornflowerblue;
  }

  .hero {                          This defines a
    --height: 7rem;         ⟵     CSS variable.

    background-color: orange;
    color: white;
    font-size: 4rem;              This uses a
    height: var(--height);   ⟵   CSS variable.
    line-height: var(--height);
    margin: 0 0 3rem 0;
    text-align: center;
    vertical-align: middle;
    width: 100vw;
  }

  main {
    color: white;
    display: flex;
    flex-direction: column;
    justify-content: flex-start;
    align-items: center;
  }
</style>
```

Modify the styling for the body element in public/global.css.

Listing 3.11   Change to body styling in public/global.css

```
body {
  padding: 0; /* was 8px */
  ... keep other properties ...
}
```

By default, Firefox displays a red box shadow around required inputs that have no value. To prevent this, add the following in public/global.css.

Listing 3.12   Styling of invalid inputs in public/global.css

```
/* This prevents Firefox from displaying a red box shadow
   around required inputs that have no value. */
input:invalid {
  box-shadow: none;
}
```

Run the app by entering `npm install` followed by `npm run dev` and browsing local-host:5000. You should see the results shown in figure 3.3.

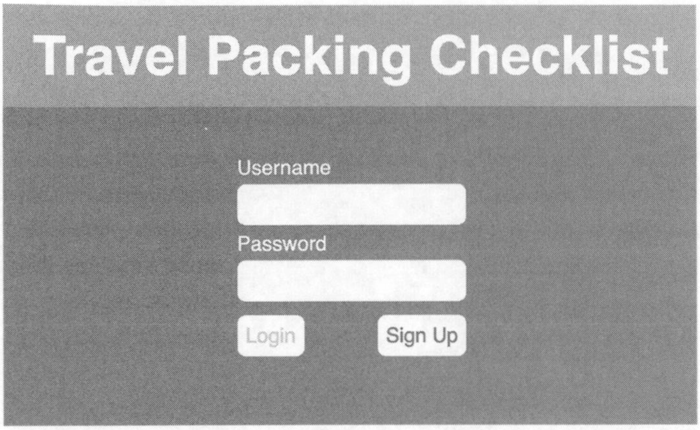

Figure 3.3   Travel Packing login

We have covered the basics of defining Svelte components, including defining what they render, styling the rendered HTML, and defining and updating component state.

In the next chapter, you will learn how to add conditional logic, iteration, and promise handling in the HTML portion of Svelte components.

Summary

- Svelte component definitions have a simple, recognizable syntax that consists of HTML elements. A `script` element holds the logic, a `style` element contains the CSS styles, and the rest is the HTML markup.
- A common way to pass data to components is through props.
- A Svelte component can import and render other Svelte components.
- CSS styling specified in a Svelte component is scoped to that component by default.
- Logic for Svelte components is implemented with plain JavaScript functions.
- Top-level variables in a Svelte component represent its state.
- Reactive statements start with `$:` and are repeated any time the value of a variable they reference changes.
- Module context is used to declare variables and define functions that are shared by all instances of the component, like static properties in many programming languages.

Block structures 4

This chapter covers
- Conditional logic in HTML with `#if`
- Iteration in HTML with `#each`
- Waiting on promises in HTML with `#await`

There are three common approaches to adding conditional and iteration logic in the markup of various web frameworks. React uses JSX (JavaScript XML) where logic is implemented by JavaScript code in curly braces (https://reactjs.org/docs/introducing-jsx.html). Angular and Vue support framework-specific attributes for logic. For example, Angular supports `ngIf` and `ngFor`, while Vue supports `v-if` and `v-for`. Svelte supports a Mustache-like (https://mustache.github.io/) custom syntax that wraps HTML and the components to render.

There are only three kinds of block structures in Svelte:

- `if` is used to specify conditional logic that determines whether something should be rendered.
- `each` is used to iterate over a collection of data, rendering something for each piece of data.
- `await` waits for a promise to resolve and renders something using that data.

Each of these defines blocks of HTML to render. They begin with {#*name*}, end with {/*name*}, and can contain {:*name*} intermediate markers. The # character indicates a block opening tag. The / character indicates a block ending tag. The : character indicates a block continuation tag. Read on to learn how to use these block structures.

4.1 Conditional logic with {#if}

Conditional logic in the HTML section of a Svelte component begins with {#if *condition*}, where the condition is any valid JavaScript expression. The end is marked with {/if}. The markup to be conditionally rendered goes between these. Other block tags that can be included between these are {:else if *condition*} and {:else}.

For example, we can render an assessment of a color as follows:

```
{#if color === 'yellow'}
  <div>Nice color!</div>
{:else if color === 'orange'}
  <div>That's okay too.</div>
{:else}
  <div>Questionable choice.</div>
{/if}
```

While this syntax may seem odd at first, it does have the benefit of being able to conditionally render multiple elements without specifying a common parent element.

The Angular/Vue approach of adding special attributes to elements requires specifying a common parent element in order to render multiple elements. In Angular this can be the special <ng-container> element, which does not produce a corresponding DOM element, as in the following listing.

Listing 4.1 Conditional logic in Angular using `ng-container`

```
<ng-container *ngIf="isMorning">
  <h1>Good Morning!</h1>
  <p>There is a lot on your plate today.</p>
</ng-container>
```

In Vue the common parent element can be a `div` element, but that element will appear in the rendered output, as in the following listing.

Listing 4.2 Conditional logic in Vue using a `div`

```
<div v-if="isMorning">
  <h1>Good Morning!</h1>
  <p>There is a lot on your plate today.</p>
</div>
```

React requires a common parent element or a React-specific "fragment." Fragments do not produce a corresponding DOM element.

Listing 4.3 Conditional logic in React using a fragment

```
{isMorning && (
  <>
    <h1>Good Morning!</h1>
    <p>There is a lot on your plate today.</p>
  </>
)}
```

Svelte does not require any wrapping element to conditionally render multiple elements. Its block syntax is used instead.

Listing 4.4 Conditional logic in Svelte

```
{#if isMorning}
  <h1>Good Morning!</h1>
  <p>There is a lot on your plate today.</p>
{/if}
```

4.2 *Iteration with {#each}*

Iteration in HTML begins with {#each array as item}. The end is marked with {/each}. The markup to be rendered for each item goes between these.

The expression that follows #each can be any JavaScript expression that results in an array or array-like object. This includes literal values, variables, and function calls.

Optionally {:else} can be used before {/each}. Content after {:else} is rendered when the array is empty.

For example, suppose the variable colors is set to ['red', 'green', 'blue']. The following example outputs each color on a separate line using the color.

```
{#each colors as color}
  <div style="color: {color}">{color}</div>
{/each}
```

The next example outputs each color on a separate line preceded by its 1-based position followed by a parenthesis:

```
{#each colors as color, index}
  <div>{index + 1}) {color}</div>
{/each}
```

The following example uses destructuring to get specific properties of the objects in the array people:

```
{#each people as {name, age}}
  <div>{name} is {age} years old.</div>
{:else}
  <div>There are no people.</div>
{/each}
```

Another option is to iterate over the keys and values of an object using `Object.entries` as follows:

```
<script>
  const person = {
    color: 'yellow',
    name: 'Mark',
    spouse: {
      color: 'blue',
      name: 'Tami'
    }
  };
</script>

{#each Object.entries(person) as [key, value]}
  <div>found key "{key}" with value {JSON.stringify(value)}</div>
{/each}
```

This renders the following:

```
found key "color" with value "yellow"
found key "name" with value "Mark"
found key "spouse" with value {"color":"blue","name":"Tami"}
```

If the items in an array will be added, removed, or modified after they are initially rendered, a unique identifier should be supplied for each element. Svelte refers to this as a "keyed each block," and it allows Svelte to optimize updating the DOM. It is similar to the need for the `key` prop in React and Vue.

In Svelte, the unique identifier is supplied as part of the #each syntax, not as a prop. In the following example, the unique identifier for each person is their `id` property.

```
{#each people as person (person.id)}
  <div>{person.name} is {person.age} years old.</div>
{/each}
```

To iterate a given number of times rather than over all the elements in an array, you can create an array with that number of elements. For example,

```
{#each Array(rows) as _, index}
  <div>line #{index + 1}</div>
{/each}
```
← **Array(rows) creates an array of length rows where all the elements are undefined.**

4.3 Promises with {#await}

Svelte provides a block structure to wait for promises to resolve or reject. It can render different output based on whether the promise is still pending, has resolved, or has rejected.

For example, suppose we have a `getDogs` function that calls an API service, perhaps using the Fetch API, to retrieve a list of dog descriptions. Calling an API service is an asynchronous operation, so a JavaScript `Promise` object is returned. It will resolve to an array of objects that describe dogs. Each has a `name` and `breed` property.

NOTE   Using the Fetch API is described in appendix B.

Any variable name can be used after `:then` and `:catch` to receive the resolved or rejected value.

```
{#await getDogs()}
  <div>Waiting for dogs ...</div>
{:then dogs}
  {#each dogs as dog}
    <div>{dog.name} is a {dog.breed}.</div>
  {/each}
{:catch error}
  <div class="error">Error: {error.message}</div>
{/await}
```

The next example omits the markup to be rendered while waiting for the `Promise` to resolve. The `:catch` portion can also be omitted, but it's typically best to render something to let the user know if the promise was rejected.

```
{#await getDogs() then dogs}
  {#each dogs as dog}
    <div>{dog.name} is a {dog.breed}.</div>
  {/each}
{:catch error}
  <div class="error">Error: {error.message}</div>
{/await}
```

If a component needs to trigger re-evaluating data from a promise, you can store the promise in a top-level variable, use that variable after `#await` (eg., `{#await myPromise}`), and modify the variable in a function.

Let's demonstrate this using a publicly available API service that returns images of a given dog breed (see figure 4.1). Copy this code to a REPL and try it!

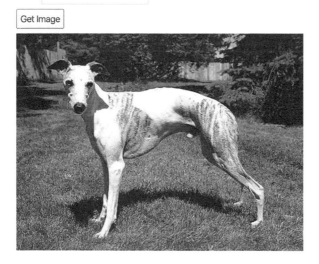

Figure 4.1   Dog breed image app

Listing 4.5   Dog breed image app

```
<script>
  let breed = 'Whippet';        ⟵┐   A Whippet is a dog breed.

  async function getDogs() {     ⟵┐   This returns a promise.
    const url =
      'https://dog.ceo/api/breed/' +
      `${breed.toLowerCase()}/images/random/1`;
    const res = await fetch(url);
    if (!res.ok || res.status === 404) return [];
    const json = await res.json();
    return json.message;
  }

  let dogsPromise = getDogs();
</script>

<label>
  Breed
  <input bind:value={breed}>
</label>
<button on:click={() => dogsPromise = getDogs()}>   ⟵┐   Changing the value of
  Get Image                                                dogsPromise causes
</button>                                                   the #await to be
                                                           evaluated again.
{#await dogsPromise}
  <div>Waiting for dogs ...</div>
{:then imageUrls}
  {#each imageUrls as url}
    <div><img alt="dog" src={url}></div>
  {:else}
    <div>Not found</div>
  {/each}
{:catch error}
  <div>Error: {error.message}</div>
{/await}
```

Listing 4.6 shows one more example of using #await that uses a publicly available API service intended for demonstration purposes, and the results are shown in figure 4.2. The service returns a JSON object containing two properties, status and data. The status property is set to the string "success" when the call is successful. The data property holds an array of objects describing employees at a company.

Employees

Name	Age
Airi Satou	33
Ashton Cox	66
Bradley Greer	41
Brielle Williamson	61

Figure 4.2   Employee table

Listing 4.6   Component that renders the employee table

```
<script>
  let employees = [];
  let message;
```

```
       async function getEmployees() {
         const res = await fetch(
           'http://dummy.restapiexample.com/api/v1/employees');
         const json = await res.json();
         if (json.status === 'success') {
           return json.data.sort(
             (e1, e2) => e1.employee_name.localeCompare(e2.employee_name));
         } else {
           throw new Error(json.status);
         }
       }
     </script>
```

This sorts the employees on their name, first before last. →

```
     {#await getEmployees()}
       <div>Loading employees ...</div>
     {:then employees}
       <table>
         <caption>Employees</caption>
         <tr><th>Name</th><th>Age</th></tr>
         {#each employees as employee}
           <tr>
             <td>{employee.employee_name}</td>
             <td>{employee.employee_age}</td>
           </tr>
         {/each}
       </table>
     {:catch message}
       <div class="error">Failed to retrieve employees: {message}</div>
     {/await}

     <style>
       caption {
         font-size: 1rem;
         font-weight: bold;
         margin-bottom: 0.5rem;
       }
       .error {
         color: red;
       }
       table {
         border-collapse: collapse;
       }
       td, th {
         border: solid lightgray 1px;
         padding: 0.5rem;
       }
     </style>
```

4.4   *Building the Travel Packing app*

Let's apply what you have learned about Svelte block structures to the Travel Packing app. The finished code can be found at http://mng.bz/vxBM.

We need to walk through a lot of code here, but it should all be understandable given what you have learned so far. This will set the stage for adding more features to the app in subsequent chapters.

The Item component uses #if to render the item name in an HTML input when in editing mode and in an HTML span otherwise. The Category component does the same for its name. It also uses #each to iterate over the items in a category. The Checklist component uses #each to iterate over the categories in a checklist.

Eventually we will create all the files shown in figure 4.3. The arrows point to files that are imported by a given file.

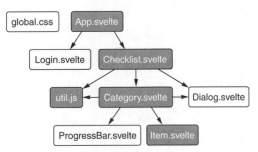

Shaded files are presented in this chapter.

Figure 4.3   Travel Packing app source files

4.4.1   *Item component*

First we need a component to represent an item to be packed. Items belong to a category, and categories have an ID. The Item component takes one prop, item, whose value is an object. An item object has the properties id (string), name (string), and packed (Boolean).

An item is represented by an li element that contains three children:

- The first child of the li is a checkbox that indicates whether the item has been packed. Clicking this toggles the packed property of the item object.
- The second child of the li is either a span element containing the name of the item or an input element that is used to edit the name. To edit the name of an item, the user clicks the text. This changes the value of the Boolean editing to true, which causes an input element to be rendered instead of a span. The editing Boolean is changed back to false when the user moves focus out of the input or presses the Enter key.
- The third child of the li is a button containing a trash can icon. In the future, clicking this will delete the item, but this is not implemented yet.

 pants

When an item is packed, its name is displayed in gray and with line-through, as shown in figure 4.4.

Figure 4.4 Item components

Listing 4.7   Item component defined in src/Item.svelte

```
<script>
  import {blurOnKey} from './util';
```

```
  export let item;

  let editing = false;
</script>

<li>
  <input type="checkbox" bind:checked={item.packed}>
  {#if editing}
    <input
      autofocus
      bind:value={item.name}
      on:blur={() => (editing = false)}
      on:keydown={blurOnKey}
      type="text" />
  {:else}
    <span class="packed-{item.packed}" on:click={() => (editing = true)}>
      {item.name}
    </span>
  {/if}
  <button class="icon">&#x1F5D1;</button>
</li>

<style>
  button {
    background-color: transparent;
    border: none;
  }

  input[type='checkbox'] {
    --size: 24px;                    This is a CSS
    height: var(--size);             variable.
    width: var(--size);
  }

  input[type='text'] {
    border: solid lightgray 1px;
  }

  li {
    display: flex;
    align-items: center;
  }

  .packed-true {
    color: gray;
    text-decoration: line-through;
  }

  span {
    margin: 0 10px;
  }
</style>
```

4.4.2 Utility functions

Some components use functions defined in util.js, shown in listing 4.8.

The getGuid function returns a unique ID. This is used to assign IDs to items to be packed. It requires the uuid npm package, which you can install by entering npm install uuid.

The sortOnName function is used to sort items within a category in a case-insensitive way.

Listing 4.8   Utility functions defined in `src/util.js`

```
import {v4 as uuidv4} from 'uuid';

export function getGuid() {
  return uuidv4();
}

export function blurOnKey(event) {
  const {code} = event;
  if (code === 'Enter' || code === 'Escape' || code === 'Tab') {
    event.target.blur();
  }
}

export function sortOnName(array) {
  array.sort((el1, el2) =>
    el1.name.toLowerCase().localeCompare(el2.name.toLowerCase())
  );
  return array;
}
```

4.4.3 Category component

Next we need a component to represent a category of items, such as "Clothing." The Category component renders the following (see figure 4.5):

- The name of the category
- The number of items in the category remaining to be packed
- The total number of items in the category
- A trash can icon for deleting the category

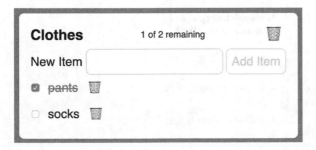

Figure 4.5   Category **component**

- An input for entering the name of a new item to be added to the category
- A button to click to add a new item
- A list of Item components, one for each item in the category

A category object has the properties id (string), name (string), and items (array of item objects).

The Category component takes three props: categories (array of category objects), category (object), and show (string). The categories prop is used to determine whether an item to be added already exists in another category. The category prop describes the category being rendered. The show prop is a string with a value of all, packed, or unpacked. It indicates which of the items should be displayed.

Clicking the name of the category changes it to an input so it can be edited. Moving focus out of the input or pressing the Enter key finalizes the change.

Listing 4.9 Category component defined in `src/Category.svelte`

```
<script>
  import Item from './Item.svelte';
  import {getGuid, blurOnKey, sortOnName} from './util';

  export let categories;
  export let category;
  export let show;

  let editing = false;
  let itemName = '';
  let items = [];
  let message = '';

  $: items = Object.values(category.items);
  $: remaining = items.filter(item => !item.packed).length;
  $: total = items.length;
  $: status = `${remaining} of ${total} remaining`;
  $: itemsToShow = sortOnName(items.filter(i => shouldShow(show, i)));

  function addItem() {
    const duplicate = Object.values(categories).some(cat =>
      Object.values(cat.items).some(item => item.name === itemName)
    );
    if (duplicate) {
      message = `The item "${itemName}" already exists.`;
      alert(message);          ◁────── This will be replaced by
      return;                          a dialog in chapter 7.
    }

    const {items} = category;
    const id = getGuid();
    items[id] = {id, name: itemName, packed: false};
    category.items = items;
    itemName = '';           ◁────── This clears the input.
  }
```

```
    function shouldShow(show, item) {
      return (
        show === 'all' ||
        (show === 'packed' && item.packed) ||
        (show === 'unpacked' && !item.packed)
      );
    }
</script>

<section>
  <h3>
    {#if editing}
      <input
        bind:value={category.name}
        on:blur={() => (editing = false)}
        on:keypress={blurOnKey} />
    {:else}
      <span on:click={() => (editing = true)}>{category.name}</span>
    {/if}
    <span class="status">{status}</span>
    <button class="icon">&#x1F5D1;</button>
  </h3>

  <form on:submit|preventDefault={addItem}>
    <label>
      New Item
      <input bind:value={itemName}>
    </label>
    <button disabled={!itemName}>Add Item</button>
  </form>

  <ul>
    {#each itemsToShow as item (item.id)}
      <!-- This bind causes the category object to update
        when the item packed value is toggled. -->
      <Item bind:item />          ⟵┐  This is equivalent to <Item bind:item={item} />.
    {:else}
      <div>This category does not contain any items yet.</div>
    {/each}
  </ul>
</section>

<style>
  button,
  input {
    border: solid lightgray 1px;
  }

  button.icon {
    border: none;
  }

  h3 {
    display: flex;
```

```
    justify-content: space-between;
    align-items: center;

    margin: 0;
  }

  section {
    --padding: 10px;

    background-color: white;
    border: solid transparent 3px;
    border-radius: var(--padding);
    color: black;
    display: inline-block;
    margin: var(--padding);
    padding: calc(var(--padding) * 2);
    padding-top: var(--padding);
    vertical-align: top;
  }

  .status {
    font-size: 18px;
    font-weight: normal;
    margin: 0 15px;
  }

  ul {
    list-style: none;
    margin: 0;
    padding-left: 0;
  }
</style>
```

4.4.4 *Checklist component*

Now we need a component to render all the categories. The Checklist component renders the following (see figure 4.6):

- An input for entering the name of a new category
- A button to click that adds the new category
- A list of suggested category names
- A set of radio buttons that determine whether to show all items, only those that have been packed, or only those that still need to be packed (unpacked items)

Figure 4.6 Checklist component

- A button to click that clears all the item checkboxes, which is useful when starting to pack for a new trip
- One Category component for each existing category

The Checklist component does not take any props.

Listing 4.10 Checklist **component defined in** src/Checklist.svelte

```
<script>
  import Category from './Category.svelte';
  import {getGuid, sortOnName} from './util';

  let categoryArray = [];
  let categories = {};
  let categoryName;
  let message = '';
  let show = 'all';

  $: categoryArray = sortOnName(Object.values(categories));

  function addCategory() {
    const duplicate = Object.values(categories).some(
      cat => cat.name === categoryName
    );
    if (duplicate) {
      message = `The category "${categoryName}" already exists.`;
      alert(message);
      return;
    }

    const id = getGuid();
    categories[id] = {id, name: categoryName, items: {}};
    categories = categories;
    categoryName = '';
  }

  function clearAllChecks() {
    for (const category of Object.values(categories)) {
      for (const item of Object.values(category.items)) {
        item.packed = false;
      }
    }
    categories = categories;
  }
</script>

<section>
  <header>
    <form on:submit|preventDefault={addCategory}>
      <label>
        New Category
        <input bind:value={categoryName}>
      </label>
      <button disabled={!categoryName}>Add Category</button>
```

This will be replaced by a dialog in chapter 7.

This triggers an update.

This clears the input.

Consider adding a confirmation here to avoid accidentally clearing all the checks.

```
        <button class="logout-btn">
          Log Out
        </button>
      </form>
      <p>
        Suggested categories include Backpack, Clothes,
        <br />
        Last Minute, Medicines, Running Gear, and Toiletries.
      </p>

      <div class="radios">
        <label>Show</label>
        <label>
          <input name="show" type="radio" value="all" bind:group={show}>
          All
        </label>
        <label>
          <input name="show" type="radio" value="packed" bind:group={show}>
          Packed
        </label>
        <label>
          <input name="show" type="radio" value="unpacked" bind:group={show}>
          Unpacked
        </label>

        <button class="clear" on:click={clearAllChecks}>Clear All Checks</button>
      </div>
    </header>

    <div class="categories">
      {#each categoryArray as category (category.id)}
        <Category bind:category {categories} {show} />
      {/each}
    </div>
</section>

<style>
  .categories {
    display: inline-flex;
    flex-wrap: wrap;
    justify-content: center;
  }

  .clear {
    margin-left: 30px;
  }

  input[type='radio'] {
    --size: 24px;
    height: var(--size);
    width: var(--size);
    margin-left: 10px;
  }

  .logout-btn {
    position: absolute;
```

There are accessibility issues here that will be fixed in chapter 12.

Using bind:group with a set of related radio buttons makes the value a single string.

```
    right: 20px;
    top: 20px;
  }

  .radios {
    display: flex;
    align-items: center;
  }

  .radios > label:not(:first-of-type) {
    display: inline-flex;
    align-items: center;

    margin-left: 1em;
  }

  .radios > label > input {
    margin-bottom: -3px;
    margin-right: 5px;
  }
  section {
    display: flex;
    flex-direction: column;
    align-items: center;

    font-size: 24px;
    margin-top: 1em;
  }
</style>
```

4.4.5   App component

For now we will render this component in the App component instead of the Login component created in the previous chapter. Later we will add logic to render only one of them at a time, depending on the state of the app.

Modify App.svelte:

1 Comment out the import of the Login component at the top of the script element.

2 Import the Checklist component at the top of the script element.

```
import Checklist from './Checklist.svelte';
```

3 In the HTML section, comment out <Login /> and add <Checklist />.

To specify global styling for the app that can affect any component, replace the contents of public/global.css with the following:

> **Listing 4.11   Global CSS defined in public/global.css**

```
body {
  font-family: sans-serif;
  height: 100vh;
```

```
    margin: 0;
    padding: 0;
  }

  button:not(:disabled),
  input:not(:disabled) {
    cursor: pointer;
  }

  button:disabled {
    color: lightgray;
  }

  button.icon {
    background-color: transparent;
    border: none;
    margin-bottom: 0;
  }

  input:disabled {
    color: #ccc;
  }

  label {
    display: inline-block;
  }

  input,
  button,
  select,
  textarea {
    --padding: 10px;

    border-radius: var(--padding);
    border: none;
    box-sizing: border-box;
    color: gray;
    font-family: inherit;
    font-size: inherit;
    margin: 0;
    padding: var(--padding);
  }
```

4.4.6   *Try it*

Run the app by entering npm run dev and browsing to localhost:5000. You should now
see the page shown in figure 4.7.

Try adding some categories and adding items in each category. Click category and
item names to modify them. Check some items to mark them as packed. Click the
Show radio buttons to switch between showing all items, only packed items, or only
unpacked items.

Clicking the trash can icons will not delete categories and items just yet. We will
implement those in chapter 5, and you will also learn about all the ways in which
Svelte components can share data.

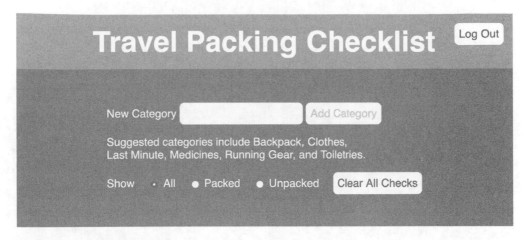

Figure 4.7   Travel Packing app

Summary

- Svelte component HTML uses Mustache-inspired syntax for specifying conditional logic, iteration, and promise handling.
- Conditional logic is specified using the syntax {#if condition}.
- Iteration is specified using the syntax {#each collection as element}.
- Promise handling is specified using the syntax {#await promise}.

Component
communication

This chapter covers

- Passing data into components using props
- Getting data out of components by binding to props
- Using slots to supply content to be rendered
- Dispatching events to notify parent elements
- Using context to pass data to descendant components

Components in non-trivial Svelte applications need to communicate with each other. For example, suppose we have a component that allows a user to enter their mailing address. It can render inputs for street, city, state, and postal code. It also contains logic to verify that the postal code matches the city. Another component that displays a map may want to know when the data in our mailing address component has been changed so it can display the location of the new address.

There are many ways for Svelte components to communicate. Table 5.1 summarizes the available options. It uses the terms "parent," "child," "descendant," and "ancestor" to refer to the relationships between components in the component hierarchy.

Table 5.1 Component communication options

Need	Solution
Parent passes data to child	Props
Parent passes HTML and components to child	Slots
Child notifies parent, optionally including data	Events
Ancestor makes data available to descendants	Context
Component shares data between all instances	Module context
Any component subscribes to data	Stores

Parent components directly render child components in their HTML sections. Ancestor components can be one or more levels removed from their descendant components. For example, if a `Bank` component renders an `Account` component, which renders a `Transaction` component, the `Bank` component is an ancestor of the `Transaction` component, and the `Transaction` component is a descendant of the `Bank` component.

Module context was discussed in chapter 3, and stores will be discussed in chapter 6. This chapter explains how to use all the other options and provides examples. It will conclude with adding component communication to the Travel Packing app.

5.1 Component communication options

There are six ways to share data between Svelte components.

1 *Props* pass data from parent components to child components, and optionally back to the parent using `bind`.
2 *Slots* pass content from parent components to child components so children can decide whether and where to render it.
3 *Events* are used to notify a parent component that something has happened in a child component, and they optionally include data in the event object that is passed to the parent.
4 *Contexts* allow ancestor components to make data available to descendant components without explicitly passing it to all the layers in between.
5 *Module context* stores data in component modules and makes it available to all instances of the component.
6 *Stores* store data outside components and can make it available to any of them.

5.2 Props

Components can accept input through props. Their values are specified as attributes on component elements. For example, a parent component can use a `Hello` component as follows.

Listing 5.1   Component that uses the `Hello` component

```
<script>
  import Hello from './Hello.svelte';
</script>

<Hello name="Mark" />
```

In this case, the value of the `name` prop is a literal string.

5.2.1   *Props go in with export*

The `Hello` component defined in `src/Hello.svelte` can be implemented as follows.

Listing 5.2   `Hello` component

```
<script>
  export let name = 'World';
</script>

<div>
  Hello, {name}!
</div>
```

Props are declared in the `script` element of a component with the `export` keyword. This uses valid JavaScript syntax, the `export` keyword, in a Svelte-specific way.

The `let` keyword must be used instead of `const` to declare props, because parent components can change the value.

Assigning default values to props is optional. In the preceding example, the `name` prop is given a default value of `'World'`. Props with no default value are required, meaning that parent components must specify them. When required props are not provided or unexpected props are provided and the app is run in dev mode (not production), warning messages are displayed in the DevTools console, and missing props have a value of `undefined`. However, the app still runs. The same is true in production mode, but the warning messages are omitted.

Prop values that are non-string literals or JavaScript expressions must be surrounded by curly braces instead of quotes. These can evaluate to any kind of JavaScript value, including objects, arrays, and functions.

The following listing shows examples of specifying non-string values for a prop.

Listing 5.3   Prop examples

```
myProp={false}
myProp={7}
myProp={{name: 'baseball', grams: 149, new: false}}    <-- An extra pair of braces
myProp={['red', 'green', 'blue']}                          is needed to pass an
myProp={myCallbackFunction}                    <--         object literal.
myProp={text => text.toUpperCase()}    <--
```

An extra pair of braces
is needed to pass an
object literal.

This passes a reference to
a named function as a
prop value.

This passes an anonymous function as a prop value.

The braces around a prop value can optionally be surrounded with quotes:

```
myProp="{{name: 'baseball'}}"
```

Some editors and syntax highlighters prefer this, but the Svelte compiler does not require quotes.

The value of Boolean props can be inferred from the absence of the prop, or its presence without specifying a value, as will be demonstrated in listing 5.4. The `Stop-Light` component renders a red or green circle. The `on` prop value is used to determine the color. When the prop is omitted, its value defaults to `false`. When the prop name is specified without a value, its value is inferred to be `true`.

Listing 5.4 `StopLight` **component in** `src/StopLight.svelte`

```
<script>
  export let on = false;              ⟵┐ Specify a default value if
  $: color = on ? 'green' : 'red';        the prop can be omitted.
</script>

<div style="background-color: {color}">
  {color}
</div>

<style>
  div {
    border-radius: 25px;
    color: white;
    height: 50px;
    line-height: 50px;
    margin-bottom: 10px;
    text-align: center;
    width: 50px;
  }
</style>
```

The `App` component in listing 5.5 renders three `Stop-light` components. The instance with no `on` prop uses a value of `false`, so it renders a red circle. The instance with an `on` prop that has no value uses a value of `true`, so it renders a green circle. The instance with an `on` prop that specifies a value uses that value, so it renders either a red or green circle. Clicking the Toggle button toggles the color of the last circle (see figure 5.1).

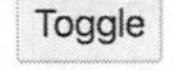

Figure 5.1 **App that uses the** `StopLight` **component**

Listing 5.5 **App that uses the** `StopLight` **component**

```
<script>
  import StopLight from './StopLight.svelte';
  let go = false;
</script>
```

```
<StopLight />
<StopLight on />
<StopLight on={go} />
<button on:click={() => go = !go}>Toggle</button>
```

5.2.2   *Reacting to prop changes*

When a parent component passes new prop values to a child component, interpolations (expressions in curly braces) in the HTML of the child component are automatically re-evaluated. However, the same is not true when the prop is used inside the script tag of the child component, unless reactive statements are used.

The following examples in listings 5.6 and 5.7 makes this clear. The Sum component is passed an array of numbers. It renders the numbers and their sum. Figure 5.2 shows an incorrect sum after Size is changed from 3 to 4.

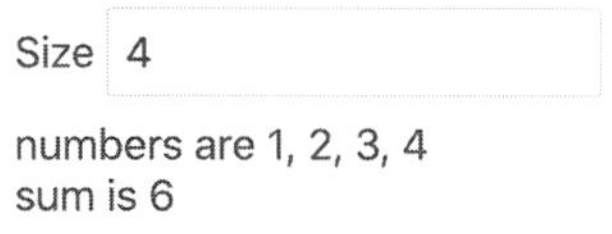

Size 4

numbers are 1, 2, 3, 4
sum is 6

Figure 5.2   An incorrect sum caused by not using a reactive statement

Listing 5.6   Sum component in .src/Sum.svelte

This computes the sum of the numbers in the numbers array. Without a reactive statement, the sum is only computed once. If a parent component modifies the numbers prop, the sum will not be recomputed.

```
<script>
  export let numbers;
  //const sum = numbers.reduce((acc, n) => acc + n);
  $: sum = numbers.reduce((acc, n) => acc + n);
</script>

<div>numbers are {numbers.join(', ')}</div><div>sum is {sum}</div>
```

Using a reactive statement fixes this.

Listing 5.7   App that uses the Sum component

```
<script>
  import Sum from './Sum.svelte';
  let size = 3;
  $: numbers = Array(size).fill().map((_, i) => i + 1);
</script>

<label>
  Size
  <input type="number" bind:value={size}>
</label>

<Sum numbers={numbers} />
```

This creates an array of numbers from 1 to size. For example, when size is 3, numbers is [1, 2, 3].

When a new value for size is entered, this passes a new numbers array to the Sum component.

5.2.3   *Prop types*

Svelte does not provide a mechanism for defining the types of props. Providing the wrong kind of value for a prop can result in a runtime error. For example, a component might expect the value of a certain prop to be a Date object, and an error could occur if a string is passed instead.

In the future, when Svelte improves support for TypeScript, it will be possible to define the types of props and catch errors in passing props to components at compile time. Until then, the best we can do is check prop types at runtime.

We can use the same library that is used by React for prop type checking (see "prop-types" in npm). Listing 5.8 shows an example of using the prop-types library. LabeledCheckboxes is a component that accepts four props:

- The className prop is an optional string CSS class name.
- The label prop is a string to be displayed in front of a list of checkboxes.
- The list prop is an array of objects that have a label property and an optional value property.
- The selected prop is an array of strings that indicates which checkboxes are currently checked.

Listing 5.8 LabeledCheckboxes **component in** src/LabeledCheckboxes.svelte

```
<script>
  import PropTypes from 'prop-types/prop-types';
  const {arrayOf, checkPropTypes, shape, string} = PropTypes;

  const propTypes = {
    className: string,
    label: string.isRequired,
    list: arrayOf(shape({
      label: string.isRequired,
      value: string
    })).isRequired,
    selected: arrayOf(string).isRequired
  }
  checkPropTypes(propTypes, $$props, 'prop', 'LabeledCheckboxes');

  ... implementation omitted ...
</script>
... implementation omitted ...
```

> $$props is an undocumented Svelte variable that is subject to change. Its value is an object where the keys are prop names and the values are their values.

If any parent component passes an invalid prop to this component or omits any required props, these errors are reported in the DevTools console.

5.2.4 *Directives*

Directives are special props that are written as a directive name followed by a colon and sometimes a value. Brief descriptions of the directives are provided here. Each is described in more detail later.

- The bind directive binds a prop value to a variable. See the next section.
- The class directive toggles the presence of a CSS class based on the truthiness of a variable. See section 3.4.
- The on directive registers an event listener. See section 5.4.1.

- The use directive specifies a function that will be passed the DOM element that is created for the element to which this directive is attached. See section 7.2.
- The directives `animate`, `transition`, `in`, and `out` support animations. See chapter 10.

Svelte does not support creating custom directives. A benefit of this is that developers only have to learn about a relatively small set of them. Reading the code of existing applications never requires learning about custom directives.

5.2.5   *The bind directive on form elements*

The value of the form elements `input`, `textarea`, and `select` can be bound to a variable using the `bind` directive. When a form element uses this, it renders the value of the variable. If a user changes the form element's value, the bound variable is updated to match. This simulates two-way data binding and is much easier than explicitly listening for a specific event, extracting the new value from the event, and explicitly updating a variable.

The Svelte compiler generates the necessary event-handling code to keep the form element and variable in sync. For `input` elements with the type `number` or `range`, using the `bind` directive automatically coerces values from strings to numbers.

The following HTML form, implemented in a single Svelte component, uses the `bind` directive with a variety of form element types. The result is shown in figure 5.3.

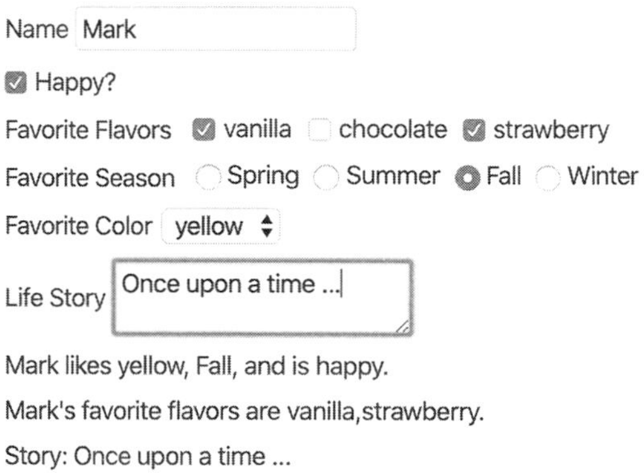

Name Mark

☑ Happy?

Favorite Flavors ☑ vanilla ☐ chocolate ☑ strawberry

Favorite Season ○ Spring ○ Summer ◉ Fall ○ Winter

Favorite Color yellow ⬍

Life Story Once upon a time ...|

Mark likes yellow, Fall, and is happy.

Mark's favorite flavors are vanilla,strawberry.

Story: Once upon a time ...

Figure 5.3   App demonstrating the use of `bind`

Listing 5.9   App demonstrating the use of `bind`

```
<script>
  const colors =
    ['red', 'orange', 'yellow', 'green', 'blue', 'purple'];
  const flavors = ['vanilla', 'chocolate', 'strawberry'];
  const seasons = ['Spring', 'Summer', 'Fall', 'Winter'];
  let favoriteColor = '';
  let favoriteFlavors = [];
  let favoriteSeason = '';
```

```
    let happy = true;
    let name = '';
    let story = '';
</script>

<div class="form">
  <div>
    <label>Name</label>
    <input type="text" bind:value={name}>
  </div>
  <div>
    <label>
      <input type="checkbox" bind:checked={happy}>
      Happy?
    </label>
  </div>
  <div>
    <label>Favorite Flavors</label>
    {#each flavors as flavor}
    <label class="indent">
      <input type="checkbox" value={flavor} bind:group={favoriteFlavors}>
      {flavor}
    </label>
    {/each}
  </div>
  <div>
    <label>Favorite Season</label>
    {#each seasons as season}
    <label class="indent">
      <input type="radio" value={season} bind:group={favoriteSeason}>
      {season}
    </label>
    {/each}
  </div>
  <div>
    <label>
      Favorite Color
      <select bind:value={favoriteColor}>
        <option />
        {#each colors as color}
        <option>{color}</option>
        {/each}
      </select>
    </label>
  </div>
  <div>
    <label>
      Life Story
      <textarea bind:value={story} />
    </label>
  </div>

  {#if name}
    <div>
      {name} likes {favoriteColor}, {favoriteSeason},
```

For checkboxes, bind to the checked property rather than the value.

Using bind:group with a set of related checkboxes makes the value an array of strings.

Using bind:group with a set of related radio buttons makes the value a single string.

To change a select to a scrollable list that allows selecting multiple options, add the multiple attribute.

option elements can also have a value attribute, and its value can be a string, number, or object.

This part just reports the variable values set by binds, but only if name has a value.

```
      and is {happy ? 'happy' : 'unhappy'}.
    </div>
    <div>{name}'s favorite flavors are {favoriteFlavors}.</div>
    <div>Story: {story}</div>
  {/if}
</div>

<style>
  div {
    margin-bottom: 10px;
  }

  .indent {
    margin-left: 10px;
  }

  input,
  select,
  textarea {
    border: solid lightgray 1px;
    border-radius: 4px;
    margin: 0;
    padding: 4px;
  }

  input[type='checkbox'],
  input[type='radio'] {
    margin: 0 5px 0 0;
  }

  label {
    display: inline-flex;
    align-items: center;
  }

  select,
  textarea {
    margin-left: 5px;
  }
</style>
```

In addition to binding to primitive variables, form elements can bind to object properties. User input then causes those objects to be mutated.

5.2.6   *bind:this*

Another form of the bind directive is bind:this={*variable*}. When used on an HTML element, this sets the variable specified as its value to a reference to the corresponding DOM element. This opens the door to arbitrary DOM manipulations. For example, it can be used to move focus into an input element. This is used in section 7.4, and there are also examples in chapter 8.

When bind:this={*variable*} is used on a component, it sets the variable specified as its value to a reference to a SvelteComponentDev object. This represents an instance of the component.

NOTE Most uses of bind:this are on HTML elements, not Svelte components. While the following example is interesting, it is somewhat contrived and just serves to demonstrate this rarely used feature.

For example, suppose we have a Tally component that allows the user to enter a series of prices (listing 5.10). It displays each price, sums them, and displays the total and the tax rate to apply.

Components that render a Tally component may want to access the tax rate and ask for the grand total, which includes tax. The Tally component can export the tax rate constant and a function that can be called to get the grand total.

Listing 5.10 Tally **component in** src/Tally.svelte

```
<script>
  export const taxRate = 0.07;

  let price;
  let prices = [];

  $: total = prices.reduce((acc, n) => acc + n, 0);

  function add() {
    prices.push(price);        This triggers an update
    prices = prices;      ⟵    of the price list.
    price = '';        ⟵
  }                            This clears the input.

  export const getGrandTotal = () => total * (1 + taxRate);
</script>

<input type="number" bind:value={price} />
<button on:click={add}>Add</button>
{#each prices as price}
  <div>{price}</div>
{/each}
<hr>
<label>Total {total}, Tax Rate {(taxRate * 100).toFixed(2)}%</label>
```

An app that uses the Tally component is shown in figure 5.4 and listing 5.11.

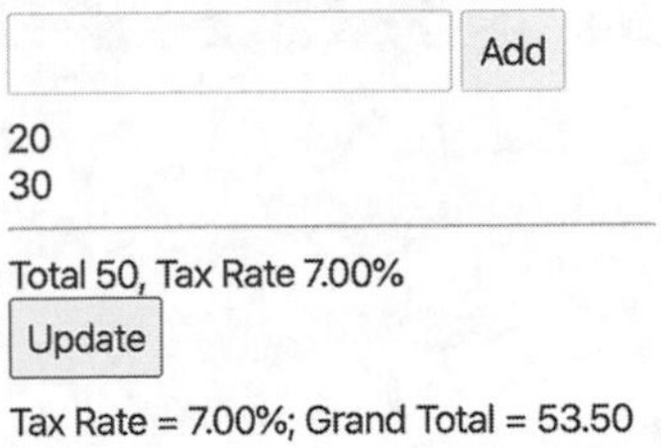

Figure 5.4 App that uses Tally **component**

Listing 5.11   App that uses `Tally` component

```
<script>
  import Tally from './Tally.svelte'

  let tally, taxRate = 0, grandTotal = 0;

  function update() {
    taxRate = tally.taxRate;
    grandTotal = tally.getGrandTotal();
  }
</script>

<Tally bind:this={tally} />

<button on:click={update}>Update</button>
<div>
  Tax Rate = {(taxRate * 100).toFixed(2)}%;
  Grand Total = {grandTotal.toFixed(2)}
</div>
```

This component does not react to changes in the properties of the Tally instance. We must explicitly ask for the new grand total.

This gets a reference to the SvelteComponentDev object that represents a Tally component instance.

The built-in properties of `SvelteComponentDev` objects have names that begin with $, which indicates they are private properties that are subject to change. If the `script` element of the component that is the target of the `bind` exports values, they become properties of this object. This is not a commonly used feature, but it is good to be aware of its existence.

5.2.7   *Props go out with bind*

Svelte can bind a child component prop to a variable in a parent component. This allows child components to change values of a parent component's variables. This is handy when a child component computes a value that parent components need. For example, listing 5.12 shows a `Parent` component, and listing 5.13 shows the `Child`.

Listing 5.12   `Parent` component in `src/Parent.svelte`

```
<script>
  import Child from './Child.svelte';
  let pValue = 1;
</script>

<Child bind:cValue={pValue} />
<div>pValue = {pValue}</div>
```

Listing 5.13   `Child` component in `src/Child.svelte`

```
<script>
  export let cValue;
  const double = () => (cValue *= 2);
</script>

<button on:click={double}>Double</button>
<div>cValue = {cValue}</div>
```

When the button in the Child component is clicked, cValue is doubled. That becomes the new value of pValue, because it is bound to cValue.

If the name of the variable in the parent component matches the name of the prop, the bind expression can be shortened. For example, these are equivalent:

```
<Child bind:cValue={cValue} />
<Child bind:cValue />
```

Child components can also use reactive declarations to modify the value of a prop. If the parent component uses bind with that prop, it will also be updated.

For example, we can add the following lines in Child.svelte:

```
export let triple;

  $: triple = cValue * 3;
```

To make use of the new triple prop, we can modify Parent.svelte as follows.

Listing 5.14 Parent component in src/Parent.svelte

```
<script>
  import Child from './Child.svelte';
  let pValue = 1;
  let triple;
</script>

<Child bind:cValue={pValue} bind:triple />
<div>pValue = {pValue}</div>
<div>triple = {triple}</div>
```

Let's implement a color-picker component that takes advantage of the bind directive. It uses sliders to select values for red, green, and blue, and it displays a swatch of the selected color below the sliders, as shown in figure 5.5.

Color Picker

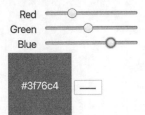

Figure 5.5 ColorPicker component

First, we need to define a ColorSlider component that can be used to select a value between 0 and 255.

Listing 5.15   ColorSlider component in src/ColorSlider.svelte

```
<script>
  export let name;
  export let value;
</script>

<div>
  <label for="slider">{name}</label>
  <input id="slider" type="range" min="0" max="255" bind:value>
</div>

<style>
  label {
    display: inline-block;
    margin-right: 10px;
    text-align: right;
    width: 45px;
  }
</style>
```

Next, we'll use the ColorSlider component in a ColorPicker component to select values for red, green, and blue, and obtain a hex value for a color that combines these. Note how this uses the bind directive to bind variables in ColorPicker to the value prop in a ColorSlider. When the user changes any slider, the corresponding bound variable in ColorPicker is updated.

Listing 5.16   ColorPicker component in src/ColorPicker.svelte

```
<script>
  import ColorSlider from './ColorSlider.svelte';
  export let hex;
  let red = 0;
  let green = 0;
  let blue = 0;

  function getHex(number) {
    const hex = number.toString(16);
    return hex.length === 1 ? '0' + hex : hex;
  }

  $: hex = '#' + getHex(red) + getHex(green) + getHex(blue);
</script>

<ColorSlider name="Red" bind:value={red} />
<ColorSlider name="Green" bind:value={green} />
<ColorSlider name="Blue" bind:value={blue} />
```

Finally, we'll use the ColorPicker component in an app to demonstrate its usage.

Listing 5.17   App that uses the `ColorPicker` component

```
<script>
  import ColorPicker from './ColorPicker.svelte';
  let hex = '000000';
</script>

<h1>Color Picker</h1>
<ColorPicker bind:hex />
<div class="swatch" style="background-color: {hex}">
  {hex}
</div>

<input type="color" bind:value={hex}>       <-- In modern browsers, clicking an
                                                 input with a type of "color" will
<style>                                          open a native color picker. This
  .swatch {                                      provides an alternative way to
    color: white;                                select a color. Note that when
    display: inline-block;                       this is used, the sliders are not
    height: 100px;                               updated to match.
    line-height: 100px;
    text-align: center;
    width: 100px;
  }
</style>
```

Note how the `ColorPicker` instance in the app uses the `bind` directive to obtain the hex value of the selected color.

There are special bind values for obtaining the size of an element. The size of an element, including padding, border, and scrollbars (if any), can be obtained from `offsetWidth` and `offsetHeight`. The size of an element including padding, but excluding everything else, can be obtained from `clientWidth` and `clientHeight`. To obtain these values, declare variables to hold them and bind them to these properties, as in the following listing.

Listing 5.18   Using element size bindings

```
<script>
  let clientH, clientW, offsetH, offsetW;
</script>

<div
  bind:clientHeight={clientH}
  bind:clientWidth={clientW}
  bind:offsetHeight={offsetH}
  bind:offsetWidth={offsetW}
>
  How big am I?
</div>
```

The client size of elements with the CSS property `display` set to "inline" will be reported as 0.

These values are read-only. Changing the bound variable values does not change the size of the element.

5.3   *Slots*

Components can allow content to be passed to them as child elements. For example, a custom `Envelope` component can accept child elements that represent a return address, a stamp, and a mailing address. It can then render all of these in the standard layout of an envelope.

The ability of a component to accept child elements is supported by *slots*. The component can decide whether and how to render each slot. Note that whitespace is included in the passed content.

The receiving component can mark the spot where all slot content is to be rendered with `<slot />`. This is called the *default slot*.

> **NOTE**   The `slot` element was added to HTML to support Web Components. Slots are not unique to Svelte. For more about Web components, see the introduction at WebComponents.org (www.webcomponents.org/introduction) and *Web Components in Action* by Ben Farrell (Manning, 2019).

A `slot` element can also provide default content to render when parent elements do not provide content for the slot. For example,

```
<slot>Thanks for nothing!</slot>
```

Named slots allow parent components to provide multiple sets of content that the receiving component can render. The parent component identifies these with a `slot` attribute on an HTML element, not a custom component. The order of the elements with a `slot` attribute in the parent component does not matter. The child component defines where they will be rendered by using `slot` elements that have a matching name attribute.

Figure 5.6 shows the results of a parent component that targets multiple named slots in the child component `ShippingLabel`. Their names are "address" and "name".

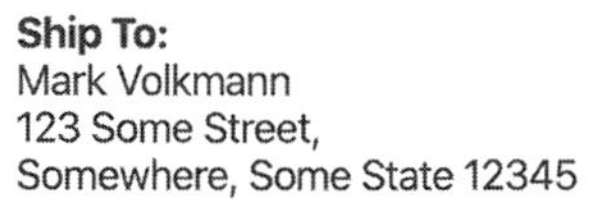

Ship To:
Mark Volkmann
123 Some Street,
Somewhere, Some State 12345

Figure 5.6   Named slots

Listing 5.19   Using the `ShippingLabel` component

```
<ShippingLabel>
  <div slot="address">
    123 Some Street,<br />
    Somewhere, Some State 12345
  </div>
  <div slot="name">Mark Volkmann</div>
</ShippingLabel>
```

Listing 5.20 `ShippingLabel` component in `src/ShippingLabel.svelte`

```
<div>
  <label>Ship To:</label>
  <slot name="name">unknown</slot>          This slot has default
  <slot name="address" />                    content of "unknown".
</div>
                                            This slot does not have
<style>                                     default content.
  label {
    display: block;
    font-weight: bold;
  }
</style>
```

If a parent component targets more than one slot with the same name, the content of all of them is used in that child component slot. For example, if we add `<div slot="address">duplicate</div>` as a new child in the `ShippingLabel` element in `App.svelte`, then "duplicate" will be rendered along with the previously specified address.

5.4 Events

Svelte components can listen for DOM events and custom events. Event handling is specified with the `on:event-name` directive. Note that `on` is followed by a colon and an event name. Its value is a function to be invoked when the event is dispatched. The event name can be the name of a DOM event or a custom event. An event object is passed to the given function.

Here's an example:

The handleClick function
must be defined in the
script section.

```
<button on:click={handleClick}>Press Me</button>

<button on:click={event => clicked = event.target}>
  Press Me
</button>
```

This demonstrates inline event handling using
an anonymous function. It just sets the variable
clicked to the DOM element for the button.

Multiple event-handling functions can be specified for the same event, and each will be invoked when the event is dispatched. For example,

```
<button on:click={doOneThing} on:click={doAnother}>
  Press Me
</button>
```

5.4.1 Event dispatching

Components can dispatch events by creating and using an event dispatcher. For example,

```
<script>
  import {createEventDispatcher} from 'svelte';
```

```
const dispatch = createEventDispatcher();          ◄────┐  This must be called when the
                                                        │  component is instantiated, not
function sendEvent() {                                   │  conditionally or later (inside a
  dispatch('someEventName', optionalData);   ◄──────┐   │  function).
}                                    The data associated with the event
</script>                            can be a primitive or an object.
```

These events only go to the parent component. They do not automatically bubble farther up the component hierarchy.

Parent components use the on directive to listen for events from child components. For example, if the parent component defines the handleEvent function, it can register that function to be invoked when a child component dispatches an event with a given name.

```
<Child on:someEventName={handleEvent} />
```

The event-handling function (handleEvent in this case) is passed an event object. This object has a detail property that is set to the data passed as the second argument to the dispatch function. Any additional arguments passed to dispatch are ignored.

To demonstrate this, we will create a Buttons component (listing 5.21) that renders several buttons and dispatches an event to let the parent component know which one was clicked (see figure 5.7).

You clicked Red.

Figure 5.7   Buttons component

Listing 5.21   Buttons component in src/Buttons.svelte

```
<script>
  import {createEventDispatcher} from 'svelte';          Parent components pass
  const dispatch = createEventDispatcher();              in an array of button
  export let labels;                       ◄────         labels.
  export let value;          ◄───
</script>                          Parent components pass
                                   in the currently selected
{#each labels as label}            label, if any.
  <button
    class:selected={label === value}
    on:click={() => dispatch('select', label)}    ◄────  Parent components listen
  >                                                       for a select event that
    {label}                                              provides the label that
  </button>                                              was selected.
{/each}

<style>
  .selected {
    background-color: darkgray;
    color: white;
  }
</style>
```

The following listing shows a component that uses the `Buttons` component.

Listing 5.22   App that uses the `Buttons` component

```
<script>
  import Buttons from './Buttons.svelte';
  let colors = ['Red', 'Green', 'Blue'];
  let color = '';
  const handleSelect = event => color = event.detail;
</script>

<Buttons labels={colors} value={color} on:select={handleSelect} />
{#if color}
  <div>You clicked {color}.</div>
{/if}
```

5.4.2   Event forwarding

Omitting the event handling function from an on directive is shorthand to forward events up to the parent component. For example, suppose part of the component hierarchy is A > B > C, and C emits a demo event. B can forward it up to A with `<C on:demo />`. Note that in this case the on directive has no value.

This approach can also be used to forward DOM events.

5.4.3   Event modifiers

The on directive can specify any number of event modifiers with vertical bars preceding modifier names. For example,

```
<button on:click|once|preventDefault={handleClick}>
  Press Me
</button>
```

These are the supported modifiers:

- `capture`—This causes the handler function to only be invoked in the capture phase, not the default bubbling phase. Typically it is not necessary to understand this distinction.

NOTE   The capture and bubbling event-handling phases are described on the Mozilla Developer Network (MDN) "Introduction to events" page at http://mng.bz/XPB6. Search for "Event bubbling and capture."

- `once`—This removes the handler after the first occurrence of the event.
- `passive`—This can improve scrolling performance. You can learn more on the MDN page for `EventTarget.addEventListener()` at http://mng.bz/yyPq.
- `preventDefault`—This prevents the default action for a DOM event from occurring. For example, it can stop a form submission from occurring. This is by far the most commonly used event modifier.
- `stopPropagation`—This prevents subsequent handlers in the capture/bubbling flow from being invoked as a result of a DOM event being dispatched.

5.5   *Context*

Context provides an alternative to using props and stores for making data in a component available in other components (stores are covered in chapter 6).

Suppose we have components A, B, and C. Component A renders component B, and component B renders component C. We want to define data in A and make it available in C. One way is to pass the data as props from A to B and do the same from B to C. But as the component hierarchy grows deeper, using props to pass data down to descendant components becomes tedious.

Context provides an easier way to do this. Data can be added to a context in an ancestor component like A and be accessed in a descendant component like C. In fact, context data can only be accessed in descendant components. Like with props, changes made to context values are not propagated upward.

To define a context in a component, import the setContext function and call it, supplying a context key and a value. The setContext function must be called when the component is instantiated, not conditionally or later (inside a function). For example,

```
import {setContext} from 'svelte';

setContext('favorites', {color: 'yellow', number: 19});
```

To use context in a descendant component, import the getContext function and call it, supplying a context key. This gets the context value from the closest ancestor component that has defined a context with that key. Like setContext, the getContext function must be called when the component is instantiated, not conditionally or later (inside a function).

```
import {getContext} from 'svelte';

const favorites = getContext('favorites');
```

Context keys can be any kind of value, not just strings. Context values can be any kind of value including functions and objects with methods that can be called by descendant components.

The following three component definitions illustrate the scenario described earlier, where A renders B, B renders C, and A wishes to define data that is available in C.

Listing 5.23   A component in `src/A.svelte`

```
<script>
  import {setContext} from 'svelte';
  import B from './B.svelte';
  setContext('favorites', {color: 'yellow', number: 19});
</script>

<div>
  This is in A.
  <B />
</div>
```

Listing 5.24 B component in `src/B.svelte`

```
<script>
  import C from './C.svelte';
</script>

<div>
  This is in B.
  <C />
</div>
```

Listing 5.25 C component in `src/C.svelte`

```
<script>
  import {getContext} from 'svelte';
  const {color, number} = getContext('favorites');
</script>

<div>
  This is in C.
  <div>favorite color is {color}</div>
  <div>favorite number is {number}</div>
</div>
```

This renders the following:

```
This is in A.
This is in B.
This is in C.
favorite color is yellow
favorite number is 19
```

If a component that has created context calls `setContext` again with the same key but a different value, descendant components will not receive updates. They only see what is available during component initialization.

Unlike props and stores, context is not reactive. This limits the usefulness of context to situations where the data an ancestor component wants to make available to descendant components is known before runtime or can be computed before the ancestor is rendered. When this is not the case, stores are a better option for sharing data, because they are reactive.

5.6 *Building the Travel Packing app*

Let's apply what you have learned about component communication to the Travel Packing app. The finished code can be found at http://mng.bz/Mdzn.

The code in chapter 4 already passes props to components. It also uses the `bind` directive on many elements.

We now want to implement the following abilities:

- Delete an item from a category
- Delete a category from a checklist

- Log in before viewing the checklist
- Log out, returning to the login page
- Persist data to localStorage

All of the preceding functionality is triggered by dispatching custom events. The Category component will dispatch persist and delete events. The Checklist component will dispatch logout events. The Item component will dispatch delete events. The Login component will dispatch login events.

Persisting to localStorage means that the data is saved across sessions. We can close the browser tab, open a new one, browse the app again, and restore the data. We can even close the browser or restart the computer and still restore the data. However, a downside of persisting data to localStorage is that it is only available in one browser on one computer.

Let's implement the ability to delete items and categories. In Item.svelte, do the following:

1 Inside the script element add

```
import {createEventDispatcher} from 'svelte';
```

2 Create the dispatch function with

```
const dispatch = createEventDispatcher();
```

3 Change the trash can button (with class icon) to dispatch a delete event when it is clicked. The Category component will listen for this.

```
<button class="icon" on:click={() => dispatch('delete')}>&#x1F5D1;</button>
```

In Category.svelte, do the following:

1 Inside the script element, add

```
import {createEventDispatcher} from 'svelte';
```

2 Create the dispatch function with

```
const dispatch = createEventDispatcher();
```

3 Add the following deleteItem function.

```
function deleteItem(item) {
  delete category.items[item.id];      ← This triggers
  category = category;                    an update.
}
```

4 Add the following on directive to the Item component instance to delete a given item when a delete event is received:

```
<Item bind:item on:delete={() => deleteItem(item)} />
```

5 Change the trash can button (with class icon) to dispatch a delete event when it is clicked. The Checklist component will listen for this.

```
<button class="icon" on:click={() => dispatch('delete')}>
  &#x1F5D1;
</button>
```

In Checklist.svelte, do the following:

1 Inside the script element, add

```
import {createEventDispatcher} from 'svelte';
```

2 Create the dispatch function with

```
const dispatch = createEventDispatcher();
```

3 Add the following deleteCategory function.

```
function deleteCategory(category) {
  delete categories[category.id];
  categories = categories;
}
```
Later we will ask for confirmation before deleting.

4 Add the following on directive to the Category component instance to delete a given category when a delete event is received:

```
on:delete={() => deleteCategory(category)}
```

With these changes, we can now click the trash can icons to delete items in a category and delete entire categories.

Now let's tackle login and logout. We want the app to begin by displaying the Login component. For now we will accept any username and password. After the Login button is pressed, we want to remove the Login component and instead display the Checklist component.

In App.svelte, do the following:

1 Uncomment the import of the Login component.

2 Add a page variable that is set to the component that should be rendered, and set it to Login:

```
let page = Login;
```

3 Replace <Checklist /> with the following. The instances of the Login and Checklist components here each listen for an event that tells App.svelte to render the other component.

```
{#if page === Login}
  <Login on:login={() => (page = Checklist)} />
{:else}
  <Checklist on:logout={() => (page = Login)} />
{/if}
```

In `Login.svelte`, do the following:

1 Inside the `script` element add

```
import {createEventDispatcher} from 'svelte';
```

2 Create the `dispatch` function with

```
const dispatch = createEventDispatcher();
```

3 Change the `login` function definition to

```
const login = () => dispatch('login');
```

In `Checklist.svelte`, do the following:

1 Add the following on directive to the Log Out button:

```
on:click={() => dispatch('logout')}>
```

With these changes made, you can log in and log out.

Now let's tackle persisting the data to `localStorage`. We want to persist the `categories` variable in the `Checklist` component whenever an item or category is modified in any way.

In `Checklist.svelte`, do the following:

1 Add the following code at the bottom of the `script` element:

```
restore();            ⟵┐  We must do this before the first call to persist.

$: if (categories) persist();      ⟵┐  This persists the categories in
                                       localStorage any time they change.
function persist() {
  localStorage.setItem('travel-packing', JSON.stringify(categories));
}

function restore() {
  const text = localStorage.getItem('travel-packing');
  if (text && text !== '{}') {
    categories = JSON.parse(text);
  }
}
```

2 Add an on directive to the `Category` element:

```
on:persist={persist}
```

In `Category.svelte`, do the following:

1 Add the following line at end of the `addItem` and `deleteItem` functions:

```
dispatch('persist');
```

With these changes made, you can now create categories, add items to them, refresh the browser, and not lose the data. You will have to log in again, but the data is retained.

In the next chapter you will learn how to use *stores* to share data between components regardless of their relationship in the component hierarchy.

Summary

- Parent components can pass data into child components using props.
- Parent components can receive updates from child components by using the `bind` directive on props.
- Parent components can provide content to be rendered by child components using slots.
- Child components can dispatch events that are handled by parent components.

Stores

6

This chapter covers

- Defining writable, readable, derived, and custom stores
- Using stores to share data between components
- Using stores in conjunction with JavaScript classes
- Persisting stores

This chapter focuses on using *stores* to share data between components, regardless of their relationship in the component hierarchy. Stores provide an alternative to using props or context. They hold application state outside any component. Each store holds a single JavaScript value, but the value can be an array or an object, which of course can hold many values.

Svelte supports several kinds of stores.

- *Writable stores* allow components to change their data.
- *Readable stores* do not allow changes.
- *Derived stores* compute their value from other stores.
- *Custom stores* can do any of these things and often provide a custom API for controlling their use.

Every store has a `subscribe` method that returns a function you can call to unsubscribe.

The built-in support for stores is so useful that there is really no need for state management libraries. Such libraries are commonly used with other frameworks. For example, Angular has @ngrx/store, React has Redux, and Vue has Vuex.

6.1 Writable stores

To create a writable store, call the `writable` function, which is defined in the `svelte/store` package. Pass an initial value and optionally a function that initializes the store. The use of such a function is described later.

In addition to the `subscribe` method, writable stores have the following methods:

- `set(newValue)`

  This sets a new value for the store.

- `update(fn)`

  This updates the store value based on its current value. `fn` is a function that is passed the current value and returns the new value. For example, the following would double the value of a store that holds a number:

  ```
  myStore.update(n => n * 2);
  ```

Here is an example of defining a writable store using just an initial value. Its purpose is to hold a collection of objects that describe dogs.

Listing 6.1 Writable store with an initial value

```
import {writable} from 'svelte/store';

export const dogStore = writable([]);
```
⟵ **The initial value is an empty array.**

Recall that declaring a variable that holds a reference to an object as `const` does not prevent modifying the object properties. The same is true for stores. Declaring a variable that holds a reference to a store does not prevent the store value from being modified.

We can also pass a function to the `writable` function that determines the initial value. This function is passed a `set` function that it calls to set the store value. For example, the function can call an API service and pass the value returned to the `set` function.

This way of initializing a store is lazy in that the function is not called until the first component subscribes to the store. It is called every time the subscriber count goes from 0 to 1, which can occur more than once.

The function passed to the `writable` function must return a "stop" function. This is called every time the subscriber count goes from 1 to 0. Any necessary cleanup can be performed here. Typically this is not needed, and the function does nothing.

The following example calls an API service to obtain an array of objects describing dogs. This becomes the value of the store.

Listing 6.2   Writable store that sets its value asynchronously

```
import {writable} from 'svelte/store';

export const dogStore = writable([], async set => {
  const res = await fetch('/dogs');
  const dogs = await res.json();
  set(dogs);
  return () => {};
});
```

The initial value is an empty array.

This uses the Fetch API, which is built into modern browsers.

This is the "stop" function.

Using a $ prefix on a store name utilizes "auto-subscription," which is explained in section 6.4.

The bind directive can be used to bind the value of a form element to a writable store. In the following example, someStore holds a string value that is used as the value of the input and is updated when the user changes the value of the input.

```
<input bind:value={$someStore}>
```

Components that use a writable store can call the set and update methods on the store to modify it.

6.2   *Readable stores*

To create a readable store, call the readable function, which is defined in the svelte/store package. As with writable stores, readable is passed an initial value and optionally a function that takes a set function.

Here is the example shown in listing 6.2, but this time it creates a readable store instead of a writable one.

Listing 6.3   Readable store example

```
import {readable} from 'svelte/store';

export const dogStore = readable([], set => {
  const res = await fetch('/dogs');
  const dogs = await res.json();
  set(dogs);
  return () => {};
});
```

The set function can use setInterval to continuously change the value of the store. For example, the readable store in the following listing provides numbers starting from 0 in increments of 10. The value changes every second.

Listing 6.4   Readable store that updates its value periodically

```
import {readable} from 'svelte/store';

let value = 0;
export const tensStore = readable(
```

```
    value,        <————— initial value
    set => {
      const token = setInterval(() => {
        value += 10;
        set(value);
      }, 1000);
      return () => clearInterval(token);
    }
);
```

Components that use a readable store cannot set or update it. This does not mean that readable stores are immutable, just that only they can change their own value.

6.3 *Where to define stores*

For stores that should be available to any component, you should define and export them in a file like src/stores.js and import the stores from that file wherever they're needed.

For stores that should only be available to descendants of a given component, define them in that component and pass them to descendants using props or context.

6.4 *Using stores*

To begin using a store, you can gain access to it in one of these ways:

- Import it from a .js file (for global stores).
- Accept it as a prop.
- Get it from a context.

There are two ways to get the value from a store:

- Call the subscribe method of the store (this is somewhat verbose).
- Use the auto-subscription shorthand (this is usually preferred).

Listing 6.5 shows an example of using the subscribe method to access the value of dogStore. The function passed to the subscribe method of the store is called initially and again every time the value changes. Here we just assign the value to the component variable dogs so it can be used in the HTML.

Listing 6.5   Store subscription example

```
<script>
  import {onDestroy} from 'svelte';
  import {dogStore} from './stores';
  let dogs;
  const unsubscribe = dogStore.subscribe(value => (dogs = value));
  onDestroy(unsubscribe);
</script>
```

Now we can use dogs in the HTML section.

We can simplify this code by using auto-subscription. All variables whose names begin with $ must be stores. Components automatically subscribe to stores when they're first used, and they automatically unsubscribe when the component is destroyed. When using auto-subscription, you only need to import the store as follows. It is not necessary to subscribe to or unsubscribe from the store.

```
<script>
  import {dogStore} from './stores';
</script>
```

Now we can use $dogStore in the HTML section. Clearly, less code is required when using auto-subscription.

The svelte/store package also exports a get function that takes a store and returns its current value. This can be used in both .svelte and .js files. For example, to get the current value of the store in the variable myStore, call get(myStore).

NOTE   The get function is somewhat inefficient. Behind the scenes it subscribes to the store, gets its value, unsubscribes from the store, and returns the value. Avoid calling this function frequently.

There are three ways to change the value of a writable store from inside a .svelte file. You have already seen the set and update methods. The value can also be directly assigned using a $ prefix on the store name:

```
$dogStore = [{breed: 'Whippet', name: 'Dasher'}];
```

Only .svelte files can use auto-subscription. Files with a .js extension must use the set or update method to change the value of a writable store.

Listing 6.6 uses the tensStore readable store (defined in listing 6.4) with auto-subscription. This component is automatically updated every time a new value is provided by the store. Each second a new value is displayed: 0, 10, 20, and so on.

Listing 6.6   App that uses `tensStore`

```
<script>
  import {tensStore} from './stores';
</script>

<div>{$tensStore}</div>
```

Let's create an app that manages a collection of dogs. For now the app will just hold objects representing dogs in memory. Later we will modify it to persist the dogs so they are not lost if the browser is refreshed.

We'll begin by defining a writable store to store objects that describe dogs. It will hold an object where the keys are dog IDs and the values are dog objects. Dog objects have id, name, breed, and size properties.

Listing 6.7   Creation of the `dogStore` in `src/stores.js`

```
import {writable} from 'svelte/store';

export const dogStore = writable({});
```

We want the ability to view, add, modify, and delete dogs. All components that subscribe to the store will see the changes.

Now we'll define the topmost component, App. It uses the DogList and DogForm components, which are defined in listings 6.9 and 6.10. The App component decides which one to render based on the value of mode, which can be list, create, or update. When mode is list, it displays the DogList component. Otherwise it displays the DogForm component.

The App component listens for two custom events. The mode event signals that the value of mode should be changed. The select event signals that a dog has been selected in the DogList component. The selected dog can then be edited.

Listing 6.8   App that uses the `DogForm` and `DogList` components

```
<script>
  import DogForm from './DogForm.svelte';
  import DogList from './DogList.svelte';

  let dog = {};                    Other modes are
  let mode = 'list';           ⟵  "create" and "update".

  function changeMode(event) {
    mode = event.detail;
    if (mode === 'create') dog = {};
  }

  const selectDog = event => (dog = event.detail);
</script>

<h1>Dogs</h1>
{#if mode === 'list'}
  <DogList on:mode={changeMode} on:select={selectDog} />
{:else}
  <DogForm {dog} {mode} on:mode={changeMode} />
{/if}
```

The DogList component displays the list of dogs, sorted on their names. It also provides buttons that can be clicked to act on the list (see figure 6.1). To add a dog, click the "+" button. To edit a dog, select one in the list and click the pencil button. To delete dogs, select them in the list and click the trash can button.

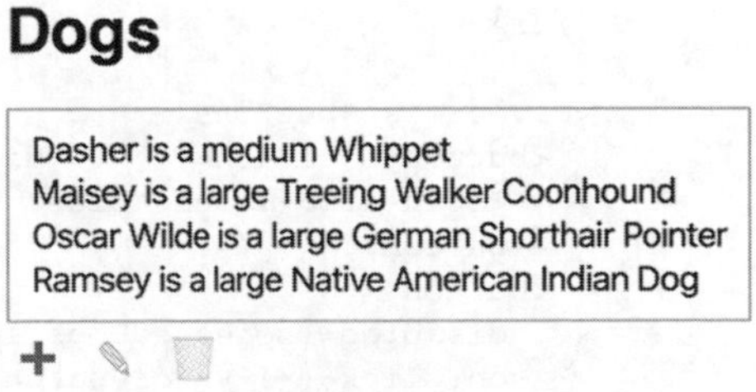

Dogs

Dasher is a medium Whippet
Maisey is a large Treeing Walker Coonhound
Oscar Wilde is a large German Shorthair Pointer
Ramsey is a large Native American Indian Dog

Figure 6.1   `DogList` **component**

Listing 6.9   DogList component in `src/DogList.svelte`

```
<script>
  import {createEventDispatcher} from 'svelte';
  import {dogStore} from './stores';
  import {sortOnName} from './util';

  const dispatch = createEventDispatcher();

  $: dogs = sortOnName(Object.values($dogStore));

  let selectedDogs = [];

  function deleteSelected() {
    const ids = selectedDogs.map(dog => dog.id);
    dogStore.update(dogMap => {
      for (const id of ids) {
        delete dogMap[id];
      }
      return dogMap;
    });
    selectedDogs = [];
  }

  const dogToString = dog => dog.name + ' is a ' + dog.size + ' ' + dog.breed
    ;

  function onSelect(event) {
    const {selectedOptions} = event.target;
    selectedDogs = Array.from(selectedOptions).map(
      option => $dogStore[option.value]        ◁─────┐  The value of each
    );                                                │  option is a dog id.
    dispatch('select', selectedDogs[0]);      ◁───┐
  }                                                │
</script>                                          │  Remember the first of the
                                                   │  selected dogs. This is the
{#if dogs.length}                                  │  one that can be edited.
  <select multiple on:change={onSelect}>
    {#each dogs as dog (dog.id)}
      <option key={dog.id} value={dog.id}>{dogToString(dog)}</option>
    {/each}
  </select>
{:else}
  <h3>No dogs have been added yet.</h3>
{/if}

<div class="buttons">
  <button on:click={() => dispatch('mode', 'create')}>
    <span aria-label="plus" role="img">&#x2795;</span>
  </button>
  <button
    disabled={selectedDogs.length === 0}       ◁────  Clicking the edit (pencil) button
    on:click={() => dispatch('mode', 'update')}>       is disabled if no dog is selected.
    <span aria-label="pencil" role="img">&#x270E;</span>
  </button>
```

```
  <button disabled={selectedDogs.length === 0} on:click={deleteSelected}>
    <span aria-label="trash can" role="img">&#x1F5D1;</span>
  </button>
</div>
```

Clicking the delete (trash can) button is disabled if no dog is selected.

```
<style>
  button {
    background-color: transparent;
    border: none;
    font-size: 24px;
  }

  option {
    font-size: 18px;
  }

  select {
    padding: 10px;
  }
</style>
```

Dogs

Name [　　　　　　]
Breed [　　　　　　]
Size ○ Small ○ Medium ○ Large
[Save] [Cancel]

Figure 6.2 DogForm component

The DogForm component displays a form that is used to enter data for a new dog or modify an existing dog (see figure 6.2).

Listing 6.10 DogForm component in src/DogForm.svelte

```
<script>
  import {createEventDispatcher} from 'svelte';
  import {dogStore} from './stores';
  import {getGuid} from './util';

  const dispatch = createEventDispatcher();
  export let dog;
  export let mode;

  let {name, breed, size} = dog;
  $: canSave = name && breed && size;

  function save() {
    const id = dog.id || getGuid();
    dogStore.update(dogMap => {
      dogMap[id] = {id, name, breed, size};
      return dogMap;
    });
    dispatch('mode', 'list');
  }
</script>
```

After saving, display the list.

```
<form on:submit|preventDefault={save}>
  <div>
    <label for="name">Name</label>
    <input autofocus id="name" bind:value={name}>
  </div>
```

```
  <div>
    <label for="breed">Breed</label>
    <input id="breed" bind:value={breed}>
  </div>
  <div>
    <label>Size</label>
    <span class="radios">
      <label>
        <input type="radio" value="small" bind:group={size}>
        Small
      </label>
      <label>
        <input type="radio" value="medium" bind:group={size}>
        Medium
      </label>
      <label>
        <input type="radio" value="large" bind:group={size}>
        Large
      </label>
    </span>
  </div>
  <div>
    <label />
    <button disabled={!canSave}>{mode === 'create' ? 'Save' : 'Update'}</button>
    <button type="button" on:click={() => dispatch('mode', 'list')}>
      Cancel
    </button>
  </div>
</form>

<style>
  div {
    display: flex;
    align-items: center;
    margin-bottom: 10px;
  }

  input {
    border: solid lightgray 1px;
    border-radius: 4px;
    font-size: 18px;
    margin: 0;
    padding: 4px;
  }

  input[type='radio'] {
    height: 16px;
  }

  label {
    display: inline-block;
    font-size: 18px;
    font-weight: bold;
    margin-right: 10px;
```

```
    text-align: right;
    width: 60px;
  }

  .radios > label {
    font-weight: normal;
    width: auto;
  }
</style>
```

The `util.js` file in listing 6.11 defines a couple of utility functions. The first generates a unique ID that is used as the ID of a dog. It uses the npm package "uuid," which must be installed by entering `npm install uuid`. The second function sorts an array of objects on their `name` properties.

Listing 6.11   Utility functions in `src/util.js`

```
import {v4 as uuidv4} from 'uuid';

export const getGuid = () => uuidv4();

export function sortOnName(array) {
  array.sort((el1, el2) =>
    el1.name.toLowerCase().localeCompare(el2.name.toLowerCase())
  );
  return array;
}
```

The following `global.css` file in the `public` directory defines CSS rules that can affect any component. We want all buttons in the app to have common default styling.

Listing 6.12   Global CSS rules in `public/global.css`

```
body {
  font-family: sans-serif;
}

button {
  border: solid lightgray 1px;
  border-radius: 4px;
  font-size: 18px;
  margin-right: 5px;
  padding: 4px;
}
```

That's it. We now have a working Svelte app that performs the common CRUD operations on a collection of dogs.

6.5   *Derived stores*

Derived stores derive their value from one or more other stores. To define one, import the `derived` function from the `svelte/store` package and call it.

The `derived` function takes two arguments. The first is the source stores. It can be a single store or an array of them. The second is a function that is passed that single store or array of stores. This function is called again each time the value of any of the source stores changes. It returns the new value of the derived store.

For example, we can create a derived store that holds only the large dogs in dog-Store. The value of this store is an array of dog objects.

Listing 6.13   Derived store defined in `src/stores.js`

```
import {derived} from 'svelte/store';

export const bigDogsStore = derived(dogStore, store =>
  Object.values(store).filter(dog => dog.size === 'large')
);
```

The preceding derived store is based on only one other store. The next example uses two stores named `itemsStore` and `taxStore`. `itemsStore` holds an array of objects that have `name` and `cost` properties. `taxStore` holds a number that is the sales tax percentage. We can create a derived store that uses these stores to hold an array of objects similar to those in `itemsStore`, but that adds a `total` property. The total of each item is computed by multiplying its cost by one plus the tax percentage.

Here is the definition of these three stores.

Listing 6.14   Stores defined in `src/stores.js`

```
import {derived, writable} from 'svelte/store';

const items = [
  {name: 'pencil', cost: 0.5},
  {name: 'backpack', cost: 40}
];
export const itemsStore = writable(items);

export const taxStore = writable(0.08);

export const itemsWithTaxStore = derived(
  [itemsStore, taxStore],
  ([$itemsStore, $taxStore]) => {
    const tax = 1 + $taxStore;
    return $itemsStore.map(item => ({...item, total: item.cost * tax}));
  }
);
```

Listing 6.15 shows a component that allows the value of taxStore to be modified. It displays the name, cost, and total for each item in itemsStore (see figure 6.3). The itemsWithTaxStore is updated any time the value of itemsStore or taxStore changes. Note that we haven't provided a way to change item-Store here.

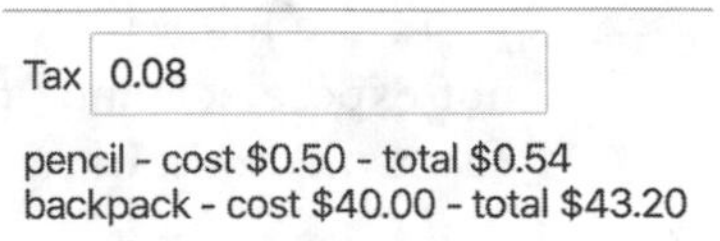

Tax 0.08

pencil - cost $0.50 - total $0.54
backpack - cost $40.00 - total $43.20

Figure 6.3   Derived store example

Listing 6.15   App that uses stores in `src/App.svelte`

```
<script>
  import {itemsWithTaxStore, taxStore} from './stores';
</script>

<label>
  Tax
  <input type="number" bind:value={$taxStore}>
</label>

{#each $itemsWithTaxStore as item}
  <div>
    {item.name} - cost ${item.cost.toFixed(2)} -
      total ${item.total.toFixed(2)}
  </div>
{/each}
```

6.6   *Custom stores*

We can also create custom stores. These can control the ways in which the code that uses them can modify the store. This is in contrast to a writable store, where the value can be changed to anything by using the set and update methods.

One use of a custom store is to provide methods that are more restrictive than set and update. These can allow only specific values or specific kinds of changes. The following count store example does this.

Another use of a custom store is to encapsulate access to API services that create, retrieve, update, and delete objects held by the store. It can expose methods that make the API calls and validate the data used to create and update the store.

The only requirement on a custom store is that it be an object with a properly implemented subscribe method. This means that the subscribe method accepts a function as its argument and returns another function that unsubscribes from the store. The subscribe method must call the function passed to it immediately and every time the store value changes, passing the function the current value of the store.

As an alternative, subscribe methods can return an object that has an unsubscribe method instead of an unsubscribe function.

Typically custom stores are created from a writable store that already has a proper subscribe method.

In the following example, count is a custom store. Unlike writable stores, it does not expose set and update methods. Instead it exposes increment, decrement, and reset methods. Users of this store can only update its value by calling those methods.

Listing 6.16   count store defined in count-store.js

```js
import {writable} from 'svelte/store';

const {subscribe, set, update} = writable(0);

export const count = {
  subscribe,
  increment: () => update(n => n + 1),
  decrement: () => update(n => n - 1),
  reset: () => set(0)
};
```

The following listing shows an example of using this custom store (see figure 6.4).

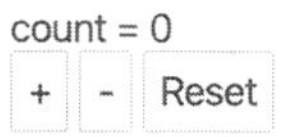

Figure 6.4   App using the count store

Listing 6.17   App using the count store in src/App.svelte

```svelte
<script>
  import {count} from './count-store';
</script>

<div>count = {$count}</div>
<button on:click={() => count.increment()}>+</button>
<button on:click={() => count.decrement()}>-</button>
<button on:click={() => count.reset()}>Reset</button>
```

6.7   *Using stores with classes*

Stores can hold instances of custom JavaScript classes. If those classes define methods that modify the properties of an instance, calling them will not notify the store that a change has been made, and subscribers to the store will not be notified.

This is no different than storing any object in a store. The only ways to trigger an update to all the subscribers are to call the set and update methods on the store or directly set the store value using the $ prefix syntax.

Fixing this is easy. In the following two listings we have the classes Point and Line. A point is defined by *x* and *y* coordinates. A line is defined by start and end Point objects. Both points and lines can be translated by given delta *x* (dx) and delta *y* (dy) values.

Listing 6.18   Point class defined in src/point.js

```js
export default class Point {
  constructor(x, y) {
    this.x = x;
    this.y = y;
  }
```

```
  toString() {
    return `(${this.x}, ${this.y})`;
  }

  translate(dx, dy) {
    this.x += dx;
    this.y += dy;
  }
}
```

Listing 6.19 Line class defined in `src/line.js`

```
import Point from './point';

export default class Line {
  constructor(start, end) {
    this.start = start;
    this.end = end;
  }

  toString() {
    return `line from ${this.start.toString()} to ${this.end.toString()}`;
  }

  translate(dx, dy) {
    this.start.translate(dx, dy);
    this.end.translate(dx, dy);
  }
}
```

To demonstrate holding instances of custom classes in stores, we can define stores in stores.js. Any component that needs these stores can import them.

Listing 6.20 Stores defined in `src/stores.js`

```
import {writable} from 'svelte/store';
import Line from './line';
import Point from './point';

export const pointStore = writable(new Point(0, 0));

export const lineStore =
  writable(new Line(new Point(0, 0), new Point(0, 0)));
```

The following listing shows a Svelte component that uses these stores.

Listing 6.21 App using the `Point` class and stores in `src/App.svelte`

```
<script>
  import Point from './point';
  import {lineStore, pointStore} from './stores';

  let point = new Point(1, 2);                    ◁—— This point is local to this
                                                       component and is not in a store.
```

```
    function translate() {          ⟵  This translates the local Point,
      const dx = 2;                     the Point in pointStore, and
      const dy = 3;                     the Line in lineStore each by
                                        the same amount.
      point.translate(dx, dy);
      point = point;                ⟵  This assignment is necessary
                                        to let Svelte know there has
      pointStore.update(point => {      been a change.
        point.translate(dx, dy);
        return point;
      });

      lineStore.update(line => {
        line.translate(dx, dy);
        return line;
      });
    }
</script>

<h1>local point = ({point.x}, {point.y})</h1>
<h1>point store = {$pointStore.toString()}</h1>
<h1>line store = {$lineStore.toString()}</h1>

<button on:click={translate}>Translate</button>
```

The main takeaway is that instance methods can be used to update objects in stores, but the updates must be performed inside the function passed to the store's update method. In addition, those functions must return the updated object.

The calls to update can be simplified as follows if the translate methods in the Point and Line classes are modified to return this.

```
pointStore.update(point => point.translate(3, 4));

lineStore.update(line => line.translate(dx, dy));
```

Another approach is to use custom stores instead of classes to represent points and lines. This moves all the logic into these stores and out of the code that uses them. For example, we can define the following custom stores for points and lines.

Listing 6.22   Stores defined in `src/stores.js`

```
import {get, writable} from 'svelte/store';

export function pointStore(x, y) {
  const store = writable({x, y});
  const {subscribe, update} = store;
  let cache = {x, y};
  return {
    subscribe,
    toString() {
      return `(${cache.x}, ${cache.y})`;
    },
```

```
    translate(dx, dy) {
      update(({x, y}) => {
        cache = {x: x + dx, y: y + dy};
        return cache;
      });
    }
  };
}

export function lineStore(start, end) {
  const store = writable({start, end});
  const {subscribe, update} = store;
  return {
    subscribe,
    translate(dx, dy) {
      update(({start, end}) => {
        start.translate(dx, dy);
        end.translate(dx, dy);
        return {start, end};
      });
    }
  };
}
```

These stores can be used as in the following listing.

Listing 6.23 App using stores in `src/App.svelte`

```
<script>
  import Point from './point';
  import {lineStore, pointStore} from './stores';
  let point = pointStore(1, 2);
  let line = lineStore(new Point(0, 0), new Point(2, 3));

  function translate() {
    const dx = 2;
    const dy = 3;

    point.translate(dx, dy);
    line.translate(dx, dy);
  }
</script>

<h1>point = ({$point.x}, {$point.y})</h1>
<h1>line = {$line.start.toString()}, {$line.end.toString()}</h1>

<button on:click={translate}>Translate</button>
```

It may seem that we could use the toString method in the object returned by the pointStore function to render its value. However, Svelte will not detect that there has been a change simply from the following:

```
<h1>point = {$point.toString()}</h1>
```

We can fix this by adding the following lines inside the `script` element,

```
let pointString = '';
point.subscribe(() => pointString = point.toString());
```

and rendering it with the following:

```
<h1>point = {pointString}</h1>
```

A similar approach can be used to add a `toString` method to `lineStore` and use it to render the current value of the store.

6.8   *Persisting stores*

If a user refreshes the browser, the code that creates stores is run again. This causes them to revert to their initial values.

It is possible to implement custom stores that persist any changes to `session-Storage` and restore their values from `sessionStorage` on refresh.

> **NOTE**   The REPL is sandboxed and cannot use `localStorage` or `session-Storage`.

The following example of a generic writable store does this. Using it is nearly the same as using the provided `writable` function. The only difference is that it needs a `session-Storage` key string.

Listing 6.24   Creating writable, persistent stores in `src/store-util.js`

```
import {writable} from 'svelte/store';

function persist(key, value) {
  sessionStorage.setItem(key, JSON.stringify(value));
}

export function writableSession(key, initialValue) {
  const sessionValue = JSON.parse(sessionStorage.getItem(key));
  if (!sessionValue) persist(key, initialValue);

  const store = writable(sessionValue || initialValue);
  store.subscribe(value => persist(key, value));
  return store;
}
```

Only save initialValue in sessionStorage if it does not already contain a value.

Create a writable store using either the value in sessionStorage or the provided initial value.

This persists any changes to the store to sessionStorage.

The following listing creates an instance of this kind of store.

Listing 6.25   Writable, persistent store of numbers in `src/stores.js`

```
import {writableSession} from './store-util';

export const numbers = writableSession('numbers', [1, 2, 3]);
```

Any number of components can import the numbers store and call its set and update methods to change the value. All changes are saved in sessionStorage and restored from there if a user refreshes the browser.

6.9 *Building the Travel Packing app*

The Travel Packing app doesn't need stores because there is no data that needs to be shared between multiple components. In chapter 17 on Sapper server routes, you will see how to call API services to persist the data in a database.

In the next chapter you will learn several ways to interact with the DOM, in addition to the DOM manipulation performed by Svelte.

Summary

- Svelte stores provide an easy way to share data between components regardless of their relationship in the component hierarchy.
- Writable stores allow components to change their data.
- Readable stores do not.
- Derived stores compute their value from other stores.
- Custom stores can do any of these things and often provide a custom API for controlling their use.
- Stores can hold instances of custom JavaScript classes.
- Stores can persist their data in a number of ways. For example, sessionStorage can be used so data is not lost if the user refreshes the browser.

DOM interactions

7

This chapter covers
- Inserting HTML from string variables
- Avoiding cross-site scripting attacks from untrusted HTML
- Using "actions" to run code when an element is added to the DOM
- Using the `tick` function to modify the DOM after Svelte updates
- Implementing a dialog component
- Implementing drag and drop

Sometimes Svelte applications need to tap into DOM functionality that is not directly supported by Svelte. Examples include

- Moving focus to an input where the user is expected to enter data
- Setting the cursor position and selected text inside an `input`
- Calling methods on a `dialog` element
- Allowing users to drag particular elements onto others

All of these require going beyond simply writing the HTML to be rendered inside a Svelte component definition. Svelte supports this by providing access to the DOM elements it creates. Component code can modify the properties of these DOM elements and call methods on them. This chapter presents several such scenarios.

7.1 Inserting HTML

Typically Svelte components render HTML by directly specifying HTML elements in .svelte files. However, sometimes it is convenient to obtain the HTML as a string from a source outside the component definition. Let's explore a scenario where this is useful.

A content management system (CMS) typically allows users to save assets such as text and images that will be used in web applications. The CMS can allow users to enter HTML into a textarea. This HTML can be stored as a string in a database. Web applications can call API services to query the CMS and obtain assets to render.

If the CMS is implemented in Svelte, it can use the @html syntax shown next to present the user with a preview of how the HTML they enter will be rendered. If consuming applications are written in Svelte, they can use the same mechanism to render the HTML.

To render a JavaScript expression whose value is an HTML string, use the following syntax:

```
{@html expression
}
```

In the following example, the user can enter any HTML in the textarea, and it will be rendered below it, as shown in figure 7.1.

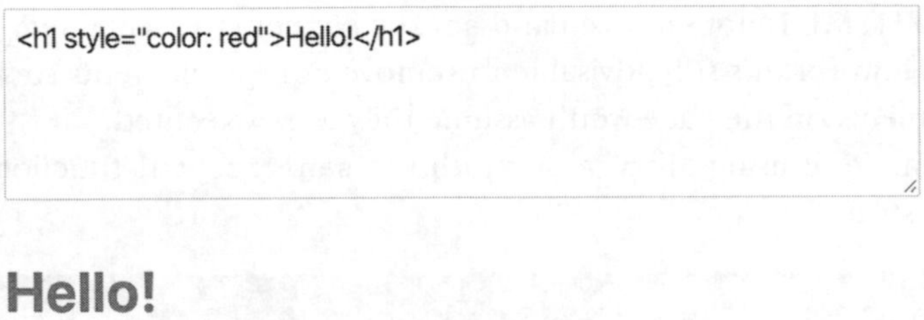

```
<h1 style="color: red">Hello!</h1>
```

Hello!

Figure 7.1 Rendering user-entered HTML

Listing 7.1 App that renders HTML entered in a textarea

```
<script>
  let markup = '<h1 style="color: red">Hello!</h1>';    ◁——  This is the initial value
</script>                                                       of the textarea.
```

```
<textarea bind:value={markup} rows={5} />
{@html markup}

<style>
  textarea {
    width: 95vw;
  }
</style>
```

In order to avoid cross-site scripting, HTML that comes from untrusted sources (such as the `textarea` in listing 7.1) should be sanitized. There are many open source libraries that remove potentially dangerous HTML from strings. One is sanitize-html, at https://github.com/apostrophecms/sanitize-html.

To use sanitize-html in a Svelte app:

1 Install it by entering `npm install sanitize-html`.
2 Import the `sanitizeHtml` function where needed.

By default `sanitizeHtml` keeps only the following elements: a, b, blockquote, br, caption, code, div, em, h3, h4, h5, h6, hr, i, iframeli, nl, ol, p, pre, strike, strong, table, tbody, td, th, thead, tr, and ul. All other elements are removed. Note that one of the elements removed is `script`.

The retained elements can have any attributes, except the a element, which can only have `href`, `name`, and `target` attributes.

By default, `img` elements are removed, but `sanitizeHtml` can be configured to retain them. It can also be configured to specify which `img` attributes are allowed. It will remove all other `img` attributes, such as `onerror` and `onload` that can run Java-Script code. See the `SANITIZE_OPTIONS` constant in listing 7.2.

`@html` inserts markup by setting the DOM property `innerHTML`. The HTML5 spec says "script elements inserted using `innerHTML` do not execute when they are inserted." So if the HTML is not sanitized and `script` elements are retained, they will not be executed. However, it's still advisable to remove `script` elements so someone inspecting the elements on the page won't assume they were executed.

Here is an example of using `@html` along with the `sanitizeHtml` function to render HTML from a string.

Listing 7.2 Using `@html` with `sanitizeHtml`

```
<script>
  import sanitizeHtml from 'sanitize-html';          Set this to false to see what
                                                     is rendered when no HTML
  const SAFE = true;                          ◁───┘  sanitizing is performed.

  const SANITIZE_OPTIONS = {
    allowedTags: [...sanitizeHtml.defaults.allowedTags, 'img'],    ◁──┐
    allowedAttributes: {img: ['alt', 'src']}
  };                                          This adds 'img' to the list of
                                              elements that are allowed by default.
```

```
function buildScript(content) {
  const s = 'script';
  return `<${s}>${content}</${s}>`;
}

function sanitize(markup) {
  return SAFE ? sanitizeHtml(markup, SANITIZE_OPTIONS) : markup;
}

const markup1 = buildScript('console.log("pwned by script")');

const markup2 = '<img alt="star" src="star.png" />';

const markup3 = '<img alt="star" src="star.png" ' +
  'onload="console.log(\'pwned by onload\')" />';

const markup4 = '<img alt="missing" src="missing.png" ' +
  'onerror="console.log(\'pwned by onerror\')" />';

const markups = [markup1, markup2, markup3, markup4];
</script>

<h1>Check the console.</h1>
{#each markups as markup}
  {@html sanitize(markup)}
{/each}
```

We have to create script elements in this way so the Svelte parser doesn't interpret them.

With the specified options, sanitizeHtml will keep this but remove the onerror attribute. It will appear as a broken image because missing.png does not exist.

With the specified options, sanitizeHtml will keep this but remove the onload attribute.

With the specified options, sanitizeHtml will keep this. The star.png file can be obtained from http://mng.bz/XPBv in the public directory.

The script created here will not be executed even if sanitizeHtml is not used to remove it. (If you're not familiar with the term "pwned," see https://en.wikipedia.org/wiki/Pwn.)

The HTML will be sanitized if the constant SAFE is set to true. When this is the case, the following HTML is rendered in the body. Note that the script element is removed, and the onerror and onload attributes are removed from the img elements. This means that output from their console.log calls will not appear in the DevTools console. The only thing that will appear in the DevTools console is a 404 error for the missing.png file, which is expected (see figure 7.2).

Check the console.

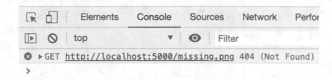

Figure 7.2 Sanitized output in the browser

```
<h1>Check the console.</h1>
<img alt="star" src="star.png">
<img alt="star" src="star.png">
<img alt="missing" src="missing.png">
```

If the SAFE constant is changed to false, the HTML will not be sanitized and the following HTML is rendered in the body (see figure 7.3). In this case, the script will not execute, but the JavaScript passed to onload and onerror will execute and write to the DevTools console.

```
<h1>Check the console.</h1>
<script>console.log("pwned by script")</script>
<img alt="star" src="star.png">
<img alt="star" src="star.png" onload="console.log('pwned by onload')">
<img alt="missing" src="missing.png" onerror="console.log('pwned by onerror')">
```

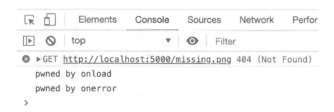

Check the console.

missing

Figure 7.3   **Unsanitized output in the browser**

7.2   *Actions*

Actions register a function to be called when a specific element in a component is added to the DOM. This is useful in cases where an application needs to modify a property of a DOM element or call a method on a DOM element after it has been added to the DOM.

> **NOTE**   Actions are somewhat related to the onMount lifecycle function (described in chapter 8), which registers a function to call when each instance of a component is added to the DOM.

Actions are specified on elements with the use directive, which has the syntax use:*fnName*={*args*}. The registered function is passed the DOM element and the arguments, if any. Omit ={*args*} if no arguments other than the element are needed.

For example, the following code moves the focus to an input element after it is added to the DOM by calling the focus function:

```
<script>
  let name = '';
```

```
  const focus = element => element.focus();
</script>
```

```
<input bind:value={name} use:focus>
```

Action functions can optionally return an object, with `update` and `destroy` properties that are functions. The `update` function is called every time an argument value changes. Of course, this doesn't apply if there are no arguments. The `destroy` function is called when the element is removed from the DOM. Returning such an object from an action function is not common.

7.3   *The tick function*

Component state is invalidated by changing the values of top-level component variables. This causes Svelte to update the parts of the DOM that rely on the modified variables, and in doing so, some properties of the previously rendered DOM elements can be lost. In some cases we need a way to restore them.

From the Svelte documentation, "When you invalidate component state in Svelte, it doesn't update the DOM immediately. Instead, it waits until the next microtask to see if there are any other changes that need to be applied, including in other components. Doing so avoids unnecessary work and allows the browser to batch things more effectively."

Also from the Svelte documentation, the `tick` function "returns a promise that resolves as soon as any pending state changes have been applied to the DOM (or immediately, if there are no pending state changes)."

The `tick` function can be used to make additional state changes after DOM updates have been applied using the following pattern.

```
<script>
  import {tick} from 'svelte';          Make some state
  ...                                    changes here.

  await tick();          Wait for previously batched state
        changes to be applied to the DOM.
  ...
</script>          Make more state changes here,
        after the DOM updates.
```

Calling `tick()` is rarely required, but let's walk through an example where it is needed.

Suppose we want to implement a masked input. Often this is an input where digits must be entered with particular delimiter characters at specific positions. For example, a phone number can be entered in the format `(123)456-7890`.

Let's create a `MaskedInput` component that takes a mask and a value as props (shown in listing 7.3). The mask is a string that contains 9 characters where digits are allowed. All other mask characters are the literal characters that must be added at specific locations. The mask for the preceding phone number format is `(999)999-9999`.

This is used as the input placeholder attribute, which is displayed until the user begins entering a value.

We want to add the appropriate delimiters in the input as the user is typing. But when Svelte updates the value of the input, the cursor position within the input is lost. To address this, we can follow these steps:

1 Capture the current cursor position before updating the value.
2 Update the value with the proper delimiter characters.
3 Wait for the DOM to finish updating, using the tick function.
4 Restore the cursor position.

Listing 7.3   `MaskedInput` component in `src/MaskedInput.svelte`

```
<script>
  import {tick} from 'svelte';
  export let mask;
  export let value;

  function getDigits(value) {
    let newValue = '';
    for (const char of value) {
      if (char >= '0' && char <= '9')  newValue += char;
    }
    return newValue;
  }

  function maskValue(digits) {
    const {length} = digits;
    if (length === 0) return '';

    let value = '';
    let index = 0;
    for (const char of mask) {
      if (char === '9') {
        const nextChar = digits[index++];
        if (!nextChar) break;
        value += nextChar;
      } else if (index < length) {
        value += char;
      }
    }
    return value;
  }

  function handleKeydown(event) {
    if (event.key !== 'Backspace') return;

    const {target} = event;
    let {selectionStart, selectionEnd} = target;

    setTimeout(async () => {
      value = maskValue(getDigits(target.value));
```

This creates a string containing only the digits in the value.

This creates a string by placing digits into the mask. For example, if the digits are "1234567" and we are using our phone number mask, this returns "(123)456-7".

This block adds a digit from digits.

This adds a mask character.

This only handles the backspace (delete) key.

This changes the value rendered by the input element.

This captures the current cursor position.

Using setTimeout gives time for the backspace key to be processed.

This waits for Svelte to update the DOM.

```
    await tick();
```

After the DOM is updated by Svelte, this restores the insert cursor position.

```
    if (selectionStart === selectionEnd) selectionStart--;
    target.setSelectionRange(selectionStart, selectionStart);
  });
}
```

This handles keys that are printable characters, like digits.

```
function handleKeypress(event) {
  setTimeout(async () => {
    const {target} = event;
    let {selectionStart} = target;
```

Using setTimeout gives time for the keypress to be processed.

This captures the current cursor position.

```
    value = maskValue(getDigits(target.value));
```

This changes the value rendered by the input element.

```
    await tick();
```

This waits for Svelte to update the DOM.

```
    if (selectionStart === value.length - 1) selectionStart++;

    const maskChar = mask[selectionStart - 1];
    if (maskChar !== '9') selectionStart++;

    target.setSelectionRange(selectionStart, selectionStart);
  });
}
</script>
```

This restores the insert cursor position.

```
<input
  maxlength={mask.length}
  on:keydown={handleKeydown}
  on:keypress={handleKeypress}
  placeholder={mask}
  bind:value={value}
/>
```

If a mask character was just inserted, this moves selectionStart ahead one.

If we are at the end of the input, this moves selectionStart ahead one.

The following listing shows an example of using the MaskedInput component.

Listing 7.4 App that uses the MaskedInput component

```
<script>
  import MaskedInput from './MaskedInput.svelte';
  let phone = '';
</script>

<label>
  Phone
  <MaskedInput
    mask="(999) 999-9999"
    bind:value={phone}
  />
</label>
<div>
  phone = {phone}
</div>
```

NOTE Listening for `keypress` events is deprecated but still supported (see http://mng.bz/6QKA). The proposed alternative is to listen for `beforeinput` events. However, at the time of writing those are not supported by Firefox. Another way of implementing a masked input that does not rely on `keypress` events can be found at http://mng.bz/oPyp.

Calling `await tick()` can also be useful in test code to wait for a change to be processed before testing for the effect.

7.4   *Implementing a dialog component*

Some applications use dialogs to present important information that users must acknowledge before continuing, or to prompt for input that must be provided before continuing. Dialogs are often *modal*, which means users cannot interact with elements outside the dialog until the dialog is dismissed. To indicate this, a *backdrop* is displayed behind the dialog and above all the other content. The backdrop blocks interaction with content outside the dialog. It typically has some opacity that shades the other content but still allows it to be visible.

In figure 7.4, a dialog is displayed when the user clicks the Open Dialog button.

Figure 7.4   A dialog example

Typically dialog components are implemented using a `div` element with a `z-index` that is higher than anything else on the page. Absolute positioning is used to position the `div` in the center of the page.

An alternative is to use the `dialog` element defined in the HTML specification. This makes using dialogs much easier. Unfortunately, browser support for the `dialog` element is still incomplete. At the time of writing, the only popular browsers that support it are Chrome and Edge.

However, a good polyfill is available in npm. It allows you to use the `dialog` element in other browsers, such as Firefox and Safari. See dialog-polyfill at www.npmjs .com/package/dialog-polyfill. To install it, enter `npm install dialog-polyfill`.

Let's implement a Svelte `Dialog` component that uses the `dialog` element and this polyfill. This component can have an icon, a title, a close "X," and any content. It is initially closed.

Parent components obtain a reference to the `dialog` element by including the `bind:dialog` prop, where `dialog` is a variable in the parent component.

To open the dialog as modal, call `dialog.showModal()`. This prevents interaction with elements outside the dialog.

To open the dialog as non-modal, call `dialog.show()`. This allows interaction with elements outside the dialog.

To close the dialog programmatically, call `dialog.close()`. Parent components can listen for the dialog being closed by the user by including the `on:close={handleClose}` prop, where `handleClose` is a function in the parent component.

The following listing shows a component that uses the `Dialog` component. This code can be found at https://github.com/mvolkmann/svelte-dialog.

Listing 7.5 App that uses the `Dialog` component

```
<script>
  import Dialog from './Dialog.svelte';
  let dialog;
</script>

<div>
  <button on:click={() => dialog.showModal()}>Open Dialog</button>
</div>

<Dialog title="Test Dialog" bind:dialog>
  My dialog content is very, very long.<br>
  It will not wrap by default.
</Dialog>
```

Here is the implementation of the `Dialog` component.

Listing 7.6 `Dialog` component in `src/Dialog.svelte`

This is a Boolean that determines whether a close "X" should be displayed.

```
<script>
  import dialogPolyfill from 'dialog-polyfill';
  import {createEventDispatcher, onMount} from 'svelte';

  export let canClose = true;
  export let className = '';
  export let dialog = null;
  export let icon = undefined;
  export let title;
```

This is an optional CSS class name to be added to the dialog element.

Parent components can use bind:dialog to get a reference so they can call show(), showModal(), and close() on it.

This is the title text to display in the dialog header.

This is an optional icon to render in the header before the title.

```
    const dispatch = createEventDispatcher();

    $: classNames = 'dialog' + (className ? ' ' + className : '');

    onMount(() => dialogPolyfill.registerDialog(dialog));
```

⟵ **onMount is a lifecycle function that is described in chapter 8. This is called when the component has been added to the DOM.**

```
    function close() {
      dispatch('close');
      dialog.close();
    }
</script>
```

⟵ **Parent components can optionally listen for this event.**

```
<dialog bind:this={dialog} class={classNames}>
```

⟵ **This sets the dialog variable to a reference to the DOM element.**

```
  <header>
    {#if icon}{icon}{/if}
    <div class="title">{title}</div>
    {#if canClose}
      <button class="close-btn" on:click={close}>
        &#x2716;
      </button>
    {/if}
  </header>
```

⟵ **This is a Unicode "heavy multiplication X."**

```
  <main>
    <slot />
  </main>
</dialog>
```

⟵ **There is an accessibility issue here that will be fixed in chapter 12.**

This is where the children of the Dialog component appear.

```
<style>
  .body {
    padding: 10px;
  }

  .close-btn {
    background-color: transparent;
    border: none;
    color: white;
    cursor: pointer;
    font-size: 24px;
    outline: none;
    margin: 0;
    padding: 0;
  }

  dialog {
```

⟵ **These properties center the dialog in the browser window.**

```
    position: fixed;
    top: 50%;
    transform: translate(0, -50%);

    border: none;
    box-shadow: 0 0 10px darkgray;
    padding: 0;
  }
```

```css
header {
  display: flex;
  justify-content: space-between;
  align-items: center;

  background-color: cornflowerblue;
  box-sizing: border-box;
  color: white;
  font-weight: bold;
  padding: 10px;
  width: 100%;
}

main {
  padding: 10px;
}

.title {
  flex-grow: 1;
  font-size: 18px;
  margin-right: 10px;
}

dialog::backdrop,
:global(dialog + .backdrop) {
  background: rgba(0, 0, 0, 0.4);
}
</style>
```

We need to define styling for the .backdrop element that is not scoped to this component, because in the polyfill that element is not nested in the root element of this component. See http://mng.bz/nPX2 for more on the ::backdrop pseudo element.

This is a transparent shade of gray.

7.5 Drag and drop

Implementing drag and drop in a Svelte app is easy. There is nothing Svelte-specific required. It can be implemented with the HTML Drag and Drop API documented on MDN at http://mng.bz/4Azj.

Let's implement a simple app that allows users to drag the names of fruits between baskets (see figure 7.5). This was inspired by an example found on the Svelte site at http://mng.bz/Qyev. The following listing presents a simpler version.

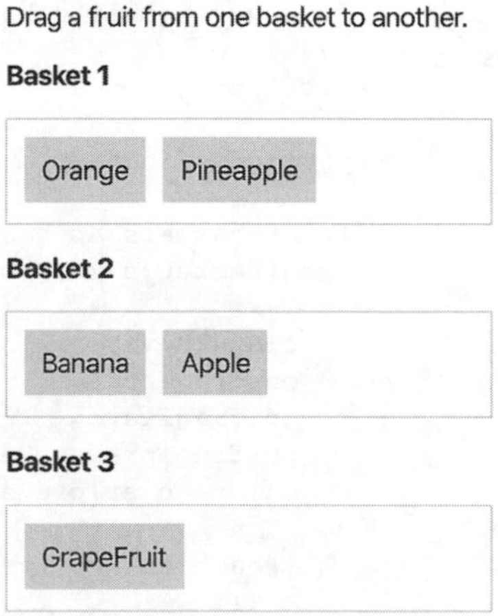

Drag a fruit from one basket to another.

Basket 1

Orange	Pineapple

Basket 2

Banana	Apple

Basket 3

GrapeFruit

Figure 7.5 Fruit drag and drop

Listing 7.7 App that demonstrates drag and drop

```html
<script>
  let baskets = [
    {
      'name': 'Basket 1',
      'items': ['Orange', 'Pineapple']
    },
```

```
      {
        'name': 'Basket 2',
        'items': ['Banana', 'Apple']
      },
      {
        'name': 'Basket 3',
        'items': ['GrapeFruit']
      }
    ];

    let hoveringOverBasket;

    function dragStart(event, basketIndex, itemIndex) {

      const data = {basketIndex, itemIndex};
      event.dataTransfer.setData('text/plain', JSON.stringify(data));
    }

    function drop(event, basketIndex) {
      const json = event.dataTransfer.getData("text/plain");
      const data = JSON.parse(json);

      const [item] = baskets[data.basketIndex].items.splice(data.itemIndex, 1);

      baskets[basketIndex].items.push(item);
      baskets = baskets;

      hoveringOverBasket = null;
    }
  </script>

  <p>Drag a fruit from one basket to another.</p>

  {#each baskets as basket, basketIndex}
    <b>{basket.name}</b>
    <ul
      class:hovering={hoveringOverBasket === basket.name}
      on:dragenter={() => hoveringOverBasket = basket.name}
      on:dragleave={() => hoveringOverBasket = null}
      on:drop|preventDefault={event => drop(event, basketIndex)}
      on:dragover|preventDefault
    >
      {#each basket.items as item, itemIndex}
        <li
          draggable="true"
          on:dragstart={event => dragStart(event, basketIndex, itemIndex)}
        >
          {item}
        </li>
      {/each}
    </ul>
  {/each}

  <style>
    .hovering {
```

This is used to highlight the basket over which an item is hovering during a drag operation.

The data we want to make available when the element is dropped is the index of the item being dragged and the index of the basket from which it is leaving.

This adds the item to the drop target basket.

This removes the item from one basket. The splice method returns an array of the deleted elements, just one in this case.

```
    border-color: orange;
  }
  li {
    background-color: lightgray;
    cursor: pointer;
    display: inline-block;
    margin-right: 10px;
    padding: 10px;
  }
  li:hover {
    background: orange;
    color: white;
  }
  ul {
    border: solid lightgray 1px;
    height: 40px; /* needed when empty */
    padding: 10px;
  }
</style>
```

For even more functionality, such as making components resizable, see the open source svelte-moveable Svelte component from Younkue Choi at http://mng.bz/vxY4.

7.6 Building the Travel Packing app

Let's apply what you have learned about dialogs to the Travel Packing app. The finished code can be found at http://mng.bz/XPKa.

First, configure use of the dialog polyfill as shown in listing 7.6. Copy the file `src/Dialog.svelte` from https://github.com/mvolkmann/svelte-dialog and place it in the `src` directory. We will use it to warn users if they attempt to create a category that already exists, add an item that already exists, or delete a category that is not empty.

In `Category.svelte`, do the following:

1 Add the following import:

```
import Dialog from './Dialog.svelte';
```

2 Add the following variable declaration that will hold a reference to the DOM dialog:

```
let dialog = null;
```

3 In the `addItem` function, change `alert(message);` to `dialog.showModal();`.

4 At the bottom of the HTML `section` element, add the following:

```
<Dialog title="Category" bind:dialog>
  <div>{message}</div>
</Dialog>
```

In `Checklist.svelte`, do the following:

1 Add the following import:

```
import Dialog from './Dialog.svelte';
```

2 Add the following variable declaration, which will hold a reference to the DOM dialog:

```
let dialog = null;
```

3 In the `addCategory` function, change `alert(message);` to `dialog.showModal();`.

4 Add the following code at the beginning of the `deleteCategory` function to prevent deleting a category that still contains items:

```
if (Object.values(category.items).length) {
  message = 'This category is not empty.';
  dialog.showModal();
  return;
}
```

5 At the bottom of the HTML `section` element, add the following:

```
<Dialog title="Checklist" bind:dialog>
  <div>{message}</div>
</Dialog>
```

With this code in place, try to create a new category that already exists, and try to add an item that already exists to a category. In both cases you will see a dialog that says it already exists, and nothing will be added.

Try to delete a category that contains one or more items. You will see a dialog that says the category is not empty, and the category will not be deleted.

Now let's apply what we have learned about drag and drop in the Travel Packing app. We want to allow users to drag items from one category to another.

In `Item.svelte`, do the following:

1 Add a `categoryId` prop so each `Item` knows its current category:

```
export let categoryId;
```

2 Add a `dnd` prop that will receive an object that has `drag` and `drop` methods:

```
export let dnd;
```

3 Add the following props to the `span` element inside the `li` element:

```
draggable="true"
on:dragstart={event => dnd.drag(event, categoryId, item.id)}
```

In `Category.svelte`, do the following:

1 Add a dnd prop that will receive an object that has `drag` and `drop` methods:

```
export let dnd;
```

2 Declare a `hovering` variable that will be set to `true` if we are currently dragging an `Item` over it, and `false` otherwise:

```
let hovering = false;
```

3 Add the following attributes to the `section` element:

```
class:hover={hovering}
on:dragenter={() => (hovering = true)}
on:dragleave={event => {

  const {localName} = event.target;
  if (localName === 'section') hovering = false;
}}
on:drop|preventDefault={event => {
  dnd.drop(event, category.id);
  hovering = false;
}}
ondragover|preventDefault
```

This only sets hovering to false when leaving the root element or the category.

4 Add the `categoryId` prop to the `Item` component instance so each `Item` knows the category to which it currently belongs:

```
categoryId={category.id}
```

5 Forward the `dnd` prop as a prop to the `Item` component:

```
{dnd}
```

6 Add styling for the `hover` class inside the `style` element:

```
.hover {
  border-color: orange;
}
```

In `Checklist.svelte`, do the following:

1 Define the `dragAndDrop` variable, which is an object that has the methods `drag` and `drop`:

```
let dragAndDrop = {
  drag(event, categoryId, itemId) {
    const data = {categoryId, itemId};
    event.dataTransfer.setData('text/plain', JSON.stringify(data));
  },
  drop(event, categoryId) {
    const json = event.dataTransfer.getData('text/plain');
    const data = JSON.parse(json);
```

This removes the item from one category.

```
const category = categories[data.categoryId];
const item = category.items[data.itemId];
delete category.items[data.itemId];

categories[categoryId].items[data.itemId] = item;

categories = categories;
  }
};
```

This adds the item to another category.

This triggers an update.

2   Add the dnd prop to the Category instance:

```
dnd={dragAndDrop}
```

With these changes in place, try dragging items from one category to another. Note how the border of a category changes to orange when you are hovering over it.

In the next chapter you will learn about Svelte "lifecycle" functions.

Summary

- Svelte components can render a string of HTML using the syntax {@html markup}.
- Depending on the source of the HTML string, it may be advisable to sanitize it.
- Svelte actions provide a way to run a given function when a specific element is added to the DOM.
- The Svelte tick function provides a way to wait for Svelte to finish updating the DOM before proceeding to the next line of code. This can be used to restore parts of the DOM state that existed before the updates.
- A Svelte Dialog component can be implemented using the HTML dialog element.
- Svelte components can implement drag and drop operations using the HTML Drag and Drop API.

Lifecycle functions

This chapters covers

- `onMount` to run code when a component is added to the DOM
- `beforeUpdate` to run code before every component update
- `afterUpdate` to run code after every component update
- `onDestroy` to run code when a component is removed from the DOM

In some applications there are actions that need to be performed when a component is added to or removed from the DOM. There are also situations where actions need to be performed before or after a component is updated. Svelte supports this by allowing the registration of functions to be invoked when four specific events occur in the lifecycle of a component instance:

- When it is mounted (added to the DOM)
- Before it is updated
- After it is updated
- When it is destroyed (removed from the DOM)

A component is "updated" if any of its props change or any of its state variables change. Recall that state variables are top-level variables in a component that are used in its HTML.

8.1   *Setup*

To register functions for these events, import the provided lifecycle functions from the `svelte` package:

```
import {afterUpdate, beforeUpdate, onDestroy, onMount} from 'svelte';
```

Call these functions, passing them a function to be called when the event occurs. They must be called during component initialization. This means they cannot be called conditionally or be called in a function that is not invoked before each component instance is mounted.

Listings 8.1 and 8.2 show examples of using each of these events. Enter the code in these listings into a REPL, and open the DevTools console (or expand the Console pane in the REPL). Click the Show checkbox and the Demo button to see when each of the lifecycle functions is called.

Listing 8.1   Demo component that uses all the lifecycle functions

```
<script>
  import {onMount, beforeUpdate, afterUpdate, onDestroy} from 'svelte';

  let color = 'red';

  function toggleColor() {
    color = color === 'red' ? 'blue' : 'red';
  }

  onMount(() => console.log('mounted'));
  beforeUpdate(() => console.log('before update'));
  afterUpdate(() => console.log('after update'));
  onDestroy(() => console.log('destroyed'));
</script>

<button on:click={toggleColor} style="color: {color}">
  Demo
</button>
```

Changing the color triggers the beforeUpdate function, updates the color of the button, and triggers the afterUpdate function.

Listing 8.2   App that uses the Demo component

```
<script>
  import Demo from './Demo.svelte';
  let show = false;
</script>

<label>
  <input type="checkbox" bind:checked={show}>
  Show
```

This determines whether the Demo component should be rendered. Changing it causes the Demo component to be mounted and unmounted. The beforeUpdate function is called before the onMount function, and the afterUpdate function is called after the onMount function.

```
</label>
{#if show}
  <Demo />
{/if}
```

The lifecycle functions can be called any number of times. For example, if onMount is called three times, passing it three functions, all of them will be called when the component is mounted, in the order in which they were registered.

Note that functions passed to beforeUpdate are called before functions passed to onMount. This happens because component props and state are evaluated before a component is added to the DOM.

8.2   *The onMount lifecycle function*

The most commonly used lifecycle function is onMount.

One use is to anticipate where a user is most likely to want to enter data in a form that is rendered by a component. An onMount function can move focus to that input when the component is first rendered. The following section shows an example of this.

Another use is to retrieve data needed by a component from API services. For example, a component that displays information about employees at a company can use an onMount function to obtain the data and store it in a top-level variable so it can be rendered. Section 8.2.2 shows an example of this.

8.2.1   *Moving focus*

Here's an example that moves the focus so the user is immediately ready to enter their name without having to click in the input or press the Tab key.

> **NOTE**   Consider the impact on accessibility when moving focus. This can cause screen readers to skip over content before the input.

```
<script>
  import {onMount} from 'svelte';
  let name = '';
  let nameInput;
  onMount(() => nameInput.focus());
</script>

<input bind:this={nameInput} bind:value={name}>
```

The bind:this directive sets a variable to a reference to a DOM element. In the preceding example, the variable nameInput is set to the DOM element of the HTML input. This is used in the function passed to onMount to move the focus to the input.

Recall that in section 7.2 you saw an even easier way to move the focus—by using an action.

8.2.2 *Retrieving data from an API service*

Here is an example that retrieves data about employees at
a company from an API service when the component is
mounted. This is the same API service described in section 4.3. The array of employee objects returned is sorted
by their names (first name before last name) and stored in
a top-level variable. The component renders the employee
data in a table (see figure 8.1).

Employees

Name	Age
Airi Satou	33
Ashton Cox	66
Bradley Greer	41
Brielle Williamson	61
Caesar Vance	21

Figure 8.1   Employee table

Listing 8.3   App that uses `onMount` to fetch data

```
<script>
  import {onMount} from 'svelte';

  let employees = [];
  let message;

  onMount(async () => {
    const res = await fetch(              For details on using the
      'http://dummy.restapiexample.com/api/v1/employees');   browser-provided Fetch
                                           API, see appendix B.
    const json = await res.json();
    if (json.status === 'success') {      This sorts the employees on
      employees = json.data.sort(         their name, first before last.
        (e1, e2) => e1.employee_name.localeCompare(e2.employee_name));
      message = '';
    } else {
      employees = [];
      message = json.status;
    }
  });
</script>

<table>
  <caption>Employees </caption>
  <tr><th>Name</th><th>Age</th></tr>
  {#each employees as employee}
    <tr>
      <td>{employee.employee_name}</td>
      <td>{employee.employee_age}</td>
    </tr>
  {/each}
</table>
{#if message}
  <div class="error">Failed to retrieve employees: {message}</div>
{/if}

<style>
  caption {
    font-size: 18px;
```

```
      font-weight: bold;
      margin-bottom: 0.5rem;
    }
    .error {
      color: red;
    }
    table {
      border-collapse: collapse;
    }
    td, th {
      border: solid lightgray 1px;
      padding: 0.5rem;
    }
  </style>
```

8.3   The onDestroy lifecycle function

To register a function to be called when a component is removed from the DOM, pass the function to onDestroy. This is typically used for cleanup operations, such as clearing timers (created with setTimeout) or intervals (created with setInterval). It can also be used to unsubscribe from stores where auto-subscribe ($ syntax) is not used.

For example, suppose we want to cycle through a set of colors for some text, changing the color every half second. Here is a Svelte component that does this.

Listing 8.4   ColorCycle component in src/ColorCycle.svelte

```
<script>
  import {onDestroy, onMount} from 'svelte';
  export let text;
  const colors = ['red', 'orange', 'yellow', 'green', 'blue', 'purple'];
  let colorIndex = 0;
  let token;

  onMount(() => {
    token = setInterval(() => {
      colorIndex = (colorIndex + 1) % colors.length;
    }, 500);
  });

  onDestroy(() => {
    console.log('ColorCycle destroyed');
    clearInterval(token);
  });
</script>

<h1 style="color: {colors[colorIndex]}">{text}</h1>
```

The following app component uses the ColorCycle component. It provides a way to remove the ColorCycle component from the DOM and add a new instance.

Listing 8.5   App that uses the `ColorCycle` component

```
<script>
  import ColorCycle from './ColorCycle.svelte';
  let show = true;
</script>

<button on:click={() => show = !show}>Toggle</button>

{#if show}
  <ColorCycle text="Some Title" />
{/if}
```

An alternative to using `onDestroy` is to return a function from the function registered with `onMount`. This function will be called when the component is removed from the DOM.

> **NOTE** This approach is a bit like the `useEffect` hook in React, but it differs in that functions passed to `useEffect` are run on both mount and updates.

Here is the `Color` component implemented with this approach.

Listing 8.6   `Color` component with `onMount` returning a function

```
<script>
  import {onMount} from 'svelte';

  const colors = ['red', 'orange', 'yellow', 'green', 'blue', 'purple'];
  let colorIndex = 0;

  onMount(() => {
    const token = setInterval(() => {
      colorIndex = (colorIndex + 1) % colors.length;
    }, 500);
    return () => clearInterval(token);
  });
</script>

<h1 style="color: {colors[colorIndex]}">Some Title</h1>
```

One advantage of this approach is that the `token` variable can be scoped to the function passed to `onMount` instead of being a top-level variable in the component. This visually groups the setup and cleanup code, making it easier to follow.

8.4   *The beforeUpdate lifecycle function*

To register a function to be called before each component update, pass the function to `beforeUpdate`. The `beforeUpdate` function is rarely used.

One reason to use it is to capture part of the DOM state before it is updated by Svelte so those values can be restored after the update using the `afterUpdate` function.

For example, the cursor position in an input can be captured and restored after its value is changed.

The following component does this when the UPPER button is clicked. This changes the value of the input to be all uppercase. Figures 8.2 and 8.3 show the component before and after the UPPER button is clicked. The cursor position, including the range of characters selected, is restored after the change.

Figure 8.2   Before clicking UPPER with "fine" selected

Figure 8.3   After clicking UPPER with "FINE" still selected

Listing 8.7   App that uses `beforeUpdate` and `afterUpdate`

```
<script>
  import {afterUpdate, beforeUpdate} from 'svelte';

  let input, name, selectionEnd, selectionStart;

  beforeUpdate(() => {
    if (input) ({selectionStart, selectionEnd} = input);      ⟵ This uses
  })                                                              destructuring to get
                                                                  two properties from
  afterUpdate(() => {                                             the DOM input object.
    input.setSelectionRange(selectionStart, selectionEnd);
    input.focus();
  });
</script>                                                       Recall that bind:this
                                                               captures the associated
<input bind:this={input} bind:value={name}>      ⟵            DOM element.
<button on:click={() => name = name.toUpperCase()}>UPPER</button>
```

8.5   *The afterUpdate lifecycle function*

To register a function to be called after each component update, pass the function to `afterUpdate`. This is typically used to perform additional DOM updates after Svelte has updated the DOM.

The previous example already used `afterUpdate`, but used it in conjunction with `beforeUpdate`. The following Svelte app provides another example. It allows the user to enter items they want for their birthday. The list displays at most three items, and new items are added at the end (see figure 8.4). After each item is added, we want to automatically scroll to the bottom so the most recently added items are visible.

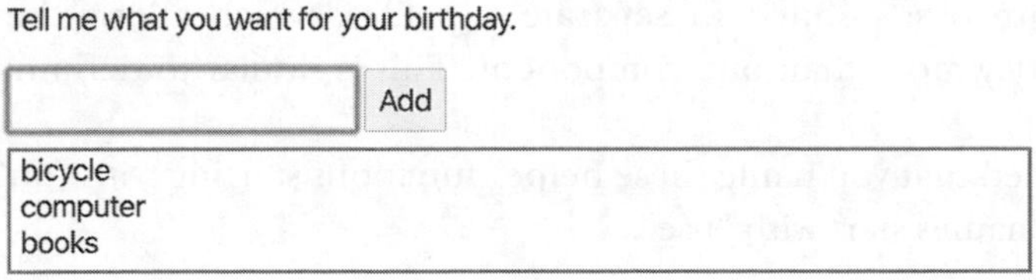

Tell me what you want for your birthday.

```
[                    ] Add
┌──────────────────────────────────────────────┐
│ bicycle                                        │
│ computer                                       │
│ books                                          │
└──────────────────────────────────────────────┘
```
Figure 8.4   Birthday list

The function passed to `afterUpdate` scrolls the list to the bottom.

Listing 8.8   App that uses `afterUpdate`

```
<script>
  import {afterUpdate} from 'svelte';
  let input;
  let item = '';
  let items = [];
  let list;

  afterUpdate(() => list.scrollTo(0, list.scrollHeight));

  function addItem() {
    items.push(item);
    items = items;
    item = '';
    input.focus();
  }
</script>

<style>
  .list {
    border: solid gray 2px;
    height: 52px;
    overflow-y: scroll;
    padding: 5px;
  }
</style>

<p>Tell me what you want for your birthday.</p>

<form on:submit|preventDefault>
  <input bind:this={input} bind:value={item}>
  <button on:click={addItem}>Add</button>
</form>

<div class="list" bind:this={list}>
  {#each items as item}
    <div>{item}</div>
  {/each}
</div>
```

- This function has access to item, which is a state variable.
- This triggers an update.
- This clears the input.
- This prepares the user for entering another item.
- This is enough height to display three items.

8.6   *Using helper functions*

Lifecycle functions can be called from helper functions whose purpose is to implement lifecycle functionality that can be shared between multiple components. These helper functions are best defined in separate `.js` files, which allows them to be imported and used by more than one component. This is similar to defining custom React hooks.

It is recommended that you name these helper functions starting with "on", similar to how React hook names start with "use".

For example, we can implement lifecycle helper functions that move the focus to the current first input and log when a component is mounted.

Listing 8.9 Helper functions defined in `src/helper.js`

```
import {onMount} from 'svelte';

export function onMountFocus() {
    onMount(() => {
    const input = document.querySelector('input');
     input.focus();
    });
}

export function onMountLog(name) {
    onMount(() => console.log(name, 'mounted'));
}
```

⟵ This finds the first input element.

Let's create two components that use these helper functions. The NameEntry component allows the user to enter the name of a person (figure 8.5 and listing 8.10). The AgeEntry component allows their age to be entered (figure 8.6 and listing 8.11). These components use both of the helper functions defined in listing 8.9.

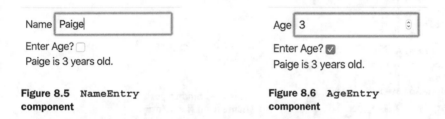

Figure 8.5 `NameEntry`
component

Figure 8.6 `AgeEntry`
component

The component that renders NameEntry and AgeEntry toggles between showing one or the other based on the value of a checkbox with the label "Enter Age?" (see listing 8.12).

Listing 8.10 `NameEntry` component in `src/NameEntry.svelte`

```
<script>
  import {onMountFocus, onMountLog} from './helper';
  export let name;
  onMountLog('NameEntry');
  onMountFocus();
</script>

<label>
  Name
  <input bind:value={name}>
</label>
```

Listing 8.11   AgeEntry component in `src/AgeEntry.svelte`

```
<script>
  import {onMountFocus, onMountLog} from './helper';
  export let age;
  onMountLog('AgeEntry');
  onMountFocus();
</script>

<label>
  Age
  <input type="number" min="0" bind:value={age}>
</label>
```

The following listing shows a component that renders AgeEntry or NameEntry.

Listing 8.12   App that uses `AgeEntry` and `NameEntry`

```
<script>
  import {onMountLog} from './helper';
  import AgeEntry from './AgeEntry.svelte';
  import NameEntry from './NameEntry.svelte';

  let age = 0;
  let enterAge = false;
  let name = '';
  onMountLog('App');
</script>

{#if enterAge}
  <AgeEntry bind:age />           ⟵  This uses bind to get age
{:else}                              from AgeEntry.
  <NameEntry bind:name />        ⟵  This uses bind to get
{/if}                                name from NameEntry.

<label>
  Enter Age?
  <input type="checkbox" bind:checked={enterAge}>
</label>

<div>{name} is {age} years old.</div>
```

8.7   *Building the Travel Packing app*

The only place where the Travel Packing app needs to use a lifecycle function is in `Dialog.svelte`. This registers the dialog polyfill with each `dialog` instance after it is mounted. (The `Dialog` component and uses of it were added to the Travel Packing app in chapter 7.)

The dialog polyfill was registered with the following line of code:

```
onMount(() => dialogPolyfill.registerDialog(dialog));
```

The `dialog` variable was set using `bind:this` with code like the following:

```
<Dialog title="some-title" bind:dialog>
```

In the next chapter you will learn how to implement routing between the "pages" of an app.

Summary

- Components can register functions to be called at specific points in their lifecycle.
- The `onMount` function registers a function to be called when each component instance is added to the DOM.
- The `onDestroy` function registers a function to be called when each component instance is removed from the DOM.
- The `beforeUpdate` function registers a function to be called before each component instance is updated due to receiving a new prop value or having a state change.
- The `afterUpdate` function registers a function to be called after each component instance is updated due to receiving a new prop value or having a state change.
- The functions passed to lifecycle functions can be defined outside component source files in plain JavaScript files. This allows them to be shared by multiple components and by other JavaScript functions.

Client-side routing

9

Client-side routing is the ability to navigate between the pages of a web application. There are many things that can trigger a route change:

- The user clicks a link or button.
- The application programmatically changes the route based on the current state of the app.
- The user manually modifies the URL in the browser's address bar.

Sapper, which builds on Svelte, provides a routing solution that is generally easier to use than adding routing to a Svelte app. This approach will be covered in chapters 15 and 16.

If you do not wish to use the other features that Sapper provides, or you wish to use a different routing approach, there are many ways to implement routing in a Svelte application. Several open source libraries support routing in Svelte. Another option is to use *hash routing*, which takes advantage of the hash portion of URLs and doesn't require installing a library. The easiest approach, however, is to simply choose a "page" component to render in the topmost component. We'll call this the "manual" approach.

We will start by exploring the manual approach before moving on to hash routing and using the page.js library. Then we will look at how to implement hash routing and routing with page.js in the Travel Packing app.

9.1 Manual routing

The downsides of the manual approach are that the browser's back button cannot be used to return to a previous "page," and the URL in the browser's address bar does not change when the "page" changes. However, for many applications these features are not necessary. This might be the case if the app begins every session on the same starting page, and users do not need to bookmark pages within the app.

The basic recipe for this approach is as follows:

1 Import all the components that represent pages in the topmost component, typically named `App`.
2 Create an object in `App` that maps page names to page components, perhaps named `pageMap`.
3 Add a variable in `App` that is set to the name of the current page.
4 Set up event handling to change this variable.
5 Use the special element `<svelte:component … />` (described more in chapter 14) to render the current page.

Let's use this approach to implement a simple shopping app. The code for this app can be found at http://mng.bz/jgq8.

The app has three page components named `Shop`, `Cart`, and `Ship`. Navigation between the pages is performed by clicking buttons at the top. The button for the `Cart` page contains a shopping cart emoji and the number of unique items in the cart, not considering their quantities. The Shop and Ship buttons just contain text labels.

All the page components share access to a writable store named `cartStore` that stores an array of items in the cart. This is defined in `stores.js` and starts as an empty array.

Listing 9.1 Defining `cartStore` in `src/stores.js`

```
import {writable} from 'svelte/store';

export const cartStore = writable([]);
```

The items available for purchase and their prices are defined in `items.js`.

Listing 9.2   Defining store items in `src/items.js`

```
export default [
  {description: 'socks', price: 7.0},
  {description: 'boots', price: 99.0},
  {description: 'gloves', price: 15.0},
  {description: 'hat', price: 10.0},
  {description: 'scarf', price: 20.0}
];
```

The NavButton component is used to allow users to navigate between the pages of the app. Three instances of this component are used in the App component.

Listing 9.3   NavButton component in `src/NavButton.svelte`

```
<script>
  export let name;          <- This is the name associated
  export let pageName;         with this button.
</script>                   <- This is the name of the currently selected page.
                              The parent component, App, will bind to this prop
<button                       to receive an update when the button is clicked.
  class:active={pageName === name}
  on:click={() => pageName = name}
>
  <slot />
</button>

<style>
  button {
    --space: 0.5rem;
    background-color: white;
    border-radius: var(--space);
    height: 38px;
    margin-right: var(--space);
    padding: var(--space);
  }

  .active {
    background-color: yellow;
  }
</style>
```

The App component is where we implement manual routing. It provides buttons that can be clicked to navigate to the three pages of the app. One page component at a time is rendered.

Listing 9.4   App that uses the NavButton component

```
<script>
  import {cartStore} from './stores';

  import NavButton from './NavButton.svelte';
```

```
import Cart from './Cart.svelte';        ◁——  These are
import Ship from './Ship.svelte';              the page
import Shop from './Shop.svelte';              components.

const pageMap = {
  cart: Cart,
  ship: Ship,
  shop: Shop
}                            This holds the name of
                             the current page to be
let pageName = 'shop';  ◁——  rendered.
</script>

<nav>
  <NavButton bind:pageName name='shop'>Shop</NavButton>
  <NavButton bind:pageName name='cart'>
    &#x1F6D2; {$cartStore.length}
  </NavButton>
  <NavButton bind:pageName name='ship'>Ship</NavButton>
</nav>

<main>
  <svelte:component this={pageMap[pageName]} />
</main>

<style>
  main {
    padding: 10px;
  }

  nav {
    display: flex;
    align-items: center;
    background-color: cornflowerblue;
    padding: 10px;
  }
</style>
```

The Unicode character here is a shopping cart. (points to `&#x1F6D2;`)

This is a special Svelte element that renders a given component. (points to `<svelte:component ...>`)

The Shop page allows the user to add items to be purchased to their cart simply by changing the quantity of an item to a number other than 0 (see figure 9.1). Deleting the quantity or setting it to 0 removes the item from the cart.

Description	Price	Quantity
socks	$7.00	2
boots	$99.00	1
gloves	$15.00	1
hat	$10.00	
scarf	$20.00	

Figure 9.1 Shop component

Listing 9.5   Shop component in src/Shop.svelte

```
<script>
  import items from './items';
  import {cartStore} from './stores';

  function changeQuantity(event, item) {
    const newQuantity = Number(event.target.value);
```

```
        cartStore.update(items => {
          // If the new quantity is not zero and the old quantity is zero ...
          if (newQuantity && !item.quantity) {
            items.push(item);
            // If the new quantity is zero and the old quantity is not zero ...
          } else if (newQuantity === 0 && item.quantity) {
            const {description} = item;
            items = items.filter(i => i.description !== description);
          }

          item.quantity = newQuantity;

          return items;
        });
      }
</script>

<h1>Shop</h1>

<table>
  <thead>
    <tr>
      <th>Description</th>
      <th>Price</th>
      <th>Quantity</th>
    </tr>
  </thead>
  <tbody>
    {#each items as item}
      <tr>
        <td>{item.description}</td>
        <td>${item.price.toFixed(2)}</td>
        <td>
          <input
            type="number"
            min="0"
            on:input={e => changeQuantity(e, item)}
            value={item.quantity}
          >
        </td>
      </tr>
    {/each}
  </tbody>
</table>

<style>
  input {
    width: 60px
  }
</style>
```

This adds the item to the cart. → (points to `items.push(item);`)

This removes the item from the cart. → (points to `items = items.filter(i => i.description !== description);`)

The Cart page merely displays the cart contents and the total price of the items in the cart (see figure 9.2).

Cart

Description	Quantity	Price
socks	2	$7.00
gloves	1	$15.00
boots	1	$99.00
Total		$128.00

Figure 9.2 Cart component

Listing 9.6 Cart component in `src/Cart.svelte`

```
<script>
  import {cartStore} from './stores';

  let total =
    $cartStore.reduce((acc, item) => acc + item.price * item.quantity, 0);
</script>

<h1>Cart</h1>

{#if $cartStore.length === 0}
  <div>empty</div>
{:else}
  <table>
    <thead>
      <tr>
        <th>Description</th>
        <th>Quantity</th>
        <th>Price</th>
      </tr>
    </thead>
    <tbody>
      {#each $cartStore as item}
        <tr>
          <td>{item.description}</td>
          <td>{item.quantity}</td>
          <td>${item.price.toFixed(2)}</td>
        </tr>
      {/each}
    </tbody>
    <tfoot>
      <tr>
        <td colspan="2"><label>Total</label></td>
        <td>${total.toFixed(2)}</td>
      </tr>
    </tfoot>
  </table>
{/if}

<style>
td[colspan="2"] {
  text-align: right;
}
</style>
```

The Ship page allows the user to enter their name and shipping address. It also displays the total before shipping, the shipping cost, and the grand total (see figure 9.3).

Ship

Name Tami Volkmann
Street 1234 Main St.
City Somewhere
State Missouri
Zip 12345

Shipping to:

Tami Volkmann
1234 Main St.
Somewhere, Missouri 12345

Total $128.00 **Shipping** $10.00 **Grand Total** $138.00   Figure 9.3   `Ship` component

---

Listing 9.7 `Ship` component in `src/Ship.svelte`

```
<script>
  import {cartStore} from './stores';

  let total = $cartStore.reduce(
    (acc, item) => acc + item.price * item.quantity, 0);

  let city = '';
  let name = '';
  let state = '';
  let street = '';
  let zip = '';

  $: shipping = total === 0 ? 0 : total < 10 ? 2 : total < 30 ? 6 : 10;

  const format = cost => '$' + cost.toFixed(2);
</script>

<h1>Ship</h1>

<form on:submit|preventDefault>
  <label>
    Name
    <input bind:value={name}>
  </label>
  <label>
    Street
    <input bind:value={street}>
  </label>
```

This computes the shipping cost based on the total cost of the items.

This function formats a cost with a dollar sign and two decimal places.

```
    <label>
      City
      <input bind:value={city}>
    </label>
    <label>
      State
      <input bind:value={state}>
    </label>
    <label>
      Zip
      <input bind:value={zip}>
    </label>
</form>

<h3>Shipping to:</h3>
<div>{name}</div>
<div>{street}</div>
<div>{city ? city + ',' : ''} {state} {zip}</div>

<div class="totals">
  <label>Total</label> {format(total)}
  <label>Shipping</label> {format(shipping)}
  <label>Grand Total</label> {format(total + shipping)}
</div>

<style>
  form {
    display: inline-block;
  }

  form > label {
    display: block;
    margin-bottom: 5px;
    text-align: right;
    width: 100%;
  }

  .totals {
    margin-top: 10px;
  }
</style>
```

Styling that can affect any component is placed in the public/global.css file.

Listing 9.8   Global CSS in `public/global.css`

```
body {
  font-family: sans-serif;
  margin: 0;
}

h1 {
  margin-top: 0;
}
```

```
input {
  border: solid lightgray 1px;
  border-radius: 4px;
  padding: 4px;
}

label {
  font-weight: bold;
}

table {
  border-collapse: collapse;
}

td,
th {
  border: solid lightgray 1px;
  padding: 5px 10px;
}
```

As you can see, very little of this code is specific to routing. In this example, only the topmost component, App, is aware of routing. The remaining components are just plain Svelte components.

9.2   *Hash routing*

An advantage of hash routing over manual routing is that the URL in the browser's address bar changes when the user navigates to a different page.

The browser's Window object dispatches a hashchange event when the portion of the URL after # changes. These events provide a simple way to implement client-side routing. All that is required is to

1 Listen for hashchange events.
2 Change the component rendered based on the hash value.
3 Navigate to URLs with different hash values to switch pages.

NOTE   Some people dislike the aesthetics of using hash values in URLs to differentiate between the pages of an app.

Let's implement the same Svelte shopping app as before, but using hash routing. The code for this app can be found at http://mng.bz/WPWl.

Users can manually change the URL in the browser's address bar to change the page that is rendered. This means it is possible to have a hash value in the URL that does not map to one of the pages of the app. When this occurs, the NotFound component, defined in the following listing, is rendered.

Listing 9.9   NotFound component in src/NotFound.svelte

```
<h1>There is nothing here to help you pack for your trip.</h1>
```

The `App` component is where we will implement hash routing. This is similar to the `App` component for manual routing in listing 9.4, but it uses anchor elements instead of the `NavButton` component to allow users to navigate between the pages. Only the `App.svelte` file needs to change. The other source files do not require any changes.

Listing 9.10 The shopping app

```
<script>
  import {cartStore} from './stores';


  import Cart from './Cart.svelte';        ◁──┐ These are
  import NotFound from './NotFound.svelte';    │ the page
  import Ship from './Ship.svelte';            │ components.
  import Shop from './Shop.svelte';

  let component;        ◁──┐ This holds the page
                           │ component to be
  const hashMap = {        │ rendered.
    '#cart': Cart,
    '#ship': Ship,
    '#shop': Shop
  };                          This function is called
                              when the hash value in
  function hashChange() {  ◁─ the URL changes.
    component = hashMap[location.hash] || NotFound;
  }
</script>

<svelte:window on:hashchange={hashChange} />       ◁──


<nav>
  <a href="/#shop" class:active={component === Shop}>Shop</a>
  <a href="/#cart" class:active={component === Cart} class="icon">
    &#x1F6D2; {$cartStore.length}
  </a>
  <a href="/#ship" class:active={component === Ship}>Ship</a>
</nav>


<main>
  <svelte:component this={component} />       ◁──
</main>

<style>
  :root {                 ◁──
    --space: 0.5rem;
  }

  a {
    background-color: white;
    border-radius: var(--space);
    margin-right: var(--space);
    padding: var(--space);
```

These are the page components.

This holds the page component to be rendered.

This function is called when the hash value in the URL changes.

This is a special Svelte element that supports adding event listeners on the window object without having to write code to remove them when the component is removed from the DOM (destroyed).

This is a special Svelte element that renders a given component.

This defines a global CSS variable that any CSS rule can use.

```
    text-decoration: none;
  }

  a.active {
    background-color: yellow;
  }

  .icon {
    padding-bottom: 6px;
    padding-top: 6px;
  }

  main {
    padding: var(--space);
  }

  nav {
    display: flex;
    align-items: center;
    background-color: cornflowerblue;
    padding: var(--space);
  }
</style>
```

As with manual routing, very little of this code is specific to routing. Only the topmost component is aware of the use of hash routing.

9.3   *Using the page.js library*

When using page.js, the URL in the browser's address bar changes if the user navigates to a different page, as it does with hash routing. An advantage of using page.js over hash routing is that page URLs do not use the hash portion. Some people prefer the look of non-hash URLs.

Page.js isn't specific to Svelte. It bills itself as a "Tiny ~1200 byte Express-inspired client-side router" (https://visionmedia.github.io/page.js). To install page.js, enter npm install page.

If any of the page URLs will use query parameters as a way of passing data, you should also install query-string by entering npm install query-string.

Let's implement the same Svelte app as before, but using page.js instead of hash routing. As in the previous routing approaches, the pages in the app are implemented as plain Svelte components. Only the App.svelte file needs to change. The other source files do not require any changes. The code for this app can be found at http://mng.bz/8p5w.

> **NOTE**   Page.js relies on the browser History API, and the Svelte REPL does not support using this. Therefore, this code will not work in the REPL. The following error will be displayed: "Failed to execute 'replaceState' on 'History': A history state object with URL 'https://svelte.dev/srcdoc' cannot be created in a document with origin 'null' and URL 'about:srcdoc'."

Listing 9.11   App using page.js

```
<script>
  import page from 'page';
  import {cartStore} from './stores';

  import Cart from './Cart.svelte';
  import NotFound from './NotFound.svelte';
  import Ship from './Ship.svelte';
  import Shop from './Shop.svelte';

  let component;

  page.redirect('/', '/shop');
  page('/cart', () => (component = Cart));
  page('/ship', () => (component = Ship));
  page('/shop', () => (component = Shop));

  page('*', () => (component = NotFound));

  page.start();
</script>

<nav>
  <a href="/shop" class:active={component === Shop}>Shop</a>
  <a class="icon" href="/cart" class:active={component === Cart}>
    &#x1F6D2; {$cartStore.length}
  </a>
  <a href="/ship" class:active={component === Ship}>Ship</a>
</nav>

<main>
  <svelte:component this={component} />
</main>

<style>
  /* styles for this component are the same as before */
</style>
```

These are the page components.

This holds the page component to be rendered.

Since this is the last registered path and it matches everything, it will be invoked for any path not already handled. If the first parameter, '*', is omitted, it will do the same thing.

This is a special Svelte element that renders a given component.

It is typical for Svelte apps to be created using the GitHub repository sveltejs/template as a starting point. This uses the sirv server application (www.npmjs.com/package/sirv) to serve static assets of the web app for local testing. Other server applications are typically used in production.

By default, the sirv app only supports HTTP requests that match files found in the public directory. If your web app routing solution uses URLs that deviate from this, such as the URLs used by the page library, those URLs will not work. To fix this, modify package.json and change the start script to the following:

```
"start": "sirv public --single"
```

With these changes in place, the app should operate as before. However, the URLs for the pages will end with a slash and a path part rather than a hash. Manually changing the URL to end with something other than /shop, /cart, or /ship will cause the NotFound page to be displayed.

9.4   *Using path and query parameters with page.js*

Now that you have seen the basic usage of page.js, let's look at how path and query parameters can be passed to a route. We don't need this capability in our shopping app, but other apps might use this to pass data to the new page component to be rendered. For example, a page that renders information about an upcoming concert might need a unique ID for the concert in order to fetch data about it.

> **Path and query parameters**
>
> As a refresher on the difference between path and query parameters, consider the following URL: https://mycompany.com/myapp/v1/v2?q1=v3&q2=v4
>
> The app represented by this URL is at the domain "mycompany.com" with a path of "myapp". The URL contains two path parameters with the values "v1" and "v2". It also contains two query parameters named "q1" and "q2". The value of "q1" is "v3" and the value of "q2" is "v4".

Let's demonstrate using path and query parameters in a simple app that only has two pages named Page1 and Page2.

The Page1 component accepts four props, two of which will come from path parameters and two of which will come from query parameters. This page simply renders the values of these parameters to show that they were received. It also renders a button that navigates to the second page when clicked (see figure 9.4). This demonstrates programmatic navigation that is not triggered by a user clicking a link.

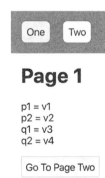

Figure 9.4
Page1 component

Listing 9.12   Page1 component in src/Page1.svelte

```
<script>
  import page from 'page';

  export let p1; // required
  export let p2 = undefined; // optional
  export let q1; // required
  export let q2 = undefined; // optional
```

```
    console.log('Page1 $$props =', $$props);
</script>
```
This shows that we can access all the props in a single object. $$props is an undocumented variable that is subject to change.

```
<h1>Page 1</h1>
<div>p1 = {p1}</div>
<div>p2 = {p2}</div>
<div>q1 = {q1}</div>
<div>q2 = {q2}</div>

<button on:click={() => page.show('/two')}>
  Go To Page Two
</button>
```
This demonstrates programmatic navigation.

```
<style>
  button {
    margin-top: 1rem;
  }
</style>
```

The Page2 component doesn't use any props (see figure 9.5). Its only purpose in this example is to show that we can navigate between multiple pages.

One   Two

Page 2

Figure 9.5
Page2 component

Listing 9.13   Page2 component in `src/Page2.svelte`

```
<h1>Page 2</h1>
```

The following listing shows the topmost component, which configures page routing.

Listing 9.14   App that uses the Page1 and Page2 components

```
<script>
  import page from 'page';
  import qs from 'query-string';

  import Page1 from './Page1.svelte';
  import Page2 from './Page2.svelte';

  let component;

  let props = {};

  function parseQueryString(context, next) {
    context.query = qs.parse(context.querystring);
    props = {};
    next();
  }

  page('*', parseQueryString);

  page('/', context => {
    component = Page1;
```

This holds the page component to be rendered.

This holds all the props to be passed to the page component.

This is a middleware function that parses query strings and puts the result back on the context object.

This clears the previous value.

This allows the next middleware to run.

This causes the parseQueryString middleware to run on every path. If the first parameter '*' is omitted, it will do the same thing.

This is the root path for the app.

```
    props = {p1: 'alpha', q1: 'beta'};
  });

  page('/one/:p1/:p2?', context => {
    component = Page1;
    const {params, query} = context;
    props = {...params, ...query};
  });

  page('/two', () => component = Page2);

  page.start();
</script>

<nav>
  <a
    class:active={component === Page1}
    href="/one/v1/v2?q1=v3&q2=v4"
  >
    One
  </a>
  <a class:active={component === Page2} href="/two">Two</a>
</nav>

<main>
  <svelte:component this={component} {...props} />
</main>

<style>

  :global(body) {
    padding: 0;
  }
  :global(h1) {
    margin-top: 0;
  }

  a {
    --padding: 0.5rem;
    background-color: white;
    border: solid gray 1px;
    border-radius: var(--padding);
    display: inline-block;
    margin-right: 1rem;
    padding: var(--padding);
    text-decoration: none;
  }

  .active {
    background-color: yellow;
  }

  main {
    padding: 1rem;
  }
```

This path requires the path parameter, p1, and accepts the optional path parameter, p2, indicated by following its name with a question mark. The associated component, Page1, also uses the query parameters q1 and q2, but there isn't a way to state in the path whether these are required or optional.

The path and query parameters are passed as props to the component to be rendered in <svelte:component> later.

This path doesn't use any path or query parameters.

Note how this link uses different path and query parameters than the previous "/" path, which sets p1 to "alpha" and q1 to "beta".

This is a special Svelte element that renders a given component.

These global CSS rules could instead be specified in public/global.css. This demonstrates an alternative way to define global styles.

```
nav {
  background-color: cornflowerblue;
  padding: 1rem;
}
</style>
```

Clearly, supporting URL paths that accept path and query parameters is a bit more complicated, but not overly so. The page.js library has additional features not demonstrated here. See https://visionmedia.github.io/page.js/ for more details.

Other routing libraries

There are also open source routing libraries that are specific to Svelte. These are some to consider:

- *navaid*—https://github.com/lukeed/navaid
- *Routify*—https://routify.dev/
- *svelte-routing*—https://github.com/EmilTholin/svelte-routing
- *svelte-spa-router*—https://github.com/ItalyPaleAle/svelte-spa-router

---

9.5 *Building the Travel Packing app*

Let's apply what you have learned about routing to the Travel Packing app. The finished code can be found at http://mng.bz/NKW1.

Currently the App component decides whether to render the Login component or the Checklist component. But the URL in the browser's address bar does not change.

Let's first use hash routing to treat these components as pages and give them unique URLs. The version you will find in GitHub uses page.js, not hash routing, but here are the steps to use hash routing.

First, copy the NotFound.svelte file shown in listing 9.9 into the src directory. Then in App.svelte, do the following:

1 Import the NotFound component with this line:

```
import NotFound from './NotFound.svelte';
```

2 Replace the line let page = Login; with the following:

```
const hashMap = {
  '#login': Login,
  '#checklist': Checklist
};

let component = Login;

const hashChange = () => (component = hashMap[location.hash] || NotFound);
```

3 Add the following at the beginning of the HTML section:

```
<svelte:window on:hashchange={hashChange} />
```

4 Replace the {#if} block that decides which component to render with the following:

```
<svelte:component
  this={component}
  on:login={() => (location.href = '/#checklist')}
  on:logout={() => (location.href = '/#login')}
/>
```

As you can see, only a small amount of code is needed to get client-side routing.

With these changes in place, the app should function as before. However, now the URL changes when the page switches between Login and Checklist. You can also switch pages by manually changing the hash portion of the URL. If an unsupported hash value is used, the NotFound component is rendered.

Now let's change the app to use page.js instead of hash routing. Install the library by entering npm install page in the top project directory.

In App.svelte, do the following:

1 Add an import for the page.js library at the top of the script element.

```
import page from 'page';
```

2 Remove the hashMap variable declaration.

3 Remove the hashChange function definition.

4 Add the following at the bottom of the script element:

```
page.redirect('/', '/login');
page('/login', () => (component = Login));
page('/checklist', () => (component = Checklist));
page('*', () => (component = NotFound));
page.start();
```

5 Remove the <svelte:window> element at the top of the HTML section.

6 Change the <svelte:component> element to match the following:

```
<svelte:component
  this={component}
  on:login={() => page.show('/checklist')}
  on:logout={() => page.show('/login')} />
```

7 Change the start script in package.json to include the --single option.

With these changes in place, the app should function as before. However, now the URL for each page no longer contains a hash.

We haven't implemented login authentication. If we did, we could prevent navigation to the Checklist page unless a valid username and password were entered.

In the next chapter you will learn how to implement animations in Svelte components.

Summary

- Client-side routing is the ability to navigate between pages of a web application.
- Svelte does not support this out of the box, but there are many ways to add routing in a Svelte app.
- A popular option is to use Sapper, which has a built-in routing solution.
- Manual routing, hash routing, and the page.js library are easy-to-use options for implementing routing in a Svelte app.
- Several additional open source libraries also add routing to Svelte apps.

Animation

10

This chapter covers

- Easing functions used by animations
- The `svelte/animate` package
- The `svelte/motion` package
- The `svelte/transition` package
- Creating custom transitions
- Transition events

Adding animation to a web application can make it more enticing to users and can make some operations more intuitive. There are libraries for many web frameworks that add animation support, but in Svelte this is a built-in feature.

Svelte provides many `transition` directive values and functions that make it easy to add CSS-based animation to elements. The fact that they are CSS-based rather than JavaScript-based means they do not block the main thread, which is good for performance. This chapter describes each of the provided animations and concludes with showing how custom transitions can be implemented.

Svelte supports two kinds of animations: adding/removing an element, and changing a value.

When elements are added to or removed from the DOM, animation allows a special effect to occur over a given number of milliseconds. For example, added elements can fade in, and removed elements can slide out of the browser window. This is more visually appealing than abruptly adding or removing an element.

Animated value changes enable a variable's value to gradually change from its current value to a new value over a given number of milliseconds. When the variable is part of the state of a component, the DOM is updated for each intermediate value. For example, the value of a given bar in a bar chart can be changed from a value of 0 to a value of 10 over a duration of 500 milliseconds. Rather than the bar jumping from a height of 0 to, say, 300 pixels, it gradually increases, resulting in an animated change.

Let's get started in our journey through Svelte animations. Each of the following sections will focus on an important animation topic or package provided by Svelte.

10.1 *Easing functions*

Animations can proceed at varying rates over their duration. This is specified with easing functions. Each animation has a default easing function that can be overridden with the `easing` option.

The `svelte/easing` package currently defines 11 easing functions. Custom easing functions can also be defined. They are simply functions that take a number between 0 and 1 and return a number in that same range.

A great way to learn about the provided easing functions is to browse the Ease Visualizer at https://svelte.dev/examples#easing (see figure 10.1). After selecting an Ease and a Type (Ease In, Ease Out, or Ease In Out), it displays a curve that describes its effect and animates the movement through the duration.

The `linear` easing function is the most basic. It provides a smooth, constant rate of animation. The easing functions `sine`, `quad`, `cubic`, `quart`, `quint`, `expo`, and `circ` are all simple curves with only minor differences in their acceleration in the middle of an animation. The most extreme of these is `expo`.

The easing functions `back`, `elastic`, and `bounce` are more interesting because they move forward and backward. `bounce` changes direction seven times, and `elastic` changes direction five times. `back` changes direction only once and so is the least bouncy.

The actual names of all of these easing functions end with `In`, `Out`, or `InOut`. For example, `bounceIn`, `bounceOut`, and `bounceInOut`.

Easings ending in `In` are applied when components are added to the DOM. Easings ending in `Out` are applied when components are removed from the DOM. Easings ending in `InOut` are applied for both.

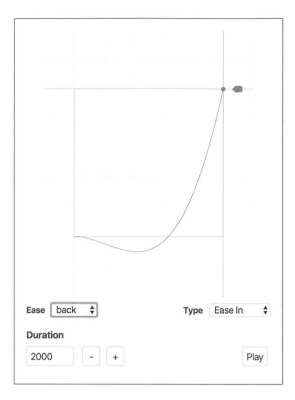

Figure 10.1   **The Ease Visualizer**

10.2   *The svelte/animate package*

The svelte/animate package provides the flip function, which stands for *first, last, invert, play*. It doesn't
actually flip anything. Instead, it determines the new
position of an element and animates changes to its *x*
and *y* values from the old to the new position. A common use is to animate the changing location of items
in a list.

Figure 10.2   flip **animations
in vertical orientation**

   In the following example, the Add button adds a
new number to a list of numbers that are each displayed
in buttons (see figure 10.2). New numbers are added to
the beginning of the list so that each one must move to
make room. Clicking a number button removes it, causing all the buttons after it to slide toward the beginning
of the list to close up the vacated space. The list can
be toggled between horizontal and vertical, and this
change is also animated (see figure 10.3).

Figure 10.3   flip **animations
in horizontal orientation**

Copy this code to the Svelte REPL and try it.

Listing 10.1 `flip` **animation demo**

```
<script>
  import {flip} from 'svelte/animate';

  let horizontal = false;
  let next = 1;
  let list = [];

  function addItem() {
    list = [next++, ...list];
  }

  function removeItem(number) {
    list = list.filter(n => n !== number);
  }

  const options = {duration: 500};
</script>

<label>
  Horizontal
  <input type="checkbox" bind:checked={horizontal}>
</label>

<button on:click={addItem}>Add</button>

{#each list as n (n)}
  <div animate:flip={options} class="container" class:horizontal>
    <button on:click={() => removeItem(n)}>{n}</button>
  </div>
{/each}

<style>
  .container {
    width: fit-content;
  }

  .horizontal {
    display: inline-block;
    margin-left: 10px;
  }
</style>
```

This adds the next number to the beginning of the list. ← `list = [next++, ...list];`

This is a keyed each block. → `{#each list as n (n)}`

The flip animation is specified here. ← `<div animate:flip={options} class="container" class:horizontal>`

Animating between the vertical and horizontal layout of the buttons only works well if the container knows its width, so this line is critical for proper animation. ← `width: fit-content;`

Toggling the Horizontal checkbox before the animation completes cancels the in-progress animations and starts new animations that cause the elements to return to their previous locations.

The animate directive that's used to request a flip animation in listing 10.1 must be applied to an HTML element. Applying it to a custom component has no effect.

The `flip` animation supports several options:

- `delay` specifies how long to wait in milliseconds before beginning the animation. It defaults to 0.
- `duration` specifies how long it should take in milliseconds to complete the animation. The value can also be a function that takes the distance to move in pixels and returns the duration to use. It defaults to the function `d => Math .sqrt(d) * 120`.
- `easing` is an easing function that defaults to `cubicOut`. Many more easing functions can be imported from the `svelte/easing` package.

Here is an example of specifying options for the `flip` animation:

```
<script>
  import {bounceInOut} from 'svelte/easing';
</script>
...
<div animate:flip={{delay: 200, duration: 1000, easing: bounceInOut}}>
```

10.3   *The svelte/motion package*

The `svelte/motion` package provides the `spring` and `tweened` functions. These create writable stores whose values animate from old to new values. As with all writable stores, the stored value can be changed by calling the store's `set` and `update` methods. The `set` method is passed a new value. The `update` method is passed a function that computes the new value based on the current value.

Typically these functions are used to interpolate between two numbers. However, they can also be used to interpolate between multiple numbers held in two arrays or between two objects that have the same shape and only have number values in their primitive properties (properties whose values are not objects).

For example, the `spring` and `tweened` functions are useful for rendering changes in a pie chart. When the value changes from say 10% to 90%, we might want the pie chart to animate showing many values in between. Rather than changing immediately, the value changes smoothly.

The `spring` and `tweened` functions both take an initial value and an options object. Supported options include `delay`, `duration`, `easing`, and `interpolate`. The first three have the same meaning as previously described for the `flip` function. The `interpolate` function is used to interpolate between values that aren't numbers or dates and is discussed a little later in this section.

Let's implement an SVG-based pie chart component that displays a given percentage value (see figure 10.4). As you learned in geometry class, 0 degrees corresponds to 3 o'clock on a clock face, and angles increase counterclockwise from there. It does not use animation, but components

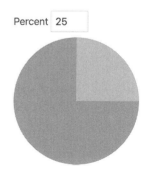

Figure 10.4   A pie chart component

that use it can animate its value. For details on creating pie charts with SVG, see Kasey Bonifacio's "How to Create an SVG Pie Chart": https://seesparkbox.com/foundry/how_to_code_an_SVG_pie_chart.

Listing 10.2 `Pie` component in `src/Pie.svelte`

```
<script>
  export let size = 200;
  export let percent = 0;
  export let bgColor = 'cornflowerblue';
  export let fgColor = 'orange';

  $: viewBox = `0 0 ${size} ${size}`;

  $: radius = size / 2;
  $: halfCircumference = Math.PI * radius;
  $: pieSize = halfCircumference * (percent / 100);
  $: dashArray = `0 ${halfCircumference - pieSize} ${pieSize}`;
</script>

<svg width={size} height={size} {viewBox}>
  <circle r={radius} cx={radius} cy={radius} fill={bgColor} />
  <circle
    r={radius / 2}
    cx={radius}
    cy={radius}
    fill={bgColor}
    stroke={fgColor}
    stroke-width={radius}
    stroke-dasharray={dashArray}
  />
</svg>
```

This renders a pie wedge whose size is a percentage of the circle.

This renders the background circle.

The following component renders a number `input` and a `Pie` component using that value. It uses the `tweened` function to animate the value.

Listing 10.3 App that uses `Pie` component

```
<script>
  import {tweened} from 'svelte/motion';
  import Pie from './Pie.svelte';

  let percent = 0;
  const store = tweened(0, {duration: 1000});
  $: store.set(percent || 0);
</script>

<label>
  Percent
  <input type="number" min="0" max="100" bind:value={percent}>
</label>
<Pie size={200} percent={$store} />
```

This updates the store every time the value of percent changes. If the input is empty, percent will be undefined, but we want the store to always contain a number.

Copy these files to the REPL and try it!

The `spring` function is similar to the `tweened` function, but it uses `stiffness`, `damping`, and `precision` parameters to give a spring-like effect to the animations. It does not use the `duration` parameter.

The previous pie chart example can be changed to use `spring` animation by simply replacing the call to `tweened` with a call to `spring`. For example, this makes it quite springy:

```
const store = spring(0, {stiffness: 0.3, damping: 0.3});
```

Make this change in the REPL, and also change the import of `tweened` to `spring` to try it!

One of the options accepted by the `spring` and `tweened` functions is an `interpolate` function. It supports interpolating between values that are *not* numbers, dates, arrays of them, or objects whose properties only have number or date values.

An `interpolate` function takes starting and ending values. It returns another function that takes a number between 0 and 1 and returns a value of the same type as the starting and ending values that is "between" them.

For example, we can use an `interpolate` function to tween over hex color values in the format "rrggbb". When changing from one color to another, such as red to green, we want to pass through colors that are in a sense between them (see figure 10.5 and listing 10.4).

Tweened Color

Figure 10.5   App that demonstrates using `tweened`

Listing 10.4   App that demonstrates using `tweened`

```
<script>
  import {tweened} from 'svelte/motion';

  let colorIndex = 0;
  const colors = ['ff0000', '00ff00', '0000ff']; // red, green, blue

  // This converts a decimal number to a two-character hex number.
  const decimalToHex = decimal =>
    Math.round(decimal).toString(16).padStart(2, '0');

  // This cycles through the indexes of the colors array.
  const goToNextColor = () => colorIndex = (colorIndex + 1) % colors.length;

  // This extracts two hex characters from an "rrggbb" color string
  // and returns the value as a number between 0 and 255.
  const getColor = (hex, index) =>
    parseInt(hex.substring(index, index + 2), 16);

  // This gets an array of red, green, and blue values in
  // the range 0 to 255 from an "rrggbb" hex color string.
```

```
const getRGBs = hex =>
  [getColor(hex, 0), getColor(hex, 2), getColor(hex, 4)];

// This computes a value that is t% of the way from
// start to start + delta where t is a number between 0 and 1.
const scaledValue = (start, delta, t) => start + delta * t;

// This is an interpolate function used by the tweened function.
function rgbInterpolate(fromColor, toColor) {
  const [fromRed, fromGreen, fromBlue] = getRGBs(fromColor);
  const [toRed, toGreen, toBlue] = getRGBs(toColor);
  const deltaRed = toRed - fromRed;
  const deltaGreen = toGreen - fromGreen;
  const deltaBlue = toBlue - fromBlue;

  return t => {                                                 ◄─┐ This returns
    const red = scaledValue(fromRed, deltaRed, t);                 a function.
    const green = scaledValue(fromGreen, deltaGreen, t);
    const blue = scaledValue(fromBlue, deltaBlue, t);
    return decimalToHex(red) + decimalToHex(green) + decimalToHex(blue);
  };
}

// Create a tweened store that holds an "rrggbb" hex color.
const color = tweened(
  colors[colorIndex],
  {duration: 1000, interpolate: rgbInterpolate}
);

// Trigger tweening if colorIndex changes.
$: color.set(colors[colorIndex]);
</script>

<button on:click={goToNextColor}>Next</button>
<span>color = {$color}</span>
<h1 style="color: #{$color}">Tweened Color</h1>          ◄─┐ The color of this h1
                                                            changes when the Next
                                                            button is clicked.
```

Copy this file to the REPL and try it!

10.4 *The svelte/transition package*

The svelte/transition package provides the crossfade function and the transition directive values blur, draw, fade, fly, scale, and slide.

These are specified using the directives in, out, and transition. An in effect is applied when an element is added to the DOM. An out effect is applied when an element is removed from the DOM. A transition effect is applied in both cases.

Like the animate directive, the in, out, and transition directives must be applied to an HTML element. Applying them to a custom component has no effect.

We will begin by looking at each of the provided transitions and their options. Then we will look at an example that demonstrates all of them, side by side, for comparison.

The `fade` transition animates a change in opacity between 0 and the current opacity value, which is typically 1. It goes from 0 to the current opacity when an element is added to the DOM, and from the current opacity to 0 when an element is removed from the DOM. It accepts the options `delay` and `duration`. The `delay` option is the number of milliseconds to wait before starting the transition. The `duration` option is the number of milliseconds over which the transition should occur.

The `blur` transition is like `fade`, but it also animates an amount of blur in pixels. In addition to the `delay` and `duration` options, it accepts the `easing`, `opacity`, and `amount` options. The `easing` option is an easing function described earlier in section 10.1. The `opacity` option specifies the starting opacity value. This defaults to 0, which is typically the desired value. The `amount` option specifies the size of the blur in pixels and defaults to 5.

The `slide` transition is like a window shade. It animates hiding and showing an element by gradually changing its height. When hiding an element, it is removed from the DOM after the height reaches 0. Elements below it in the normal DOM flow will move up to occupy the vacated space. It accepts `delay`, `duration`, and `easing` options.

The `scale` transition animates the size and opacity of an element. It accepts `delay`, `duration`, `easing`, `start`, and `opacity` options. The `start` option specifies the smallest scale to use before the element is removed. It defaults to 0, which is typically the desired value.

The `fly` transition animates the *x* and *y* location of an element. It accepts `delay`, `duration`, `easing`, `opacity`, x, and y options. The x and y options can be set to negative values to slide the element off the left and top sides of the page. By default, it also animates opacity to 0, but this can be changed by specifying the `opacity` option. To slide an element off the screen without changing its opacity during the slide, set this to 1.

The `draw` transition animates the stroke of an SVG element. It accepts `delay`, `duration`, `easing`, and `speed` options. The `speed` option is an alternate way to specify the duration, computed based on the SVG path length using `length / speed`.

The following example (figure 10.6 and listing 10.5) demonstrates each of these transitions. Copy the following code to the REPL to try it. Click the Toggle button to toggle between hiding and showing each of the `h1` elements, which triggers their transitions. Focus your eyes on one element at a time to get a clear understanding of the effect of a particular transition.

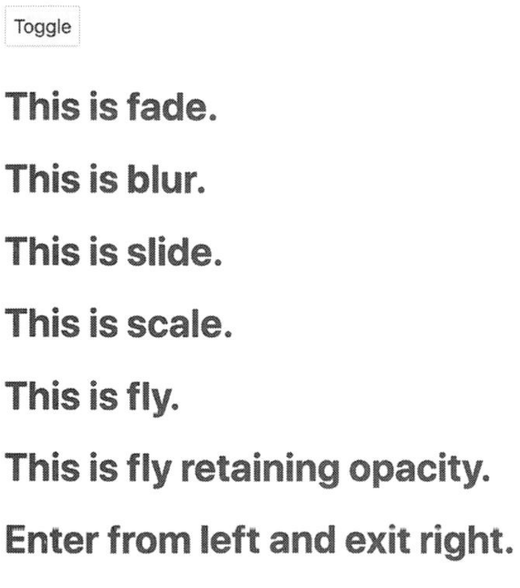

Toggle

This is fade.

This is blur.

This is slide.

This is scale.

This is fly.

This is fly retaining opacity.

Enter from left and exit right.

Figure 10.6   Transitions demo app

Listing 10.5 Transitions demo app

```
<script>
  import {linear} from 'svelte/easing';
  import {blur, fade, fly, scale, slide} from 'svelte/transition';
  let show = true;
  let options = {duration: 1000, easing: linear};
</script>

<button on:click={() => show = !show}>
  Toggle
</button>
{#if show}
  <h1 transition:fade={options}>This is fade.</h1>
  <h1 transition:blur={options}>This is blur.</h1>
  <h1 transition:slide={{...options, x: -150}}>This is slide.</h1>
  <h1 transition:scale={options}>This is scale.</h1>
  <h1 transition:fly={{...options, x: -150}}>This is fly.</h1>
  <h1 transition:fly={{...options, opacity: 1, x: -400}}>
    This is fly retaining opacity.
  </h1>
  <h1
    in:fly={{...options, opacity: 1, x: -400}}
    out:fly={{...options, opacity: 1, x: 500}}
  >
    Enter from left and exit right.
  </h1>
{/if}
```

Setting the easing function to linear makes it more obvious that all the animations are happening simultaneously.

Only transitions specified with the transition directive can be canceled. Canceling a transition means the element returns to its previous state of either being in the DOM or not being in the DOM. Transitions specified using the in and out directives cannot be canceled. This makes sense because, for example, it would be odd to stop the addition of an element with a blur transition partway through, and to remove the element using a fly transition.

10.5 *The fade transition and flip animation*

The following example moves buttons between left and right lists as each button is clicked (see figure 10.7). It uses the fade transition, so the clicked button fades out of its current list and fades into its new list. It also uses the flip animation so buttons below the button being moved slide up to fill the vacated space.

We will implement this using two components to avoid duplicating code. The following listing shows the ButtonList component that is used for both the left and right lists.

Click a button to move it to the other list.

Figure 10.7 Moving buttons with fade and flip

Listing 10.6   `ButtonList` component in `src/ButtonList.svelte`

```
<script>
  import {flip} from 'svelte/animate';
  import {fade} from 'svelte/transition';

  export let list;                          ◁      This is an array of
  export let moveFn;                        ◁      button text values.

  const options = {duration: 1000};                This is a function that
</script>                                           moves the clicked button
                                                    to the other list.
<div class="list">
  {#each list as item (item)}
    <button
      class="item"
      on:click={moveFn}
      animate:flip={options}
      transition:fade={options}>
      {item}
    </button>
  {/each}
</div>

<style>
  .item {
    display: block;
    margin-bottom: 10px;
    padding: 5px;
  }

  .list {
    display: inline-block;
    vertical-align: top;
    width: 100px;
  }
</style>
```

The next listing shows a component that uses two instances of the `ButtonList` component.

Listing 10.7   App that uses the `ButtonList` component

```
<script>
  import ButtonList from './ButtonList.svelte';        trim is needed because
                                                        ButtonList includes whitespace
  let left = ['red', 'orange', 'yellow', 'green'];      in the button text.
  let right = ['blue', 'purple'];
                                                        This adds the text to
  function move(event, from, to) {                      the "to" list.
    const text = event.target.textContent.trim();  ◁
    to.push(text);                                  ◁   This removes the text
    return [from.filter(t => t !== text), to];      ◁   from the "from" list.
  }
```

```
function moveLeft(event) {
  [right, left] = move(event, right, left);
}

function moveRight(event) {
  [left, right] = move(event, left, right);
}
</script>

<p>Click a button to move it to the other list.</p>
<ButtonList list={left} moveFn={moveRight} />
<ButtonList list={right} moveFn={moveLeft} />
```

New values must be assigned to left and right to trigger updates.

Copy these files to the REPL and try it!

10.6 *The crossfade transition*

The crossfade transition creates send and receive transitions. These are used to coordinate the movement of an element from one parent to another. This is also referred to as a *deferred transition* (see https://svelte.dev/tutorial/deferred-transitions).

One example of using crossfade is to move items between lists (see figure 10.8). An item is sent out of one list and received into another. The send transition defers to see if the element is being received in the other location. Then it animates a transition

Click a button to move it to the opposite list.

Figure 10.8 crossfade **demo app**

of the element from its current location to its new location. This provides a much nicer visual effect than what we achieved earlier using the fade transition.

The following listing shows an example of using crossfade. Like before, this example also uses the flip animation so that the remaining list items animate closing up the vacated space.

Listing 10.8 crossfade **demo app**

```
<script>
  import {flip} from 'svelte/animate';
  import {crossfade} from 'svelte/transition';
  const [send, receive] = crossfade({});

  let left = ['red', 'orange', 'green', 'purple'];
  let right = ['yellow', 'blue'];

  function move(item, from, to) {
    to.push(item);
    return [from.filter(i => i !== item), to];
  }
```

The crossfade function must be passed an options object, but it can be an empty object to use the defaults.

```
    function moveLeft(item) {
      [right, left] = move(item, right, left);
    }

    function moveRight(item) {
      [left, right] = move(item, left, right);
    }
</script>

<main>
  <p>Click a button to move it to the opposite list.</p>
  <div class="list">
    {#each left as item (item)}
      <button
        animate:flip
        in:receive={{key: item}}
        out:send={{key: item}}
        on:click={() => moveRight(item)}
      >
        {item}
      </button>
    {/each}
  </div>

  <div class="list">
    {#each right as item (item)}
      <button
        animate:flip
        in:receive={{key: item}}
        out:send={{key: item}}
        on:click={() => moveLeft(item)}
      >
        {item}
      </button>
    {/each}
  </div>
</main>

<style>
  button {
    background-color: cornflowerblue;
    border: none;
    color: white;
    padding: 10px;
    margin-bottom: 10px;
    width: 100%;
  }

  .list {
    display: inline-block;
    margin-right: 30px;
    vertical-align: top;
    width: 70px;
  }
</style>
```

Copy this code to the REPL and try it. It's amazing!

10.7 The draw transition

The `draw` transition animates the stroke of an SVG element.

The example in listing 10.9 draws a house with a single SVG `path` element that uses `transition:draw`. Click the Toggle button to cause the drawing and erasing of the house to be animated (see figure 10.9).

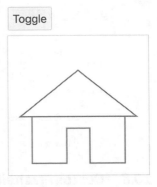

Figure 10.9   `draw` demo app

SVG refresher

Here's a quick SVG refresher:

- The `M` command moves to a given `x` and `y` location.
- The `h` command draws a horizontal line with a given `dx`.
- The `v` command draws a vertical line with a given `dy`.
- The `l` command draws a line with a given `dx` and `dy`.

By default, the origin is the upper-left corner. The SVG `scale` and `translate` functions can be used to flip the coordinate system so the origin is in the lower-left corner.

Listing 10.9   `draw` demo app

```
<script>
  import {draw} from 'svelte/transition';
  const commands =
    'M 2 5 v-4 h3 v3 h2 v-3 h3 v4 h-9 l 5 4 l 5 -4 h-1';    ◁── This draws
  const max = 12;                                                a house.
  let show = true;
</script>

<div>
  <button on:click={() => show = !show}>
    Toggle
  </button>
</div>

{#if show}
  <svg width={200} height={200} viewBox="0 0 {max} {max}">    ◁──
    <g transform="translate(0 {max}) scale(1 -1)">   ◁──
      <path transition:draw={{duration: 1000}}
        d={commands}
        fill="none"
        stroke="red"
```

This gives a coordinate system that goes from 0 to max on both the x and y axes.

The scale function flips the coordinate system.

```
        stroke-width="0.1px"
      />
    </g>
  </svg>
{/if}

<style>
  svg {
    outline: solid lightgray 1px;
  }
</style>
```

◁—┐ **In the coordinate system
       we have configured, 1px
       is very wide.**

10.8   *Custom transitions*

Implementing custom transitions is easy. All that is required is to write a function that follows a few basic rules. The function should take two arguments: the DOM node to be transitioned and an options object. Examples of options include

- delay—This is the number of milliseconds to wait before the transition begins.
- duration—This is the number of milliseconds over which the transition should occur.
- easing—This is an easing function that takes a value between 0 and 1 and returns a value in that same range.

Options that are specific to a given transition can also be provided. For example, the fly transition accepts x and y options.

The function must return an object whose properties include the transition options and a css method. The css method must return the appropriate CSS string for the number between 0 and 1 that is returned by calling the easing function. Svelte takes care of honoring the delay and duration options.

The transition options returned can be given default values that are used when options are not passed to the custom function. For example, default values for duration and easing can be provided.

The css method is passed a time value between 0 and 1. It must return a string containing CSS properties to be applied to the DOM node for that time value. Examples of CSS properties that might vary over time include opacity, size, font size, position, rotation, and color.

Listing 10.10 is an example of a custom transition. It animates the scale and rotation of an element to make it appear to spiral down a drain when removed from the DOM. We will apply this to a div element containing the text "Take me for a spin!" sized to wrap to two lines (see figure 10.10). Click the Toggle button to toggle between hiding and showing the div element. Check the "Springy" checkbox to use the backInOut easing function instead of the linear easing function.

Copy this code to the REPL to try it.

Figure 10.10 Custom transition app

Listing 10.10   Custom transition app

```
<script>
  import {backInOut, linear} from 'svelte/easing';

  let springy = false;
  $: duration = springy ? 2000 : 1000;
  $: easing = springy ? backInOut : linear;
  $: options = {duration, easing, times: 2};

  let show = true;
  const toggle = () => show = !show;

  function spin(node, options) {
    const {easing, times = 1} = options;
    return {
      ...options,
      css(t) {
        const eased = easing(t);
        const degrees = 360 * times;
        return `transform: scale(${eased}) rotate(${eased * degrees}deg);`;
      }
    };
  }
</script>

<label>
  <input type="checkbox" bind:checked={springy} /> Springy
</label>
<div>duration = {duration}</div>
<button on:click={toggle}>Toggle</button>
```

The value of t passed to the css method varies between 0 and 1 during an "in" transition and between 1 and 0 during an "out" transition.

Recall that easing functions return a value between 0 and 1 inclusive.

This is the degrees through which to spin.

```
{#if show}
  <div class="center" in:spin={options} out:spin={options}>
    <div class="content">Take me for a spin!</div>
  </div>
{/if}

<style>
  .center {
    position: absolute;
    left: 50%;
    top: 50%;
    transform: translate(-50%, -50%);
  }

  .content {

    position: absolute;
    transform: translate(-50%, -50%);

    font-size: 64px;
    text-align: center;
    width: 300px;
  }
</style>
```

The reasons for using in and out instead of transition is explained in the next section.

This has a width and height of 0 and is only used to center the content on the page.

These CSS properties give rotation about the center.

10.9 *The transition vs. in and out props*

Recall that we can specify separate in and out transition props instead of specifying a transition prop that is used for both the "in" and "out" portions. There is a difference between these approaches even if the same transition is specified for in and out. When the transition prop is used, the same transition options will be used for the "out" portion as the "in" portion even if the options are changed after the "in" portion occurs. To allow option changes made after the "in" portion occurs to be honored by the "out" portion, use the in and out props instead of the transition prop.

In the previous example, the transition options are changed when the "Springy" checkbox is changed. This is why we use in:spin={options} out:spin={options} instead of transition:spin={options}.

10.10 *Transition events*

Events are dispatched at specific points in a transition. An introstart event is dispatched when an "in" transition begins. An introend event is dispatched when an "in" transition ends. An outrostart event is dispatched when an "out" transition begins. An outroend event is dispatched when an "out" transition ends.

Like with other events, the on directive can be used to register a function to be called when these events are dispatched. For example, to run a function when the transition for an element being removed from the DOM completes, use on:outro-end={*someFunction*}. These functions can trigger changes to the affected component or to other components. For example, focus can be moved to a particular input

element after the transition for an element being added to the DOM completes using
`on:introend`.

10.11 *Building the Travel Packing app*

Let's apply what you have learned about animation to the Travel Packing app. The finished code can be found at http://mng.bz/rrlD.

We want to add four animations:

- Animate adding and deleting items in a category so they slide to their new positions.
- Animate adding and deleting categories so they slide to their new positions.
- Animate adding a category so it scales from 0 to full size.
- Animate deleting a category by rotating and scaling it so it appears to spin down a drain.

In `Category.svelte`, do the following:

1 Import the `flip` transition:

```
import {flip} from 'svelte/animate';
```

2 Wrap the `Item` component and the comment that precedes it with the following `div`:

```
<div animate:flip>
  ...
</div>
```

The first animation for adding and deleting items is now complete.

In `Checklist.svelte`, do the following:

1 Import the `flip` transition:

```
import {flip} from 'svelte/animate';
```

2 Declare an `options` constant:

```
const options = {duration: 700};
```

3 Wrap the `Category` component with the following `div`:

```
<div class="wrapper" animate:flip={options}>
  ...
</div>
```

NOTE In Safari, items are not visible while they are being dragged if the
`<Category>` in `Checklist.svelte` is wrapped in a `div` element. Removing the
`div` fixes it, but then we lose animation of `Category` components.

4 Add the following CSS rules in the `style` element:

```css
.animate {
  display: inline-block;
}

.wrapper {
  display: inline;
}
```

The second animation for adding and deleting categories is now complete.

In `Category.svelte`, do the following:

1 Import the `linear` easing function and the `scale` transition:

```js
import {linear} from 'svelte/easing';
import {scale} from 'svelte/transition';
```

2 Add an `options` constant:

```js
const options = {duration: 700, easing: linear};
```

3 Add the following attribute to the `section` element that wraps all the HTML for a category:

```
in:scale={options}
```

The third animation for scaling new categories from 0 to full size is now complete.

In `Category.svelte`, do the following:

1 Add the `times` property, which specifies the number of times to spin, to the `options` constant to match the following:

```js
const options = {duration: 700, easing: linear, times: 2};
```

2 Add the custom transition function `spin`, which scales and rotates a given DOM node over the duration of an animation:

```js
function spin(node, options) {
  const {easing, times = 1} = options;
  return {
    ...options,
    css(t) {
      const eased = easing(t);
      const degrees = 360 * times;
      return 'transform-origin: 50% 50%; ' +
        `transform: scale(${eased}) ` +
        `rotate(${eased * degrees}deg);`;
    }
  };
}
```

This is the total degrees through which to spin.

3   Add the following attribute to the `section` element that wraps all the HTML for a category:

```
out:spin={options}
```

The fourth animation for making categories appear to spin down a drain when they are deleted is now complete.

That was really a small amount of code to add in order to gain all those animations! In the next chapter you will learn some tips for debugging Svelte applications.

Summary

- Svelte has great built-in support for CSS-based, rather than JavaScript-based, animation, which means the animation won't block the main thread.
- Easing functions control the rate of change in an animation over its duration. Many easing functions are provided, and custom easing functions can be defined.
- Animation is supported by the provided packages `svelte/easing`, `svelte/animate`, `svelte/transition`, and `svelte/motion`.
- Custom transitions can be easily implemented.

Debugging

11

This chapter covers

- Using the @debug tag
- Using reactive statements for debugging
- Using Svelte Devtools

There are three popular ways to debug issues in Svelte applications. The most basic approach to debugging is to add @debug tags that pause execution and output variable values.

Another approach is to use reactive statements to output the values of JavaScript expressions any time variables they use change. Both of these use features built into Svelte.

A final approach covered here is to use a browser extension called Svelte Devtools to view the component hierarchy. After selecting a component, its props and state can be viewed and modified.

> **NOTE** Like in all web applications, the debugger statement can be added in JavaScript code to pause execution when the statement is reached if DevTools is open.

11.1 The @debug tag

The @debug tag pauses execution (breaks) when given top-level variables change, and it outputs those variables' values in the browser's DevTools console. It is only honored if DevTools is open. The browser debugger can then be used to examine the code and other variables that are in scope.

> **NOTE** Both debugger and the @debug tag can be used when running apps in the REPL, but they only pause execution if DevTools is open.

To use the @debug tag, place it at the top of the HTML section, not inside a script element. For example, the following listing shows a Svelte component that allows the user to enter the radius of a circle and then computes its area. We want to break any time the value of radius or area changes.

Listing 11.1 App that uses @debug

```
<script>
  export let radius = 1;
  $: area = 2 * Math.PI * radius**2;
</script>

{@debug radius, area}
<main>
  <label>
    Circle Radius:
    <input type="number" bind:value={radius}>
  </label>
  <label>
    Circle Area: {area}
  </label>
</main>
```

If the browser's DevTools is not open when the app is run, the @debug tag will have no effect. If DevTools is open, it will pause and display what's shown in figure 11.1. Here we can examine the source code and see the values of all variables that are in scope.

Clicking the Console tab will display what's shown in figure 11.2. Click the play button (blue in Chrome, hollow in Firefox) to resume execution.

Now we can change the value in the Radius input, which will trigger another break and show updated values in the Console tab. The variables being watched can have any kind of value, including an object or array.

To break when any state in the current component changes, omit the variable names:

```
{@debug}
```

Let's try this in the Travel Packing app. Add the following line at the top of the HTML section in Category.svelte:

```
{@debug status}
```

Start the app by entering npm run dev. Log in to get to the Checklist page.

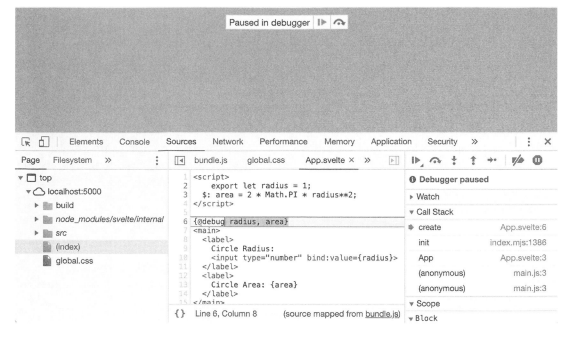

Figure 11.1   Chrome DevTools Sources tab

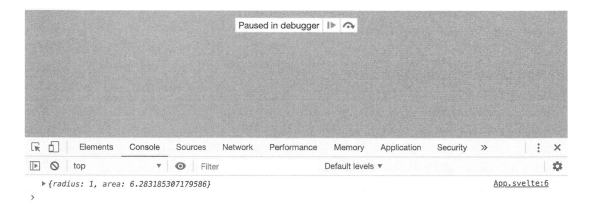

Figure 11.2   Chrome DevTools Console tab

The status variable holds a string that indicates the number of items in the category that have not yet been packed and the total number of items in the category. Any change that affects its value will now cause execution to stop. This includes adding an item, deleting an item, or toggling the checkbox for an item. Try doing these things and verify that the new value of `status` is output in the DevTools Console and that execution is paused.

Note that the `@debug` tag is not useful for determining which line of code caused the state change. By the time execution pauses, the code in question will have already executed, and the debugger will show that it stopped on the line containing `{@debug}`.

To stop at a particular line of code, use the browser debugger to set a breakpoint there. This is done by clicking its line number which toggles a breakpoint. Alternatively, you can add the statement `debugger;` before a line in the JavaScript code.

Back in the circle example, if we set a breakpoint at line 3 and change the value of the radius, execution will pause as shown in figure 11.3.

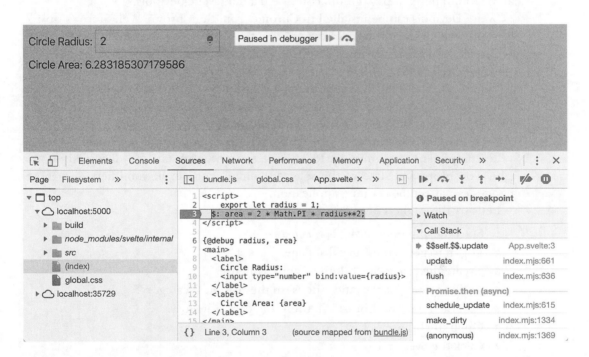

Figure 11.3   Chrome DevTools when paused at a breakpoint

11.2   Reactive statements

The `$:` syntax can be used to output the value of variables if any of their values change. You saw this approach in section 3.10. For example, if a component has the top-level variables `date` and `count`, we can log their values whenever they change with the following line:

```
$: console.log('count on date', date, 'is', count);
```

Let's try this in the Travel Packing app. Add the following inside the `script` element of `Item.svelte`:

```
$: if (editing) console.log('editing item', item.name);
```

Start the app by entering `npm run dev`. Log in to get to the Checklist page. Open the browser's DevTools and click the Console tab. Click the text of an item to edit it. Output from the preceding `console.log` call will appear in the DevTools Console.

11.3   *Svelte Devtools*

Svelte Devtools is a Chrome and Firefox extension for debugging Svelte apps that are running in development mode (npm run dev). It was created by Timothy Johnson and can be found here: https://github.com/RedHatter/svelte-devtools.

Svelte Devtools can be installed in Chrome from the Chrome Web Store (https://chrome.google.com/webstore/category/extensions). It can be installed in Firefox from the Firefox Add-ons page (https://addons.mozilla.org/en-US/firefox/).

To use Svelte Devtools, browse a Svelte app, open the browser's DevTools, and click the Svelte tab. A tree representing the hierarchy of the Svelte application is displayed on the left. This contains Svelte components, the HTML elements they render, Svelte blocks (#if, #each, and #await), slots, and text nodes.

Expand and collapse parts of this tree by clicking the disclosure triangles. Select a Svelte component to examine it. Its attributes, props, and state are displayed on the right. The props and state of the selected component can be modified, and those changes can affect the running application.

Let's try this in the Travel Packing app.

1 Start the app by entering `npm run dev`.
2 Log in to get to the Checklist page.
3 Create the categories "Clothes" and "Toiletries".
4 Add the items "socks" and "shoes" in the "Clothes" category.
5 Add the item "toothbrush" in the "Toiletries" category.
6 Open the browser's DevTools.
7 Click the Svelte tab.
8 Click disclosure triangles on the left side to open parts of the hierarchy to be examined. Click a component on the left side to see its props and state on the right side.

For example, click the `Category` component for "Clothes". Figures 11.4, 11.5, and 11.6 show what you'll see on the left and right sides.

Hover over an element on the left side of the Svelte tab to highlight it in the browser. Right-click a rendered HTML element and select Inspect to see that element in DevTools' Elements tab. Click the Svelte tab again to see the Svelte component that rendered that HTML element.

```
▼ <App>
  ▼ <main class="svelte-1n0fmy6">
    ▶ <h1 class="hero svelte-1n0fmy6">…</h1>
    ▼ <Checklist on:login on:logout>
      ▼ <section class="svelte-rmek2h">
        ▶ <header>…</header>
        ▼ <div class="categories svelte-rmek2h">
          ▼ {#each categoryArray as category (category.id)}
              ↳
            ▼ <div class="animate svelte-rmek2h">
              ▼ <Category on:delete on:persist> == $s
                ▼ <section ondragover="return false" class="svelte-fin4p6" on:dragenter on:dragleave on:drop>
                  ▶ <h3 class="svelte-fin4p6">…</h3>
                  ▶ <form on:submit|preventDefault>…</form>
                  ▼ <ul class="svelte-fin4p6">
                    ▼ {#each itemsToShow as item (item.id)}
                        ↳
                      ▼ <div>
                        ▼ <Item on:delete>
                          ▼ <li draggable="true" class="svelte-ft3yg2" on:dragstart>
                            <input type="checkbox" class="svelte-ft3yg2" on:change />
                            ▼ {:else}
                              ▼ <span class="packed-false svelte-ft3yg2" on:click>
                                  socks
                                </span>
                            {/else}
                            ▼ <button class="icon svelte-ft3yg2" on:click>
                                🗑
                              </button>
                          </li>
                        </Item>
                      </div>
                        ↳
                      ▶ <div>…</div>
                    {/each}
                  </ul>
                </section>
                ▶ <Dialog>…</Dialog>
              </Category>
            </div>
              ↳
            ▼ <div class="animate svelte-rmek2h">
              ▼ <Category on:delete on:persist>
                ▶ <section ondragover="return false" class="svelte-fin4p6" on:dragenter on:dragleave on:drop>…</section>
                ▶ <Dialog>…</Dialog>
              </Category>
            </div>
          {/each}
        </div>
      </section>
      ▶ <Dialog>…</Dialog>
    </Checklist>
  </main>
</App>
```

Figure 11.4 Svelte Devtools left side

```
Props

  None

State

▼ 0: Object {…}
     id: "bc0c3460-2807-11ea-9586-69befcd5a720"

   name: "Clothes"

  ▼ items: Object {…}
     ▼ c20103f0-2807-11ea-9586-69befcd5a720: Object {…}
          id: "c20103f0-2807-11ea-9586-69befcd5a720"

        name: "socks"

        packed: false

     ▼ c34347f0-2807-11ea-9586-69befcd5a720: Object {…}
          id: "c34347f0-2807-11ea-9586-69befcd5a720"

        name: "shoes"

        packed: false
```

Figure 11.5   Svelte Devtools right side with Clothing category selected

```
Props

  None

State

▼ 0: Object {…}
     id: "beb4e630-2807-11ea-9586-69befcd5a720"

   name: "Toiletries"

  ▼ items: Object {…}
     ▼ c65039d0-2807-11ea-9586-69befcd5a720: Object {…}
          id: "c65039d0-2807-11ea-9586-69befcd5a720"

        name: "toothbrush"

        packed: false
```

Figure 11.6   Svelte Devtools right side with Toiletries category selected

Click the eye icon inside the Svelte tab to select the kinds of things that should be displayed on the left. For example, it can be configured to only show components, not HTML elements, blocks, slots, anchors, or text (see figure 11.7). Anchors, in this context, are special comment nodes that Svelte adds for internal use. There is little reason to want to see them, and that is why they are not shown by default.

In the next chapter you will learn how to test Svelte applications.

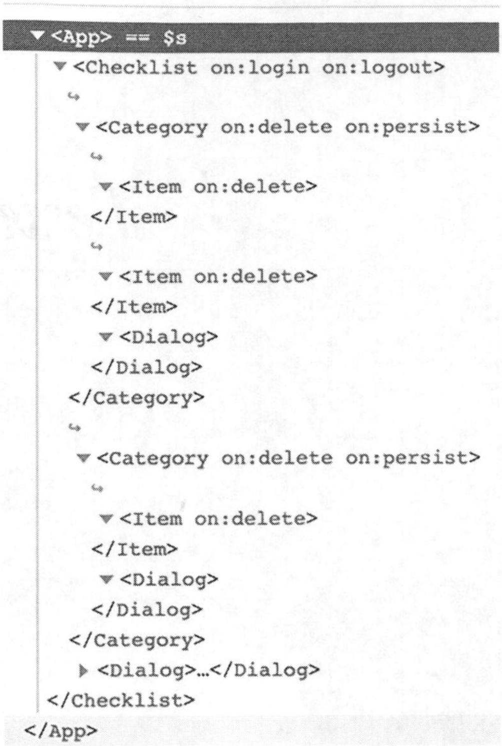

```
▼ <App> == $s
    ▼ <Checklist on:login on:logout>
      ↳
      ▼ <Category on:delete on:persist>
        ↳
        ▼ <Item on:delete>
        </Item>
        ↳
        ▼ <Item on:delete>
        </Item>
        ▼ <Dialog>
        </Dialog>
      </Category>
      ↳
      ▼ <Category on:delete on:persist>
        ↳
        ▼ <Item on:delete>
        </Item>
        ▼ <Dialog>
        </Dialog>
      </Category>
      ▶ <Dialog>...</Dialog>
    </Checklist>
</App>
```

Figure 11.7   Svelte Devtools left side showing only components

Summary

- The @debug tag can be used to pause execution when the values of specific component state variables change, or when any state variables change if none are specified.
- Reactive statements can be used to write to the DevTools console when the values of specific component state variables change.
- Svelte Devtools can be used in Chrome and Firefox to examine the runtime component hierarchy of a Svelte application.

12

Testing

This chapter covers

- Unit tests with Jest
- End-to-end tests with Cypress
- Accessibility tests with the Svelte compiler, Lighthouse, axe, and WAVE
- Demonstrating and debugging Svelte components with Storybook

Now that we've covered most of the features of Svelte, it's time to turn our focus to testing. We want to feel confident that our applications have properly implemented their intended functionality in a way that is accessible to a variety of users and that will remain that way through repeated updates. Three primary kinds of tests to consider are unit, end-to-end, and accessibility.

Unit tests are intended to test a piece of code in isolation from the rest of an application. These are great for testing individual functions and components. We will cover implementing unit tests using the Jest testing framework.

End-to-end tests are intended to test an application in the same way that a user would interact with it. This includes logging in (if the app requires it), navigating to each page within the app (if there are multiple pages), and generally putting the app into each of the states a user would encounter. We will cover implementing end-to-end tests using the Cypress testing framework.

Accessibility tests verify that users with special needs will be able to successfully use the application. Often they focus on supporting users with vision impairments that require more color contrast or the use of screen readers. We will cover implementing accessibility tests using the Svelte compiler, Lighthouse, axe, and WAVE.

Storybook is a tool that catalogs and demonstrates individual components that are used by an app. It works with many web frameworks, including Svelte.

Proper use of the tools described in this chapter can help developers identify issues in their Svelte and Sapper applications. These tools can also help reduce the issues users might encounter when apps are released for production use.

This chapter is a bit longer than previous ones due to the many code examples and screenshots. But it's well worth working through them all to get better at testing Svelte apps, which results in better apps overall!

12.1 *Unit tests with Jest*

Jest (https://jestjs.io) bills itself as "a delightful JavaScript Testing Framework with a focus on simplicity." It can be used to implement unit tests for many web frameworks, including Svelte.

By default, Jest tests are run in jsdom (https://github.com/jsdom/jsdom), which supports headless execution of DOM-based tests. This enables us to run Jest tests from a command prompt and in continuous integration (CI) environments.

Jest can watch source and test files and automatically rerun the tests if any of these files are modified. This is a convenient feature when debugging test failures.

Jest supports *snapshot tests*. These are simple tests that assert that some output should be the same as it was the last time the test was run. They make implementing many tests much easier, but they require extra diligence in examining test failures.

Jest test suites are defined by functions that are passed to the `describe` function . These functions can

- Declare constants and variables used by all the tests in the suite
- Specify functions to be called
  - Before any of the tests in the suite run (`beforeAll`)
  - After all the tests in the suite have run (`afterAll`)
  - Before each test in the suite runs (`beforeEach`)
  - After each test in the suite runs (`afterEach`)
- Call the `test` function once for each test in the suite, passing it a function that contains the code for the test. Note that `it` is an alias for `test`.

Typically each test suite is defined in a separate file with an extension of `.spec.js`. These files can be colocated with the `.js` and `.svelte` source files they test, or they can be placed in the `__tests__` directory at the same level as the `src` directory.

NOTE   Recall that Svelte bundles only include code that is actually used. This means that test code will not be included.

The functions passed to the `test` function can

- Render a Svelte component, optionally providing prop values.
- Find DOM nodes in the rendered output.
- Simulate user interactions by firing events that can trigger DOM updates.
- Make assertions about what should be found in the DOM using the `expect` function.

For details on using the `expect` function and "matchers" that specify what to expect, see the Jest documentation for "Using Matchers" (https://jestjs.io/docs/en/using-matchers). Many examples are provided in this section.

The Svelte Testing Library (https://testing-library.com/docs/svelte-testing-library/intro) can be used in conjunction with Jest to make implementing tests of Svelte components easier. It is built on the DOM Testing Library (https://testing-library.com/docs/dom-testing-library/intro), which provides functions for implementing tests that are not specific to any web framework.

The most important functions provided by the Svelte Testing Library are `render` and `fireEvent`.

The `render` function takes a Svelte component and an object containing props to pass to the component. It returns an object containing a `container` property and query functions that can be called to find nodes in the DOM created by the component. The `container` property value is the topmost DOM element of the rendered component. Tests can find DOM nodes inside this using the DOM methods `querySelector` and `querySelectorAll`.

For details on the query functions returned by the `render` function, see the DOM Testing Library's "Queries" documentation (https://testing-library.com/docs/dom-testing-library/api-queries). Some of the most commonly used query functions are `getByText`, `getByLabelText`, and `getByTestId`.

The `fireEvent` function fires a given event on a specific DOM node. This can trigger a Svelte component to update the DOM. Calls to the `expect` function that follow can verify that the expected DOM updates were made.

To install everything needed to implement unit tests for Svelte components, `cd` to the project directory and enter `npm install -D` *name*, where *name* is each of the following:

- `@babel/core`
- `@babel/preset-env`
- `@testing-library/svelte`
- `babel-jest`
- `jest`
- `svelte-jester`

Babel compiles modern JavaScript code to JavaScript that runs in current browsers. Configure the use of Babel by creating the following file in the top project directory.

Listing 12.1　Babel configuration in `babel.config.js`

```
module.exports = {
  presets: [
    [
      '@babel/preset-env',
      {
        targets: {
          node: 'current'
        }
      }
    ]
  ]
};
```

This setting avoids the error message "regenerator-runtime not found."

Configure the use of Jest by creating the following file in the top project directory.

Listing 12.2　Jest configuration in `jest.config.js`

```
module.exports = {
  bail: false,
  moduleFileExtensions: ['js', 'svelte'],
  transform: {
    '^.+\\.js$': 'babel-jest',
    '^.+\\.svelte$': 'svelte-jester'
  },
  verbose: true
};
```

This tells Jest not to exit a test suite when one of its tests fails, which allows you to get results for other tests in the suite.

This causes Jest to show the result of each test rather than just a summary of the results for each test suite.

Add the following npm scripts in `package.json`.

```
"test": "jest src",
"test:watch": "npm run test -- --watch"
```

To run the unit tests once, enter `npm test`. To run the unit tests in watch mode so they are automatically rerun when code changes are detected, enter `npm run test:watch`.

12.1.1　*Unit tests for the Todo app*

Here is a Jest test suite for the `Todo` component shown at the end of chapter 2.

Listing 12.3　Jest test for `Todo` component in `src/Todo.spec.js`

```
import {cleanup, render} from '@testing-library/svelte';

import Todo from './Todo.svelte';

describe('Todo', () => {
  const text = 'buy milk';
  const todo = {text};
```

```
    afterEach(cleanup);
```

⟵ **This unmounts any components mounted in the previously run test.**

```
    test('should render', () => {
      const {getByText} = render(Todo, {props: {todo}});
      const checkbox = document.querySelector('input[type="checkbox"]');
      expect(checkbox).not.toBeNull(); // found checkbox
      expect(getByText(text)); // found todo text
      expect(getByText('Delete')); // found Delete button
    });
});
```

There is no easy way to test that events are fired when the checkbox state is changed or when the Delete button is clicked. These are covered by tests for the `TodoList` component.

The following listing shows a Jest test suite for the `TodoList` component from the end of chapter 2.

Listing 12.4 Jest test for `TodoList` component in `src/TodoList.spec.js`

```
import {cleanup, fireEvent, render, waitFor} from '@testing-library/svelte';

import TodoList from './TodoList.svelte';

describe('TodoList', () => {
  const PREDEFINED_TODOS = 2;
```
⟵ **This is the number of todos that are automatically added in the TodoList component.**

```
  afterEach(cleanup);

  function expectTodoCount(count) {
    return waitFor(() => {
      const lis = document.querySelectorAll('li');
      expect(lis.length).toBe(count);
    });
  }
```
⟵ **This is used by many of the test functions below.**

This waits for the DOM to be updated.

⟵ **Each Todo component has an li root element.**

```
  test('should render', async () => {
    const {getByText} = render(TodoList);
    expect(getByText('To Do List'));
    expect(getByText('1 of 2 remaining'));
    expect(getByText('Archive Completed')); // button
    await expectTodoCount(PREDEFINED_TODOS);
  });

  test('should add a todo', async () => {
    const {getByTestId, getByText} = render(TodoList);

    const input = getByTestId('todo-input');
    const value = 'buy milk';
    fireEvent.input(input, {target: {value}});
    fireEvent.click(getByText('Add'));
```
⟵ **This requires adding the following attribute to the input element in src/TodoList.svelte: data-testid="todo-input":.**

```
    await expectTodoCount(PREDEFINED_TODOS + 1);
    expect(getByText(value));
  });
```

```
test('should archive completed', async () => {
  const {getByText} = render(TodoList);
  fireEvent.click(getByText('Archive Completed'));
  await expectTodoCount(PREDEFINED_TODOS - 1);
  expect(getByText('1 of 1 remaining'));
});
```

This is the text in the first todo.
```
test('should delete a todo', async () => {
  const {getAllByText, getByText} = render(TodoList);
  const text = 'learn Svelte';
  expect(getByText(text));
```
→

This deletes the first todo.
```
  const deleteBtns = getAllByText('Delete');
  fireEvent.click(deleteBtns[0]);
  await expectTodoCount(PREDEFINED_TODOS - 1);
});
```
→

```
test('should toggle a todo', async () => {
  const {container, getByText} = render(TodoList);
  const checkboxes = container.querySelectorAll('input[type="checkbox"]');

  await fireEvent.click(checkboxes[1]);
  expect(getByText('0 of 2 remaining'));
```
◁ ─┐ **This toggles the second todo.**

```
  await fireEvent.click(checkboxes[0]);
  expect(getByText('1 of 2 remaining'));
});
});
```
◁ ─┐ **This toggles the first todo.**

12.1.2 *Unit tests for the Travel Packing app*

Let's add some unit tests in the Travel Packing app. The finished code can be found at http://mng.bz/QyNG.

Change the button element in src/Item.svelte to include a data-testid attribute to make it easier to find this button in a test.

Listing 12.5   Change to Item component in src/Item.svelte

```
<button class="icon" data-testid="delete"
  on:click={() => dispatch('delete')}>
  &#x1F5D1;
</button>
```

The following listing shows a Jest test suite for the Item component.

Listing 12.6   Jest test for Item component in Item.spec.js

```
import {cleanup, render} from '@testing-library/svelte';

import Item from './Item.svelte';

describe('Item', () => {
  const categoryId = 1;
```

```
  const dnd = {};
  const item = {id: 2, name: 'socks', packed: false};

  afterEach(cleanup);

  test('should render', () => {
    const {getByTestId, getByText} = render(Item, {categoryId, dnd, item});
    const checkbox = document.querySelector('input[type="checkbox"]');
    expect(checkbox).not.toBeNull();
    expect(getByText(item.name));
    expect(getByTestId('delete'));
  });
});
```

The Item component requires this prop, but it won't be used in the test, so an empty object suffices.

Tests that the checkbox can be found

Tests that the item name can be fond

Tests that the Delete button can be found

The preceding test simply verifies that the Item component renders the expected DOM elements. This can also be accomplished using a "snapshot" test. The first time snapshot tests are run, a __snapshots__ directory is created, and files containing rendered output are saved in this directory. In subsequent runs the rendered output is compared to these files. Any differences are reported as failed tests.

Relying on snapshot tests requires attention to detail on the part of the developers who run them. When tests are run the first time, developers should verify that components are currently rendering correctly. In subsequent test runs, if any tests fail, developers should carefully examine the differences reported and determine whether they are expected based on recent code changes. If they are expected, press the "U" key to update all the snapshot files that differ. Otherwise, fix the errors and rerun the tests.

The following listing shows a snapshot test for the Item component. Note how much simpler this is to write than the previous "should render" test.

Listing 12.7   Snapshot test for `Item` component in `Item.spec.js`

```
test('should match snapshot', () => {
  const {container} = render(Item, {categoryId, dnd, item});
  expect(container).toMatchSnapshot();
});
```

Tests for the Category component need to be able to find the input element that binds to the variable itemName. To simplify this, change the input element to include a data-testid attribute.

Listing 12.8   Adding `data-testid` attribute to `input` in `src/Category.svelte`

```
<input data-testid="item-input" required bind:value={itemName} />
```

The following listing shows a Jest test suite for the Category component.

Listing 12.9 Jest tests for `Category` component in `Category.spec.js`

```
import {cleanup, fireEvent, render, waitFor} from '@testing-library/svelte';

import Category from './Category.svelte';

describe('Category', () => {
  let itemCount = 0;
```
> This will be set to the number of items that are added to the category inside the function that is passed to beforeEach.

```
  const category = {id: 1, name: 'Clothes', items: {}};
  const categories = [category];
  const dnd = {};
  const props = {categories, category, dnd, show: 'all'};
```
> The Category component requires this prop, but it won't be used in the test, so an empty object suffices.

```
  beforeEach(() => {
    category.items = {
      1: {id: 1, name: 'socks', packed: true},
      2: {id: 2, name: 'shoes', packed: false}
    };
    itemCount = Object.keys(category.items).length;
  });

  afterEach(cleanup);

  test('should match snapshot', () => {
    const {container} = render(Category, props);
    expect(container).toMatchSnapshot();
  });

  function expectItemCount(count) {
    return waitFor(() => {
      const lis = document.querySelectorAll('li');
      expect(lis.length).toBe(count);
    });
  }
```
> Each Item component has an li root element.

```
  test('should render', async () => {
    const {getByText} = render(Category, props);
    expect(getByText('Clothes'));
    expect(getByText('1 of 2 remaining'));
    expect(getByText('New Item'));
    expect(getByText('Add Item'));
    await expectItemCount(itemCount);
  });

  test('should add an item', async () => {
    const {getByTestId, getByText} = render(Category, props);

    const input = getByTestId('item-input');
    const value = 't-shirts';
    fireEvent.input(input, {target: {value}});
    fireEvent.click(getByText('Add Item'));
```

```
    await expectItemCount(itemCount + 1);
    expect(getByText(value));
  });

  test('should delete an item', async () => {
    const {getAllByTestId} = render(Category, props);

    const deleteBtns = getAllByTestId('delete');
    fireEvent.click(deleteBtns[0]); // deletes first item
    await expectItemCount(itemCount - 1);
  });

  test('should toggle an item', async () => {
    const {container, getByText} = render(Category, props);

    const checkboxes = container.querySelectorAll('input[type="checkbox"]');
    expect(checkboxes.length).toBe(2);

    const [shoesCheckbox, socksCheckbox] = checkboxes;

    expect(socksCheckbox.nextElementSibling.textContent).toBe('socks');
    await fireEvent.click(socksCheckbox);
    expect(getByText('2 of 2 remaining'));

    expect(shoesCheckbox.nextElementSibling.textContent).toBe('shoes');
    await fireEvent.click(shoesCheckbox);
    expect(getByText('1 of 2 remaining'));
  });
});
```

> The items are sorted so that "shoes" comes before "socks".

> Now nothing in this category is packed.

> Now one item in this category is packed.

When the Jest tests for the Travel Packing app are run, DialogPolyfill, which is used in the custom Dialog component, will not be defined. To account for this, modify the call to onMount in src/Dialog.svelte to match the following:

Listing 12.10 Dialog component onMount in src/Dialog.svelte

```
onMount(() => {
  if (dialogPolyfill) dialogPolyfill.registerDialog(dialog);
});
```

You might be tempted to wrap an if around the call to onMount instead of placing the if inside the function passed to onMount. However, that would not be correct because lifecycle functions cannot be called conditionally.

To temporarily skip running certain test suites, change their describe function to describe.skip. To temporarily skip running certain tests within a suite, change their test function to test.skip. To temporarily run only certain tests in a suite, change their test function to test.only.

We are now ready to run the Jest tests using the npm scripts added earlier in package.json.

When tests fail, output similar to the following will appear in the terminal where the tests ran. This test failure is caused by searching for "SOCKS" instead of "socks".

Listing 12.11   Failed Jest output

```
FAIL  src/Item.spec.js
  Item
    ✕ should render (32ms)
    ✓ should match snapshot (4ms)

  ● Item › should render

    Unable to find an element with the text: SOCKS.
    This could be because the text is broken up by multiple elements.
    In this case, you can provide a function for your
    text matcher to make your matcher more flexible.

    <body>
      <div>
        <li
          class="svelte-ft3yg2"
          draggable="true"
        >
          <input
            class="svelte-ft3yg2"
            type="checkbox"
          />

          <span
            class="packed-false svelte-ft3yg2"
          >
            socks
          </span>

          <button
            class="icon svelte-ft3yg2"
            data-testid="delete"
          >
            🗑
          </button>
        </li>
      </div>
    </body>

      15 |     const checkbox = document.querySelector('input[type="checkbox"]');
      16 |     expect(checkbox).not.toBeNull(); // found checkbox
    > 17 |     expect(getByText(item.name.toUpperCase())); // found item name
         |            ^
      18 |     expect(getByTestId('delete')); // found delete button
      19 |   });
      20 |

      at getElementError (node_modules/@testing-library/dom/dist/query-
    helpers.js:22:10)
      at node_modules/@testing-library/dom/dist/query-helpers.js:76:13
      at getByText (node_modules/@testing-library/dom/dist/query-
    helpers.js:59:17)
      at Object.<anonymous> (src/Item.spec.js:17:12)
```

```
Test Suites: 1 failed, 1 passed, 2 total
Tests:       1 failed, 6 passed, 7 total
Snapshots:   2 passed, 2 total
Time:        1.964s, estimated 2s
Ran all test suites matching /src/i.

Watch Usage: Press w to show more.
```

When tests are successful, output similar to the following will appear in the terminal where the tests ran.

Listing 12.12   Successful Jest output

```
PASS  src/Item.spec.js
  Item
    ✓ should render (22ms)
    ✓ should match snapshot (5ms)

 PASS  src/Category.spec.js
  Category
    ✓ should match snapshot (48ms)
    ✓ should render (16ms)
    ✓ should add an item (14ms)
    ✓ should delete an item (32ms)
    ✓ should toggle an item (11ms)

Test Suites: 2 passed, 2 total
Tests:       7 passed, 7 total
Snapshots:   2 passed, 2 total
Time:        1.928s, estimated 2s
Ran all test suites matching /src/i.

Watch Usage: Press w to show more.
```

12.2 End-to-end tests with Cypress

Cypress (www.cypress.io/) bills itself as "fast, easy and reliable testing for anything that runs in a browser." It supports end-to-end testing of web applications written using any framework (including Svelte) or even no framework. This means that the tests can exercise the functionality of a web application without focusing on specific components as is done in unit tests.

All the functionality of Cypress is accessed through the global variable cy. Queries to find elements on the page can search by text and CSS selectors. By default they wait 4 seconds for elements to appear.

Suppose a web application renders a button containing the text "Press Me" that when clicked renders the text "Success". The following code finds this button, clicks it, and verifies that "Success" is found.

```
cy.get('button').contains('Press Me').click();
cy.contains('Success');
```

The following code finds an `input` and types text into it. It assumes that the `input` has a `data-testid` attribute that can be used in tests to find it.

```
cy.get('[data-testid=some-id]').type('some text');
```

Cypress tests benefit greatly from you writing and using utility functions that navigate to various application states and make assertions. For example, a function that navigates to the login page, enters a username and password, and clicks the Login button is useful in nearly all tests of a web app that requires logging in. You will see several examples of these kinds of functions shortly, in tests for the Travel Packing app.

To install Cypress in a Svelte app, enter `npm install -D cypress`. Then add the following npm scripts in `package.json`:

```
"cy:open": "cypress open",          ⟵  This runs Cypress in
"cy:run": "cypress run",            ⟵  interactive mode.
                                        This runs Cypress in
                                        command-line mode.
```

To launch the Cypress test tool in interactive mode, enter `npm run cy:open`. The tests are automatically rerun if any source files or test files are modified. This command also creates a `cypress` directory, if it doesn't already exist, containing the following subdirectories:

- `fixtures`—Fixtures can hold data used by tests. The data is typically in `.json` files that are imported into tests. Using fixtures is optional.
- `integration`—Test implementation files (a.k.a. specs) go here, either at the top of this directory or in subdirectories.
- `plugins`—Plugins extend the functionality of Cypress. For examples of Cypress plugins, see https://github.com/bahmutov/cypress-svelte-unit-test. Cypress automatically runs the code in the `index.js` file in this directory before running each spec file. Using plugins is optional.
- `screenshots`—This subdirectory holds screenshots produced by calling `cy.screenshot()`. These are useful when debugging tests.
- `support`—Files in this subdirectory add custom Cypress commands, making them available in tests. Cypress automatically runs the code in the `index.js` file in this directory before running each spec file. Using custom Cypress commands is optional.

These subdirectories are populated with sample files, all of which can be deleted. Create your test files under the `cypress/integration` directory with extensions of `.spec.js`.

12.2.1 *End-to-end tests for the Todo app*

Here are some end-to-end tests for the Todo application shown at the end of chapter 2.

Listing 12.13   Cypress tests for the `TodoList` component in
`cypress/integration/TodoList.spec.js`

```
const baseUrl = 'http://localhost:5000/';

describe('Todo app', () => {
  it('should add todo', () => {
    cy.visit(baseUrl);
    cy.contains('1 of 2 remaining');
    cy.contains('Add')
      .as('addBtn')
      .should('be.disabled');

    const todoText = 'buy milk';
    cy.get('[data-testid=todo-input]')
      .as('todoInput')
      .type(todoText);

    const addBtn = cy.get('@addBtn');
    addBtn.should('not.be.disabled');
    addBtn.click();

    cy.get('@todoInput').should('have.value', '');
    cy.get('@addBtn').should('be.disabled');
    cy.contains(todoText);
    cy.contains('2 of 3 remaining');
  });

  it('should toggle done', () => {
    cy.visit(baseUrl);
    cy.contains('1 of 2 remaining');

    cy.get('input[type=checkbox]')
      .first()
      .as('cb1')
      .click();
    cy.contains('2 of 2 remaining');

    cy.get('@cb1').check();
    cy.contains('1 of 2 remaining');
  });

  it('should delete todo', () => {
    cy.visit(baseUrl);
    cy.contains('1 of 2 remaining');

    const todoText = 'learn Svelte'; // first todo
    cy.contains('ul', todoText);
```

The Add button should be disabled until text is entered.

This saves a reference to found elements for later use.

This enters todo text.

This finds the first checkbox and toggles it.

This toggles the same checkbox again to show that status text returns to its previous value.

```
      cy.contains('Delete').click();
      cy.contains('ul', todoText).should('not.exist');
      cy.contains('1 of 1 remaining');
  });

  it('should archive completed', () => {
    cy.visit(baseUrl);

    const todoText = 'learn Svelte'; // first todo
    cy.contains('ul', todoText);

    cy.contains('Archive Completed').click();
    cy.contains('ul', todoText).should('not.exist');
    cy.contains('1 of 1 remaining');
  });
});
```

This clicks the first Delete button.

This clicks the Archive Completed button.

To run the tests in interactive mode, start the local server with `npm run dev`, enter `npm run cy:open`, and click the Run All Specs button in the upper-right corner of the Cypress tool. This opens a browser window where all the tests are run. When you're finished running the tests, close this browser window and the Cypress tool.

To aid in debugging, add `console.log` calls in the application code. When there are several of these in the code, it is helpful if they identify the source file and function where they are located. For example, `console.log('TodoList.svelte toggle-Done: todo =', todo);`. To see their output, open the DevTools Console in the browser window where the tests are running.

To run the tests in command-line mode, start the local server with `npm run dev`, open another terminal, and enter `npm run cy:run`. This outputs test results in the terminal window, records an MP4 video of the test run, and outputs the file path of the video, which is in the `cypress/videos` subdirectory. Double-click the video file to watch it.

12.2.2 *End-to-end tests for the Travel Packing app*

Let's add end-to-end tests in the Travel Packing app. The finished code can be found at http://mng.bz/eQqQ.

1 Install Cypress by entering `npm install -D cypress`.
2 Add the npm scripts suggested for Cypress in section 12.2.
3 Start the app by entering `npm run dev`.
4 In another terminal, enter `npm run cy:open` to create the `cypress` directory and starting files inside it.
5 Move the `cypress/integration/examples` directory to `cypress/examples` so these example tests don't appear in the Cypress app but can be referred to later for examples.

6 Add a `data-testid` attribute to the `input` element that binds to the `category-Name` variable in `src/Checklist.svelte` so the `input` element is easy to find in a test:

```
<input
  data-testid="category-name-input"
  required
  bind:value={categoryName}
/>
```

7 Create a `travel-packing.spec.js` file in the `cypress/integration` directory containing the code in listing 12.14.

Listing 12.14 Cypress tests for the Travel Packing app in `cypress/integration/travel-packing.spec.js`

```
const baseUrl = 'http://localhost:5000/';

function login() {
  cy.visit(baseUrl);
  cy.contains('Username')
    .children('input')
    .type('username');
  cy.contains('Password')
    .children('input')
    .type('password');
  cy.get('button')
    .contains('Login')
    .click();
}

function addCategories() {
  login();

  cy.get('[data-testid=category-name-input]')
    .as('nameInput')
    .type('Clothes');
  cy.get('button')
    .contains('Add Category')
    .click();

  cy.get('@nameInput').type('Toiletries{enter}');
}

function addItems() {
  addCategories();

  cy.get('[data-testid=item-input]')
    .first()
    .as('item-input-1')
    .type('socks');
  cy.get('button')
    .contains('Add Item')
```

We must log in before adding categories.

Including "{enter}" in a string passed to the type method simulates a user pressing the Enter key.

We must add categories before adding items.

This finds the input item in the "Clothes" category.

```
      .first()
      .click();
  cy.get('@item-input-1').type('shoes{enter}');
  verifyStatus('Clothes', '2 of 2 remaining');

  cy.get('[data-testid=item-input]')
      .last()
      .type('razor{enter}');
  verifyStatus('Toiletries', '1 of 1 remaining');
}
```

> **This finds the input item in the "Toiletries" category.**

```
function deleteCategory(categoryName) {
  cy.contains(new RegExp(`^${categoryName}$`))
      .siblings('button')
      .click();
}

function deleteItem(itemName) {
  cy.contains(new RegExp(`^${itemName}$`))
      .siblings('button')
      .click();
}

function togglePacked(itemName) {
  cy.contains(new RegExp(`^${itemName}$`))
      .siblings('input[type="checkbox"]')
      .click();
}

function verifyStatus(categoryName, expectedStatus) {
  cy.contains(new RegExp(`^${categoryName}$`))
      // This is useful to verify that the correct element is found.
      // It draws a red outline around all the matching elements.
      //.then(el => el.css('outline', 'solid red'))
      .siblings('span')
      .contains(expectedStatus);
}

describe('Travel Packing app', () => {
  it('should login', login);

  it('should add categories', addCategories);

  it('should add items', addItems);

  it('should toggle packed', () => {
    addItems();
    verifyStatus('Clothes', '2 of 2 remaining');

    togglePacked('shoes');
    verifyStatus('Clothes', '1 of 2 remaining');
```

```
    togglePacked('shoes');
    verifyStatus('Clothes', '2 of 2 remaining');
  });

  it('should delete item', () => {
    addItems();
    verifyStatus('Clothes', '2 of 2 remaining');

    deleteItem('shoes');
    verifyStatus('Clothes', '1 of 1 remaining');
  });

  it('should delete category', () => {
    addItems();
    verifyStatus('Toiletries', '1 of 1 remaining');

    deleteItem('razor');
    verifyStatus('Toiletries', '0 of 0 remaining');

    const categoryName = 'Toiletries';
    // Verify that the category exists.
    cy.get('.categories h2 > span').contains(categoryName);
    deleteCategory(categoryName);
    // Verify that the category no longer exists.
    cy.get('.categories h2 > span')
      .contains(categoryName)
      .should('not.exist');
  });

  it('should logout', () => {
    login();
    cy.get('button')
      .contains('Log Out')
      .click();
    cy.contains('Login');
  });
});
```

We must delete all items in a category before the category can be deleted.

To run these end-to-end tests, enter npm run cy:open. This renders the results shown in figure 12.1. Note the green check marks next to the successful tests.

To run these end-to-end tests in command-line mode, enter npm run cy:run. This outputs listing 12.15 in the terminal window.

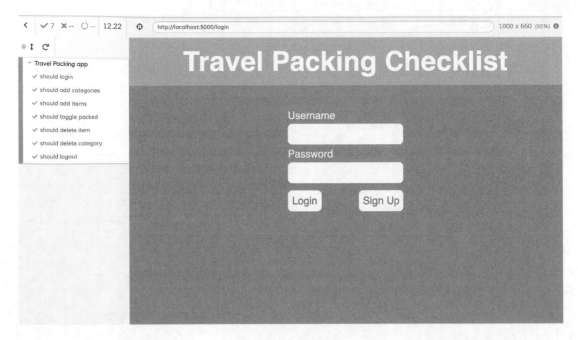

Figure 12.1 Cypress in Chrome

Listing 12.15 Cypress command-line output

```
(Run Starting)

  ┌─────────────────────────────────────────────────────────┐
  │ Cypress:    3.8.1                                        │
  │ Browser:    Electron 78 (headless)                      │
  │ Specs:      1 found (travel-packing.spec.js)           │
  └─────────────────────────────────────────────────────────┘


─────────────────────────────────────────────────────────────

  Running:  travel-packing.spec.js                              (1 of 1)

  Travel Packing app
    ✓ should login (888ms)
    ✓ should add categories (1196ms)
    ✓ should add items (1846ms)
    ✓ should toggle packed (2057ms)
    ✓ should delete item (1973ms)
    ✓ should delete category (2037ms)
    ✓ should logout (1938ms)

  7 passing (13s)

(Results)
```

```
| Tests:        7                                                    |
| Passing:      7                                                    |
| Failing:      0                                                    |
| Pending:      0                                                    |
| Skipped:      0                                                    |
| Screenshots:  0                                                    |
| Video:        true                                                 |
| Duration:     12 seconds                                           |
| Spec Ran:     travel-packing.spec.js                              |
```

(Video)

- Started processing: Compressing to 32 CRF
- Finished processing: /Users/mark/Documents/programming/languages/ (0 seconds)
                       javascript/svelte/book/svelte-and-sapper-in-action/
                       travel-packing-ch11/cypress/videos/
                       travel-packing.spec.js.mp4

```
====================================================================================
```

(Run Finished)

Spec		Tests	Passing	Failing	Pending	Skipped
✓ travel-packing.spec.js	00:12	7	7	-	-	-
✓ All specs passed!	00:12	7	7	-	-	-

12.3   *Accessibility tests*

There are many tools for detecting web UI accessibility issues, such as the following.

- *Svelte compiler*—The Svelte compiler flags some accessibility issues. These are described in the following section.
- *Lighthouse* (https://developers.google.com/web/tools/lighthouse)—This is a free tool. It is used by Chrome DevTools on the Audits tab and can also be run from a command line or a Node application. Lighthouse audits many aspects of a web app, including performance, progressive web app metrics, accessibility, and search engine optimization (SEO).
- *axe* (www.deque.com/axe/)—This is a free Chrome extension. axe PRO is an enterprise version of axe that identifies even more issues.
- *WAVE* (https://wave.webaim.org/)—This is a free Chrome and Firefox extension. Pope Tech (https://pope.tech/) is an enterprise-level accessibility tool built on WAVE.

These tools can identify different issues, so it is recommended that you use more than one. As you will see below, sometimes it is not desirable to address all the identified issues.

12.3.1 *Svelte compiler*

The Svelte compiler detects some accessibility issues and outputs warning messages that begin with "A11y:". You will see a list of the messages, along with their codes, in table 12.1. Note that some codes are used for more than one message.

Table 12.1 Svelte accessibility warning codes and messages

Code	Message
a11y-distracting-elements	Avoid <{name}> elements
a11y-structure	<figcaption> must be an immediate child of <figure>
a11y-structure	<figcaption> must be first or last child of <figure>
a11y-aria-attributes	<{name}> should not have aria-* attributes
a11y-unknown-aria-attribute	Unknown aria attribute 'aria-{type}'
a11y-hidden	<{name}> element should not be hidden
a11y-misplaced-role	<{name}> should not have role attribute
a11y-unknown-role	Unknown role '{value}'
a11y-accesskey	Avoid using accesskey
a11y-autofocus	Avoid using autofocus
a11y-misplaced-scope	The scope attribute should only be used with <th> elements
a11y-positive-tabindex	Avoid tabindex values above zero
a11y-invalid-attribute	'{value}' is not a valid {attribute-name} attribute
a11y-missing-attribute	<a> element should have an href attribute
a11y-missing-content	<{name}> element should have child content
a11y-missing-attribute	<{name}> element should have {article} {sequence} attribute

In some cases it may be desirable to suppress certain warnings. To do this, add a special comment above the offending lines. For example, to suppress the warning "Avoid using autofocus," add the following line before all `input` elements that use it:

```
<!-- svelte-ignore a11y-autofocus -->
```

12.3.2 *Lighthouse*

The easiest way to use Lighthouse to identify accessibility issues is as follows:

1 Open the website to be tested in Chrome.
2 Open the DevTools.
3 Click the Audits tab (see figure 12.2).
4 Verify that the Accessibility checkbox is checked.

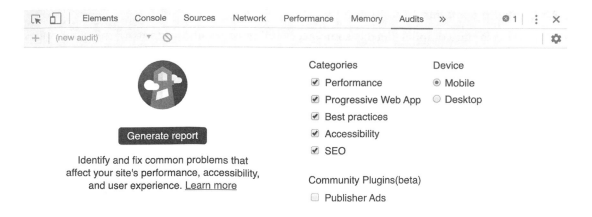

Figure 12.2   Lighthouse setup in Chrome DevTools

5   Click the Generate Report button.

6   To keep current test results and open a new tab for the next test, press the "+" in the upper-left corner of the Audits tab.

7   Visit another page or state of the site.

8   Click the Generate Report button again.

9   Repeat steps 6 to 8 for each page or state of the site, noting the reported accessibility issues for each.

NOTE   The issues have already been fixed in this chapter's version of the Travel Packing app. To see these issues, run Lighthouse on the chapter 11 version.

To rerun tests after code changes, click the Clear All icon (a circle with a diagonal line) and then click the Run Audits button.

Lighthouse reported two issues for the Login page. The color contrast on the Login and Sign Up buttons, gray on white, is insufficient. These can be fixed by changing gray to black in `public/global.css`.

Lighthouse only reported one issue for the Checklist page of the Travel Packing app after adding a category and an item in it. It was "Background and foreground colors do not have a sufficient contrast ratio," as shown in figures 12.3 and 12.4. The color contrast between the white text and the orange and cornflowerblue backgrounds is not sufficient from an accessibility standpoint. These color contrast issues can be fixed by choosing a color other than orange for `.hero` in `src/App.svelte` and choosing a color other than cornflowerblue for `main` in `src/App.svelte` and `header` in `src/Dialog.svelte`.

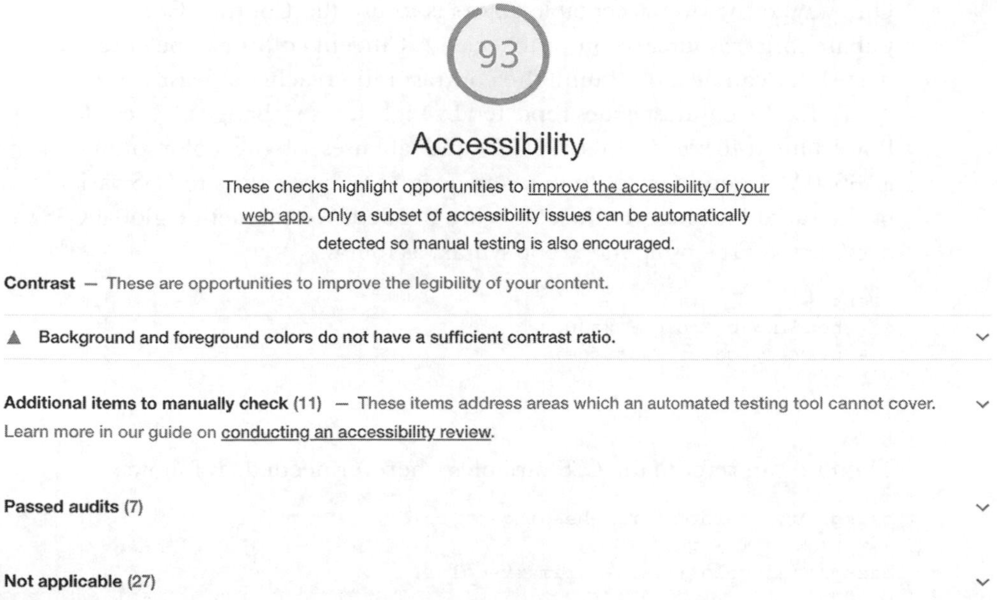

Accessibility

These checks highlight opportunities to improve the accessibility of your web app. Only a subset of accessibility issues can be automatically detected so manual testing is also encouraged.

Contrast — These are opportunities to improve the legibility of your content.

⚠ Background and foreground colors do not have a sufficient contrast ratio.   ⌄

Additional items to manually check (11) — These items address areas which an automated testing tool cannot cover. ⌄
Learn more in our guide on conducting an accessibility review.

Passed audits (7)   ⌄

Not applicable (27)   ⌄

Figure 12.3 Lighthouse results in Chrome DevTools (top of page)

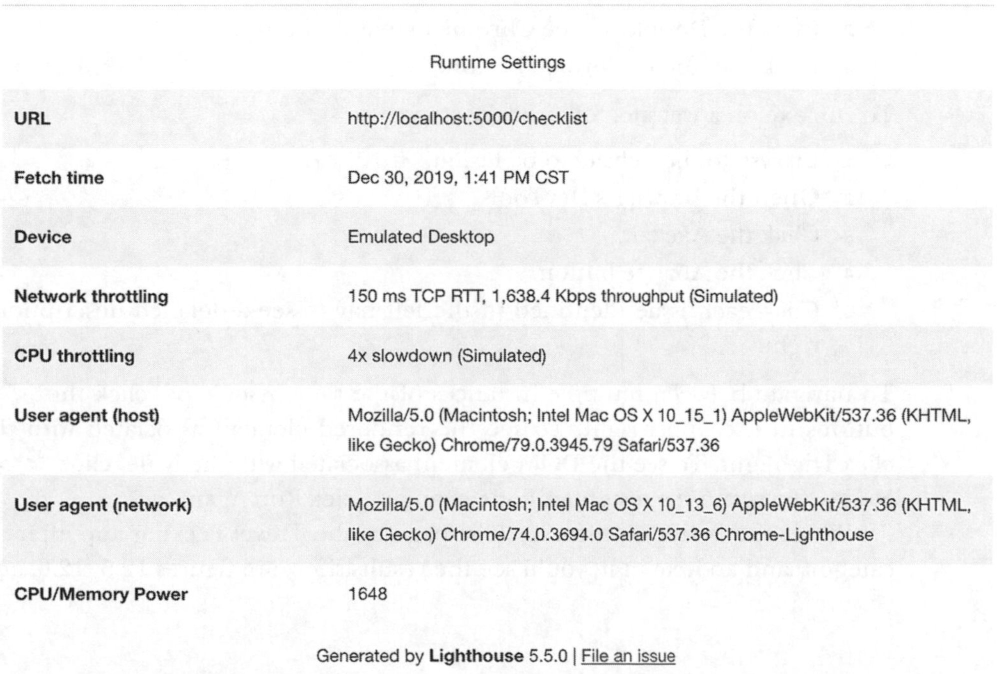

Runtime Settings

URL	http://localhost:5000/checklist
Fetch time	Dec 30, 2019, 1:41 PM CST
Device	Emulated Desktop
Network throttling	150 ms TCP RTT, 1,638.4 Kbps throughput (Simulated)
CPU throttling	4x slowdown (Simulated)
User agent (host)	Mozilla/5.0 (Macintosh; Intel Mac OS X 10_15_1) AppleWebKit/537.36 (KHTML, like Gecko) Chrome/79.0.3945.79 Safari/537.36
User agent (network)	Mozilla/5.0 (Macintosh; Intel Mac OS X 10_13_6) AppleWebKit/537.36 (KHTML, like Gecko) Chrome/74.0.3694.0 Safari/537.36 Chrome-Lighthouse
CPU/Memory Power	1648

Generated by **Lighthouse** 5.5.0 | File an issue

Figure 12.4 Lighthouse results in Chrome DevTools (bottom of page)

One way to discover acceptable colors is to use the Contrast Checker tool at https://webaim.org/resources/contrastchecker/. Current colors can be entered, and a Lightness slider can be moved until the contrast ratio reaches at least 4.5.

To fix the contrast issues reported by Lighthouse, change all uses of the color cornflowerblue (#6495ed) to #3F6FDE and all uses of the color orange (#ffa500) to #A3660A. A good way to do this is to assign the new colors to CSS variables and refer to the variables wherever the colors are needed. We can define global CSS variables in src/App.svelte using the :root syntax, as follows:

```
:root {
  --heading-bg-color: #a3660a;
  --primary-color: #3f6fde;
  ...
}
```

Then we can refer to the CSS variables wherever needed, as follows:

```
background-color: var(--heading-bg-color);

background-color: var(--primary-color);
```

12.3.3 *axe*

To install axe in Chrome, follow these steps:

1 Browse to https://www.deque.com/axe/.
2 Click the Download free Chrome extension button.
3 Click the Add to Chrome button.

To run axe on a website, follow these steps:

1 Browse to the website to be tested.
2 Open the browser's DevTools.
3 Click the Axe tab.
4 Click the Analyze button.
5 Click each issue identified in the left nav to see a detailed description on the right.

To navigate between multiple instances of the same issue type, click the "<" and ">" buttons in the upper-right. To see the rendered element associated with the issue, click Highlight. To see the DOM element associated with the issue, click "</> Inspect Node". To rerun the tests after code changes, click Run Again.

When axe is run on the Checklist page of the Travel Packing app after adding a category and an item in it, you'll see the results shown in figures 12.5, 12.6, and 12.7.

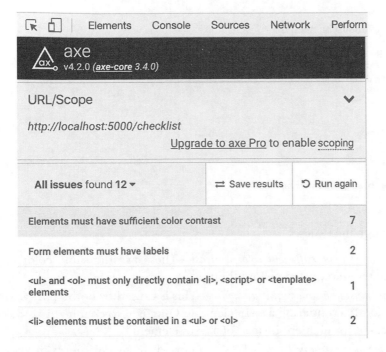

Figure 12.5   axe results

Elements must have sufficient color contrast
</> Inspect Node   ⭘ Highlight

Issue description   Impact: **serious**
Ensures the contrast between foreground and background colors meets WCAG 2 AA   ☑Learn more
contrast ratio thresholds

Element location

    h1

Element source

    <h1 class="hero svelte-iyru9t">Travel Packing Checklist</h1>

Figure 12.6   axe detail for an issue

To solve this violation, you need to:

Fix the following:
Element has insufficient color contrast of 1.97 (foreground color: #ffffff, background color: #ffa500, font size: 48.0pt (64px), font weight: bold). Expected contrast ratio of 3:1

Related node:
</>Inspect

```
h1
```

Figure 12.7   axe fix suggestion for an issue

Let's walk through the issues.

- *Elements must have sufficient color contrast*—These are the same color contrast issues that were reported by Lighthouse.
- *Document must have one main landmark*—This is caused by both App.svelte and Dialog.svelte rendering a main element. One fix is to change Dialog.svelte to use a section element instead of a main element.
- *Form elements must have labels*—This is reported for two elements in src/Item/svelte. The first is the checkbox input for marking an item as packed. The second is the text input for editing an item name that is rendered when the name of an item is clicked. Both of these omit a label. We don't want to display label elements in these cases. One fix is to add an aria-label attribute to these input elements as follows:

```
<input
  aria-label="Toggle Packed"
  type="checkbox"
  bind:checked={item.packed}
/>
{#if editing}
  <input
    aria-label="Edit Name"
    autofocus
    bind:value={item.name}
    on:blur={() => (editing = false)}
    on:keydown={blurOnKey}
    type="text"
  />
```

- *<ul> and <ol> must only directly contain <li>, <script> or <template> elements*—This issue is in Category.svelte where Item components that render an li element are wrapped in a div with the attribute animate:flip. We cannot remove the div and move this attribute to the li in Item.svelte because doing so causes the

Svelte error "An element that use the animate directive must be the immediate child of a keyed each block." So it seems we have to live with this accessibility issue if we want to keep this particular animation.

- *<li> elements must be contained in a <ul> or <ol>*—This identifies the same issue as the previous one.
- *Heading levels should only increase by one*—This issue is caused by using an h3 for the name of a category when the previous heading is an h1 in the "hero" at the top of the page. One fix is to change all occurrences of h3 in Category.svelte to h2. CSS can be used to reduce the font size of the h2 elements if desired.

12.3.4 *WAVE*

To install WAVE in Chrome, follow these steps:

1. Browse to https://wave.webaim.org/.
2. Click the Browser Extensions link.
3. Click the link for the extension for your browser.
4. Click the Add to Chrome button.

To run WAVE on a website, follow these steps:

1. Click the WAVE icon ( ) to the right of the browser's address bar.
2. An accessibility report will open on the left side of the page.
3. Click the View Details button.

WAVE reports both issues and the good things it finds (such as having alt text for images). Click an icon for an issue to scroll to it on the web page.

WAVE reported the issues shown in figures 12.8 and 12.9 for the Checklist page of the Travel Packing app after adding a category and an item in it.

Let's walk through the issues.

- *Missing form label*—These are the same issues that axe reported as "Form elements must have labels."
- *Very low contrast*—These are the same color contrast issues that were reported by Lighthouse.
- *Orphaned form label*—This means that a form label is not associated with a form control. It refers to the Show label in Checklist.svelte. A fix is shown after the next issue because they are related.
- *Missing fieldset*—This means that a group of checkboxes or radio buttons is not enclosed in a fieldset element.

One fix for the last two issues is to edit Checklist.svelte and use a fieldset element to surround the radio buttons. We want the radio buttons to be laid out in a row. But there is a browser issue where flexbox layout is not honored on fieldset elements.

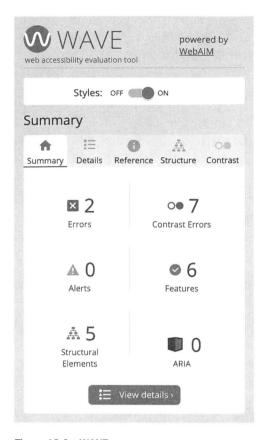

Figure 12.8   WAVE summary

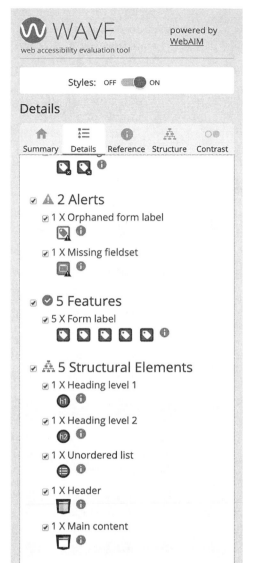

Figure 12.9   WAVE detail

A workaround is to wrap all the `fieldset` children in a `div` and apply flexbox layout to that. Here is a replacement for the `<div class="radios">` element that fixes the accessibility issues.

```
<fieldset>
  <div>
    <legend>Show</legend>
    <label>
      <input name="show" type="radio" value="all" bind:group={show} />
      All
    </label>
```

```
    <label>
      <input name="show" type="radio" value="packed" bind:group={show} />
      Packed
    </label>
    <label>
      <input name="show" type="radio" value="unpacked" bind:group={show} />
      Unpacked
    </label>
    <button class="clear" on:click={clearAllChecks}>Clear All Checks</button>
  </div>
</fieldset>
```

Replace the CSS rules for .radios with the following:

```
fieldset {
  border: none;
  margin: 0;
  padding: 0;
}

fieldset > div {
  display: flex;
  align-items: center;
}

fieldset input {
  margin-left: 1.5rem;
}

fieldset legend {
  padding: 0;
}
```

12.4 *Component demos and debugging with Storybook*

Storybook (https://storybook.js.org) bills itself as "an open source tool for developing UI components in isolation." It works with many web frameworks including React, Vue, Angular, Svelte, and more.

Storybook displays a list of components in specific states in its left nav (see figure 12.10). Selecting a component or state renders it in the main area of the UI. It also allows interaction with the component in all ways supported by the component. For example, if a Category component from the Travel Packing app is rendered, it can be renamed, and items can be added, renamed, marked as packed, and deleted.

Storybook has many uses. One is for showcasing the set of components that have been developed. Another is for testing and debugging components separately from web apps that use them. This is much faster than having to navigate to the use of a particular component in a web app.

Detailed instructions for using Storybook with Svelte components can be found in the Storybook documentation at https://storybook.js.org/docs/guides/guide-svelte/.

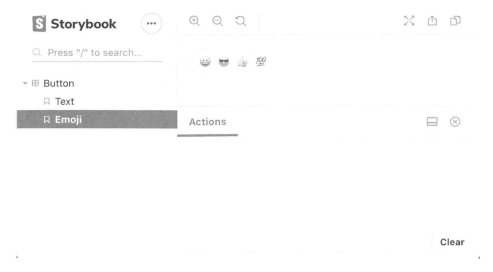

Figure 12.10   Storybook before adding components

To add the use of Storybook to an existing Svelte application, `cd` to the top application directory and enter the following:

```
npx -p @storybook/cli sb init --type svelte
```

This takes a couple of minutes to complete and results in the following changes:

- It installs all the development dependencies needed by Storybook.
- It adds the following npm scripts:

  ```
  "storybook": "start-storybook",
  "build-storybook": "build-storybook"
  ```

- It creates the `.storybook` directory, which contains the `addons.js` file that registers the use of Storybook actions and links. Actions provide a way to log user interactions, such as a certain button being pressed. Links provide a way to add links in stories that can be clicked to navigate to other stories, as an alternative to clicking a link in the left nav.

  This directory also contains the `config.js` file that configures the use of Storybook to automatically import all files found in the `stories` directory whose names end with `.stories.js`.

- It creates the `stories` directory, which contains the `button.svelte` file that defines a simple Svelte component. It also contains the `index.stories.js` file that registers the `Button` component with Storybook. These files just provide an example of registering a component with Storybook. Typically source files for the components being demonstrated are found in the src directory rather than the stories directory.

The supplied Button component dispatches an event when it is clicked. The index.stories.js file listens for the event and calls the action function that it imports from @storybook/addon-actions. Strings passed to the action function are logged at the bottom of the main section of the Storybook UI. The Clear button in the lower-right corner of the Actions area clears the list of logged actions.

To run Storybook locally, enter npm run storybook.

To add components to Storybook, add one .stories.js file for each component in the stories directory. These files should be similar to the provided index.stories.js file.

Each story renders a component in a different state. It is common for a .stories.js file to define multiple stories that render the same component in different states. Each state has a name that is displayed in the left nav below the component name. The two states for the provided Button component are "Text" and "Emoji".

When new .stories.js files are created, refresh the browser where Storybook is running to see them in the left nav. When an existing .stories.js file is modified, Storybook automatically detects the changes and displays the modified story at the bottom of the left nav.

12.4.1 Storybook for Travel Packing app

Let's define Storybook stories for the Travel Packing app components. The finished code can be found at http://mng.bz/pBqz.

The following listing shows stories for the Item component (see figure 12.11).

Listing 12.16 Storybook stories for the Item component in stories/Item.stories.js

```
import {action} from '@storybook/addon-actions';
import Item from '../src/Item.svelte';
import '../public/global.css';          ⟵  This applies global
                                            styles from the Travel
export default {title: 'Item'};             Packing app.

const getOptions = packed => ({
  Component: Item,                            This writes to the Actions area
  props: {                                    of the Storybook UI to indicate
    categoryId: 1,                            that the action occurred.
    dnd: {},
    item: {id: 2, name: 'socks', packed}      Each story is defined by an
  },                                          exported function that returns
  on: {delete: action('item delete dispatched')}   ⟵  an object describing the
});                                              component to be rendered,
                                                props to be passed to it, and
export const unpacked = () => getOptions(false);   handling of events dispatched
export const packed = () => getOptions(true);      by the component.
```

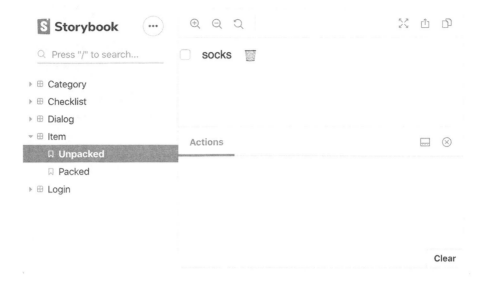

Figure 12.11   `Item` component in Storybook

Now that we have developed stories of our own, we no longer need the provided example files. The files `button.svelte` and `index.stories.js` can be deleted so they no longer appear inside Storybook.

The following listing shows stories for the `Category` component (see figure 12.12).

**Listing 12.17   Storybook stories for the `Category` component in
`stories/Category.stories.js`**

```
import {action} from '@storybook/addon-actions';
import Category from '../src/Category.svelte';
import '../public/global.css';

export default {title: 'Category'};

function getOptions(items) {
  const category = {id: 1, name: 'Clothes', items};
  return {
    Component: Category,
    props: {
      category,
      categories: {[category.id]: category},
      dnd: {},
      show: 'all'
    },
    on: {delete: action('category delete dispatched')}    ⟵── This writes to the
  };                                                            Actions area of the
}                                                               Storybook UI to
                                                                indicate that the
                                                                action occurred.
```

```
export const empty = () => getOptions({});
export const nonEmpty = () =>
  getOptions({
    1: {id: 1, name: 'socks', packed: true},
    2: {id: 2, name: 'shoes', packed: false}
  });
```

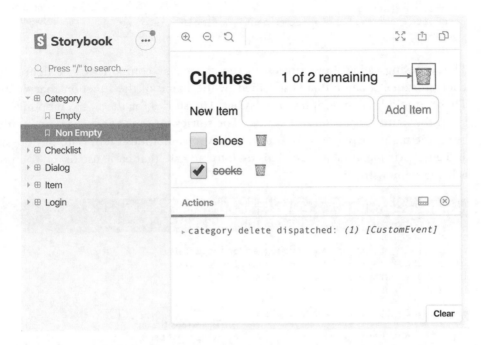

Figure 12.12 `Category` **component in Storybook**

In the Travel Packing app, the App component provides some styling that will be missing in Storybook when we render components not nested in an App component. But we can simulate this by defining a StyleWrapper component that renders a given component in a div with specified styling applied to the div. The StyleWrapper component is used in a couple of the stories that follow.

Some of the components dispatch events to which their parent component listens. Recall that events only go to parent components. Inserting the StyleWrapper component between them breaks the ability of parent components to receive the events. To fix this, the StyleWrapper component must forward the events. The events in question are login and logout, so those are the events that are forwarded.

Listing 12.18   StyleWrapper component in stories/StyleWrapper.svelte

```
<script>
  export let component;
  export let style;
</script>

<div style={style}>
  <svelte:component this={component} on:login on:logout />    ←┐ This forwards
</div>                                                           login and
                                                                logout events.
```

The following listing shows stories for the Checklist component (see figure 12.13). Each story has a name that is specified by the name of the function that defines it. These should be as descriptive as possible. The stories for the Item component were given the names unpacked and packed. The stories for the Category component were given the names empty and nonEmpty. However, sometimes there is no obvious name, and a generic name such as basic is used to indicate that basic use of the component is being demonstrated.

Listing 12.19   Storybook stories for the Checklist component in stories/Checklist.stories.js

```
import {action} from '@storybook/addon-actions';
import Checklist from '../src/Checklist.svelte';
import StyleWrapper from './StyleWrapper.svelte';
import '../public/global.css';

export default {title: 'Checklist'};

export const basic = () => ({          This wraps the
  Component: StyleWrapper,      ←┐     component being
  props: {                             demonstrated in
    component: Checklist,              the StyleWrapper
    style: `                           component.
      background-color: cornflowerblue;
      color: white;
      height: 100vh;
      padding: 1rem
    `
  },
  on: {logout: action('logout dispatched')}
});
```

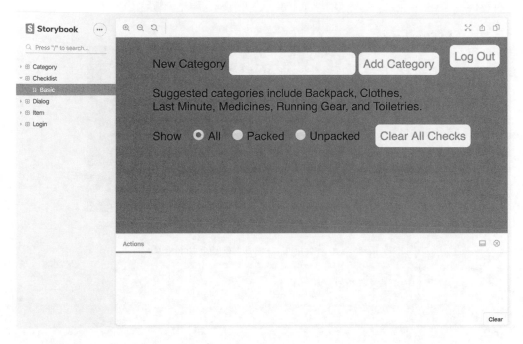

Figure 12.13 `Checklist` **component in Storybook**

The following listing shows stories for the `Login` component (see figure 12.14).

Listing 12.20 Storybook stories for the `Login` component in `stories/Login.stories.js`

```js
import {action} from '@storybook/addon-actions';
import StyleWrapper from './StyleWrapper.svelte';
import Login from '../src/Login.svelte';
import '../public/global.css';

export default {title: 'Login'};

export const basic = () => ({
  Component: StyleWrapper,
  props: {
    component: Login,
    style: `
      background-color: cornflowerblue;
      height: 100vh;
      padding: 1rem
    `
  },
  on: {login: action('login dispatched')}
});
```

Figure 12.14   Login **component in Storybook**

We want to allow Storybook users to configure the title and content of a Dialog component. To enable this, we can define the following DialogWrapper component that provides inputs for the title and content. This component is only used by Storybook, not the Travel Packing app.

Listing 12.21   DialogWrapper **component in** stories/DialogWrapper.svelte

```
<script>
  import Dialog from '../src/Dialog.svelte';
  let content = 'This is some\\nlong content.';
  let dialog;
  let title = 'My Dialog Title';

  $: lines = content.split('\\n');          ⟵┐  The content string is split
</script>                                        on occurrences of \n,
                                                 which is the escape
<section>                                        sequence for a newline
  <label>                                        character, to support
    Title                                        multiline content.
    <input bind:value={title} />
  </label>

  <label>
    Content
```

```
    <textarea bind:value={content} />
    Insert \n to get multi-line content.
  </label>

  <button on:click={() => dialog.showModal()}>Show Dialog</button>

  <Dialog {title} bind:dialog={dialog} on:close={() => dialog.close()}>
    {#each lines as line}
      <div>{line}</div>
    {/each}
  </Dialog>
</section>

<style>
  input, textarea {
    margin: 0 1rem 1rem 1rem;
  }

  label {
    color: white;
    display: flex;
    align-items: flex-start;
  }

  section {
    background-color: cornflowerblue;
    height: 100vh;
    padding: 1rem;
  }
</style>
```

The following listing shows stories for the `Dialog` component (see figure 12.15).

Listing 12.22 Storybook stories for the `Dialog` component in `stories/Dialog.stories.js`

```
import DialogWrapper from './DialogWrapper.svelte';
import '../public/global.css';

export default {title: 'Dialog'};

export const basic = () => ({Component: DialogWrapper});
```

We have now added all the components in the Travel Packing app to Storybook.

It may be desirable to generate and deploy a static version of Storybook, including all the registered components, to allow others to view the components. To generate a static version of Storybook, enter `npm run build-storybook`. This creates the `story-book-static` directory containing all the required HTML and JavaScript files. All required CSS rules are compiled into the JavaScript. This directory can be copied to a web server. To view it locally, simply open the `index.html` file in a web browser.

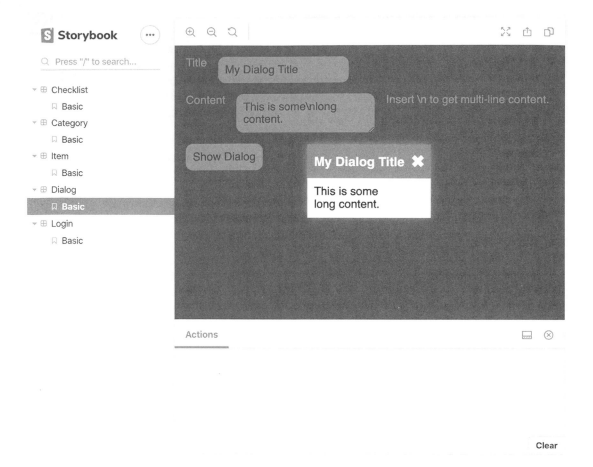

Figure 12.15   `Dialog` **component in Storybook**

Storybook provides a quick way to see a list of all the components used by an app and to interact with them. If a bug is discovered in a component, it can be debugged in the context of Storybook, which is easier than debugging in an app that uses it.

In the next chapter you'll see options for deploying Svelte applications.

Summary

- Jest is a good choice for implementing unit tests for Svelte applications, and using the Svelte Testing Library in conjunction with it makes this even easier.
- Cypress is a good choice for implementing end-to-end tests for Svelte applications.
- Lighthouse, axe, and WAVE are good choices for testing the accessibility of Svelte applications. The Svelte compiler also identifies many accessibility issues.
- Storybook is a good tool for demonstrating Svelte components and debugging issues in them.

Deploying 13

This chapter covers
- Deploying to any HTTP server
- Using Netlify
- Using Vercel (formerly ZEIT)
- Using Docker

Writing a Svelte app is lots of fun, and they are easy to run locally. But eventually you'll want to deploy apps to a server that enables others to use them. There are many more deployment options than we will cover here, but we will discuss some popular choices.

Some services, such as Netlify and Vercel, support registering a source repository (such as GitHub, GitLab, or Bitbucket). After you do this, they watch the repository for changes. Every time changes are pushed, they rebuild the web app and serve the resulting files.

13.1   Deploying to any HTTP server

It is easy to deploy a Svelte application to any HTTP server. To demonstrate this, we will use the Node-based Express server. Here are the steps:

1 cd to the top project directory.
2 Enter npm run build to create files in the public/build directory.
3 Create a server directory in the top project directory.
4 cd to the server directory.
5 Enter npm init and answer the questions it asks in order to create a package .json file. Alternatively enter npm init --yes to use the default values instead of having to answer questions.
6 Install Express by entering npm install express.
7 Create a server.js file containing the following:

```
const express = require('express');
const path = require('path');

const app = express();

app.use(express.static(path.resolve(__dirname + '/..', 'public')));

const PORT = 1234;
app.listen(PORT, () => console.log('listening on port', PORT));
```

This specifies that files will be served from the public directory, which is a sibling of the server directory.

Other port numbers can be used.

8 Add the following script in package.json:

```
"start": "node server.js"
```

9 Start the server by entering npm start, still in the server directory.
10 Browse to localhost:1234 (or whatever port you chose) to run the app.

When using a cloud-based server, upload the public directory to its recommended location.

13.2   Using Netlify

Netlify (www.netlify.com) bills itself as an "all-in-one platform for automating modern web projects."

To get started using Netlify, browse to https://www.netlify.com/, click the Get Started in Seconds button, and sign up. Netlify sites are automatically secured with HTTPS using a "Let's Encrypt" certificate.

There are two ways to create and deploy sitcs in Netlify: using the website and working from the command line.

13.2.1 *Netlify from the website*

When you use Netlify from the website, code for your site must be in a GitHub, Git-Lab, or Bitbucket repository. Once the repository is associated with your site, pushing changes to it will trigger a new build and deploy.

To create a site and build and deploy it, follow these steps:

1 Browse to https://www.netlify.com/.
2 Log in and enter your email address and password.
3 Click the New Site From Git button in the upper right.
4 Click a button for one of the supported repository services. A dialog will open.
5 Click the Authorize button to grant Netlify access to repositories.
6 Select the account where Netlify should be installed to allow it to host applications in repositories found there.
7 Choose between allowing Netlify to access all repositories or only selected repositories (preferred). If the latter is selected, choose a specific repository.
8 Click the Install button.
9 Enter your password for the repository service.
10 Click a repository name to configure its Netlify options. These include the branch to deploy, the build command to run, and the directory to publish that contains build artifacts. In the case of Svelte and Sapper, the build command should be `npm install; npm run build`. The directory to publish should be `public` for Svelte and `__sapper__/build` for Sapper.
11 If your build process requires environment variables to be set, click the Show Advanced button. For each environment variable needed, click the New Variable button and enter a name and value.
12 Click the Deploy Site button. The message "Site deploy in progress" will appear for a few seconds, and then the URL of the newly deployed application will be displayed. If the build fails, a red link that says "Site deploy failed" will be displayed. Click this to see the error messages.
13 The provided URL is fine for testing, but you will want a better URL for users. To change the URL, click the Site Settings button and the Change Site Name button. Enter a new site name. It must be unique among all domains that end in .netlify.com. For example, you can try changing the site name to "travel-packing".
14 To add a custom domain, click the Domain Settings and Add Custom Domain buttons. Of course, you need to own a domain to do this.
15 To run the app, click its URL link or enter the URL in a browser.

When changes are pushed to the repository, Netlify will automatically rebuild and redeploy the site. This can be seen by browsing the Netlify site and clicking the Deploys tab. There will be a row at the top of the list of deploys that says "Building." If you are already viewing this page, refresh the browser to get an updated list of deploys. To monitor the build progress, click the "Building" row that displays the "Deploy log."

To manually trigger a new deploy, click Deploys near the top of the page, click the Trigger Deploy drop-down, and select Deploy Site. This is useful after making changes to the deploy settings, such as changing the build command.

13.2.2 *Netlify from the command line*

To install the Netlify CLI for operating on Netlify sites from the command line, follow these steps:

1 Enter `npm install -g netlify-cli`.
2 Enter `netlify login`, which launches a website.
3 Click the Authorize button. This stores an access token in your home directory in the file `.netlify/config.json`. The access token is automatically used by the Netlify CLI commands.

For help on the `netlify` command, enter `netlify help` or just `netlify`.

To create a Netlify site from code in the current directory, enter `netlify init` and answer a few questions. If the current directory is a local source repository, this will associate the site with it, so that pushes will trigger deploys. However, the current directory is not required to be a local source repository.

If the current directory becomes a source repository later, it can be linked to the Netlify site by entering `netlify link`. This is an optional step that causes pushes to automatically trigger a deploy.

To deploy the current directory site using the latest code changes when it is unlinked (not associated with a remote repository), follow these steps:

1 If the dependencies of the site have not yet been installed, enter `npm install`.
2 Build the site locally by entering `npm run build`.
3 Enter `netlify init` to create a Netlify site for this app.
4 Select Yes, Create and Deploy Site Manually.
5 Select a team, likely your own.
6 Optionally enter a site name with no spaces.
7 Enter `netlify deploy --dir build`.
8 Select Create & Configure a New Site.
9 Select a team name, which is typically the one associated with your account.
10 Optionally enter a site name.

This will output a "live draft URL" at which the site can be tested.

You can deploy the site to its production URL by entering `netlify deploy --prod --dir build`. This will output a "live URL" at which users can visit the site.

The same steps can be used to deploy a site that was created through the Netlify website.

To open the web-based Netlify admin UI for the current directory site, enter `netlify open:admin`. To open the current directory site, enter `netlify open:site`.

To delete the Netlify site for the current directory, follow these steps:

1 Enter `netlify open`.
2 Click the Site Settings button.
3 Scroll to the bottom and click the red Delete This Site button.
4 Enter the site name in the input.
5 Click the red Delete button.

For more details on Netlify, see the documentation: https://docs.netlify.com/cli/get-started/.

13.2.3 *Netlify plans*

At the time of this writing, Netlify has three plans. For details on pricing, see www.netlify.com/pricing/.

- *Starter*—This plan is free. It only supports a single team member. Only one build can run at a time. This plan is great for enabling individual web developers to show their applications to others during development and for hosting applications that do not require advanced features or large amounts of bandwidth. It provides up to 100 GB of bandwidth per month for free, and it charges beyond that.
- *Pro*—This plan adds support for three team members, three concurrent builds, and password-protected sites. Additional team members incur added costs.
- *Business*—This plan adds support for five team members and five concurrent builds. Additional team members incur added costs. It also adds support for single sign-on (SSO), role-based access control (RBAC), full audit logs, 24/7/365 support options, a CDN, and a 99.99% uptime SLA. Pricing is also based on bandwidth usage and total monthly build times.

In addition to hosting web apps, Netlify also hosts serverless functions and FaunaDB, but no other databases.

13.3 *Using Vercel*

Vercel (https://vercel.com/) bills itself as "the optimal workflow for frontend teams." To get started using Vercel, browse to https://vercel.com/ and click the Start Deploying button. Click the appropriate button to continue with GitHub, GitLab, or Bitbucket. Follow the instructions to finish creating an account.

By default, Vercel projects that are associated with a source repository build and deploy the default branch, which defaults to "master." This can be changed by modifying the default branch in the source repository. Deploying a non-default branch requires custom CI/CD tooling such as GitHub Actions (https://github.com/features/actions).

There are two ways to create and deploy projects in Vercel: using the website and working from the command line.

13.3.1 *Vercel from the website*

Code for a new site can be created from a template. There are templates for many kinds of projects, including Create-React-App, Next.js, Gatsby, Vue.js, Nuxt.js, Svelte, Sapper, and more.

Alternatively, code for a new site can be obtained from a GitHub, GitLab, or Bit-Bucket repository. Pushing changes to the repository will trigger a new build and deploy.

To create a project and build and deploy it, follow these steps:

1 Browse to https://vercel.com.
2 Click Login in the upper right and log in to your account.
3 Click the Import Project button.
4 The first time a given repository service is used, Now integration must be installed. For example, for GitHub, click the Install Now for GitHub button.
5 Select a repository account, and enable it for All Repositories or Only Select Repositories (preferred).
6 Click the Install button.
7 Enter your password for the repository service.
8 To use an existing repository, select it and click the Import button.
9 Wait for the initial project build to complete.
10 To run the project, browse to the provided URL, which will have the format `project-name.username.now.sh`. Alternatively, just click the Visit button.

Now when changes are pushed to the repository, Vercel will automatically build and deploy the project. To customize the build process, modify the npm `build` script in the `package.json` file in the top project directory.

13.3.2 *Vercel from the command line*

To install the `vercel` command for operating on Vercel projects from the command line, follow these steps:

1 Enter `npm install -g vercel`.
2 Enter `vercel login`.
3 After being prompted, enter your email address.
4 Click the Verify button in the email you receive.

For help on using the `vercel` command, enter `vercel help`.

To create and deploy a Vercel project from the current directory, enter `vercel`. The project does not need to be in a source repository. This is by far the easiest way to deploy a web application.

To list all your deployments, enter `vercel ls`.

To delete a deployment from the command line, `cd` to the top project directory and enter `vercel projects rm project-name`.

13.3.3 *Vercel tiers*

At the time of this writing, Vercel has three tiers. For details on pricing, see https://vercel.com/pricing.

- *Free*—This tier only supports a single user. It also supports use of serverless functions. Only one build can run at a time.
- *Pro*—This tier adds support for 10 team members and concurrent builds. Additional team members incur added costs.
- *Enterprise*—This tier adds an SLA for 99.99% uptime, enterprise support, audit logs, and more.

13.4 *Using Docker*

Svelte applications can be deployed as Docker images. To create and run a Docker image for a Svelte application locally, follow these steps:

1 Install Docker from https://docs.docker.com/get-docker/.
2 Create a `Dockerfile` file containing the following:

```
FROM node:12-alpine
WORKDIR /usr/src/app
COPY package*.json ./
RUN npm install
COPY . .
EXPOSE 5000
ENV HOST=0.0.0.0
CMD ["npm", "start"]
```

3 Add the following scripts in `package.json`:

```
"docker:build": "docker build -t svelte/app-name .",
"docker:run": "docker run -p 5000:5000 svelte/app-name",
```

4 Enter npm run docker:build.
5 Enter npm run docker:run.

Details on deploying a Docker image to the cloud are provider-specific. Examples include Amazon Web Services (AWS), Google Cloud Platform (GCP), and Microsoft Azure.

In the next chapter we will explore some advanced features of Svelte.

Summary

- Deploying Svelte apps is easy.
- Using a service like Netlify or Vercel makes it even easier.
- Vercel provides the easiest command-line option, only requiring you to enter the single command `vercel` to create and deploy a new project.

Advanced Svelte

This chapter covers

- Form validation
- Using CSS libraries
- Special elements
- Importing JSON files
- Creating component libraries
- Web components

This chapter will wrap up our coverage of Svelte with a collection of relatively unrelated topics. What they have in common is that they may not be needed for basic Svelte applications.

Web applications that require form input from users typically need to validate that input. There are third-party libraries for other web frameworks that assist with this. However, the form validation that is part of HTML is often sufficient and is easy to use. We will look at how to do so in a Svelte application.

CSS libraries generally provide three things. First is a set of common styles that make it easy to produce polished user interfaces. Second is help with page layout and making user interfaces responsive to a variety of screen sizes. Third is a set of reusable UI components. Examples of CSS libraries include Bootstrap, Foundation, and Material UI. We will look at how one of these libraries, Bootstrap, can be used in Svelte applications.

Svelte supports a set of elements whose names begin with `svelte:`. These enable functionality that is needed in a variety of special circumstances, such as rendering a component identified by an expression, listening to DOM window and body events, binding variables to DOM window properties, inserting elements into the document head element, and specifying options for the Svelte compiler.

It can be convenient in some applications to import data from JSON files. Svelte does not support this by default, but the module bundler being used can be configured to support it. We will look at how to do this.

It is common to want to develop collections of components that can be reused across multiple Svelte applications. The steps involved in creating component libraries are only slightly different from the steps for creating a Svelte application. You will see how to implement such a library.

The Svelte compiler can generate web components from Svelte components. If you're new to web components, see www.webcomponents.org/ and *Web Components in Action* by Ben Farrell (Manning, 2019). Web components can be used in applications that are built with other frameworks, such as React, Vue, and Angular. They can even be used in applications that do not use a framework. We will create a couple of web components from Svelte components and use them in a React application.

Changes to the Travel Packing app suggested in this chapter can be found at http://mng.bz/YrlA.

14.1 Form validation

Svelte components can use built-in HTML form validation to validate user inputs. When this is done, the browser provides nice error messages for invalid fields.

A `form` element can contain the form control elements `input`, `textarea`, and `select`. To require users to enter or select a value, add the attribute `required`. The `input` element accepts a `type` attribute that can have many values. Some values such as `email` and `url` provide validation.

When an invalid value is entered in an input, it is given the CSS pseudo-class `:invalid`. Invalid inputs can be styled to indicate this, perhaps by adding a red border.

Figure 14.1 shows an example form that requires a user to enter their name, age, email address, home page URL, and postal code. The required format for postal code changes based on whether they are in the United States or Canada.

Figure 14.1 Form with valid data

Figures 14.2 through 14.8 show the error messages that are displayed if the user omits required data or enters invalid data. These are provided by the browser based on the requirements specified on the `input` elements.

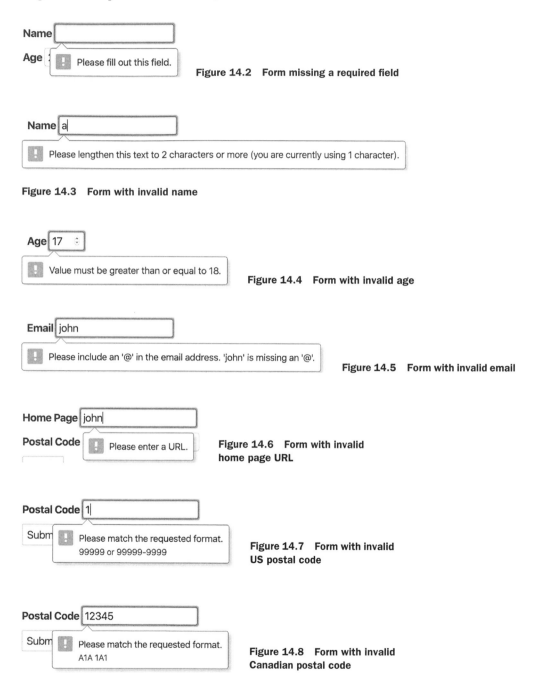

Figure 14.2   Form missing a required field

Figure 14.3   Form with invalid name

Figure 14.4   Form with invalid age

Figure 14.5   Form with invalid email

Figure 14.6   Form with invalid home page URL

Figure 14.7   Form with invalid US postal code

Figure 14.8   Form with invalid Canadian postal code

The following listing shows a Svelte component that implements the preceding form.

Listing 14.1 App that demonstrates form validation

```
<script>
  // The input pattern attribute does not recognize character classes like \d.
  const canadaRegExp = '[A-Z][0-9][A-Z] [0-9][A-Z][0-9]';
  const usRegExp = '[0-9]{5}(-[0-9]{4})?';
  const countries = ['Canada', 'United States'];

  let age = 18;
  let email = '';
  let homePage = '';
  let name = '';
  let postalCode = '';
  let postalCodeType = countries[1];

  $: isCanada = postalCodeType === countries[0];
  $: postalCodeExample = isCanada ? 'A1A 1A1' : '99999 or 99999-9999';
  $: postalCodeRegExp = isCanada ? canadaRegExp : usRegExp;

  function submit() {
    alert(`You submitted
      name = ${name}
      age = ${age}
      email = ${email}
      home page = ${homePage}
      postal code = ${postalCode}
    `);
  }
</script>

<form on:submit|preventDefault={submit}>
  <fieldset>
    <legend>Country</legend>
    <div>
      {#each countries as country}
      <label>
        <input
          type="radio"
          name="postalCodeType"
          value={country}
          bind:group={postalCodeType}
        />
        {country}
      </label>
      {/each}
    </div>
  </fieldset>
  <label>
    Name
    <input
      required
      minlength={2}
      maxlength={40}
```

The input pattern attribute does not recognize regular expression character classes like \d.

This allows 5-digit zip codes or the 9-digit ZIP+4 format.

It is customary for the text associated with checkboxes and radio buttons to come after the input element.

```
        placeholder=" "
        bind:value={name}
      />
    </label>
    <label>
      Age
      <input required type="number" min={18} max={105} bind:value={age} />
    </label>
    <label>
      Email
      <input required placeholder=" " type="email" bind:value={email} />
    </label>
    <label>
      Home Page
      <input
        required
        placeholder="http(s)://something"
        type="url"
        bind:value={homePage}
      />
    </label>
    <label>
      Postal Code
      <input
        required
        pattern={postalCodeRegExp}
        placeholder={postalCodeExample}
        title={postalCodeExample}
        bind:value={postalCode}
      />
    </label>
    <button>Submit</button>
</form>

<style>
  fieldset {
    display: inline-block;
    margin-bottom: 1rem;
  }

  input {
    border-color: lightgray;
    border-radius: 4px;
    padding: 4px;
  }

  input:not(:placeholder-shown) {
    border-color: red;
  }

  input:valid {
    border-color: lightgray;
  }
```

⟵ This displays example values in a tooltip.

⟵ This adds a red border to all inputs where a value has been entered, which is detected by the lack of a placeholder. Of course, this requires all inputs that need this border to have a placeholder attribute, but it can be just a single space.

⟵ This adds a lightgray border to all valid inputs, which removes the red border.

```
label {
    font-weight: bold;
  }
</style>
```

Adding a red border only to `input` elements that contain an invalid value is tricky! The preceding approach, using placeholders, seems to be the easiest.

14.2 *Using CSS libraries*

As an example of using a CSS library in a Svelte app, let's look at Bootstrap. If Material UI is more your style, Svelte implementations of Material UI-themed components are available on the Svelte Material UI site (https://sveltematerialui.com/).

Bootstrap provides CSS classes that help with page layout and make user interfaces responsive to a variety of screen sizes. Some developers think that these are no longer needed. Layout is well-supported by using CSS flexbox and grid layout. Using CSS media queries in conjunction with these works well. For example, elements that use flexbox can change the value of `flex-direction` between `row` and `column` to switch between laying out elements horizontally and vertically. However, all the CSS classes provided by Bootstrap, including those for its grid system, can be used for layout in Svelte apps.

Bootstrap components can be used in Svelte applications. However, many of them require including jQuery which bloats the bundle size of the app. An alternative is to use the sveltestrap library (https://bestguy.github.io/sveltestrap/), which re-implements nearly all the Bootstrap components as Svelte components These components use Bootstrap CSS classes, but sveltestrap does not include Bootstrap CSS, so that must be downloaded and added with a `link` element.

Bootstrap components typically require the developer to write several nested HTML elements with special CSS classes applied to them. Sveltestrap components are easier to use because they require less markup.

Here are the steps to use sveltestrap in a Svelte application:

1 Enter `npm install bootstrap sveltestrap`.
2 Copy the files `bootstrap.min.css` and `bootstrap.min.css.map` from `node_modules/bootstrap/dist/css` to the `public` directory.
3 Add the following line in `public/index.html` after the other `link` elements:

```
<link rel='stylesheet' href='/bootstrap.min.css'>
```

NOTE In order to use Bootstrap styles in a REPL app, all the required files must be imported from a CDN.

Figures 14.9 through 14.12 show an example Svelte app that uses Bootstrap. Listing 14.2 shows the code for the app.

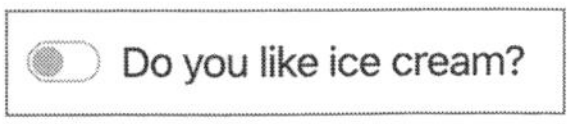

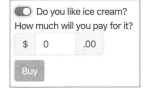

Figure 14.9   Before liking

Figure 14.10   After liking

Figure 14.11   After entering an amount and clicking Buy (shows spinner)

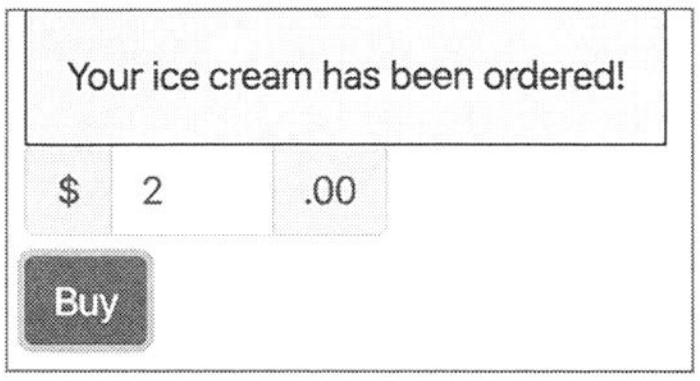

Figure 14.12   Showing toast after order is processed

Listing 14.2   App that demonstrates use of sveltestrap

```
<script>
  import {CustomInput, Spinner} from 'sveltestrap';        ◁ ── These are Bootstrap
  import Toast from './Toast.svelte';    ◁                     components
                                                              implemented as
  let amount = 0;                    Code for this            Svelte components.
  let like = false;                  component
  let status = '';                   is shown in
                                     listing 14.3.
  function buy() {
    status = 'buying';
    // Show the toast after 1 second.
    setTimeout(
      () => {
        status = 'bought';
        // Hide the toast after 3 seconds.
        setTimeout(() => status = '', 3000);
      },
      1000);
  }
</script>

                        This is a Bootstrap
<main>                  switch component.
  <CustomInput      ◁
    type="switch"
    id="like"
    label="Do you like ice cream?"
    bind:checked={like} />
```

```
{#if like}
  <label>
    How much will you pay for it?
    <div class="input-group">
      <div class="input-group-prepend">
        <span class="input-group-text">$</span>
      </div>
      <input type="number" class="form-control" min="0" bind:value={amount}>
      <div class="input-group-append">
        <span class="input-group-text">.00</span>
      </div>
    </div>
  </label>
  <div class="btn-row">
    <button class="btn btn-success" disabled={!amount} on:click={buy}>
      Buy
    </button>
    {#if status === 'buying'}
      <div class="spinner-container">
        <Spinner color="warning" />
      </div>
    {/if}
  </div>
{/if}


{#if status === 'bought'}
  <Toast>Your ice cream has been ordered!</Toast>
{/if}
</main>


<style>
  .btn-row {
    display: flex;
    align-items: center;
  }

  button {
    border: none;
  }

  .input-group {
    width: 150px;
  }

  .row > div {
    outline: solid red 1px;
  }

  .spinner-container {
    display: inline-block;
    margin-left: 1rem;
  }
</style>
```

This uses Bootstrap styling to build a fancy input.

This button uses Bootstrap styling.

This is a Bootstrap spinner component.

The following listing shows the code for the `Toast` component. It uses the `fly` transition to animate a toast coming into view and leaving from the top.

Listing 14.3   Toast component in `src/Toast.svelte`

```
<script>
  import {fly} from 'svelte/transition';
  let height = 0;                    ⟵   The default value of
</script>                                0 will be changed by
                                         the bind below.

<div
  class="my-toast"
  bind:clientHeight={height}
  transition:fly={{duration: 1000, opacity: 1, y: -height}}
>
  <slot />
</div>
                              Bootstrap defines a CSS
                              class named "toast", so I
<style>                       named this "my-toast".
  .my-toast {              ⟵
    display: inline-flex;
    align-items: center;

    background-color: linen;
    border: solid black 1px;
    border-top: none;
    box-sizing: border-box;
    padding: 1rem;
    position: absolute;
    top: 0;
  }
</style>
```

This gets the height of this div.

14.3   *Special elements*

Svelte supports many special elements that have the form `<svelte:nameprops>`. They are placed in the HTML section of `.svelte` files.

- `<svelte:component this={expression} optionalProps />`

  This renders the component specified by *expression*. If *expression* is falsy, it renders nothing. The optional props are passed to the component that is rendered.

  We used this in chapter 9 for manual routing, hash routing, and the page library. For example, when we implemented hash routing, the `pageMap` variable held an object that mapped a page name to a page component. The current page was rendered with the following:

  ```
  <svelte:component this={pageMap[pageName]} />
  ```

  The `App.svelte` file of the Travel Packing app also uses this special element for manual routing.

- `<svelte:self props />`

  This allows a component to render an instance of itself. It supports recursive components and is needed because a component cannot import itself.

  This special element is rarely needed, but one case where it is used is when a component represents a tree node. For example, a genealogy application that renders a family tree might define a `Person` component. Rendering one of these might also render its children, which are also represented by `Person` components.

- `<svelte:window on:eventName={handler} />`

  This registers a function to be called when a given event is dispatched by the DOM `window` object. One example is the `resize` event. Listening for this event allows an application to change the layout of its components based on the window size. It could even remove certain components when the window becomes small and add them back when it becomes large.

  We used this in chapter 9 to implement hash-based page routing. In that case we listened for the `hashchange` event.

NOTE When possible, it is better to use CSS media queries to change page layout based on window size. See the MDN web docs for more on using media queries: http://mng.bz/GVMO.

- `<svelte:window bind:propertyName={variable} />`

  This binds a variable to a window property. The supported window properties are `innerHeight`, `innerWidth`, `outerHeight`, `outerWidth`, `scrollX`, `scrollY`, and `online`.

  For example, a component can use the following code to obtain the value of `innerWidth` and change its layout based on the value.

  ```
  <svelte:window bind:innerWidth={windowWidth} />
  ```

  The scroll properties can be modified to trigger scrolling the window. All the other properties are read-only. Here's an example:

  ```
  <script>
    const rows = 100;
    const columns = 150;
    let scrollX;
    let scrollY;
  </script>

  <svelte:window bind:scrollX={scrollX} bind:scrollY={scrollY} />

  <button on:click={() => scrollX += 100}>Right</button>
  <button on:click={() => scrollY += 100}>Down</button>

  <!-- This just creates content that can be scrolled. -->
  {#each Array(rows) as _, index}
  ```

This iterates a given number of times instead of over an existing array.

```
    <div>{index + 1}{'#'.repeat(columns)}</div>
  {/each}
```

NOTE   A component can only include one `svelte:window` element. but it can listen to any number of events *and* bind to any number of properties.

- `<svelte:body on:eventName={handler} />`

  This registers a function to be called when a given event is dispatched by the DOM `body` element. Examples include `mouseenter` and `mouseleave`. A component can only include one `svelte:body` element, but it can bind to any number of body events.

  For example, this can be used to change the background color of an app when the mouse enters and leaves the browser window:

  ```
  <script>
    let bgColor = 'white';
  </script>

  <svelte:body
    on:mouseenter={() => bgColor = 'white'}
    on:mouseleave={() => bgColor = 'gray'}
  />
  <main style="background-color: {bgColor}">
    ...
  </main>
  ```

- `<svelte:head>elements</svelte:head>`

  This inserts elements in the `head` element of the DOM document. Examples include inserting `link`, `script`, and `title` elements. Including a `title` element changes what is displayed in the browser title bar and in bookmarks.

  For example, for the Travel Packing app we can add the following in the HTML section of `src/Login.svelte`:

  ```
  <svelte:head>
    <title>Login</title>
  </svelte:head>
  ```

  Add the following in the HTML section of `.src/Checklist.svelte`:

  ```
  <svelte:head>
    <title>Checklist</title>
  </svelte:head>
  ```

  Interpolation can be used in the `title` element content to compute a title, as the following example shows in `src/App.svelte`:

  ```
  <script>
    const days = [
      'Sunday', 'Monday', 'Tuesday', 'Wednesday',
      'Thursday', 'Friday', 'Saturday'
    ];
  ```

```
  const dayName = days[new Date().getDay()];
</script>
<svelte:head>
  <title>Today is {dayName}</title>
</svelte:head>
<!-- More page content goes here. -->
```

If multiple components insert elements into the head that cannot be duplicated, such as the title element, the value of the element will be updated by the last one rather than adding multiple elements.

NOTE Using <svelte:head> has no impact inside the REPL.

- <svelte:options *option*={*value*} />

This is used to specify options for the Svelte compiler. Most applications do not need to set any of these options, but it's important to be aware of them so you can recognize when they are needed.

This element is placed at the top of a .svelte file, before any other elements (not inside the script element).

The following compiler options can be specified:

- immutable—This means props will be treated as immutable, which provides an optimization. The default value is false.

Being *immutable* means parent components will create new objects for all object props rather than modifying properties of existing objects. This allows Svelte to determine whether a prop has changed by comparing object references rather than object properties.

When this option is set to true, if a parent component modifies the object properties of a child component, the child will not detect the change and will not re-render.

In the Travel Packing app, we can add <svelte:options immutable={true} /> or the equivalent of <svelte:options immutable /> at the top of the Dialog component source file. We cannot add it to the Category component because that takes the prop categories, which is an object whose properties are modified in its parent component Checklist. We cannot add it to the Item component because that takes the prop item, which is an object whose packed property is modified when the checkbox for an item is toggled. There is no point in adding it to the Login or Checklist components because those do not take any props.

- accessors—This adds getter and setter methods for the component props. The default is false. This option isn't really needed when components are used in a Svelte app because the bind directive can be used instead to attach a variable to a prop. It can be useful when Svelte components are compiled to custom elements and those are used in non-Svelte apps. You will learn how to do this in section 14.6.

Having a setter method allows non-Svelte code to modify the value of a component prop after it has been rendered. Having a getter method allows non-Svelte code to obtain the current value of a component prop after it has been rendered.

- `namespace="value"`—This specifies the namespace of the component. One use is for Svelte components that only render SVG. Those can use a namespace of `svg`.
- `tag="value"`—This specifies the name to use when a Svelte component is compiled as a custom element. It allows Svelte components to be used as custom elements in non-Svelte apps. See section 14.6 for examples of using this option.

14.4 *Importing JSON files*

Svelte applications can import JSON files if the module bundler is configured to support this. By default, Svelte applications use the Rollup module bundler. Here are the steps to configure it:

1 Install the required Rollup plugin by entering `npm install -D @rollup/plugin-json`.
2 Edit `rollup.config.js`.
3 Add `import json from '@rollup/plugin-json';` near the top with the other imports.
4 Add `json()` in the `plugins` array. For example, it should already contain `commonjs()`.

After restarting the Svelte server, you will be able to process code like the following:

```
import myData from './myData.json';
```

14.5 *Creating component libraries*

Svelte components can be reused by multiple Svelte applications. For example, suppose we implement a component that renders a bar chart. We might want to use it in an application that shows company profits by quarter and also in a separate application that shows changes in utility bills by month.

A good way to achieve Svelte component reuse is to create an npm package that defines the components, install that package in the apps that will use the components, and import them where needed.

To create an npm package that defines Svelte components, follow these steps:

1 Choose a library name that is not already registered in npm.
2 Create a Svelte project for the library by entering the following:

```
npx degit sveltejs/component-template library-name
```

3 Enter `cd library-name`.

4 Create a `.svelte` file for each component in the `src` directory.

5 Delete the provided example file, `src/Component.svelte`.

6 Replace the content of `src/index.js` with a line like the following for each component:

```
export {default as MyComponentName} from './MyComponentName.svelte';
```

7 Edit `package.json`.

- Change the `name` property value to the library name.
- Add a `version` property such as `"version": "0.1.0",`.

8 Build the component library by entering `npm run build`. This creates a `dist` directory and the files `index.js` and `index.mjs` inside it, which contain all the required Svelte library code and the definitions of all the components. The `index.js` file contains CommonJS definitions. The `index.mjs` file contains ES Module definitions. Svelte applications that use the components will get their definitions from one of these files.

9 Create a GitHub repository for the library.

10 Add the contents of this directory to the GitHub repository.

11 If you're not already logged into npm, enter `npm login`.

12 Every time changes need to be published, bump the version in `package.json` and tag the GitHub repository by entering the following commands:

```
npm version patch|minor|major     ◁——  Choose one of these
git push --tags                         options based on the kind
git push                                of change being made.
```

13 Publish the library to npm by entering `npm pub`.

To use Svelte components defined in an npm package in a Svelte app, follow these steps:

1 Install the library by entering `npm install *library-name*`. For example, `npm install rmv-svelte-components`.

2 Import the components to be used. For example, `import {LabeledInput, Select} from rmv-svelte-components;`

3 Use the components like any other Svelte components. For example, the app in listing 14.9 uses the components `LabeledInput` and `Select` from the `rmv-svelte-component` library (see figure 14.13).

Figure 14.13   App that uses library components

Listing 14.4   App that uses library components

```
<script>
  import {LabeledInput, Select} from 'rmv-svelte-components';
  let color = '';
  let name = 'Mark';
  let options = ['', 'red', 'green', 'blue'];
</script>

<main>
  <LabeledInput label="Name" bind:value={name} />
  <p>Hello, {name}!</p>
  <Select options={options} on:select={event => color = event.detail} />
  <p>You selected the color {color}.</p>
</main>
```

14.6   *Web components*

The Web Components standard defines the ability to create custom elements. These are custom HTML elements that can be used in web frameworks (such as React, Vue, and Angular) and when using no framework (just JavaScript and the DOM).

Svelte components can be compiled into custom elements. However, there are some limitations to keep in mind:

- The styles for these components are copied to the generated JavaScript code and used as inline styles. This means they cannot be overridden by external CSS rules. For this reason, it is best for such Svelte components to include minimal CSS to maximize the degree to which applications that use them can apply styling.
- In Svelte components that use slots to render child content, {#if} and {#each} blocks surrounding slots are ignored.
- The slot directive :let is ignored. This is a rarely used feature.
- Using Svelte-based custom elements in older browsers requires polyfills.

Follow these steps to generate custom elements from a set of Svelte components:

1 Create a new Svelte project with npx degit sveltejs/template *project-name*.
2 Enter cd *project-name*.
3 Enter npm install.
4 Add .svelte files defining components in the src directory.

   Here is one example of a basic component, the Greet component in src/ Greet.svelte:

```
<script>
  export let name = 'World';
</script>

<div>Hello, {name}!</div>
```

And here is another, the `Counter` component in `src/Counter.svelte`:

```
<script>
  export let count = 0;
</script>

<div class="counter">
  <button on:click={() => count--}>-</button>
  <span>{count}</span>
  <button on:click={() => count++}>+</button>
</div>

<style>
  button {
    border: solid lightgray 1px;
    border-radius: 4px;
    padding: 10px;
  }

  .counter {
    font-size: 24px;
  }
</style>
```

5   Specify a tag at the top of each component `.svelte` file. Tags must contain at least one hyphen. Typically they consist of a common prefix string followed by a hyphen and an element name. We will use "svelte" for the prefix.

    For example, we can add this to `src/Greet.svelte`:

```
<svelte:options tag="svelte-greet" />
```

And we can add this to `src/Counter.svelte`:

```
<svelte:options tag="svelte-counter" />
```

If the tag is {null} instead of a string, applications that import the custom element can specify the name of the custom element. This changes the way applications configure the use of custom elements, and is explained below.

6   To verify that the components work as expected, render them in `App.svelte`, as in this example:

```
<script>
  import Counter from './Counter.svelte';
  import Greet from './Greet.svelte';
</script>

<Greet name="Mark" />
<Counter />
```

7   Test the components by entering `npm run dev` and browsing to `localhost:5000`.

8   Create a `custom-elements.js` file that imports the components. For example, if the components are `Counter` and `Greet`, the contents should be as follows:

```
import Counter from './Counter.svelte';
import Greet from './Greet.svelte';
export {Counter, Greet};
```

9   Copy `rollup.config.js` to `rollup.ce-config.js`.
    – ce stands for custom elements, but the actual name is not important.

10 Modify `rollup.ce-config.js`:
    – Change the `input` property value from `'src/main.js'` to `'src/custom-elements.js'`.
    – Change the `format` property of `output` from `iife` to `es`.
    – Add `customElement: true` to the object passed to the `svelte` function in the `plugins` array.

11 Add the following npm script in `package.json`:

```
"custom-elements": "rollup -c rollup.ce-config.js",
```

12 Enter `npm run custom-elements`. This generates files in the `public/build` directory that define custom elements for the components.

The following steps show how you can use these custom elements in a new React application:

1   Create a new React application by entering `npx create-react-app` *app-name*.
2   Enter `cd` *app-name*.
3   Copy the file `public/build/bundle.js` from the Svelte project to the `src` directory of the React application, and rename it `svelte-elements.js`.
4   If using ESLint (and why wouldn't you?), edit `svelte-elements.js` to ignore some ESLint issues:

```
/* eslint-disable eqeqeq, no-self-compare, no-sequences, no-unused-
    expressions */
```

5   Edit `src/index.js`.

If the custom elements used a {null} tag, add the following after the existing imports to import JavaScript classes that define the custom elements and assign names to them.

```
import {Counter, Greet} from './svelte-elements';
customElements.define('svelte-greet', Greet);
customElements.define('svelte-counter', Counter);
```

If the custom elements each specified a tag name, the preceding code that defines custom elements will already be in the `svelte-elements.js` file. This frees users of the custom elements from needing to do this. In this case, just add the following line after the existing imports to import the custom elements that already have names.

```
import './svelte-elements';
```

NOTE Specifying a {null} tag is often preferred because it allows users of the component to choose the name. This matches the way components work in Svelte, where a component is defined by a source file but does not specify the name of the component. When web components are given names, there is the possibility that two component authors might select the same name. This makes it difficult to use both components in the same app.

1   Render the custom elements in React components. For example, the following lines can be added in the JSX of src/App.js:

```
<svelte-greet name="Mark" />
<svelte-counter />
```

Empty custom elements

The self-closing versions of the custom elements above only work in the context of JSX. When using them in a setting where JSX is not supported, they must be written as follows:

```
<svelte-greet name="Mark"></svelte-greet>
<svelte-counter></svelte-counter>
```

2   Enter npm start to run the React app.

3   Verify that the custom elements render correctly.

NOTE React currently only supports passing primitive values as props to custom elements. Objects and arrays cannot be passed. See the notes on React at https://custom-elements-everywhere.com/. This is a significant limitation. React relies on its own *synthetic events* for representing DOM events. It cannot currently listen for DOM events emitted by custom elements.

A similar approach can be employed to use custom elements in other frameworks such as Vue and Angular.

For another approach to creating custom elements from Svelte components, see the video "How to create a web component in sveltejs" at http://mng.bz/zjqQ.

The command-line tool publish-svelte (or "pelte" for short) at https://github.com/philter87/publish-svelte automates the previous steps to generate custom elements from a set of Svelte components.

It compiles and bundles a single Svelte component into a custom element. Then it publishes the custom element to npm for use in applications. The author of publish-svelte plans to enhance it to support publishing multiple Svelte components to a single npm package.

In the next chapter we will begin exploring Sapper, which is a framework built on Svelte that adds many features.

Summary

- Form validation can be added to Svelte apps using features provided by HTML.
- CSS libraries such as Bootstrap, Foundation, and Material UI can be used in Svelte apps.
- Svelte provides special elements to implement features that cannot be implemented in a Svelte app using HTML elements alone.
- Svelte apps can import JSON files if the module bundler is configured to support this.
- It is possible to create libraries of Svelte components that can be reused across multiple applications.
- It is possible to generate custom elements from Svelte components so they can be used in web applications that use any web framework or no framework.

Part 3

Deeper into Sapper

Part 3 explores Sapper, a tool that builds on Svelte to add more features. We'll build our first Sapper application, which will recreate the shopping app we developed earlier in the book, and take a closer look at Sapper's unique features, such as page routes, page layouts, preloading, prefetching, and code splitting. We'll also cover server routes, which enable API service implementation in the same project as the client side of a web app. Sapper apps can be "exported" to generate static sites, which can be desirable when you want to generate the HTML for every page at build time. This part will cover that topic and look at an example app that builds on it, along with service worker caching strategies and events. Finally, we'll look at techniques to verify the offline behavior of a Sapper app.

Your first Sapper app

This chapter covers

- Reasons to use Sapper
- Creating a new Sapper app
- Redeveloping the shopping application with Sapper

In this chapter we will review the benefits of using Sapper and walk through developing a Sapper app.

As you learned in chapter 1, Sapper (https://sapper.svelte.dev/) is a framework built on top of Svelte. It is used to create more advanced web applications that take advantage of one or more of the features summarized below.

- *Sapper provides page routing*, which associates URLs with the "pages" in an app and defines how navigation between pages is described in markup. Having a unique URL for each page allows those pages to be bookmarked so users can begin subsequent sessions on different pages.
- *Sapper supports page layouts*, which define a common layout for sets of pages within an app. This can include common areas of a page such as headers, footers, and navigation.

- *Sapper provides server-side rendering* (SSR), which allows the generation of HTML for pages to occur on the server instead of in the browser. This can provide a better user experience for rendering the initial page, because it is typically faster to generate this HTML on the server than to download the JavaScript required to render it in the browser and then do so. JavaScript for rendering subsequent pages can then be downloaded in the background before the user navigates away from the initial page.

- *Sapper supports server routes,* which provide an easy way to implement Node-based API services in the same project as the frontend web application. This allows API services to be implemented in the same programming language that is used to implement the user interface, avoiding a mental switch between languages. Having frontend and backend code in the same project naturally leads toward storing it in the same source repository, which is convenient for developers who maintain both kinds of code.

- *Sapper supports code splitting,* which allows the JavaScript required for each page of the application to be downloaded only when a page is visited for the first time. This reduces the initial load time because it is no longer necessary to download all the code for the app at startup. It also avoids downloading code for pages that are never visited.

- *Sapper supports prefetching,* which provides faster page loads by anticipating the next page a user will visit based on mouse hovers. Page links can be configured so if a user hovers over it, Sapper will begin downloading the code needed to render the page before the user clicks the link. This provides a better user experience because it decreases the time required to render the next page.

- *Sapper supports static site generation* by crawling a Svelte web app at build time and generating the HTML that each page renders. This produces a site where all the pages a user might visit have already been rendered to HTML files. It provides a better user experience because when users visit each page, no server-side or client-side HTML generation is required. Static sites can include JavaScript code that provides dynamic behavior.

- *Sapper supports offline usage* by using a service worker in order for some portions of an application to remain usable when network connectivity is lost. This includes issues with internet providers and cell phone connectivity.

- *Sapper supports end-to-end testing* using Cypress. This enables you to write comprehensive tests that exercise an application in ways that a user would. It can simulate user actions such as typing text into input fields, selecting items from dropdowns, and clicking buttons. Everything nccdcd to implcmcnt and run Cyprcss tests is preconfigured in Sapper projects created using a template described in the next section.

In this chapter we will recreate the shopping application from chapter 9 using Sapper. It will use page routing, page layouts, server-side rendering, and code splitting. This will serve to demonstrate how easy it is to take advantage of some of the features of Sapper.

15.1 Creating a new Sapper app

Let's walk through the steps to create and run a Sapper application. It will have Home, About, and Blog pages, along with a way to navigate between them. The Sapper home page recommends that you start any Sapper application from this beginning point and then customize the pages and their navigation to suit the app you would like to create.

1 If you haven't already, install Node.js from https://nodejs.org.
2 Create the starting directory structure and files for a new application. Choose between using the Rollup or Webpack module bundler. To use Rollup, enter `npx degit sveltejs/sapper-template#rollup` *app-name*. To use Webpack, enter `npx degit sveltejs/sapper-template#webpack` *app-name*.
3 Enter `cd` *app-name*.
4 Enter `npm install`.
5 Enter `npm run dev`. This starts a local HTTP server and provides live reload, unlike `npm start`, which omits live reload. Then browse to localhost:3000.

The default Sapper app contains three "pages" or "routes" with navigation links at the top. The routes are Home, About, and Blog. Links on the Blog page open sub-pages that render specific blog content. These pages are shown in figures 15.1, 15.2, and 15.3.

Figure 15.1 Home page

Figure 15.2   About page

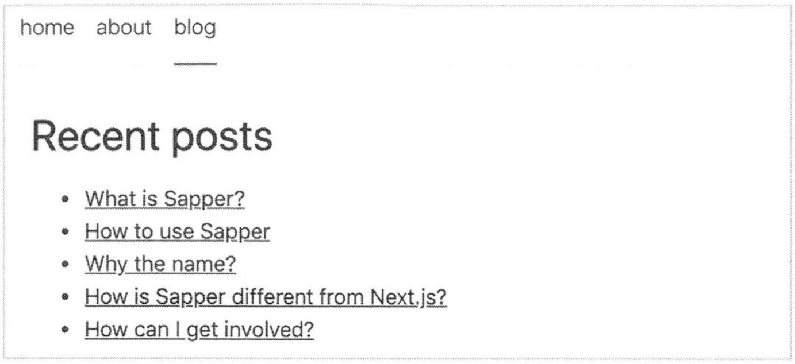

Figure 15.3   Blog page

The page in figure 15.4 is rendered when the first link on the Blog page is clicked.

Figure 15.4   Blog page for "What is Sapper?"

Now we can begin modifying the app.

15.2   *Recreating the shopping app with Sapper*

Let's recreate the shopping application from chapter 9 using Sapper. The code for this app can be found at http://mng.bz/NKG1.

This is a simpler app to start with than the Travel Packing app. We will tackle creating a Sapper version of that in chapter 16.

Change the links at the top of the pages to be "Shop", "Cart", and "Ship". To do this, modify `Nav.svelte` and change the `li` elements to match the following.

Listing 15.1 Nav component in `src/components/Nav.svelte`

```
<li>
  <a aria-current={segment === undefined ? 'page' : undefined}
    href=".">Shop</a>
</li>
<li>
  <a aria-current={segment === "cart" ? 'page' : undefined}
    href="cart">Cart</a>
</li>
<li>
  <a aria-current={segment === "ship"? 'page' : undefined}
    href="ship">Ship</a>
</li>
```

NOTE For details on the `aria-current` attribute, see the W3C documentation (www.w3.org/TR/wai-aria-1.1/#aria-current), which says "Indicates the element that represents the current item within a container or set of related elements."

NOTE Perhaps you don't want the page links to be at the top of the page, or you want to style them differently. You'll see how to change them in section 16.2.

Files in the `src/routes` directory represent the pages in the app. These define Svelte components, but the filenames are all lowercase. This is because these names become part of the URLs for visiting the pages, and it is common for URLs to be lowercase.

Make the following changes to files in the `src/routes` directory:

1 Rename `about.svelte` to `cart.svelte`.

2 Modify `cart.svelte` to match the following:

```
<svelte:head>
  <title>Cart</title>
</svelte:head>

<h1>Cart</h1>

<p>This is the 'cart' page.</p>
```

3 Copy `cart.svelte` to `ship.svelte`.

4 Modify `ship.svelte` to match the following:

```
<svelte:head>
  <title>Ship</title>
</svelte:head>
```

```
<h1>Ship</h1>

<p>This is the 'ship' page.</p>+
```

5   Delete the `blog` directory in `src/routes`.

6   Modify the bottom of `index.svelte`, which represents the Home page of the app, to match the following:

```
<svelte:head>
  <title>Shop</title>
</svelte:head>

<h1>Shop</h1>
```

7   Delete the following line in `src/routes/_layout.svelte`:

```
max-width: 56em;
```

Removing this left-justifies the content of each page. Page layouts will be discussed in the next chapter.

We now have the three pages we need for the shopping app. Assuming the app is still running, click the links at the top to verify that navigating between the pages still works.

Another way to navigate to a page is to manually change the URL in the browser's address bar. Change it to end with `/cart` or `/ship` to switch to those pages. Remove the path at the end to switch to the Shop page, since it is the Home page.

Now let's copy code from chapter 9 to finish implementing the three pages:

1   Copy `public/global.css` from the chapter 9 version of the shopping application to the `static` directory, replacing the existing file. This includes styling for tables.

2   Copy `src/items.js` from chapter 9 to the `src` directory. This defines the items available for sale.

3   Copy `src/stores.js` from chapter 9 to the `src` directory. This defines a writable store that holds items in the cart.

4   Copy the code in `src/Shop.svelte` from chapter 9 into the existing `src/routes/index.svelte` file. The only code currently in `index.svelte` that should be retained is the `<svelte:head>` element, which should be the first element after the `script` element. Change the path for the imports at the top of the `script` element to begin with `..` since those files are in the parent directory of the routes directory.

5   Repeat what was done with `src/Shop.svelte` to copy code in `src/Cart.svelte` from chapter 9 into `src/routes/cart.svelte` and to copy code in `src/Ship.svelte` from chapter 9 into `src/routes/ship.svelte`.

The app should now be operational. Figures 15.5, 15.6, and 15.7 show screenshots of the three pages with some data entered.

Figure 15.5   Shop page

Figure 15.6   Cart page

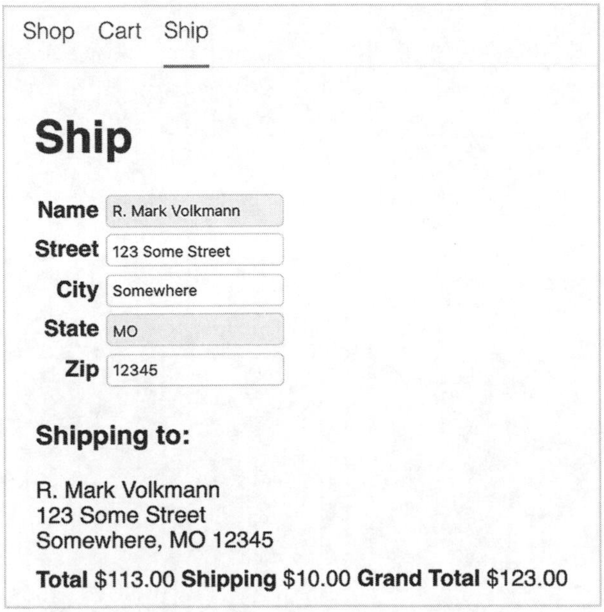

Figure 15.7   Ship page

What did we gain by using Sapper instead of straight Svelte? We now have simple page routing, server-side rendering, and code splitting.

To see server-side rendering in action, open the DevTools in the browser window where the app is running, click the Network tab, and refresh the browser. There will be a GET request to http://localhost:3000/ that returns HTML for the first page, which is the Shop page. The remaining pages are created in the browser by downloaded JavaScript code.

To see code splitting in action within the DevTools Network tab, click the Cart or Ship link at the top of the page. The first time each page is rendered, new files are downloaded with names like `cart.hash.js`, `ship.hash.js`, and `ship.hash.css`. The Cart page does not contain a `style` element, so no `cart.hash.css` is downloaded.

In the next chapter we will dive deeper into Sapper projects and learn about their directory structure, more on routes, page layouts, preloading, prefetching, code splitting, and more.

Summary

- Sapper builds on Svelte to add many features.
- Creating a new Sapper app is as easy as running `npm degit`.
- Pages in a Sapper app are defined by files in the `src/routes` directory.
- Navigation to pages is implemented with HTML anchor elements (`<a>`).
- Sapper automatically provides many benefits.

16
Sapper applications

This chapter covers

- The file structure of Sapper projects
- Page routes
- Page layouts
- Handling errors
- Running on both server and client
- The Fetch API wrapper
- Preloading data needed by pages
- Prefetching for faster page loads
- Code splitting

The previous chapter provided a taste of using Sapper. Now it's time to dig deeper into a series of topics covering its most commonly used features:

- *File structure*—While it is not technically necessary to understand the purpose of every directory and file in a Sapper project, being exposed to this information will give you a better understanding of what Sapper provides and how the pieces fit together. By the time you've finished this chapter, you will feel comfortable navigating a Sapper project.

- *Page routes*—Sapper routes greatly simplify creating apps where users can navigate to multiple pages, like the three pages in the Shopping app from chapter 15.
- *Page layouts*—Page layouts are Svelte components that provide a common layout to a set of pages. A scenario supported by page layouts is when multiple pages in an app have common sections, such as a header, footer, or left nav. We will explore implementing custom page layouts.
- *Error handling*—Things can go wrong when web apps invoke server APIs. Maybe the URL of the service has changed, the service is down, invalid data is passed, a database error occurs, or there is a logic error in the server-side code. These kinds of errors should typically be described on a dedicated, nicely formatted, informative error page. Sapper supports configuring such a page, and you will see how to do this.
- *Client and server code*—When writing Sapper apps, it is important to consider where each piece of JavaScript code will run. It may run only in the browser, only on the server, or in both places. You will learn how to determine this, why it matters, and how to avoid errors from code running in the wrong environment.
- *Preloading and prefetching*—The Sapper concepts of preloading and prefetching coordinate data loading and provide performance benefits. We'll explore when and how to use these features.
- *Code splitting*—Finally, we will dig into the details of code splitting to understand the benefit it brings and its relationship with prefetching.

We have a lot of exciting concepts to learn and material to cover, so let's get to it!

> **NOTE**   This chapter uses the term "API service" when referring to any kind of remote service to which a request can be sent from the client side of a web app. This includes REST services.

16.1 Sapper file structure

Sapper apps created from `sveltejs/sapper-template` begin with the directory structure described in this section. Typically most of the files described here do not require modification. Those that do are noted in their descriptions.

Let's take a high-level look at the project structure.

- `__sapper__` directory—This contains the following subdirectories:
  - `build` subdirectory—This is the destination for generated build artifacts. This directory and the files in it are created by entering `npm run build`, if they do not already exist. A simple way to serve the app locally is to enter `npm start` and browse to localhost:3000.
  - `dev` subdirectory—This is the destination for generated, development-mode artifacts. This directory and the files in it are created by entering `npm run dev`, if they do not already exist.

- export subdirectory—This is the destination for files generated by npm run export, which generates a static site. Using Sapper in this way is similar to using Gatsby to generate a static site from React components. We will cover this in detail in chapter 18.

- cypress directory—This contains directories and files for running end-to-end tests. The Cypress test tool was described in chapter 12. Using Cypress with Sapper apps works in much the same way as it does with Svelte apps.

- node_modules directory—This contains dependency package files installed by running npm install. All project dependencies are described in package.json.

- src directory—This contains application code and is where most of your changes will take place.

  - components subdirectory—This contains Svelte components that are used in pages of the app.

    - Nav.svelte—This file defines nav bar links for navigating to the pages in the app. Modify it to change page navigation.

    - routes subdirectory—This contains Svelte components that represent the pages in the app.

    - client.js—This file is the starting point of the client-side Sapper app. It is not typically modified.

    - server.js—This file configures the server used for server-side routes (API services). It uses Polka (https://github.com/lukeed/polka) by default but can easily be modified to use another library such as Express (https://expressjs.com/) if desired. You will see how in chapter 17. Another reason to modify this file is to configure the use of additional server middleware libraries for special needs, such as body parsing and request logging.

      The environment variable PORT can be set to specify the port on which the server should listen for requests. By default it listens on port 3000.

      The server will run in dev mode if the NODE_ENV environment variable is set to development. Running in dev mode has several effects.

      - It causes the Sapper error page to include a stack trace for errors that have one.

      - It causes the sirv middleware, which is used by Polka to serve static files, to disable file caching and ignore the sirv options etag, immutable, maxAge, and setHeaders. The benefit is that code changes will be reflected immediately.

      - It passes a dev option to the Rollup Svelte plugin in rollup.config.js. The plugin doesn't use this option, but any unsupported options are passed on to the Svelte compiler. Enabling the dev option of the Svelte compiler causes it to generate extra code that performs runtime checks and output debugging information.

- – service-worker.js—This file defines the service worker caching strategy to use. This will be covered in chapter 19.
- – template.html—This file contains the HTML template used by the app. It defines the DOM ID sapper that is targeted by client.js. It also includes several files from the static directory described next.
- static directory—This contains static assets such as images. Add images needed by the app here, and delete any provided images that are not needed. It also contains the following files, which are included by template.html described previously.
    - – static/global.css defines global styling. Edit this to change or add global styles that can affect any component.
    - – static/manifest.json is important for progressive web apps (PWAs), which are described in chapter 19.
    - – static/favicon.png is the icon displayed in the browser tab where the app is running.
- cypress.json—This file contains configuration details for Cypress end-to-end tests.
- package.json—This file lists package dependencies. It also defines the npm scripts dev, build, export, start, cy:run, cy:open, and test.
- README.md—This file contains basic documentation on using Sapper. Modify it to provide details on your application.
- rollup.config.js—This file contains configuration details for the Rollup module bundler. Modify this to use preprocessors like Sass and TypeScript.

There is also a directory named node_modules under the src directory. Sapper generates this directory and the files inside it when the commands npm run dev, npm run build, and npm run export are run. Placing files here allows them to be imported using Node resolution rules. Otherwise imports of these files would have to use relative paths.

Here is the content of the src/node_modules directory:

- @sapper directory—This directory and its subdirectories contain files provided or generated by Sapper that should not be modified.
    - – app.mjs—This file exports the Sapper API functions, including
        - goto for programmatic navigation.
        - start, which configures event handling for page navigation and is called by client.js, which was described earlier.
    - – server.mjs—This file exports the Sapper middleware function that processes IITTP requests sent to the app. It is called by server.js, which was described earlier.
    - – service-worker.js—This file exports the following constants used by src/service-worker.js, described earlier.
        - files is an array of static files to be cached by the service worker.

- shell is an array of files generated by Sapper to be cached by the service worker.
  - internal directory—This contains the following files:
    - App.svelte—This displays the current page, or an error page if there is an error.
    - error.svelte—This is the default error page component that is used if src/routes/_error.svelte is not found. It displays the status code and an error message. It also displays a stack trace if the NODE_ENV environment variable is set to development.
    - layout.svelte—This is the default layout component that is used if src/routes/_layout.svelte is not found. It only contains a <slot> for rendering the current page component.
    - manifest-client.mjs—This provides data about components and routes (pages). It is used by app.mjs, which was described earlier.
    - manifest-server.mjs—This provides data about server routes (see chapter 17) and pages. It is used by server.mjs, which was described earlier.
    - shared.mjs—This currently doesn't seem to provide anything useful. Perhaps it will have some purpose in the future.

That's it! You now know, at least at a high level, the purpose of each directory and file provided by sveltejs/sapper-template.

16.2 Page routes

Think of a *route* as a path to a page, like the Shopping app pages you saw in chapter 15. Each page in a Sapper app is implemented as a Svelte component defined in the src/routes directory. Route names are derived from the names of the .svelte files and directories found there.

The default Sapper app renders a Nav component at the top of every page. The Nav component renders a page navigation link for each page.

It is important to use anchor elements (<a>) for page navigation instead of alternative elements such as buttons. This is because Sapper page navigation requires changing the URL, and clicking anchor elements does this. Also, as you will see in chapter 18, exporting a Sapper app to generate a static site version relies on crawling the anchor elements that are reachable starting from the first page.

We can modify src/components/Nav.svelte to add or remove page navigation anchor elements.

In the default Sapper app, the Nav component renders each anchor element with code like the following:

```
<li>
  <a aria-current={segment === 'about' ? 'page' : undefined} href="about">
    about
  </a>
</li>
```

The `href` attribute is set to the URL path for the corresponding page. In the case of the home page described by `src/routes/index.svelte`, the `href` attribute can be set to "." or "/". Either works.

Sapper passes a `segment` prop to all layout components. The provided layout defined in `routes/_layout.svelte` passes this on to the `Nav` component. The `segment` prop indicates the current page and can be used to style the anchor element for the current page differently than the others. This is why the anchor element is given the `aria-current` attribute value of `page` if it corresponds to the current page. The default `Nav` component styles the selected nav item with a red underline in the CSS rule for `[aria-current]::after`.

We can define additional pages by creating components in the `src/routes` directory. To add navigation links for new pages, add an anchor element in `src/components/Nav.svelte` for each new page using the same markup as is used for the other anchor elements.

As an example, the path to the page component source file for a route named `dogs` is `src/routes/dogs.svelte` or `src/routes/dogs/index.svelte`. The latter is preferred when a page has associated server routes (see chapter 17). Creating a `dogs` directory provides a common location for these related files.

Nested directories under the `routes` directory create pages with additional URL path parts. For example, the file `src/routes/baseball/cardinals/roster.svelte` defines a page component that is rendered by browsing a URL with the path /baseball/cardinals/roster. This can be useful for grouping related pages.

Files in route directories with names that begin with an underscore are considered helper files and are not interpreted as routes. These typically define and export JavaScript functions that are imported and used by multiple routes.

> **NOTE** A result of these naming conventions is that there can be many source files within an app that have names that are not meaningful on their own (such as `index.svelte` and `_layout.svelte`). Some editors support displaying the directory name along with the filename in the tab of each open file. In VS Code, this is enabled by setting the `workbench.editor.labelFormat` option to a value like `short`.

16.3 *Page layouts*

A page layout is a Svelte component that provides a common layout for a set of pages. For example, a page layout can be used to add a common header, footer, and left nav to each rendered page.

The topmost page layout is defined in `src/routes/_layout.svelte`. This is a special file that Sapper looks for because it defines the layout for all pages.

Layout components can use conditional logic to vary the layout depending on the current app state. For example, suppose the app has a login page that requires a different layout than all the other pages. Typically the login page does not render links to navigate to other pages.

The path to the page being rendered can be determined from a provided store. The package `@sapper/app` provides a `stores` function that returns an object containing three stores named page, `preloading`, and `session`.

The page store holds an object containing `host`, `path`, `query`, and `params` properties. The properties `host` and `path` are strings. The properties `query` and `params` are objects that hold query and path parameters. Pages can use this data to determine what to render.

The `prefetching` store holds a Boolean that indicates whether the component is currently prefetching data. An example is a page that invokes an API service to obtain data to render. Prefetching will be described in more detail in section 16.8.

The `session` store holds session data. It is a writable store that is set to `undefined` by default, meaning there is currently no session data. Placing data here is one way to share data between the pages of an app.

The following layout implementation renders only the page component if the path is "/". This is the case for the login page. For all other paths, it renders a `Nav` component and a `main` element that contains a `section` element that contains the corresponding page component.

Listing 16.1 Topmost page layout in `src/routes/_layout.svelte`

```
<script>
  import {stores} from '@sapper/app';
  import Nav from '../components/Nav.svelte';

  export let segment;              ⟵┐ This prop is
                                     │ automatically passed
  const {page} = stores();          │ to all layouts.
</script>

{#if $page.path === '/'}
  <slot />
{:else}
  <Nav {segment} />
  <main>
    <section>
      <slot />
    </section>
  </main>
{/if}

<style>
  main {
    display: flex;
    justify-content: center;
                                          The CSS variable
    background-color: linen;              --nav-height can
    box-sizing: border-box;               be defined in
    height: calc(100vh - var(--nav-height));  ⟵  static/global.css.
    padding: 2em;
```

```
    width: 100vw;
  }
</style>
```

Page layouts can be nested. The top page layout defined in src/routes/_layout.svelte applies to all pages. Each route subdirectory can define its own _layout.svelte file that specifies the layout of its content within the slot element of its parent layout.

In the sample Sapper app, we can add the following file in src/routes/blog to place the content of each blog entry inside a div with a light blue background (see figure 16.1).

Listing 16.2   Blog layout in `src/routes/blog/_layout.svelte`

```
<div>
  <p>It's blog time!</p>
  <slot />
</div>

<style>
  div {
    background-color: lightblue;
    padding: 0.2rem 1rem;
  }
</style>
```

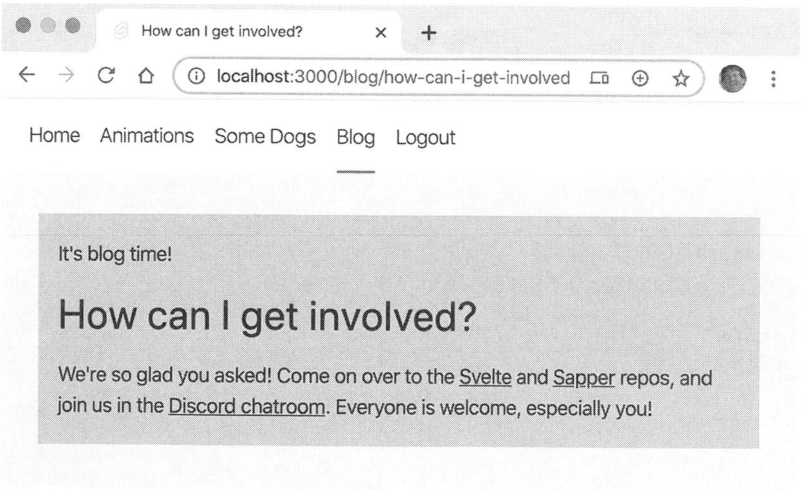

Figure 16.1   Nested layout for blog pages

16.4 Handling errors

When certain kinds of errors occur, the component defined in `src/routes/_error.svelte` is rendered. These errors include page navigation and server-side errors. For example, this component is rendered if there is an attempt to navigate to an undefined route. We can modify this file to customize the error page.

For example, the following error page handles 404 errors differently than other errors. The path to the page where the error occurred can be determined from a provided store.

> **Listing 16.3   Error page in `src/routes/_error.svelte`**

```
<script>
  import {stores} from '@sapper/app';
  const {page, preloading, session} = stores();

  export let status;
  export let error;

  const dev = process.env.NODE_ENV === 'development';
</script>

{#if status === 404}
  There is no page mapped to {$page.path}.
{:else}
  <h1>Error: {error.message}</h1>
  <p>status: {status}</p>
  {#if dev && error.stack}
    <pre>{error.stack}</pre>
  {/if}
{/if}
```

A Sapper app defines a single error page. Unlike page layout components, nested directories under `src/routes` cannot define different error pages that only apply to subsets of the routes.

16.5 Running on both server and client

When the server for a Sapper app is started, the code in the `<script context="module">` element of all routes and all components they import is run. This provides a way to perform any necessary setup tasks, such as establishing WebSocket connections. Often a module context only defines a `preload` function and does not contain any code to be executed immediately.

Sapper apps render the first page visited on the server. The JavaScript code in the `script` element for this page runs twice: once on the server, and once in the browser. The JavaScript code in the `script` element of subsequently rendered pages only runs in the browser.

If the code in the `script` element accesses things that are only available in a browser, such as the `window` object, `sessionStorage`, or `localStorage`, care must be taken to avoid running the code on the server. One way to do this is to place such code in a function that is passed to the onMount, beforeUpdate, or afterUpdate lifecycle functions. These functions are only run in browsers. Another way is to check the value of process.browser, which is true when running in a browser.

16.6   *Fetch API wrapper*

The Fetch API (http://mng.bz/xWqe) defines the global function fetch and interfaces for Body, Headers, Request, and Response objects. The fetch function is commonly used to invoke API services. It is built into browser environments but not Node.js environments.

Recall that the module context is used to define variables and functions that are associated with the module, not with each instance of the component. The module context includes everything defined inside a <script context="module"> element.

In normal script elements, the fetch function provided by browsers can be used to call API services. In <script context="module"> elements, use this.fetch instead of fetch. This is required to ensure the availability of a fetch function when it is invoked on the server, as happens during server-side rendering. An example of using this.fetch is presented in the next section.

16.7   *Preloading*

Pages that require data to be fetched from API services before they can be rendered can do so in a preload function. This must be defined in the module context (<script context="module">) of the page component. The preload function has two parameters, typically named page and session. These values were described earlier in section 16.3.

The preload function can call any number of API services to obtain data. It can also obtain data in other ways, such as GraphQL queries, WebSocket connections, and so on. The preload function should return an object whose property names are the names of props accepted by the page component and whose property values will become the prop values.

Defining a preload function in a component that is not a route has no purpose, because it will never be invoked.

Let's demonstrate this by adding an Employees page to the default Sapper app (see figure 16.2).

Create an employees.svelte file in the routes directory containing the following content.

home   about   employees   blog
──────────

Employees

Name	Age	Salary
Yuri Berry	40	$675,000
Paul Byrd	64	$725,000
Jenette Caldwell	30	$345,000
Herrod Chandler	59	$137,500

Figure 16.2   Employees page

Listing 16.4   Employees page in `src/routes/employees.svelte`

```
<script context="module">
  export async function preload(page, session) {
    try {
      const url = 'http://dummy.restapiexample.com/api/v1/employees';
      const res = await this.fetch(url);
      if (res.ok) {
        const result = await res.json();
        const employees = result.data;

        // Sort the employees on their last name, then first name.
        employees.sort((emp1, emp2) => {
          const [first1, last1] = emp1.employee_name.split(' ');
          const [first2, last2] = emp2.employee_name.split(' ');
          const compare = last1.localeCompare(last2);
          return compare ? compare : first1.localeCompare(first2);
        });

        return {employees};
      } else {
        const msg = await res.text();
        this.error(res.statusCode, 'employees preload error: ' + msg);
      }
    } catch (e) {
      this.error(500, 'employees preload error: ' + e.message);
    }
  }
</script>

<script>
  export let employees;

  const formatter = new Intl.NumberFormat('en-US', {
    style: 'currency',
    currency: 'USD',
    minimumFractionDigits: 0
  });
</script>

<svelte:head>
  <title>Employees</title>
</svelte:head>

<table>
  <caption>Employees</caption>
  <tr>
    <th>Name</th>
    <th>Age</th>
    <th>Salary</th>
  </tr>
  {#each employees as employee}
    <tr>
      <td>{employee.employee_name}</td>
      <td class="right">{employee.employee_age}</td>
```

This is a free, public API service that returns fake employee data.

Note the use of this.fetch instead of fetch.

The API service returns a JSON object with a data property whose value is an array of employee objects.

The object returned provides prop values to the component.

Note the way errors are handled.

This formats a number as US currency and only includes cents when they are not zero.

```
      <td class="right">{formatter.format(employee.employee_salary)}</td>
    <tr>
  {/each}
</table>

<style>
  caption {
    font-size: 2rem;
    font-weight: bold;
  }

  table {
    border-collapse: collapse;
  }

  td, th {
    border: solid lightgray 1px;
    padding: 0.5rem;
  }

  .right {
    text-align: right;
  }
</style>
```

Edit routes/_layout.svelte and remove the CSS properties position, max-width, and margin from the rule for main, so the table is left-aligned on the page.

Edit components/Nav.svelte and add a link for the new Employees page by adding the following after the li element for the About page:

```
<li>
  <a [aria-current]={segment === 'employees' ? 'page' : undefined}
    href="employees">
    employees
  </a>
</li>
```

That's it! We now have a component that calls an API service to get the data it needs before it is rendered.

Note that it is not possible to register the same component for multiple route paths because the route path also specifies the path to the component .svelte file.

Consider how the onMount lifecycle function differs from the preload function. onMount can directly set top-level component variables that represent the state of the component. preload returns an object whose properties are supplied to the component as props. It does not have access to the state variables of the component.

16.8   *Prefetching*

Routes can be configured so the data they require is downloaded when the user simply hovers over their anchor element. This anticipates that the user will click the anchor element and results in faster page loads.

Prefetching is configured by adding the `rel="prefetch"` attribute to the anchor element for a page component. This is under consideration for being added as a standard HTML anchor attribute and value (see http://mng.bz/AAnK).

Prefetching works in conjunction with code splitting. The first time a user hovers over an anchor element that uses prefetch (or taps on it when using a mobile device), the JavaScript required by the page is downloaded and its `preload` function, if any, is called. This occurs before the component is rendered.

Should you opt into prefetching on every page link? It's great for performance! But also consider whether there are any negative consequences to invoking API services for pages that may not actually be visited because the user only hovered over a link and never clicked it. The consequences could include consuming server resources unnecessarily or logging server-side activity that didn't need to occur. It's okay to make a different decision for each page link in the app.

When prefetching is not configured, the `preload` function is called each time the anchor for a route is clicked and it is not the current route.

When prefetching is configured, the `preload` function is called when the user hovers over the anchor for a route. It will not be called again due to a hover unless the user first navigates to another route or hovers over another route that has a `preload` function.

To enable prefetching for the Employees page created in the previous section, edit `components/Nav.svelte` and add `rel="prefetch"` to the anchor element for employees as follows:

> **Listing 16.5 Nav component changes in `src/components/Nav.svelte`**

```
<li>
  <a
    aria-current={segment === 'employees' ? 'page' : ''}
    href="employees"
    rel="prefetch">
    employees
  </a>
</li>
```

To verify that this works as expected, add a `console.log` call inside the `preload` function in `employees.svelte` so you can detect when it is called.

> **Listing 16.6 Employees page changes in `src/routes/employees.svelte`**

```
<script context="module">
  export async function preload(page, session) {
    console.log('employees.svelte preload: entered');
    ...
  }
</script>
```

Now follow these steps:

1 In the browser tab where the app is running, open the DevTools, click the Console tab, and refresh the page.
2 Hover over the Employees link and note that the `preload` function is called.
3 Hover over another link and then back to the Employees link. Note that the `preload` function is not called again.
4 Click another link, such as About.
5 Hover over the Employees link. Note that the `preload` function is called again.

The `rel="prefetch"` attribute cannot be applied to `button` elements. However, anchor elements can be styled to look like buttons, as in the following listing.

Listing 16.7 Nav component style changes in `src/components/Nav.svelte`

```
<style>
  a {
    border: solid gray 1px;
    border-radius: 4px;
    padding: 4px;
    text-decoration: none;
  }
</style>
```

16.9 Code splitting

Svelte produces bundles that are much smaller than those produced by other frameworks. But the initial download size can be decreased even further by code splitting. This removes the need to download all the JavaScript for the app when the first page is rendered. Code splitting provides a significant improvement for apps that are run with slow internet connections or on mobile devices. Sapper provides this automatically.

When a browser first loads a Sapper app, only the JavaScript code necessary to render the first page/route is downloaded. The JavaScript for each remaining route is not downloaded until the page is rendered. This typically happens in response to a user clicking on an anchor element that triggers a route change.

For routes whose anchor element includes `rel="prefetch"`, the download of their JavaScript code begins when the user hovers over their anchor element. In the Sapper starter app, this is specified on anchor elements in `src/components/Nav.svelte`. The Blog route uses prefetching, and we added this to the Employees route in the previous section.

Follow these steps using our app with the Employees route to see code splitting in action:

1 Open the DevTools and click the Network tab.
2 Click the Home link to return to the first page.
3 Refresh the browser tab.

4 Note that three files are downloaded:
   – `client.`*`some-hash`*`.js` contains code corresponding to `src/client.js` that bootstraps the Sapper app. No page-specific code is included in this file.
   – `sapper-dev-client.`*`some-hash`*`.js` is only downloaded when running in development mode. It provides a small amount of additional debugging output.
   – `index.`*`some-hash`*`.js` contains code for the Home page.

5 Click the `index.`*`some-hash`*`.js` file in DevTools to see its contents. Note that it contains "Great success!" from the Home page but does not contain "About this site" from the About page.

6 Click the About link in the web app. Note that a file named `about.`*`some-hash`*`.js` is downloaded.

7 Click this file in DevTools to see its contents. Note that it contains "About this site" from the About page, but it does not contain "Great success!" from the Home page.

8 Hover over the Employees link in the web app. Note that a file named `employees.`*`some-hash`*`.js` is downloaded without you clicking the link, because it uses `rel="prefetch"`.

9 Click the Employees link in the web app. Note that no new file is downloaded because the JavaScript for this page has already been downloaded.

Code splitting is a great feature for improving the performance of web applications, and Sapper provides this automatically.

16.10 *Building the Travel Packing app*

Let's create a Sapper version of the Travel Packing app. It will have two routes, use a page layout, and take advantage of code splitting. The finished code can be found at http://mng.bz/Z2BO.

This code will not use preloading or prefetching because we do not yet use API services in the app. Those features will be added in chapter 17.

First, create the new Sapper application:

1 `cd` to the directory where you want it to reside.
2 Enter `npx degit sveltejs/sapper-template#rollup sapper-travel-packing`.
3 Enter `cd sapper-travel-packing`.
4 Enter `npm install`.
5 Enter `npm install` *`name`* for any packages needed that are not included in `sveltejs/sapper-template`. For the Travel Packing app, this includes `dialog-polyfill` and `uuid`.

Now copy files from the Svelte version of the app to the Sapper version. This is going to seem like a lot of work, but that's only because we need to modify several things to work with Sapper. Starting an app with Sapper is a more natural path.

1 Copy `public/global.css` to `static/global.css`, replacing the provided version.

2 Delete `static/great-success.png` because it will not be used.

3 Delete supplied page component files that will not be used from the `src/routes` directory. These are `index.svelte`, `about.svelte`, and the `blog` directory.

4 Copy components that represent pages from `src` to `src/routes`. These are `Login.svelte` and `Checklist.svelte`.

5 Rename these `.svelte` files to snake-case. For example, the filename `TwoWords.svelte` should be renamed to `two-words.svelte`. This is preferred because these names will appear in page URLs. Also, rename the Home page source file to `index.svelte`. In this case, this means renaming `Login.svelte` to `index.svelte` and `Checklist.svelte` to `checklist.svelte`.

6 Copy components that do not represent pages from `src` to `src/components`. These include `Category.svelte`, `Dialog.svelte`, `Item.svelte`, and `NotFound.svelte`.

7 Copy `.js` files to the same directory in the new project. For this project, copy `util.js` from the `src` directory in the Svelte app to the `src` directory in the Sapper app.

8 Correct the paths of the imports in the `.svelte` files that were copied to `src/routes`. In this case, change the following in `checklist.svelte`:

```
import Category from '../components/Category.svelte';
import Dialog from '../components/Dialog.svelte';
import {getGuid, sortOnName} from '../util';
```
We changed
`.` to `..`

And change the following in `Item.svelte`:

```
import {blurOnKey} from '../util';
```

9 Correct the paths of the imports in the `.svelte` files that were copied to `src/components`. In this case, all the changes are in `Category.svelte`:

```
import {getGuid, sortOnName} from '../util';
```

10 Modify `src/routes/_layout.svelte`:
   - Delete the `script` element and its contents because nothing there is being used.
   - Remove the `Nav` element.
   - Add the following line before the `slot` element:

     ```
     <h1 class="hero">Travel Packing Checklist</h1>
     ```

   - Replace the `style` element and its contents with those found in the Svelte version of `src/App.svelte`.

11 Delete `src/components/Nav.svelte`, since it is not being used.

12 Modify `src/routes/index.svelte` to handle the Login button differently:

- Add an import of the `goto` function.

```
import {goto} from '@sapper/app';
```

- Remove the import of the `createEventDispatcher` function.
- Remove the `dispatch` variable.
- Change the `login` function to the following:

```
const login = () => goto('/checklist');
```

13 Modify `src/routes/checklist.svelte`:

- At the top, add `import {onMount} from 'svelte';`.
- Change the call to `restore()` to `onMount(restore)` so the `restore` function is only called in the browser.
- Remove the import of the `createEventDispatcher` function.
- Remove the `dispatch` variable.
- Add a `let restored = false;` variable declaration inside the `script` element near the other variable declarations.
- Make changes to ensure that code that calls methods on `localStorage` only happens in the browser, because `localStorage` is not defined on the server. Recall that functions passed to lifecycle functions are only executed in the browser. In this case, change the `persist` and `restore` functions to the following:

```
function persist() {
    if (process.browser && restored) {
      localStorage.setItem('travel-packing',
        JSON.stringify(categories));
    }
}

  function restore() {
    const text = localStorage.getItem('travel-packing');
    if (text && text !== '{}') categories = JSON.parse(text);
    restored = true;
  }
```

- Replace the Log Out button with the following:

```
<a class="button logout-btn" href="/">Log Out</a>
```

14 Add the following CSS rule in `static/global.css` to style anchor elements that should look like buttons:

```
.button {
  background-color: white;
  border-radius: 10px;
  color: gray;
```

```
    padding: 1rem;
    text-decoration: none;
}
```

15   Modify `src/components/Dialog.svelte`:

  – Remove `import dialogPolyfill from 'dialog-polyfill'`; because this runs code that accesses the `window` global variable, which is not available when this code is run on the server side.

  – Change the call to `onMount`, which is only run in the browser, to match the following:

This uses an asynchronous import.

```
onMount(async () => {
    const {default: dialogPolyfill} = await import('dialog-polyfill');
    dialogPolyfill.registerDialog(dialog);
});
```

Now run the app by entering `npm run dev`.

Whew, that was a lot of work! But consider what we have gained. Adding new pages will be much easier now, we gained code splitting and preloading, and we introduced a common page layout. Larger apps benefit greatly from the features that Sapper provides.

In the next chapter you will learn how to implement Node-based API services in Sapper apps.

Summary

- Sapper apps have a well-defined file structure.
- Pages within a Sapper app are defined by files and directories under the `src/routes` directory.
- A Sapper app has a top page layout that applies to all pages.
- Nested routes can define their own layout that supplies the `slot` content in their parent layout.
- A Sapper app has a single error page.
- Sapper apps must avoid running certain JavaScript code on the server side, but doing this is easy.
- The Fetch API wrapper supports using the Fetch API in code that is run on the server, such as `preload` functions.
- Preloading allows pages to load data they need before the page is rendered.
- Prefetching downloads the code and data needed by a page before the user navigates to the page.
- Sapper provides code splitting so the code for a page is not downloaded until the user navigates to the page or hovers over its link (when prefetching is enabled).

Sapper server routes

This chapter covers

- Server routes
- Server route source files
- Server route functions
- A create/retrieve/update/delete (CRUD) example
- Switching to Express

Server routes are Node-based API/REST services. Sapper supports implementing these, and it hosts them so the client-side code can send requests to them. It enables collocating server-side code with client-side code in the same project. This is convenient for full-stack developers because it avoids having to maintain multiple source code repositories, one for client-side code and one for server-side code. It also has the benefit of using the same programming language, JavaScript, for all of the code.

> **NOTE** It is possible to host a Svelte app and Node-based API server in the same repository (a monorepo) without using Sapper. However, in that case they would typically be implemented in separate source trees, each with their own package.json file. With Sapper, the frontend and backend code are in the same source tree, and the same HTTP server is used to serve frontend assets and respond to API requests.

Server route source files define functions for server-side code that is part of a Sapper application. This code can perform tasks like managing data persistence using a relational database such as PostgreSQL or a NoSQL database such as MongoDB. For example, an app that manages employee data can use API services to create, retrieve, update, and delete this data.

Using server routes to implement server-side functionality is optional. Sapper apps are not restricted to only invoking services that are implemented using server routes. The services used by a Sapper app can be implemented outside the app, using any programming language and any framework.

We will explore how to implement Sapper server routes, including where to place the source files, how to name them, and what functions to implement in these files.

17.1 *Server route source files*

The source files that define server routes are placed under the `src/routes` directory. As you saw earlier, this is also where the definitions of Svelte components that correspond to pages in the app reside.

API services are defined in source files with a `.js` extension containing JavaScript code. There is a convention to use an extension of `.json.js` to indicate that response bodies contain JSON data.

Each directory below `src/routes` can contain both a page `.svelte` file and a server routes `.js` file. This is useful when a page is the only one that uses the colocated server routes. If a page doesn't use server routes that are only intended for it, its directory can just contain the page `.svelte` file. If particular server routes are not intended for use by a single page, their directory can only contain server route source files. The bottom line is that there is a lot of flexibility in where page and server routes are defined, as long as they are defined under the `src/routes` directory.

Sapper has a convention for naming the source files that define server routes. The example code in this chapter assumes the resources are descriptions of dogs, and the page route that will use the services has the name `dogs`. A particular dog might have the following JSON representation:

```
{
  "id": "5e4984b33c9533dfdf102ac8",
  "breed" : "Whippet",
  "name" : "Dasher"
}
```

Server routes that do not require a path parameter in their URL, such as retrieving all instances of a resource or creating a new resource, are typically defined in `src/routes/dogs/index.json.js`.

Server routes that do require a path parameter in their URL, such as updating or deleting an existing resource, are typically defined in `src/routes/dogs/[id].json.js`. The syntax `[id]` here represents a path parameter, where `id` is a unique identifier for a resource.

Server routes can only have one path parameter per path part. Having more than one path part is useful when the data exists in a hierarchy. For example, if we wanted to segregate dogs based on the families that own them, we might create a server route source file in `src/routes/families/[familyId]/dogs/[dogId].json.js`. Note that the square brackets are actually part of the directory and file names. We could update the dog with an ID of "d7" that is owned by the family with an ID of "f3" by sending a `PUT` request to `/families/f3/dogs/d7`.

17.2 Server route functions

Server route source files define server route functions. These process HTTP requests and are similar to Express (https://expressjs.com/) middleware functions. Typically they examine a request object and call methods on the response object to provide response data.

Express middleware functions

Express middleware functions are used to process HTTP requests. They are run in the order in which they were registered. Each is passed three arguments: a request object, a response object, and a `next` function. These functions typically perform one of the following actions:

- Modify the request object and call `next`, allowing the next middleware function to process the request.
- Call methods on the response object to provide response data.
- Modify the response object and call `next`, allowing the next middleware function to make additional modifications.

Some middleware functions only handle errors, perhaps logging them. Passing an error description to the `next` function triggers the next (or first) error middleware function to run. Passing nothing to the `next` function triggers the next normal (non-error) middleware function to run.

The names of server route functions correspond to HTTP verbs, as you can see in table 17.1.

Table 17.1 CRUD operations

CRUD operation	HTTP verb	Function name
Create	POST	post
Retrieve	GET	get
Update	PUT	put
Delete	DELETE	del

17.3 A create/retrieve/update/delete (CRUD) example

Let's walk through the steps to implement a page that supports CRUD operations on dogs using a MongoDB database. The code to use a relational database such as PostgreSQL would not be dramatically different. It would just involve substituting SQL in place of MongoDB-specific calls. Figure 17.1 shows a screenshot of what we want to create.

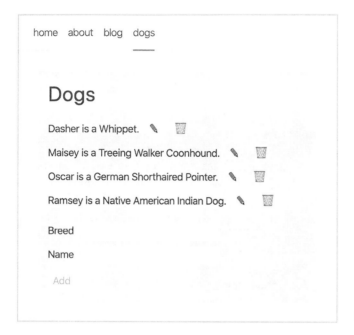

Figure 17.1   Dogs page

With this UI we can

- See all the dogs that are currently in a database.
- Add a new dog to the database by entering a breed and name and clicking the Add button.
- Modify the breed or name of an existing dog in the database by clicking the pencil icon next to one, modifying the values, and clicking the Modify button. The Add button changes to Modify when a pencil icon is clicked.
- Delete an existing dog from the database by clicking the trash can icon next to one.

Start by creating a new Sapper app with the following commands:

```
1  npx degit sveltejs/sapper-template#rollup dog-app
2  cd dog-app
3  npm install
4  npm install body-parser mongodb
```

The `body-parser` library parses HTTP request bodies.

The `mongodb` library lets us communicate with a MongoDB database. See appendix C for details on installing MongoDB, starting the MongoDB server, and interacting with MongoDB databases from both the MongoDB shell and JavaScript.

By default, server routes are managed by Polka (https://github.com/lukeed/polka). Polka is described as "a micro web server so fast, it'll make you dance!" It is an alternative to Express and claims to be 33% to 50% faster. Polka supports a nearly identical API and the same middleware functions. It was created by Luke Edwards, who is also a Sapper contributor.

To enable your code to pass HTTP request bodies, make two changes in `src/server.js`:

1 Add the following `require` call:

```
import {json} from 'body-parser';
```

2 Add the following as the first call chained onto `polka()`:

```
.use(json())
```
← **The use method registers a middleware function.**

Create the directory `src/routes/dogs`. In this directory, create the following files:

- `index.svelte`—This defines the component that renders the page shown in figure 17.1.
- `index.json.js`—This exports middleware functions that get all dogs and create a new dog. These are API services that could be implemented with many frameworks using many programming languages, but you will see how easy it is to define them using Sapper.
- `[id].json.js`—This exports middleware functions that update or delete an existing dog. These are more API services.
- `_helpers.js`—This exports a helper function that returns an object for operating on the `dogs` MongoDB collection.

Listing 17.1 shows the code for the dogs page component. There is a lot of code here, but it should all be understandable, given what you have already learned about Svelte and Sapper.

> **Listing 17.1** dogs page component in `src/routes/dogs/index.svelte`

```
<script context="module">
  export async function preload() {
    try {
      const res = await this.fetch('dogs.json');
      if (res.ok) {
        const dogs = await res.json();
```
← **This function is called before each time this component is rendered in order to get the dog data. Preload functions were described in chapter 16.**

← **This invokes the get middleware function defined in dogs/index.json.js.**

```
      const dogMap = dogs.reduce((acc, dog) => {
        acc[dog._id] = dog;
        return acc;
      }, {});

      return {dogMap};
    } else {
      // Handle errors.
      const msg = await res.text();
      this.error(res.statusCode, 'Dogs preload: ' + msg);
    }
  } catch (e) {
    this.error(500, 'Dogs preload error: ' + e.message);
  }
}
</script>

<script>
  export let dogMap = {};

  let breed = '';
  let breedInput;
  let error = '';
  let id = '';
  let name = '';

  $: saveBtnText = id ? 'Modify' : 'Add';

  $: sortedDogs = Object.values(dogMap).sort((dog1, dog2) =>
    dog1.name.localeCompare(dog2.name)
  );

  function clearState() {
    id = breed = name = '';
    breedInput.focus();
  }

  async function deleteDog(id) {
    try {
      const options = {method: 'DELETE'};
      const res = await fetch(`dogs/${id}.json`, options);
      if (!res.ok) throw new Error('failed to delete dog with id ' + id);
      delete dogMap[id];
      dogMap = dogMap;
      clearState();
    } catch (e) {
      error = e.message;
    }
  }

  function editDog(dog) {
    ({breed, name} = dog);
    id = dog._id;
  }
```

This creates a map of dog IDs to dog objects.

Properties in the object returned here are passed to this component as props, in this case only dogs.

The previous preload function provides this prop.

If we have a dog ID, we can modify the dog. Otherwise we can add a new dog.

This invokes the del middleware function defined in [id].json.js.

This triggers an update to parts of the UI that use dogMap.

```
    async function saveDog() {
      const dog = {breed, name};
      if (id) dog._id = id;

      try {
        const options = {
          method: id ? 'PUT' : 'POST',
          headers: {'Content-Type': 'application/json'},
          body: JSON.stringify(dog)
        };
        const path = id ? `dogs/${id}.json` : 'dogs.json';
        const res = await fetch(path, options);
        const result = await res.json();

        if (!res.ok) throw new Error(result.error);

        dogMap[result._id] = result;
        dogMap = dogMap;

        clearState();
      } catch (e) {
        error = e.message;
      }
    }
  }
</script>

<svelte:head>
  <title>Dogs</title>
</svelte:head>

<section>
  <h1>Dogs</h1>

  {#if error}
    <div class="error">Error: {error}</div>
  {:else}
    {#each sortedDogs as dog}
      <div class="dog-row">
        {dog.name} is a {dog.breed}.
        <button class="icon-btn" on:click={() => editDog(dog)}>
          <!-- pencil icon -->
          &#x270E;
        </button>
        <button class="icon-btn" on:click={() => deleteDog(dog._id)}>
          <!-- trash can icon -->
          &#x1F5D1;
        </button>
      </div>
    {/each}
  {/if}

  <form>
    <div>
      <label>Breed</label>
      <input bind:this={breedInput} bind:value={breed} />
```

◁— **This handles both creating and updating dogs.**

◁— **If id is set, we are updating a dog. Otherwise we are creating a new dog.**

◁— **This invokes either the post middleware function defined in index.json.js or the put middleware function defined in [id].json.js.**

◁— **This triggers an update to parts of the UI that use dogMap.**

```
      </div>
      <div>
        <label>Name</label>
        <input bind:value={name} />
      </div>

      <button disabled={!breed || !name} on:click|preventDefault={saveDog}>     ◁──┐
        {saveBtnText}
      </button>

      {#if id}
        <button on:click|preventDefault={clearState}>Cancel</button>            ◁──┤
      {/if}
    </form>
</section>
```

**Using preventDefault
prevents a form
submission.**

```
<style>
  button {
    border: none;
    font-size: 1rem;
    padding: 0.5rem;
  }

  .dog-row {
    display: flex;
    align-items: center;
  }

  form {
    margin-top: 1rem;
  }

  form > div {
    margin-bottom: 0.5rem;
  }

  .icon-btn {
    background-color: transparent;
    font-size: 18px;
    margin-left: 0.5rem;
  }

  .icon-btn:hover {
    background-color: lightgreen;
  }

  input {
    border: none;
    padding: 0.5rem;
    width: 200px;
  }

  label {
    margin-right: 0.5rem;
  }
```

```
    section {
      background-color: linen;
      padding: 1rem;
    }
</style>
```

Now we are ready to turn our attention to the server-side code for this application.

The following listing shows the code for a helper function that is used by functions in other source files to obtain the MongoDB dogs collection.

Listing 17.2   MongoDB helper function in `src/routes/dogs/_helpers.js`

MongoDB thinks localhost is a different database instance than 127.0.0.1. The mongo shell uses 127.0.0.1, so we use that to hit the same instance.

These are recommended MongoDB options to avoid deprecation warnings.

```
const {MongoClient} = require('mongodb');

const url = 'mongodb://127.0.0.1:27017';       ◁
const options = {useNewUrlParser: true, useUnifiedTopology: true};   ◁
let collection;                                ◁

export async function getCollection() {
  if (!collection) {
    const client = await MongoClient.connect(url, options);
    const db = client.db('animals');           ◁
    collection = await db.collection('dogs');  ◁
  }

  return collection;
}
```

This holds the dogs collection, so we only retrieve it once per session.

This gets the "dogs" collection from the "animals" database.

This gets access to the "animals" MongoDB database. There is no need to call the close method on db (see http://mng.bz/qMqw).

The following listing shows the code that implements the server routes for GET and POST requests. These server routes do not require any path parameters. The functions exported here must have the names get and post.

Listing 17.3   GET and POST server routes in `src/routes/dogs/index.json.js`

```
import {getCollection} from './_helpers';

export async function get(req, res) {
  try {
    const collection = await getCollection();
    const result = await collection.find().toArray();   ◁
    res.end(JSON.stringify(result));         ◁
  } catch (e) {
    console.error('index.json.js get:', e);
    res.status(500).json({error: e.message});
  }
}

export async function post(req, res) {
  const dog = req.body;
```

This gets all the documents (objects) in the dogs MongoDB collection.

This returns an array of dog objects as JSON.

```
    try {
      const collection = await getCollection();
      const result = await collection.insertOne(dog);
      const [obj] = result.ops;
      res.end(JSON.stringify(obj));
    } catch (e) {
      console.error('index.json.js post:', e);
      res.status(500).json({error: e.message});
    }
}
```

This adds a dog to the dogs MongoDB collection.

This gets the inserted document, which contains all the dog data plus its assigned unique ID.

This returns the dog object to the client as JSON, primarily so it has access to its ID.

The next listing shows the code that implements the server routes for DELETE and PUT requests. These server routes require one path parameter named id. The functions exported here must have the names del and put.

Listing 17.4   DELETE and PUT server routes in `src/routes/dogs/[id].json.js`

```
const {ObjectId} = require('mongodb');
import {getCollection} from './_helpers';

export async function del(req, res) {
  const {id} = req.params;
  try {
    const collection = await getCollection();
    const result = await collection.deleteOne({_id: ObjectId(id)});
    if (result.deletedCount === 0) {
      res.status(404).send(`no dog with id ${id} found`);
    } else {
      res.end();
    }
  } catch (e) {
    console.error('[id].json.js del:', e);
    res.status(500).json({error: e.message});
  }
}

export async function put(req, res) {
  const {id} = req.params;
  const replacement = req.body;

  delete replacement._id;

  try {
    const collection = await getCollection();
    const result = await collection.replaceOne(
      {_id: ObjectId(id)},
      replacement
    );
    const [obj] = result.ops;
    obj._id = id;
    res.end(JSON.stringify(obj));
```

This function is used to create objects that represent document IDs.

This gets the ID of the dog to delete from a path parameter.

This attempts to delete the document with a given ID from the dogs collection.

This gets the ID of the dog to update from a path parameter.

The object passed to the MongoDB replaceOne method cannot have an _id property, so we remove it.

This updates a document in the dogs collection identified by its unique ID.

This restores the _id property in the object that will be returned as JSON.

```
  } catch (e) {
    console.error('[id].json.js put:', e);
    res.status(500).json({error: e.message});
  }
}
```

Now we that we have implemented all the necessary server-side functionality, we are ready to add our `dogs` route to the navigation bar. Add a navigation link for this route by adding the following in the provided `Nav` component.

Listing 17.5 Change to `Nav` component in `src/components/Nav.svelte`

```
<li>
  <a
    rel="prefetch"
    aria-current={segment === 'dogs' ? 'page' : undefined}
    href="dogs"
  >
    dogs
  </a>
</li>
```

The impact of `rel="prefetch"` was described in chapter 16. It causes the `preload` function in `src/routes/index.svelte` to be called as soon as the user hovers over the link for that page in the nav bar. Hovering also triggers downloading the JavaScript required for the Dogs page. Recall that you can see this happening by opening the browser's DevTools and clicking on the Network tab before hovering over the Dogs link.

To run the app, enter `npm run dev` and browse to localhost:3000.

That's it! We have implemented a new route that supports all the CRUD operations on dogs. Copy this pattern to implement similar functionality for other kinds of data.

17.4 *Switching to Express*

Sapper applications can easily be modified so that server routes are managed by another Node.js server library such as Express. Here are the steps to switch a Sapper app from using Polka to using Express:

1 Enter `npm uninstall polka`.
2 Enter `npm install express`.
3 Edit `src/server.js`.
    – Remove `import polka from 'polka';`.
    – Add `import express from 'express';`.

By default, Sapper uses Sirv to serve static files.

Assuming the preceding changes have been made, here are the additional steps to use Express for serving static files:

1 Enter `npm uninstall sirv`.
2 Edit `src/server.js`.
   - Remove `import sirv from 'sirv';`.
   - Replace `sirv('static', {dev})`, with `express.static('static')`,.
3 Restart the server.

17.5   Building the Travel Packing app

Let's modify the Sapper Travel Packing app created in chapter 16 to use server routes. It will persist the travel-packing checklist in a MongoDB database. The finished code can be found at http://mng.bz/7XN9.

The MongoDB database will be named "travel-packing". It will contain a single collection named `categories`. Each document in this collection will represent a category and all of its items.

Enter the following command to install a few npm packages that perform HTTP request-body parsing, enable the use of MongoDB, and provide an easier way to send HTTP responses:

```
npm install body-parser mongodb @polka/send-type
```

Make the following changes in `src/server.js` for parsing HTTP request bodies:

1 Add the following import:

```
const {json} = require('body-parser');
```

2 Add the following as the first call after `polka()`:

```
.use(json())
```

Here is a summary of the API services we need to implement:

1 *Create a category*—This is currently implemented in the `addCategory` function of `routes/checklist.svelte`. We will implement this as a POST to `/categories` by defining and exporting a `post` function in `src/routes/categories/index.json.js`.
2 *Retrieve all categories*—This is currently implemented in the `restore` function of `routes/checklist.svelte`. We will implement this as a GET to `/categories` by defining and exporting a `get` function in `src/routes/categories/index.json.js`.
3 *Delete a category*—This is currently implemented in the `deleteCategory` function of `routes/checklist.svelte`. We will implement this as a DELETE to

/categories/{category-id} by defining and exporting a del function in src/routes/categories/[categoryId]/index.json.js. Note that [categoryId] is the actual name of a directory, including the square brackets.

4 *Update a category name*—This is currently implemented in the persist function of routes/checklist.svelte, which is called if any data in the categories object changes. We will implement this as a PUT to /categories/{category-id} by defining and exporting a put function in src/routes/categories/[categoryId]/index.json.js.

5 *Create an item in a category*—This is currently implemented in the addItem function of components/Category.svelte. We will implement this as a POST to /categories/{category-id}/items by defining and exporting a post function in src/routes/categories/[categoryId]/items/index.json.js.

6 *Delete an item from a category*—This is currently implemented in the deleteItem function of components/Category.svelte. We will implement this as a DELETE to /categories/{category-id}/items/{item-id} by defining and exporting a del function in src/routes/categories/[categoryId]/items/[itemId].json.js.

7 *Update an item name or packed status*—This is currently implemented in the persist function of routes/checklist.svelte, which is called if any data in the categories object changes. We will implement this as a PUT to /categories/{category-id}/items/{item-id} by defining and exporting a put function in src/routes/categories/[categoryId]/items/[itemId].json.js.

Note that we do not need an API service to retrieve all the items in a given category because those are included when a category is retrieved.

The directory structure for the files that implement these API services looks like this:

- src directory
  - routes directory
  - categories directory
  - index.json.js—get and post category
  - [categoryId] directory
  - index.json.js—put and del category
  - items directory
  - index.json.js—post item
  - [itemId].json.js—put and del item

Here are the steps to implement these API services:

1 Create the categories directory under src/routes.

2 Create the following src/routes/categories/_helpers.js file that defines a function for getting the checklist collection from the "travel-packing" MongoDB database. This is nearly identical to the file src/routes/dogs/_helper.js shown in listing 17.2. See the annotations in that code.

```
const {MongoClient} = require('mongodb');

const url = 'mongodb://127.0.0.1:27017';
const options = {useNewUrlParser: true, useUnifiedTopology: true};
let collection;

export async function getCollection() {
  if (!collection) {
    const client = await MongoClient.connect(url, options);
    const db = client.db('travel-packing');
    collection = await db.collection('categories');
  }
  return collection;
}
```

3 Implement the API services to retrieve and create categories in `src/routes/`
`categories/index.json.js`:

```
const send = require('@polka/send-type');        ◄———  Using this send function
import {getCollection} from './_helpers';               simplifies returning HTTP
                                                        responses.

export async function get(req, res) {          ◄——————
  try {                                                    This gets all the
    const collection = await getCollection();              categories from
    const result = await collection.find().toArray();      the database.
    res.end(JSON.stringify(result));
  } catch (e) {
    console.error('categories/index.json.js get:', e);
    send(res, 500, {error: e});
  }
}
                                               This adds a category
                                               to the database.
export async function post(req, res) {   ◄————
  const category = req.body;
  try {
    const collection = await getCollection();
    const result = await collection.insertOne(category);
    const [obj] = result.ops;
    res.end(JSON.stringify(obj));
  } catch (e) {
    console.error('categories/index.json.js post:', e);
    send(res, 500, {error: e});
  }
}
```

The object added
to the database
is returned so
the client can get
its assigned _id
value.

4 Implement the API services to delete and update categories in `src/routes/`
`categories/[categoryId]/index.json.js`:

```
const send = require('@polka/send-type');          This function is used
const {ObjectId} = require('mongodb');       ◄——   to create objects that
import {getCollection} from '../_helpers';         represent document IDs.

export async function del(req, res) {   ◄——   This deletes a category
  const {categoryId} = req.params;            from the database.
```

```
    try {
      const collection = await getCollection();
      const result =
        await collection.deleteOne({_id: ObjectId(categoryId)});
      if (result.deletedCount === 0) {
        send(res, 404, `no category with id ${categoryId} found`);
      } else {
        res.end();
      }
    } catch (e) {
      console.error(
        'categories/[categoryId]/index.json.js del:',
        e
      );
      send(res, 500, {error: e});
    }
}

export async function put(req, res) {          ⟵  **This updates a category**
  const {categoryId} = req.params;                 **in the database.**
  const replacement = req.body;

  delete replacement._id;          ⟵  **The object passed to the**
                                       **MongoDB replaceOne method**
                                       **cannot have an _id property.**
  try {
    const collection = await getCollection();
    const result = await collection.replaceOne(
      {_id: ObjectId(categoryId)},
      replacement
    );
    const [obj] = result.ops;          **This restores the value**
    obj._id = categoryId;         ⟵    **of the _id property.**
    res.end(JSON.stringify(obj));
  } catch (e) {
    console.error(
      'categories/[categoryId]/index.json.js put:',
      e
    );
    send(res, 500, {error: e});
  }
}
```

5 Implement the API service to create items in a category in `src/routes/` `categories/[categoryId]/items/index.json.js`:

```
const {ObjectId} = require('mongodb');
const send = require('@polka/send-type');
import {getCollection} from '../../_helpers';

export async function post(req, res) {          ⟵  **This adds an item to a**
  const {categoryId} = req.params;                 **category in the database.**
  const item = req.body;
  try {
    const collection = await getCollection();
    const itemPath = `items.${item.id}`;
```

```
      await collection.updateOne(
        {_id: ObjectId(categoryId)},
        {$set: {[itemPath]: item}}
      );
      res.end();
    } catch (e) {
      console.error(
        'categories/[categoryId]/items/index.json.js post:',
        e
      );
      send(res, 500, {error: e});
    }
  }
}
```

6 Implement the API services to delete and update items in a category in
   src/routes/categories/[categoryId]/items/[itemId].json.js:

```
const {ObjectId} = require('mongodb');
const send = require('@polka/send-type');
import {getCollection} from '../../_helpers';

export async function del(req, res) {          ⟵┐  This deletes an item
  const {categoryId, itemId} = req.params;         │  from a category in
  try {                                            │  the database.
    const collection = await getCollection();
    const itemPath = `items.${itemId}`;
    const result = await collection.updateOne(
      {_id: ObjectId(categoryId)},
      {$unset: {[itemPath]: ''}}
    );
    if (result.deletedCount === 0) {
      res
        .status(404)
        .send(
          `no item with id ${itemId} found ` +
          `in category with id ${categoryId}`
        );
    } else {
      res.end();
    }
  } catch (e) {
    console.error(
      'categories/[categoryId]/items/[itemId].json.js del:',
      e
    );
    send(res, 500, {error: e});
  }
}

export async function put(req, res) {          ⟵┐  This updates an item
  const {categoryId} = req.params;                 │  in a category in the
  const item = req.body;                           │  database.

  try {
    const collection = await getCollection();
```

```
      const itemPath = `items.${item.id}`;
      await collection.updateOne(
        {_id: ObjectId(categoryId)},
        {$set: {[itemPath]: item}}
      );
      res.end();
    } catch (e) {
      console.error(
        'categories/[categoryId]/items/[itemId].json.js put:',
        e
      );
      send(res, 500, {error: e});
    }
  }
}
```

Here are the steps to use these API services in the client-side code of the Sapper app:

1 *Update the* id *property of category objects.* The objects returned from the MongoDB database that represent categories contain an _id property that holds their unique ID. The current client-side code expects category objects to have an id property. Change all these references to _id.

2 *Modify* src/routes/checklist.svelte. Many changes to this file are required. Calls to the API services implemented above can be found in the preload, drop, deleteCategory, and saveCategory functions. Check out checklist.svelte (http://mng.bz/mBqr) for details.

3 *Modify* src/components/Category.svelte. Many changes to this file are required. Calls to the API services implemented above can be found in the deleteItem and saveItem functions. Check out Category.svelte (http://mng.bz/5a8B) for details.

4 *Modify* src/components/Item.svelte. Minor event handling changes to dispatch a persist event are needed. Check out Item.svelte (http://mng.bz/6QEo) for details.

To try all these changes, follow these steps:

1 Start the MongoDB server.
2 Start the server from a terminal by entering npm run dev.
3 Add a few categories.
4 Change a category name by clicking it, modifying the name, and pressing Enter.
5 Delete a category by clicking its trash can icon.
6 Add a few items to a category.
7 Change the name of an item by clicking it, modifying the name, and pressing Enter.
8 Delete an item by clicking its trash can icon.
9 Drag an item from one category to another.
10 Refresh the browser to see that all the categories and items are retained.

With these changes in place, we have transformed the Travel Packing app into one that no longer just saves data in browser `localStorage`, which is tied to a single web browser. It now saves the data in a MongoDB database.

As an exercise, you can modify the app to store the data separately for each user. Currently there is one travel packing checklist that would be shared by all users.

In the next chapter you will learn how to create a static site from a Sapper application.

Summary

- Server routes are Node-based API/REST services that enable collocating server-side code with client-side code in the same Sapper project.
- Server route source files are placed under the `src/routes` directory along with the `.svelte` files that define page components. They follow a special naming convention.
- Server route functions are like Express middleware functions. They handle HTTP requests.
- Server routes can implement all the common CRUD operations.
- It is easy to switch from using the Polka server library to using Express, though there is not a strong reason to do so.

Exporting static sites with Sapper

This chapter covers

- Exporting Sapper apps to generate static sites
- When to export apps
- An example exported app

Exporting can be desirable for apps where it is possible to generate the HTML for every page at build time.

A common example is a blog site, where users can navigate to specific posts. Authors periodically add blog posts, and the new posts only become available when the site is regenerated. Site generation can be automated so it occurs on a regular basis, such as every night. The site can also be automatically regenerated every time there is a push to its source repository.

Static sites have excellent runtime performance. One reason is that the HTML for each page only has to be downloaded, not generated in the browser or on the server. Another reason is that typically far less JavaScript code is downloaded. In some cases no JavaScript is required, such as for sites that do not require user interaction other than page navigation.

Static sites are also more secure because most or all API interactions occur during site generation, not when users interact with the site. This means there is little to no chance that server hacking can affect the content of the site.

Exporting a Sapper app is somewhat similar to the functionality provided by Gatsby (www.gatsbyjs.org/) for React. In this chapter, we will dive deep into the details of exporting and use it in an example app.

The Travel Packing app is not a candidate for creating a static site because it uses server routes to query and update a MongoDB database. Server routes are not available for use at runtime in exported Sapper apps. Instead we will build a site that does two things: it provides information about the rock-paper-scissors game, and it provides information about selected dog breeds.

18.1   Sapper details

Sapper apps that are not exported only provide server-side rendering for the first page that is visited. All other pages are rendered in the browser.

Exporting a Sapper app generates the HTML for every page at build time. No pages are rendered on the server or in the browser. Sapper does this by recursively crawling the pages of an app starting at the first page, looking for anchor elements (`<a>`), and prerendering every reachable page. This static version of the app can be deployed using any static hosting solution. No Node-based server is required because no JavaScript that is part of the Sapper app is processed on the server.

When a Sapper app is exported, the `preload` functions defined in reachable pages are invoked. If these functions call API services that are implemented outside of the Sapper app (in other words, not implemented by a Sapper server route), the servers that support them must be running.

The `preload` functions are only called during the export, not when users visit the site. The data retrieved in these functions is typically used to render the component defined in the same `.svelte` file. This data will be from a snapshot in time, which is the time that the site was last exported. The responses are written to `.json` files, and when the static site is browsed, these `.json` files are used in place of the API calls. For some types of apps, this is an acceptable limitation, but exporting is certainly not appropriate for all apps.

API calls made outside of `preload` functions can still be made at runtime. However, server routes are not available at runtime in exported apps, so API services that need to be called at runtime cannot be implemented as server routes.

To build a static site from a Sapper app, enter `npm run export`. This generates files in the `__sapper__/build` and `__sapper__/export` directories.

18.2   When to export

Before deciding to export a Sapper app, some questions should be considered.

First, is it possible to determine and generate all the pages required by the site at build time? This is related to requirements on data being up to date. For example, if the site provides a catalog of items for sale, is it acceptable to only show the items that were available at the time the site was last generated? If not, using a normal, unexported Sapper app is better, because it can generate pages when users visit the site.

Second, how long does it take to generate a new version of the site? The need to present up-to-date data might lead to automating site builds, perhaps nightly. But if the data needs to be more current, say within the last hour, you could automatically generate a new site every hour. Whether this is reasonable depends on how long it takes to generate the site. Returning to our catalog example, if there are thousands of items available and we need to generate a separate page for each item, the site generation time and cost of computing resources might make this an unreasonable approach. Using an unexported Sapper app may be a better option.

18.3   *Example app*

Let's walk through an example of building a static site starting with the Sapper app template. The finished code for this app and all the images it uses can be found at http://mng.bz/oPqd.

It's best to build and test the app as a dynamic site (non-static) before exporting it. This provides live reload after changes, which provides great feedback.

First, create a new Sapper app using the provided template:

1 Enter `npx degit "sveltejs/sapper-template#rollup" my-static-site`.
2 Enter `cd my-static-site`.
3 Enter `npm install`.
4 To test the app as a dynamic site, enter `npm run dev`.
5 Browse to http://localhost:3000.
6 Verify that the app works by clicking each of the navigation links at the top and verifying that the pages render correctly.
7 Stop the server by pressing Ctrl-C.
8 To test the app as a static site, enter `npm run export`.
9 Enter `npx serve __sapper__/export`, as suggested in the output from the previous command.
10 Browse to http://localhost:5000.
11 Verify that the app still works by again clicking each of the navigation links at the top and verifying that the pages render correctly.
12 Stop the server by pressing Ctrl-C.

During the development of a static site, it will be necessary to run the export and serve commands many times. To simplify this, install a couple of npm packages by entering `npm install -D npm-run-all serve`. Then add the following npm scripts in `package.json`:

```
"serve": "serve __sapper__/export",
"static": "npm-run-all export serve",
```

Now both the export and serve scripts can be run by entering the single command npm run static. Browse to http://localhost:5000 to see the result.

Next, let's replace the contents of the home page:

1 Enter npm run dev to start the server so the app can be run as a dynamic site.

2 Browse to http://localhost:3000.

3 Edit src/routes/index.svelte and replace its contents with the following:

```
<svelte:head>
  <title>Home</title>
</svelte:head>

<h1>Purpose</h1>

<p>
  This is a Sapper app that can be used
  to demonstrate exporting a static site.
</p>
```

4 Since we are no longer using the default image, delete the file static/great-success.png.

5 Edit src/routes/_layout.svelte:
   – Delete the max-width and margin CSS properties from the CSS rule for main elements. This will allow page content to be left-aligned.

6 Verify that the Home page shown in figure 18.1 is rendered in the browser.

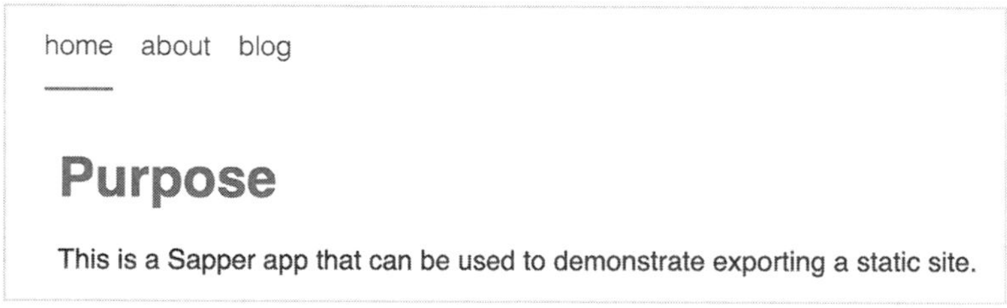

home   about   blog
_____

Purpose

This is a Sapper app that can be used to demonstrate exporting a static site.

Figure 18.1   Home page

Now let's replace the About page with a new RPS page (for "Rock, Paper, Scissors").

1 Create the following files. Note the use of anchor elements to link to other pages. First, create src/routes/rps.svelte:

```
<svelte:head>
  <title>Rock Paper Scissors</title>
</svelte:head>

<h1>Rock Paper Scissors</h1>
<p>This is a game for two players.</p>
<p>Meet <a href="./rock">rock!</a></p>
```

Next, create `src/routes/rock.svelte`:

```
<svelte:head>
  <title>Rock</title>
</svelte:head>

<h1>Rock</h1>
<img alt="rock" src="./images/rock.jpg" />
<p>I beat <a href="./scissors">scissors</a>.</p>
```

Next, create `src/routes/paper.svelte`:

```
<svelte:head>
  <title>Paper</title>
</svelte:head>

<h1>Paper</h1>
<img alt="paper" src="./images/paper.jpg" />
<p>I beat <a href="./rock">rock</a>.</p>
```

And next, create `src/routes/scissors.svelte`:

```
<svelte:head>
  <title>Scissor</title>
</svelte:head>

<h1>Scissors</h1>
<img alt="scissors" src="./images/scissors.jpg" />
<p>I beat <a href="./paper">paper</a>.</p>
```

2 Edit `src/components/Nav.svelte` and change the second `li` to match the following:

```
<li>
  <a
    aria-current={segment === "rps" ? 'page' : undefined}
    href='rps'
  >
    RPS
  </a>
</li>
```

3 Capitalize the text for the Home link so it is "Home", just to be consistent with the "RPS" and "Dogs" links (created later).

4 Add images like those in figures 18.2, 18.3, and 18.4 in the `static/images` directory.

Figure 18.2 `static/images/rock.jpg`

Figure 18.3 `static/images/paper.jpg`

Figure 18.4 `static/images/scissors.jpg`

5   Delete the file `src/routes/about.svelte`, since it is no longer being used.

6   In the browser, click the RPS navigation link and verify that the RPS page shown in figure 18.5 is rendered.

Home   RPS   blog

Rock Paper Scissors

This is a game for two players.

Meet rock!

Figure 18.5   RPS page

7   Click the Rock link and verify that the Rock page shown in figure 18.6 is rendered.

8   Click the Scissors link and verify that the Scissors page shown in figure 18.7 is rendered.

9   Click the Paper link and verify that the Paper page shown in figure 18.8 is rendered.

10   Click the Rock link and verify that the Rock page is again rendered.

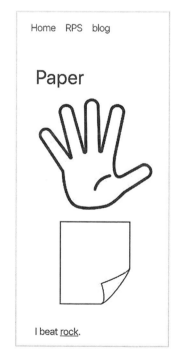

Figure 18.6   Rock page   **Figure 18.7   Scissors page**   **Figure 18.8   Paper page**

Finally, let's replace the Blog page with a new Dogs page.

1 Configure Rollup to enable importing JSON files:
   – Enter `npm install -D @rollup/plugin-json`.
   – Edit `rollup.config.js`:
   – Add `import json from '@rollup/plugin-json';` after the existing imports.
   – Add `json()` after `commonjs()` in the plugins array for both the `client` and server objects. Be sure to add commas where needed after elements in the plugins arrays.
2 Create a dogs directory under `src/routes`.
3 Create the following files in the dogs directory.

First, create `src/routes/dogs/dogs.json`:

```
{
  "Dasher": {                    ⟵┐  Feel free to substitute
    "name": "Dasher",             │  dogs you know.
    "gender": "male",
    "breed": "Whippet",
    "imageUrl": "./images/whippet.jpg",
    "description": "The sleek, sweet-faced Whippet, ..."
  },
  "Maisey": {
    "name": "Maisey",
    "gender": "female",
    "breed": "Treeing Walker Coonhound",
    "imageUrl": "./images/treeing-walker-coonhound.jpg",
    "description": "A smart, brave, and sensible hunter, ..."
  },
  "Ramsay": {
    "name": "Ramsay",
    "gender": "male",
    "breed": "Native American Indian Dog (NAID)",
    "imageUrl": "./images/native-american-indian-dog.jpg",
    "description": "The NAID is one of friendliest dog breeds. ..."
  },
  "Oscar": {
    "name": "Oscar ",
    "gender": "male",
    "breed": "German Shorthaired Pointer (GSP)",
    "imageUrl": "./images/german-shorthaired-pointer.jpg",
    "description": "Male German Shorthaired Pointers stand between ..."
  }
}
```

The next file, `src/routes/dogs/index.json.js`, implements an API service that retrieves a sorted array of dog names:

This gets the dog names from dogs.json and sorts them.

```
import dogs from './dogs.json';
const names = Object.values(dogs).map(dog => dog.name).sort();  ⟵
```

```
export function get(req, res) {
  res.end(JSON.stringify(names));
}
```

⟵ This implements the **GET /dogs** API service. Alternatively, we could implement this to get the dog names from a database.

The next file, `src/routes/dogs/[name].json.js`, implements an API service that retrieves an object that describes the dog with a given name:

```
import dogs from './dogs.json';

export function get(req, res, next) {
  const {name} = req.params;
  const dog = dogs[name];

  if (dog) {
    res.end(JSON.stringify(dog));
  } else {
    const error = {message: `${name} not found`};
    res.statusCode = 404;
    res.end(JSON.stringify(error));
  }
}
```

⟵ This implements the **GET /dogs/{name}** API service. Alternatively, we could implement this to get the dog data from a database.

The next file, `src/routes/dogs/index.svelte`, implements the Dogs page, which renders an anchor for each dog, styled to look like a button. Clicking a button navigates to the page for that dog.

```
<script context="module">
  export async function preload(page, session) {
    try {
      const res = await this.fetch('dogs.json');
      if (res.ok) {
        const names = await res.json();
        return {names};
      } else {
        const msg = await res.text();
        this.error(res.statusCode, 'error getting dog names: ' + msg);
      }
    } catch (e) {
      this.error(500, 'getDogs error:', e);
    }
  }
</script>

<script>
  // The preload function above makes this available as a prop.
  export let names;
</script>

<svelte:head>
  <title>Dogs</title>
</svelte:head>

<h1>Dogs</h1>
```

⟵ This retrieves an array of dog names by invoking an API service.

⟵ This supplies the value of the names prop used in the #each block.

```
{#each names as name}
  <div>
    <a rel="prefetch" href="dogs/{name}">{name}</a>
  </div>
{/each}
<div>
  <a rel="prefetch" href="dogs/Spot">Spot</a>
</div>

<style>
  div {
    --padding: 0.5rem;
    box-sizing: border-box;
    height: calc(22px + var(--padding) * 2);
    margin-top: var(--padding);
  }

  div > a {
    border: solid lightgray 2px;
    border-radius: var(--padding);
    padding: var(--padding);
    text-decoration: none;
  }
</style>
```

This is only here to demonstrate what happens when there is a link to a non-existent page.

The next file, src/routes/dogs/[name].svelte, implements the page that renders data for a specific dog.

```
<script context="module">
  export async function preload({params}) {
    const {name} = params;
    const res = await this.fetch(`dogs/${name}.json`);
    if (res.ok) {
      const data = await res.json();
      if (res.status === 200) {
        return {dog: data};
      } else {
        this.error(res.status, data.message);
      }
    } else {
      const {message} = await res.json();
      const status = message && message.endsWith('not found') ? 404 : 500;
      this.error(status, 'error getting dog data: ' + message);
    }
  }
</script>
```

This retrieves an object describing a dog with a given name by invoking an API.

This supplies the value of the dog prop used in the HTML of this component.

```
<script>
  import {goto} from '@sapper/app';

  export let dog;

  function back() {
    goto('/dogs');
  }
</script>
```

The goto function navigates to a page at a given path.

```
<svelte:head>
  <title>{dog.name}</title>
</svelte:head>

{#if dog.message}
  <h1>{dog.message}</h1>
  <button on:click={back}>Back</button>
{:else}
  <h1>{dog.name} - {dog.breed}</h1>
  <div class="container">
    <div class="left">
      <p>{dog.description}</p>
      <button on:click={back}>Back</button>
    </div>
    <img alt="dog" src={dog.imageUrl} />
  </div>
{/if}

<style>
  .container {
    display: flex;
  }

  img {
    height: 400px;
    margin-left: 1rem;
  }

  p {
    max-width: 300px;
  }
</style>
```

> The dog object has a message property when there is an error retrieving data for a given dog name, as is the case with "Spot".

4   Edit `src/components/Nav.svelte` and change the third `li` element to match the following:

```
<li>
  <a
    aria-current={segment === 'dogs' ? 'page' : undefined}
    href='dogs'
  >
    Dogs
  </a>
</li>
```

5   Delete the `src/routes/blog` directory, since it is no longer being used.

6   Add images for each of the dogs in the `static/images` directory. The `dogs.json` file defined earlier in this section specifies that we need the following files:

   – `german-shorthaired-pointer.jpg`
   – `native-american-indian-dog.jpg`
   – `treeing-walker-coonhound.jpg`
   – `whippet.jpg`

The Dogs page should now be operational. Click the Dogs navigation link and verify that the page in figure 18.9 is rendered.

Figure 18.9   Dogs page

Click each dog name button and verify that the pages shown in figures 18.10 through 18.14 are rendered. After each of these pages is rendered, click the Back button to return to the Dogs page.

Figure 18.10   Dasher page

Home   RPS   Dogs

Maisey - Treeing Walker Coonhound

A smart, brave, and sensible hunter, the Treeing Walker Coonhound is a genuine American favorite, nicknamed "The People's Choice." Don't let the name fool you. Walkers are runners and are capable of covering a lot of ground in a hurry.

Back

Figure 18.11   Maisey page

Home   RPS   Dogs

Oscar Wilde - German Shorthaired Pointer (GSP)

Male German Shorthaired Pointers stand between 23 and 25 inches at the shoulder and weigh anywhere from 55 to 70 pounds; females run smaller. The coat is solid liver (a reddish brown), or liver and white in distinctive patterns. The dark eyes shine with enthusiasm and friendliness. Built to work long days in the field or at the lake, GSPs are known for power, speed, agility, and endurance. "Noble" and "aristocratic" are words often used to describe the overall look. GSPs make happy, trainable pets who bond firmly to their family. They are always up for physical activities like running, swimming, organized dog sports - in fact, anything that will burn some of their boundless energy while spending outdoors time with a human buddy.

Back

Figure 18.12   Oscar page

Figure 18.13   Ramsay page

Figure 18.14   Spot page

Now that all the pages in the app are working when run as a dynamic (non-static) app, we are ready to export the app, creating a static version.

1 Enter `npm run static`. This will export the site, creating many files under the `__sapper__/export` directory. It will also start a local HTTP server for testing the site.

2 Browse to http://localhost:5000.

3 Verify that the Home, RPS, and Dogs pages all work as before.

NOTE   Exporting a Sapper app does not currently perform any image optimization. This is a desired feature that may be added in the future. At the time of writing, it is being discussed in the issue at https://github.com/sveltejs/sapper/issues/172.

In the next chapter you will learn how to make Sapper apps usable, at least in a limited sense, when offline.

Summary

- Sapper apps can be "exported" to generate a static site.
- This is done by crawling all the anchor (`<a>`) elements, starting from the first page.
- API calls in `preload` functions can retrieve data that is used to generate the pages.
- Static sites can be periodically regenerated to include updated data.

ER 961 9062

Sapper offline support

19

This chapter covers

- Progressive web applications (PWAs)
- Service worker overview
- Caching strategies used by service workers
- Sapper service worker configuration
- Service worker events
- Managing service workers in Chrome
- Enabling the use of HTTPS in the Sapper server
- Verifying offline behavior

Progressive web applications (PWAs) are apps created using browser-supported technologies such as HTML, CSS, and JavaScript. They can run on any platform with a standard web browser, including desktop computers, tablets, and phones. Their primary features are the ability to run when offline, receive push notifications, and interact with device features such as cameras.

NOTE When an app attempts to use device features, users are typically prompted to give permission to the app. For example, an app that uses the camera to identify a food item or diagnose a skin condition would be required to ask for permission to use the camera.

Users must be online the first time they browse a PWA so the files that implement it can be downloaded to the browser. After downloading a PWA, it can optionally be installed. This typically adds an icon to the home screen and allows it to be invoked by tapping or double-clicking an icon instead of explicitly browsing the app URL. It also makes the PWA appear more like a native application because it can run without displaying browser chrome (such as a browser menubar and tabs).

Sapper apps are PWAs by default, enabled through the use of a service worker, which will be described in the next section (see "Using Service Workers" in the MDN docs: http://mng.bz/nPqa). Offline behavior, with some limitations, is provided automatically. Modifications are only required to use a different caching strategy.

Web apps generally must be served over HTTPS in order to use service workers. This is a safety measure aimed at preventing man-in-the-middle attacks, where a substitute service worker could modify network responses. Some browsers can be configured to allow the use of service workers with localhost URLs using HTTP, but this is only for debugging purposes.

In this chapter, we will dive into the details of using service workers with Sapper apps. Then we will apply what we have covered to the Travel Packing app.

19.1 Service worker overview

A service worker is a kind of *web worker*, which means its functionality is defined by a JavaScript source file and it runs in a background thread (see "Using Web Workers" in the MDN docs: http://mng.bz/vxq7). Service workers have many use cases. They can listen for external events, periodically fetch data, and send notifications to their associated web app using push notifications. Their most common use is enabling offline functionality by acting as a proxy between a web app and the network, deciding how to handle each resource request.

Service workers can allow parts of a web application to continue functioning after network connectivity is lost. They do this by returning cached responses when requests for inaccessible resources are received.

Common tasks performed by service workers include

- Creating caches
- Storing resources in caches
- Intercepting network requests and deciding how to respond to them

There is a limit to how much data each application domain can cache and to the total amount of data that can be cached across all domains. The limits differ across web browsers, but they are mostly consistent for Chrome, Edge, and Firefox. The limit for a single domain is 20% of the overall limit. Typically the limits are based on the available space as summarized in table 19.1.

Currently Safari is an outlier in this regard. It limits each application domain to 50 MB of cache storage regardless of available disk space, and it purges this after two weeks of not being used. An alternative is to store data in IndexedDB, which has a

Table 19.1 Cache limits

Available space	Total cache limit
Up to 8 GB	50 MB
8 to 32 GB	500 MB
32 to 128 GB	4% of volume size
Over 128 GB	The smaller of 20 GB or 4% of volume size

limit of 500 MB per application domain in Safari (see "Using IndexedDB" in the MDN docs: http://mng.bz/4AWw).

When the total limit has been reached, some browsers remove the least recently used caches to make room for new caches. Currently Chrome and Firefox do this.

Service workers do not have access to the DOM of their associated web application, so they cannot directly change what is rendered in the browser. However, they can communicate with the associated web application via message passing. The `Worker-postMessage` method is used to send a message from a web worker to the associated web app or from the web app to a web worker.

Figure 19.1 illustrates one possible scenario. Here the client app posts a message to the service worker. The service worker uses data in the message to invoke an API service. It then returns data from the API service to the client by posting a message. The client app can use the data it receives to change what is rendered.

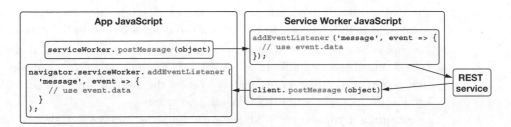

Figure 19.1 Service worker flow

As stated earlier, web workers run in a background thread. A user can close the browser tab or window where the web application is running, and its web workers can continue executing.

19.2 *Caching strategies*

Service workers can implement many caching strategies. Different strategies can be used for different kinds of resources being requested. Resources can be files with content such as HTML, CSS, JavaScript, JSON, and image data. Resources can also be the results of API calls.

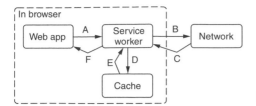

Figure 19.2   Service worker flow

Figure 19.2 is helpful for understanding the differences between these strategies. In all cases, if the requested resource cannot be obtained from the network or the cache, and the service worker cannot generate the resource, a "not found" (404) status is returned.

These are some examples of caching strategies:

- *Network only*—This strategy is applicable when using cached versions of a resource is unacceptable. For example, a banking app might decide it is better to let the user know when they are offline and not show stale data.

  All resource requests are forwarded to the network, and only resources obtained from the network are returned. No caching is used. In figure 19.2 this is represented by the path A-B-C-F.

- *Cache only*—This strategy is applicable for resources that never change or that change very rarely. Examples include a CSS file that defines site styling or an image file for a company logo.

  The service worker is responsible for initially populating the caches and thereafter only returns resources from the caches. Resource requests are never forwarded to the network. In figure 19.2 this is represented by the path A-D-E-F.

- *Network or cache*—This strategy is applicable when having the latest data is preferred, but it is acceptable to use previously fetched data. For example, a site that reports basketball scores prefers to show the latest scores, but showing the last known scores is better than showing no scores.

  Resource requests are first forwarded to the network. If a response is obtained from the network, that is returned. Then cache is updated with the response, so it can be used again later if the same resource is requested while offline. If no response is obtained from the network and a previously cached response is available, that is returned. In figure 19.2 this is represented by the path A-B-C-(D-E)-F where steps D and E are optional.

- *Cache and update*—This strategy is applicable when fast responses are prioritized over having the latest data. It's difficult to think of a case when this strategy might be preferred, but the next strategy augments this to make it more applicable.

  If the requested resource is available in a cache, that is returned. Then the request is forwarded to the network to obtain an up-to-date value. If the network returns a different value, the cache is updated so the next request for the same resource will receive the updated value. This is great for performance but has the downside of potentially using stale data. In figure 19.2 this is represented by the path A-D-E-F-B-C-D.

- *Cache, update, and refresh*—This strategy starts the same way as the "cache and update" strategy, but after new data is received from the network, the UI is triggered to refresh using the new data.

  For example, a theater website might use this approach to quickly display the known shows and ticket availability from the cache. As soon as new data becomes available, it can update this information in the browser.

- *Embedded fallback*—In this strategy, the service worker provides default responses for cases when the resource cannot be obtained from the network or a cache. For example, a service worker that returns photos of specific dogs can return stock images that match the breeds of requested dogs when the requested photos are unavailable. This, of course, assumes that the stock images have already been cached.

  This strategy can be employed as a supplement to the previously described strategies to provide an alternative to returning a "not found" (404) status.

For some web applications it is possible to define a subset of functionality that can be supported for offline use and then only cache resources related to that. For example, in the Travel Packing app we can cache the checklist of items to be packed, along with all the JavaScript and CSS required by the site, making the checklist available for viewing while offline. But we can forego support for changing the checklist in any way.

For some web applications it is acceptable to accumulate transactions when offline and execute them later when online again. For example, suppose a timesheet web app allows users to enter the hours they worked on various projects. If network connectivity is lost, the app can save the hours entered in a cache. When connectivity is restored, it can read data from the cache, make the appropriate API calls to save it on a server, and delete the data from the cache.

This can be challenging to implement due to special cases that must be considered. For example, what should be done in the timesheet app if we are saving hours for a project that has been deleted by someone else after network connectivity was lost for the user that entered the hours? Perhaps the new hours should just be ignored, or perhaps the project should be recreated and the hours should be applied to it. There can be many such cases to consider.

The current state of network connectivity can be determined from the Boolean value of `navigator.onLine`. The best way to access the current value of this variable in a Svelte/Sapper app is to do the following:

```
<script>
  let online = true;
  ...use online in JavaScript code and {#if} blocks ...
</script>

<svelte:window bind:online />
```

online is an alias for
window.navigator.onLine.

Another option is to register functions to be called when connectivity changes by listening for `offline` and `online` events on the `window` object. In a Svelte/Sapper app, this is best done as follows, where `handleOffline` and `handleOnline` are functions to be invoked:

```
<svelte:window on:offline={handleOffline} on:online={handleOnline} />
```

19.3   *Sapper service worker configuration*

By default, Sapper apps configure a `ServiceWorker` in `src/service-worker.js`. This file can be modified to change the default caching strategy. When debugging this code, it can be useful to write to the DevTools Console using calls like `console.log`.

The `src/service-worker.js` file imports four variables defined in the generated file `src/node_modules/@sapper/service-worker.js`. That file should not be modified. The variables are `timestamp`, `files`, `shell`, and `routes`.

The `timestamp` variable is set to the timestamp of the last time the app was built. It is used as part of cache names so that new builds use new caches containing new resources, and old caches can be deleted.

The `files` variable is set to an array of the names of all the files found in the `static` directory. This includes the `global.css` file and media files such as images. It also includes the `manifest.json` file, which configures how the PWA will appear to users, including names, colors, and icons. When the service worker receives the `install` event (described in the next section), these files are saved in a cache with a name formed by concatenating "cache" with the value of the `timestamp` variable.

The `shell` variable is set to an array of the paths to all the files found in the `__sapper__/build/client` directory. These files are generated by code splitting each route and contain minimized JavaScript. When the service worker receives the `install` event (described in the next section), these files are saved in the same cache used for files in the `files` array.

The `routes` variable is set to an array of objects with a `pattern` property whose value is a regular expression that matches the URL of each route in the app. The default service worker configuration does not use this variable. However, the function that handles `fetch` events (described in the next section) contains a commented-out `if` statement that uses this variable to determine if the URL being fetched matches any of the app routes. Study this code to determine if uncommenting it might be appropriate for your application.

The Sapper app can be built by entering `npm run build`, and the server can be started by entering `npm start`. In this case, changes to the code, such as `src/service-worker.js`, will not be reflected in the running application unless the app is rebuilt, the server is restarted, and the page is manually refreshed.

Alternatively, if `npm run dev` is used to build the app and start the server, the server will be restarted when code changes are detected. It is still necessary to manually refresh the page in the browser. This differs from Svelte and Sapper apps that do not use a service worker, in which case the browser is automatically reloaded after code changes.

Until each page is visited, the cache will not contain everything needed to render the page. After a page has been visited once while online, it can be visited again while offline.

The results of API calls made from the `preload` function in a page are cached when the page is visited while online. If visited pages are revisited later while offline, the cached API responses are used. However, if a page that was not visited while online is visited while offline, the error page will be displayed with a 500 error and the message "Failed to fetch."

For apps where it is possible to proactively cache all pages, a better option may be to export the app. This is the case for the default Sapper app.

19.4 *Service worker events*

Service workers listen for events and act on them.

The first event received is `install`. This is a one-time event. The default Sapper service worker configuration handles this event by doing the following:

1. Open a cache whose name is "cache" concatenated with the value of the `timestamp` variable. If this cache does not exist, it is created.
2. Add all the files listed in the `shell` and `files` arrays to the cache. These files are always served from the cache. They are available without a network connection after the app is initially loaded from the network.

The second event received is `activate`. This is also a one-time event. The default Sapper service worker configuration handles this event by deleting any old caches for this app that were created when previous builds of the app were run. This is determined by checking whether their names contain the current value of the `timestamp` variable.

The third event type received is `fetch`. This can be received many times. The caching strategy is implemented here. The default Sapper service worker caching strategy defined in `service-worker.js` evaluates each request using the following steps in this sequence:

1. Only process `GET` requests.
2. Don't process requests asking for just part of a document, using an HTTP "Range" header (not commonly used).
3. Only process URLs with a protocol beginning with "http". For example, URLs with the "data" protocol are ignored.
4. Serve all static files and bundler-generated assets (such as those from code splitting) from the cache.
5. If the file was not found in the cache and the request has a `cache` property of `only-if-cached`, don't attempt to find the file using the network.
6. Otherwise, attempt to satisfy the request using the network.
7. If found, add the file to the cache and return its contents.
8. If not found and a match for the URL is in the cache, return that content.

This caching strategy means that the results of API service calls are cached. Later, if the same request is made again and the service is offline, the cached value will be returned.

19.5   *Managing service workers in Chrome*

The Chrome DevTools provide a way to interact with service workers and the caches they create.

To view service workers for the current site, click the DevTools Application tab. Then click Service Workers in the left nav. The main area will display information about each of the service workers for the site (see figure 19.3).

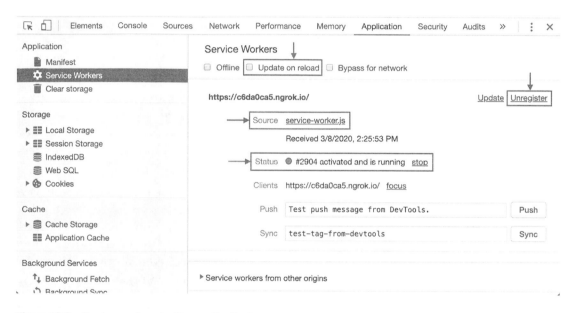

Figure 19.3   Service workers in Chrome DevTools

The status of a service worker is displayed after the Status label. For example, it may say "activated and is running." To stop the service worker, click the Stop link after the status. The Stop link will change to Start, and this can be clicked to restart it.

Unregistering a service worker allows it to run through its lifecycle again one time, when the page is refreshed. This includes processing the `install` and `activate` events again. This is useful for debugging the code that handles those events. To do this, click the Unregister link to the right of a service worker description.

To cause service workers to install and activate again every time the page is reloaded, and without creating a new build, check the Update on Reload check box at the top of the main area, and refresh the page.

To view the source code for a service worker, click the link after the Source label. This switches to the Sources tab and displays the code. Typically the code will have been minified (see figure 19.4). To see a pretty-printed version of this, as displayed in figure 19.5, click the "{}" shown at the bottom of figure 19.4.

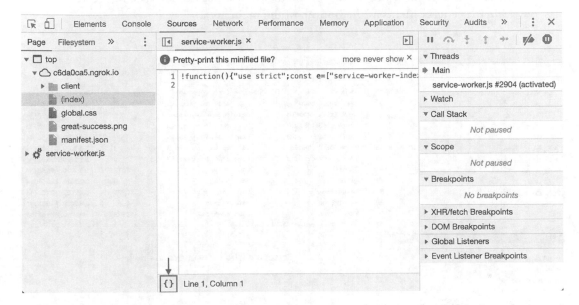

Figure 19.4 Minimized service worker code in Chrome DevTools

Figure 19.5 Pretty-printed service worker code in Chrome DevTools

To see the files that have been cached, click the DevTools Application tab. Then click the disclosure triangle before Cache Storage in the left nav. This will display a list of all the current caches for the site. The caches that Sapper apps create by default have names that begin with "cache" and "offline" and end with a build timestamp.

Click one of these to see a list of the files that it has cached (see figure 19.6). Click a file to see its contents at the bottom of the main area.

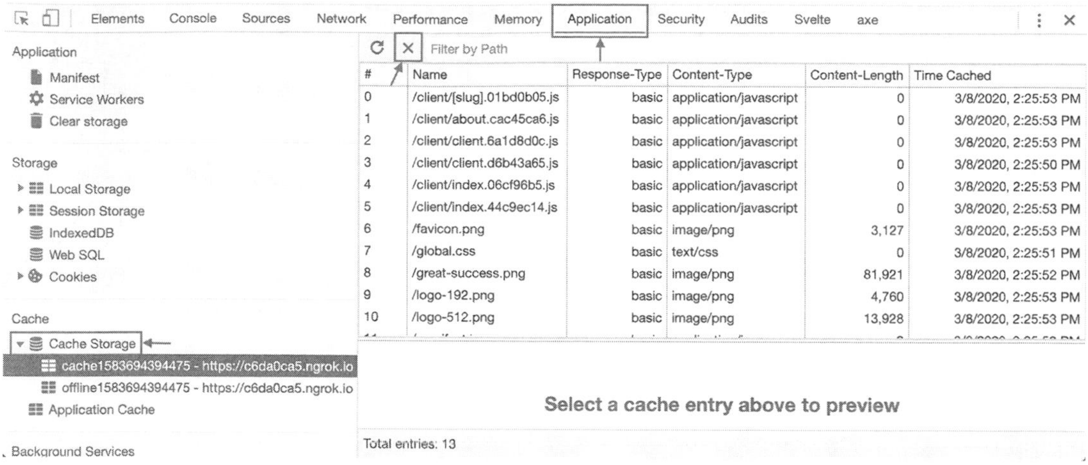

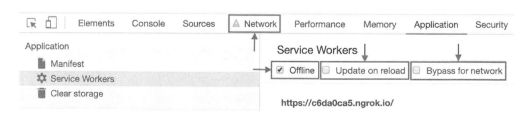

Figure 19.6   Cached files in Chrome DevTools

To remove an individual file from a cache, select the file in the main area and press the Delete key or click the "X" above the list of files. To delete an entire cache, right-click a cache name and select Delete.

To simulate being offline, click Service Workers in the left nav and check the Offline check box at the top of the main area (see figure 19.7). This is an alternative to going to the Network tab and changing the Online drop-down to Offline. A warning icon will appear in the Network tab to remind you that you are offline. This is useful for testing the ability of service workers to use cached files.

Figure 19.7   Simulating being offline in Chrome DevTools

To bypass the use of service workers, causing all requests to go to the network, check the Bypass for Network check box at the top of the main area. This, of course, requires being online.

The list of requested files in the Network tab has a gear icon before each file that was loaded from a cache (see figure 19.8). This is useful for determining whether specific files were served from the network or from a cache.

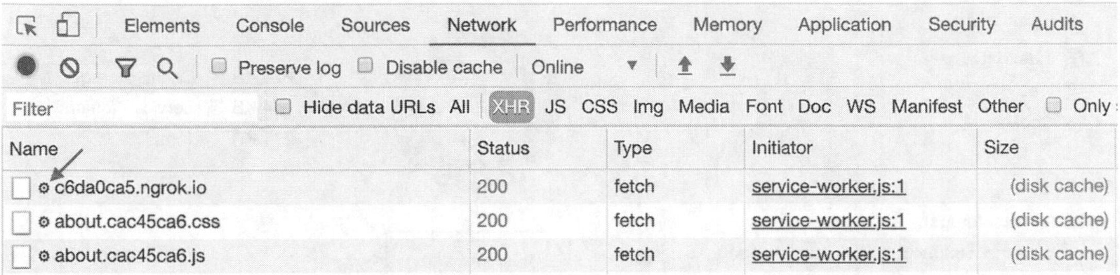

Name	Status	Type	Initiator	Size
☐ ⚙ c6da0ca5.ngrok.io	200	fetch	service-worker.js:1	(disk cache)
☐ ⚙ about.cac45ca6.css	200	fetch	service-worker.js:1	(disk cache)
☐ ⚙ about.cac45ca6.js	200	fetch	service-worker.js:1	(disk cache)

Figure 19.8   Files loaded from cache in Chrome DevTools

To clear many things at once, click the Application tab and click Clear Storage (preceded by a trash can icon) in the left nav (see figure 19.9). This displays a series of check boxes in the main area for categories of things that can be cleared. By default, all the check boxes are checked. This includes Unregister Service Workers and Cache Storage. Click the Clear Site Data button to clear the data associated with every checked category.

A great video covering most of the topics in this section, created by the Chrome team, can be found at http://mng.bz/oPwp. A similar video for Firefox, also from the Chrome team, can be found at http://mng.bz/nPw2.

Figure 19.9   Clearing storage in Chrome DevTools

19.6   *Enabling the use of HTTPS in the Sapper server*

By default, Sapper apps use the Polka server library and configure it to use HTTP, not HTTPS. As discussed earlier, service workers must be served over HTTPS for security reasons.

The following steps show one approach to enable serving a Sapper app using HTTPS:

1 Install ngrok at https://ngrok.com/. This is a tool that provides a public URL that tunnels to a local server. Anyone can then browse this URL, but the URL is

only temporary and the number of connections per minute is limited to 40. The benefit we are after is being able to browse a local server using HTTPS. The free version of ngrok is sufficient for this.

2 Create a Sapper app:
   - Enter npx degit sveltejs/sapper-template#rollup *app-name*.
   - cd to the new *app-name* directory.
   - Enter npm install.

3 If you do not already have suitable SSL key and certificate files, generate temporary, self-signed ones using the openssl command and answering the questions it asks. Anything can be entered for Organizational Unit, and localhost can be entered for Common Name.

```
openssl req -newkey rsa:2048 -nodes -x509 -days 365 \
  -keyout key.pem \
  -out cert.pem
```

NOTE If you do not already have openssl, you'll need to install it. Windows users can install openssl from www.openssl.org. MacOS users can install a newer version of openssl using Homebrew (see https://brew.sh/).

1 Modify server.js to use HTTPS by matching the following:

```
const {createServer} = require('https');        ◁──  The function imported
const {readFileSync} = require('fs');                 here creates a server
                                                      that listens for HTTPS
import sirv from 'sirv';                               requests.
import polka from 'polka';
import compression from 'compression';
import * as sapper from '@sapper/server';

const {PORT, NODE_ENV} = process.env;
const dev = NODE_ENV === 'development';

const options = {                               ◁──  The files referenced
  key: readFileSync('key.pem'),                      here can be created
  cert: readFileSync('cert.pem')                     using the openssl
};                                                    command.

const {handler} = polka().use(
  compression({threshold: 0}),
  sirv('static', {dev}),
  sapper.middleware()
);

createServer(options, handler).listen(PORT, err => {
  if (err) {
    console.error('error', err);
  } else {
    console.info('listening for HTTPS requests on', PORT);
  }
});
```

2 Build the Sapper app by entering `npm run build`.

3 Start the Sapper server by entering `npm start`. This listens on port 3000 by default.

4 Establish a tunnel by entering `ngrok http https://localhost:3000`.

5 Browse the Forwarding URL output from ngrok that begins with "https:", not the one that begins with "http:".

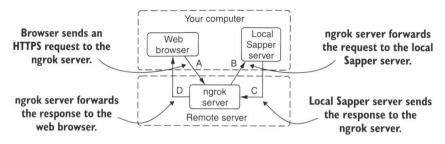

Figure 19.10   Flow of HTTPS requests using ngrok

Issue with running in development mode

If the Sapper server is run in development mode by entering `npm run dev`, the following error message will appear in the DevTools console:

```
Mixed Content: The page at 'https://{some-id}.ngrok.io/' was loaded over
HTTPS, but requested an insecure EventSource endpoint
'http://{some-id}.ngrok.io:10000/__sapper__'.
This request has been blocked; the content must be served over HTTPS.
```

This is why the previous steps use `npm run build` and `npm start`.

19.7   *Verifying offline behavior*

When developing apps that use service workers for offline behavior, it is important to know how to use tools to verify that they are working correctly. Here are some steps that can be followed to do this using the Chrome DevTools.

1 Browse the app in Chrome.

2 Open the DevTools.

3 Verify that browser caching is not disabled. (When this is disabled, service workers will not cache any downloaded files.)

   – Click the Network tab.

   – Verify that Disable Cache is not checked.

   – Click the vertical ellipsis in the upper right of the DevTools.

   – Select Settings.

  - Scroll to the Network section.
  - Verify that Disable Cache (While DevTools Is Open) is not checked.
4 Browse all the pages of the app so they are cached.
5 View the status of the service worker:
  - Click the Application tab.
  - Click Service Workers in the left nav.
6 View lists of files that have been cached.
  - Expand Cache Storage in the left nav.
  - Click the cache names that begin with "cache" and "offline." Each of these displays a list of cached files.
7 Go offline using one of several options:
  - The easiest option is to ask the browser to simulate being offline. Click the Application tab and check the Offline check box.
  - If you're using Wi-Fi, another option is to turn it off.
  - If you're using a wired connection, another option is to disconnect the Ethernet cable.
8 Now that you are offline, browse all the pages of the app and verify that they render properly.
9 Return to being online.

Another approach to testing the offline behavior of a Sapper app is to export it using the export npm script. Recall that this crawls all the pages of the app and generates a static site. After doing this, you can manually test the behavior of the static site.

There are many tools that assist in testing all the pages of a web application. One to consider is BrowserStack at www.browserstack.com.

19.8 Building the Travel Packing app

There are a couple of aspects of the Travel Packing app that make implementing offline use challenging.

The first issue is handling authentication. Of course, we haven't really implemented that yet, but if we had, how would we authenticate a user when they are offline? One option would be to assume it is the same user that authenticated last when they were online on the current computer. This might be acceptable if the app is only used on non-shared devices. Otherwise this is a risky assumption.

The second issue is deciding what to do when the user is offline and wants to make changes. Examples include adding/modifying/deleting categories and items, and checking and unchecking items. One option is to disallow these when offline. The user could still view their travel packing checklist in the state it was in the last time they used the app online.

Another option is to save any change transactions, simulate their effect in the UI, and replay them when the user is back online. As you might imagine, implementing this introduces a fair amount of complexity. Code to do this would have to consider many transactional scenarios. For example, what should happen if a user performs the following steps:

1 Add a category named "Clothing".
2 Add an item named "socks" to the "Clothing" category.
3 Lose connectivity.
4 Delete the "socks" item, creating a saved transaction.
5 Delete the "Clothing" category, creating a saved transaction.
6 Go to another computer with connectivity.
7 Browse the app and notice that the "Clothing" category and the "socks" item are still there.
8 Rename "Clothing" to "Clothes".
9 Return to the first computer and restore connectivity.

What should happen now? There are pending transactions to delete the "socks" item and the "Clothing" category, but that category no longer exists because it was renamed.

As you can see, this is a difficult problem to solve and one that the Travel Packing app will avoid for now by making the data read-only while offline. Users can still view their checklists. They just cannot modify them while offline. The finished code can be found at http://mng.bz/vxw4.

Let's start by making it clear to users when they are offline. We will do this in two ways. First, we will add the text "Offline" to the page title when offline. Second, we will change the background color of the main area from its current shade of blue to gray when offline. We only need to modify src/routes/_layout.svelte to achieve both of these.

Listing 19.1 Top layout defined in `src/routes/_layout.svelte`

```
<script>
  let mainElement;
  let online = true;
  $: title = 'Travel Packing Checklist' + (online ? '' : ' Offline');    ◁—— This updates the title every time the value of online changes.
  $: if (mainElement) {
    mainElement.style.setProperty(          ◁—┐ This updates the value of the CSS
      '--main-bg-color',                        variable, --main-bg-color, every
      online ? '#3f6fde' : 'gray'               time the value of online changes.
    );
  }
</script>

                                              ┌ This causes the online variable
                                              │ to be updated when the value of
<svelte:window bind:online />    ◁——          └ window.navigator.onLine changes.

<main bind:this={mainElement}>   ◁——┐ This sets the mainElement
  <h1 class="hero">{title}</h1>        variable to the DOM element
  <slot />                             for the main element.
</main>
```

```
<style>
  .hero {
    /* no changes here */
  }

  main {
    --main-bg-color: #3f6fde; /* shade of blue */
    background-color: var(--main-bg-color);
    /* no other changes here */
  }
</style>
```

Next, let's ensure that API calls made while offline are handled gracefully. We won't save the requests and re-execute them when connectivity is restored. We will just ignore them.

Add the following function in `src/util.js`:

Listing 19.2 `fetchPlus` **function in** `src/util.js`

```
export async function fetchPlus(path, options = {}) {
  if (navigator.onLine) return fetch(path, options);

  alert(`This operation is not available while offline.`);
  return {offline: true};
}
```

> We could implement a nicer looking notification than using the alert function. This is left as an exercise.

Replace all client-side calls to the `fetch` function, not calls to `this.fetch` in `preload` functions, with calls to `fetchPlus`. There are four occurrences in `src/routes/checklist.svelte` and two occurrences in `src/components/Category.svelte`. These files already import from `util.js`. Modify the existing `import` statement to also import the `fetchPlus` function.

> **NOTE** To understand why the calls to `this.fetch` cannot be changed to use the `fetchPlus` function, see section 16.6.

The response returned by `fetchPlus` when offline is a JSON object containing the property `offline` set to `true`. Check for this immediately after calls to `fetchPlus`, as follows, and just return if it is `true` to avoid performing the requested update in the UI.

```
if (res.offline) return;
```

Prevent use of the Clear All Checks button when offline by modifying `src/routes/checklist.svelte`. Add the following variable inside the `script` element:

```
let online = true;
```

Add the following at the top of the HTML section to update this variable when connectivity changes:

```
<svelte:window bind:online />
```

Add a `disabled` attribute to the Clear All Checks button as follows:

```
<button class="clear" disabled={!online} on:click={clearAllChecks}>
  Clear All Checks
</button>
```

Prevent the editing of category names when offline by modifying `src/components/Category.svelte`. Add the following variable inside the `script` element:

```
let online = true;
```

Add the following at the top of the HTML section to update this variable when connectivity changes:

```
<svelte:window bind:online />
```

Change the line that renders the category name to the following so the `editing` variable is only set to `true` when online:

```
<span on:click={() => (editing = online)}>{category.name}</span>
```

Prevent the editing of item names when offline by modifying `src/components/Item.svelte`. Add the following variable inside the `script` element:

```
let online = true;
```

Add the following at the top of the HTML section to update this variable when connectivity changes:

```
<svelte:window bind:online />
```

Prevent the toggling of item check boxes by adding a `disabled` attribute to them that is set to `true` when offline, as follows:

```
<input
  aria-label="Toggle Packed"
  type="checkbox"
  disabled={!online}
  bind:checked={item.packed}
  on:change={() => dispatch('persist')} />
```

Change the line that renders the item name to the following so the `editing` variable is only set to `true` when online:

```
<span
  class="packed-{item.packed}"
  draggable="true"
  on:dragstart={event => dnd.drag(event, categoryId, item.id)}
  on:click={() => (editing = online)}>
  {item.name}
</span>
```

When using a tunnel like that provided by ngrok, API calls in `preload` functions will need help knowing the domain that ngrok provides. We have only one case like this in the Travel Packing app. It is the `preload` function in `src/routes/checklist.svelte`.

A solution is to modify it to begin as follows. Note the use of `page.host` in the URL passed to `this.fetch`.

```
export async function preload(page) {
  try {
    const res = await this.fetch(`https://${page.host}/categories.json`);
```

Follow these steps to build and run the app:

1 Open a terminal window.
2 Enter `npm run build`.
3 Enter `npm start`.
4 Open another terminal window.
5 Enter `ngrok http https://localhost:3000`.
6 Run the app by browsing the forwarding URL for https that is output.

Now we can load the app, go offline, and refresh the browser. The page will still display the current travel packing checklist.

In the next chapter you will learn about using preprocessors to support alternate syntaxes for JavaScript, HTML, and CSS.

Summary

- Service workers can act as proxies for network requests, deciding how to fulfill them. This typically involves caching.
- Many caching strategies can be implemented.
- Sapper provides a default service worker that implements a particular caching strategy, but this can be customized.
- Service workers respond to events. The most important of these are `install`, `activate`, and `fetch`.
- The Polka-based server provided by Sapper does not use HTTPS by default, but it can be modified to do so.

Part 4

Beyond Svelte and Sapper

The last part of the book goes beyond Svelte and Sapper to explore preprocessing source files that can add support for alternate syntaxes. Examples include Sass, TypeScript, and Markdown. We'll return to Svelte Native and build mobile applications for Android and iOS. In particular, we'll focus on components for display, forms, actions, dialogs, layout, and navigation, as well as details about styling them, all through an example app that demonstrates how to implement them.

Preprocessors

20

This chapter covers

- Custom preprocessing
- Using svelte-preprocess and its auto-preprocessing mode
- Using Sass instead of CSS
- Using TypeScript instead of JavaScript
- Using Markdown instead of HTML
- Using multiple preprocessors
- Image compression as a preprocessing step

By default, Svelte and Sapper only support using JavaScript, HTML, and CSS. Preprocessors enable the use of alternate syntaxes for these files that can simplify writing the code or provide additional features not otherwise present.

This chapter assumes that if you're interested in adding preprocessing, you will have some familiarity with Sass, TypeScript, and Markdown. You may have also heard of less popular options such as CoffeeScript, Pug, Less, PostCSS, and Stylus, but knowing about those is less important because no examples of using them are shown here.

Svelte apps can optionally configure the use of preprocessors that transform the content of `.svelte` files before they are passed to the Svelte compiler. This is typically specified in the configuration file for the bundler being used, such as Rollup or Webpack.

Examples of preprocessing include

1 Converting Sass syntax to CSS
2 Compiling TypeScript code to JavaScript
3 Converting Markdown or Pug syntax to HTML
4 Custom search and replace

Many npm packages can be used to implement preprocessing, and some examples are identified in the sections that follow. When multiple preprocessors are configured, they are executed one at a time, with the output of each being used as input for the next.

Internally, Svelte preprocessing is managed by the function `svelte.preprocess`, documented at https://svelte.dev/docs#svelte_preprocess. This function can be called directly, but it is more common to configure a module bundler to use it, as shown in the next section.

20.1 *Custom preprocessing*

Let's implement an example of custom preprocessing that changes `color: red` to `color: blue` inside `style` elements. We will accomplish this using the JavaScript `Stringreplace` method and a regular expression with the `global` flag as follows:

```
content.replace(/color: red/g, 'color: blue')   ◁—┐  The value of the content
                                                     variable will be the
                                                     content of a style element.
```

Create a Svelte app by entering `npx degit sveltejs/template` *app-name*. This uses Rollup as the module bundler. Later you will see how to use Webpack if you prefer.

Edit `rollup.config.js` to configure the use of the custom preprocessor. This file defines a default export that is an object with several properties, including one named `plugins`. The value of `plugins` is an array, and one of the elements in this array is a call to the `svelte` function. It is passed an object with the properties `dev` and `css` (not shown here). Add a `preprocess` property to this object whose value is an object as shown in the following listing.

Listing 20.1   Rollup configuration in `rollup.config.js`

```
plugins: [
  svelte({
    ...
    preprocess: {              This specifies a
      style({content}) {       transformation for code
                        ◁—     inside style elements.
        return {
          code: content.replace(/color: red/g, 'color: blue')
        };
      }
```

```
    }
  }),
  ...
]
```

To test this, follow these steps:

1 Enter npm install.
2 Edit src/App.svelte and change the color for h1 inside the style element to red.
3 Enter npm run dev.
4 Browse to localhost:5000.
5 Note that "Hello world!" is blue.

The value of the preprocess property in the object passed to the svelte function is an object where the properties can be script, markup, and style. Each of these is a function that takes an object with content and filename properties. These functions must return an object, or a promise that resolves to an object, that has a code property whose value is a string representing the preprocessing result.

The returned object can also have a dependencies property, but this is not frequently used. It is an array of file paths to watch. Changes in these files can trigger reprocessing of the file that depends on them. See the Svelte documentation for preprocess for details (https://svelte.dev/docs#svelte_preprocess).

20.1.1 *Using Webpack*

A Svelte app that uses Webpack as its module bundler can be created by entering npx degit sveltejs/template-webpack {app-name}.

To configure the same custom preprocessing shown in the previous section for a Svelte app that uses Webpack, edit the file webpack.config.js. This defines a default export that is an object with several properties, including one named module. The value of module is an object that has a rules property. The value of rules is an array of objects. These objects have a test property that specifies the files to which they apply, and a use property that specifies what to do to those files. Add a preprocess property to the options object for .svelte files as shown in the following listing.

Listing 20.2 One of the rules objects in webpack.config.js

```
{
  test: /\.svelte$/,
  use: {
    loader: 'svelte-loader',
    options: {
      ...
      preprocess: {
        style({content}) {
          return {
            code: content.replace(/color: red/g, 'color: blue')
          };
```

```
          }
        }
      }
    }
}
```

The value of the `preprocess` property is the same kind of object used by the Rollup `svelte` plugin. Its properties can be `script`, `markup`, and `style` functions.

To test this, follow the same steps as for the Rollup-based app in the preceding section, but browse localhost:8080.

> **NOTE** When using Sapper, configure the desired preprocessing in both the `client` and `server` sections of the bundler configuration file so preprocessing is performed for both server-side and client-side rendered pages.

You have seen how easy adding preprocessing can be. But, of course, you will want to perform more advanced transformations than color substitutions. The preprocessing functions can invoke compilers such as Sass and TypeScript to obtain their `code` result, but doing this is a bit more involved. The svelte-preprocess package described next simplifies this.

20.2   *The svelte-preprocess package*

The svelte-preprocess package (https://github.com/kaisermann/svelte-preprocess) makes configuring the use of certain preprocessors easier. These include

- Transforming TypeScript and CoffeeScript to JavaScript
- Transforming Pug to HTML
- Transforming Sass, Less, PostCSS, and Stylus to CSS

There are two ways to add the svelte-preprocess package to a Svelte project. When using `npx degit sveltejs/template {project-name}` to start a project, cd to the directory created and enter `node scripts/setupTypeScript.js`. This adds svelte-preprocess to the `devDependencies` in `package.json`. Otherwise it can be installed by entering `npm install -D svelte-preprocess`. Each supported preprocessor to be used requires additional installs.

To configure the use of svelte-preprocess with Rollup, modify `rollup.config.js`. Add the following `import` near the top:

```
import sveltePreprocess from 'svelte-preprocess';
```

Add the following property to the object passed to the `svelte` function in the `plugins` array:

```
preprocess: sveltePreprocess()
```

An options object can be passed to the `sveltePreprocess` function, but one is not required. For details on the supported options, see the documentation for svelte-preprocess: https://github.com/kaisermann/svelte preprocess#options.

20.2.1 Auto-preprocessing mode

The easiest way to use the svelte-preprocess package is in auto-preprocessing mode. This mode determines the preprocessors to use based on `lang` and `type` attributes on `script`, `style`, and `template` elements in `.svelte` files, such as these:

```
<script lang="ts">

<template lang="pug">

<style lang="scss">
```

Note that alternative HTML syntaxes, such as Pug, must be surrounded by a `template` element in order to specify its language.

20.2.2 External files

The svelte-preprocess package also adds external file support. To get content from an external file, add `src` attributes whose values are file paths to `script`, `template`, and `style` elements, such as these:

```
<script src="./name.js">

<template src="./name.html">

<style src="./name.css">
```

The language of an external file is determined by its file extension. This allows preprocessing to be performed on its content.

To demonstrate, let's create an app that renders information about dogs, as shown in figure 20.1.

The `Dog` component implemented in the following listing uses JavaScript, HTML, and CSS stored in separate files rather than in the `.svelte` file that defines the component. Any of the elements with `src` attributes could be replaced by the content of the referenced file without changing the component definition.

Dasher
His breed is Whippet.

Maisey
Her breed is Treeing Walker Coonhound.

Ramsay
His breed is Native American Indian Dog.

Oscar
His breed is German Shorthaired Pointer.

Figure 20.1 Dogs UI with external files

Listing 20.3 `src/Dog.svelte` referring to three external files

```
<script src="./Dog.js"></script>

<template src="./Dog.html"></template>

<style src="./Dog.css"></style>
```

The following listing shows the JavaScript used by the `Dog` component.

Listing 20.4   JavaScript for the `Dog` component in `src/Dog.js`

```
export let name;          The props of this
export let breed;         component are name,
export let gender;        breed, and gender.

let color = gender === 'male' ? 'lightblue' : 'pink';
```

The following listing shows the HTML used by the `Dog` component.

Listing 20.5   HTML for the `Dog` component in `src/Dog.html`

```
<h1 style="color: {color}">{name}</h1>
<div class="breed">{gender === 'male' ? 'His' : 'Her'} breed is {breed}.</div>
```

Next is the CSS used by the `Dog` component.

Listing 20.6   CSS for the `Dog` component in `src/Dog.css`

```
h1 {
  margin-bottom: 0;
}

.breed {
  color: green;
}
```

The following listing shows the topmost component in the app that renders several `Dog` components.

Listing 20.7   App that uses the `Dog` component in `src/App.svelte`

```
<script>
  import Dog from './Dog.svelte';

  const dogs = [
    {name: 'Dasher', gender: 'male', breed: 'Whippet'},
    {name: 'Maisey', gender: 'female', breed: 'Treeing Walker Coonhound'},
    {name: 'Ramsay', gender: 'male', breed: 'Native American Indian Dog'},
    {name: 'Oscar ', gender: 'male', breed: 'German Shorthaired Pointer'}
  ];
</script>

{#each dogs as {name, breed, gender}}
  <Dog {name} {breed} {gender} />
{/each}
```

20.2.3 *Global styles*

The svelte-preprocess package also provides a new way to specify global styles that is an alternative to the `:global(selector)` syntax you learned about in chapter 3. All CSS placed inside a `<style global>` element becomes global instead of being scoped to the component. Using this feature leads to spreading global styling across component source files. Consider placing global styles in the `global.css` file instead, to avoid this.

This global style feature requires PostCSS. To install it, enter `npm install -D postcss`.

For example, one way to change the background color of the `body` element is to add the following code in the `App` component.

Listing 20.8   Global styles in `src/App.svelte`

```
<style global>
  body {
    background-color: linen;
  }
</style>
```

20.2.4 *Using Sass*

Sass is a very popular CSS preprocessor. For details on Sass, see https://sass-lang.com/.

To enable Sass support, install the node-sass package by entering `npm install -D node-sass`. All features of Sass will be available, including variables, nested rules, mixins, and Sass functions.

The following listing shows an example of using Sass inside a component. It takes advantage of variables, nested rules, and single-line comments.

Listing 20.9   Using Sass in a `.svelte` file

```
<style lang="scss">
  $color: green;
  $space: 0.7rem;

  form {
    // a nested CSS rule
    input {
      $padding: 4px;
      border-radius: $padding;
      color: $color;
      padding: $padding;
    }

    // another nested CSS rule
    label {
      color: $color;
      margin-right: $space;
    }
  }
</style>
```

NOTE   Now that there is widespread support for CSS variables in popular browsers (not including IE), there is little reason to use Sass variables unless you want a more compact syntax for referring to them.

The style element `global` attribute can be used in conjunction with Sass:

```
<style global lang="scss">
  // define global styles here using Sass syntax.
</style>
```

20.2.5 *Using TypeScript*

TypeScript is a programming languages that is a superset of JavaScript. Its primary benefit is that it adds types to JavaScript. For details on TypeScript, see www.typescriptlang.org.

There are two ways to enable TypeScript support in a Svelte project. When using `npx degit sveltejs/template {project-name}` to start a project, cd to the directory created and enter `node scripts/setupTypeScript.js`. Otherwise, install the TypeScript compiler by entering `npm install -D typescript`.

The preprocessor only runs the TypeScript compiler on code within `script` elements, not on code in HTML interpolations (curly braces). This means that no errors will be reported if JavaScript code inside HTML interpolations calls TypeScript functions with invalid arguments. The VS Code extension Svelte for VS Code described in appendix F catches TypeScript errors in opened `.svelte` files, including those in HTML interpolations.

The svelte-check tool (http://mng.bz/4Agj) checks all `.svelte` files in an application and reports many kinds of errors, including TypeScript errors. The `setupType-Script` script mentioned earlier adds this to the `devDependencies` in `package.json` and adds an npm script so it can be run by entering `npm run validate`. Otherwise, enter `npm install -D svelte-check` to install it and manually add an npm script to run it.

Here is a simple example of using TypeScript inside a component that illustrates where type checking occurs:

```
<script lang="ts">
  function add(n1: number, n2: number): number {
    return n1 + n2;
  }

  const sum = add(1, '2');   ⟵
</script>
```

The TypeScript compiler will give the following error: "error TS2345: Argument of type "'2'" is not assignable to parameter of type 'number'." However, the code will run, and the value assigned to sum will be 1 concatenated with '2' resulting in '12'. To fix the error, pass the number 2 instead of the string '2'.

```
<div>sum in ts = {sum}</div>
<div>sum in HTML = {add(1, '2')}</div>   ⟵
```

The same type error occurs here, but it will not be flagged because it is outside the script element and so will not be processed by the TypeScript compiler.

Let's see how we can move the `add` function out of the Svelte component and into a separate `.ts` file. This will allow it to be imported by any number of components.

TypeScript source files can export any number of values, including functions, classes, and constants.

Listing 20.10 `add` **function in** `src/math.ts`

```
export function add(n1: number, n2: number): number {
  return n1 + n2;
}
```

This return type can be inferred by the compiler.

To enable importing TypeScript source files in Svelte components, follow these steps:

1 Install the required npm packages by entering the following:

```
npm install -D @rollup/plugin-typescript tslib
```

2 Edit `rollup.config.js`:

– Add the following `import` near the top:

```
import typescript from '@rollup/plugin-typescript';
```

– Add a call to `typescript()` in the `plugins` array:

```
plugins: [
  svelte({
    ...
    preprocess: sveltePreprocess()
  }),
  typescript(),
  ...
]
```

We can now modify `src/App.svelte` to match the following:

Listing 20.11 App that uses the `add` **function in** `src/App.svelte`

```
<script lang="ts">
  import {add} from './math';

  const sum = add(1, '2');
</script>

<div>sum in ts = {sum}</div>
<div>sum in HTML = {add(1, '2')}</div>
```

The TypeScript compiler will report the same error described earlier.

The TypeScript compiler will not run on this line, so no error will be reported.

When using TypeScript, there is a specific way to declare the type of variables that are the target of a reactive declaration: declare the variable being assigned, including its type, before the reactive declaration. Here is an example:

```
let upperName: string;
$: upperName = name.toUpperCase();
```

NOTE   Another option to consider for TypeScript support in Svelte is svelte-type-checker (https://github.com/halfnelson/svelte-type-checker). There is a corresponding svelte-type-checker-vscode VS Code extension (https://github .com/halfnelson/svelte-type-checker-vscode).

20.2.6 *A VS Code tip*

Code editors may flag the use of non-JS syntax inside `script` elements, non-HTML syntax such as Pug, and non-CSS syntax inside `style` elements. For VS Code this can be addressed by creating the `svelte.config.js` file in the root application directory with the following content, and restarting VS Code:

```
const sveltePreprocess = require('svelte-preprocess');

module.exports = {
  preprocess: sveltePreprocess()
};
```

20.3   *Using Markdown*

Svelte component content can be specified using Markdown instead of HTML. The svelte-preprocessor package does not currently support Markdown, but two libraries that do are svelte-preprocess-markdown and MDsveX. Currently svelte-preprocess-markdown better supports the syntax of `.svelte` files, so only that option is described here.

The svelte-preprocess-markdown package can be found at https://alexxnb.github .io/svelte-preprocess-markdown/. It uses the popular "marked" library at https:// marked.js.org to process Markdown syntax.

This package supports implementing Svelte components in `.md` files that include Markdown syntax. These files can contain everything that can be present in `.svelte` files, including `script` elements, HTML elements, `style` elements, and the use of other Svelte components.

To style the Markdown, add CSS that targets the HTML elements produced by the Markdown syntax. For example, # creates an `h1` element. For details on the mapping from Markdown syntax to HTML elements, see the "Basic Syntax" section of the Markdown Guide: www.markdown-guide.org/basic-syntax.

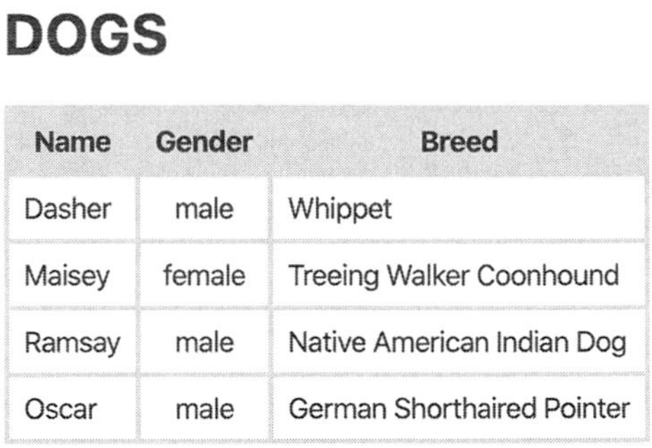

To demonstrate, let's create an app that renders a table of information about dogs using Markdown syntax (see figure 20.2).

DOGS

Name	Gender	Breed
Dasher	male	Whippet
Maisey	female	Treeing Walker Coonhound
Ramsay	male	Native American Indian Dog
Oscar	male	German Shorthaired Pointer

Figure 20.2   Dogs UI with Markdown

Starting from the default Svelte app, rename `src/App.svelte` to `src/App.md` and modify `src/main.js` to import from `App.md` instead of `App.svelte`. Then change the content of `src/App.md` to use Markdown syntax instead of HTML.

Listing 20.12 Component that uses Markdown syntax in `src/App.md`

```
<script>
  const dogs = [
    {name: 'Dasher', gender: 'male', breed: 'Whippet'},
    {name: 'Maisey', gender: 'female', breed: 'Treeing Walker Coonhound'},
    {name: 'Ramsay', gender: 'male', breed: 'Native American Indian Dog'},
    {name: 'Oscar ', gender: 'male', breed: 'German Shorthaired Pointer'}
  ];
</script>

# dogs

| Name | Gender | Breed |
| ---- | :----: | ----- |
{#each dogs as {name, gender, breed}}
  | {name} | {gender} | {breed} |
{/each}

<style>
  h1 {
    color: blue;
    margin-top: 0;
    text-transform: uppercase;
  }

  table {
    border-collapse: collapse;
  }

  td, th {
    border: solid lightgray 3px;
    padding: 0.5rem;
  }

  th {
    background-color: pink;
  }
</style>
```

This is Markdown syntax for a heading.

This is Markdown syntax for a table heading row.

The colons here specify that data in this column should be centered.

This is Markdown syntax for a table data row.

Note that it is important to not have a blank line before the #each. The table will not render properly if any lines of Markdown that define the table are separated.

To configure svelte-preprocess-markdown, follow these steps:

1 Enter `npm install -D svelte-preprocess-markdown`.
2 Edit `rollup.config.js`:
  - Add `import {markdown} from 'svelte-preprocess-markdown';` after the imports at the top of the file.
  - Add the following in the object passed to the `svelte` plugin:

```
extensions: ['.svelte','.md'],
preprocess: markdown()
```

To run this app, follow these steps:

1 Enter npm install.
2 Enter npm run dev.
3 Browse to localhost:3000.

20.4 *Using multiple preprocessors*

It is possible to use multiple preprocessors to transform content before it is passed to the Svelte compiler. To do so, edit the module bundler configuration file and specify an array for the value of the preprocess property.

For example, to use the svelte-preprocess and svelte-preprocess-markdown packages, specify the following in rollup.config.js:

```
preprocess: [sveltePreprocess(), markdown()],
```

After following the steps described earlier to install svelte-preprocess and type-script, you can change the script element in App.md from the previous example to use TypeScript as follows:

Listing 20.13 Using TypeScript in src/App.md

```
<script lang="ts">
  type Dog = {
    name: string;
    gender: string;
    breed: string;
  };

  const dogs: Dog[] = [
    {name: 'Dasher', gender: 'male', breed: 'Whippet'},
    {name: 'Maisey', gender: 'female', breed: 'Treeing Walker Coonhound'},
    {name: 'Ramsay', gender: 'male', breed: 'Native American Indian Dog'},
    {name: 'Oscar ', gender: 'male', breed: 'German Shorthaired Pointer'}
  ];
</script>
```

With this in place, if there is a typo in a dog property name such as "bred" instead of "breed," the TypeScript compiler will flag the error.

20.5 *Image compression*

Another Svelte preprocessor to consider is svelte-image (https://github.com/matyunya/svelte-image). This uses the sharp image processing package (https://github.com/lovell/sharp) to automate image optimization.

This preprocessor looks for img elements to refer to local image files and replaces the src attribute value with a reference to an optimized image that it generates.

The svelte-image package also provides an Image component, which provides lazy loading of images. It also supports the srcset attribute for serving an appropriate image size based on screen width.

In the next chapter you will learn about implementing Android and iOS mobile applications using Svelte Native.

Summary

- Svelte is quite flexible when it comes to using alternative syntaxes for specifying code, markup, and styling.
- Any syntax can be supported if you are willing to write a preprocessor.
- The easiest way to configure preprocessing is to use svelte-preprocess and its auto-preprocessing mode.

21

Svelte Native

This chapter covers
- Svelte Native and NativeScript components
- Developing Svelte Native apps locally
- NativeScript styling
- Predefined NativeScript CSS classes
- The NativeScript UI component library

Svelte Native (https://svelte-native.technology/) enables implementing Android and iOS applications using Svelte by building on top of NativeScript (https://nativescript.org/). It's a big topic. The learning path includes how to structure a Svelte Native app, use provided components, use provided layout mechanisms, implement page navigation, use NativeScript-specific styling and themes, use third-party libraries, and integrate with device capabilities. We will only scratch the surface here, but we will cover enough to enable you to start building mobile apps.

NativeScript uses XML syntax (with custom elements), CSS, and JavaScript/TypeScript to create apps that run on Android and iOS devices. It renders native components rather than web views. NativeScript was created and is maintained by Telerik Corp., which was acquired by Progress Software in 2014.

NativeScript can be used without any web framework. In addition, there are integrations of several popular web frameworks with NativeScript. The NativeScript team supports Angular and Vue integrations, and the community at large supports React and Svelte implementations.

Svelte Native provides a thin layer over the NativeScript API that makes it relatively easy to remain compatible with future NativeScript versions. It was created by David Pershouse, who goes by halfnelson on GitHub and @halfnelson_au on Twitter.

The official Svelte Native tutorial and API documentation can be found on the Svelte Native website: https://svelte-native.technology/.

We will cover all the provided components at a high level. Then we will look at the steps for getting started creating Svelte Native applications. Finally, we will walk through a few example apps, including a basic Hello World app, one that demonstrates nearly all the provided components, and one that uses an add-on library to implement a hamburger (side-drawer) menu.

21.1 Provided components

NativeScript provides many components, and you can build more by combining them. A list of provided components can be found at https://docs.nativescript.org/ui/overview.

Svelte Native exposes all of these components as DOM elements to Svelte, and they are used as alternatives to the HTML elements used in Svelte apps. They are globally available and so can be used in custom Svelte components without importing them. Documentation on these Svelte components can be found at https://svelte-native .technology/docs.

The names of the provided NativeScript components are camel case and begin with a capital letter. However, the Svelte components that wrap them have names that begin with a lowercase letter. This distinguishes them from custom Svelte components whose names must start with an uppercase letter. For example, instead of `<Label text="Hello" />` you would write `<label text="Hello" />`. We will use the Svelte Native names here when discussing them.

The following sections describe each of the provided components at a high level. Section 21.6 provides examples of using each component.

21.1.1 Display components

The Svelte Native components that display data are listed in table 21.1 after the closest HTML element to which they correspond.

The `label` component can specify its content using a `text` attribute, text content, or a `formattedString` child with `span` children.

The `activityIndicator` component displays a platform-specific spinner to indicate that some activity, such as waiting for a response from an API service, is occurring.

Table 21.1   Display components

HTML element	Svelte Native component
`<label>`	`label`
`<img>`	`image`
`<progress>`	`progress`
None	`activityIndicator`
`<ul>` or `<ol>` plus `<li>`	`listView`
None	`htmlView`
None	`webView`

The `listView` component displays a scrolling list of items. Its `items` attribute is set to an array of values that can be any JavaScript type. To specify how each item should be rendered, include a `Template` child element whose content is components that render the item. To take action when an item is clicked, set `on:itemTap` to a function.

The `htmlView` and `webView` components are used to render a string of HTML. Using `webView` is preferred because `htmlView` has a very limited ability to apply CSS styling. The HTML string for an `htmlView` component is specified with an `html` attribute. The HTML string for a `webView` component is specified with a `src` attribute whose value can be an HTML string, a URL, or a path to an HTML file. Often instances of the `webView` component must be given a height because that isn't calculated based on its content. HTML from untrusted sources should be sanitized before it's passed to a `WebView` component because it is capable of executing JavaScript code.

21.1.2   *Form components*

The Svelte Native components that allow user input are listed in table 21.2 after the closest HTML element to which they correspond.

The `searchBar` component is similar to the `textField` component, but it adds a magnifying glass icon to the left of the input.

21.1.3   *Action components*

Components for actions include `actionBar`, `actionItem`, and `navigationButton`.

An `actionBar` is a toolbar that is displayed at the top of the screen. It typically contains a title and can also contain `actionItem` and `navigationButton` components.

`actionItem` components are buttons with platform-specific icons and positioning. An example is the iOS share icon that looks like a square with an arrow pointing up. For Android, the icon is identified by one of the `R.drawable` constants documented at

Table 21.2 Form components

HTML element	Svelte Native component
`<button>`	`button`
`<input type="text">`	`textField` (for single-line)
`<textarea>`	`textView` (for multiline)
`<input type="checkbox">`	`switch`
`<input type="radio">`	`segmentedBar` and `segmentedBarItem`
`<select>` and `<option>`	`listPicker`
`<input type="range">`	`slider`
`<input type="date">`	`datePicker`
`<input type="time">`	`timePicker`
None	`searchBar`

https://developer.android.com/reference/android/R.drawable. For iOS, the icon is one of the `SystemItem` constants documented at https://developer.apple.com/documentation/uikit/uibarbuttonitem/systemitem.

21.1.4 Dialog components

Functions that render a dialog include `action`, `alert`, `confirm`, `login`, and `prompt`. Table 21.3 describes the contents of each kind of dialog.

Table 21.3 Dialog components

Function name	Dialog contents
`action`	Message, vertical list of buttons, and a cancel button
`alert`	Title, message, and a close button
`confirm`	Title, message, cancel button, and OK button
`login`	Title, message, username input, password input, cancel button, and OK button
`prompt`	Title, message, input, cancel button, and OK button

21.1.5 Layout components

Provided components that organize their child components in a certain way are listed in table 21.4 after the closest CSS property value to which they correspond.

A `page` component can optionally contain an `actionBar` component, and it can only contain one top-level layout component.

Table 21.4   Layout components

CSS property	Svelte Native layout component
display: inline	wrapLayout
display: block	stackLayout
display: flex	flexboxLayout
display: grid	gridLayout
position: absolute	absoluteLayout
None	dockLayout

absoluteLayout requires its children to specify their absolute location with left and top attributes.

dockLayout positions its children on a given side of the screen: left, right, top, or bottom. The example in listing 21.1 shows how to create the classic layout with a header, footer, and left nav (see figure 21.1). Note that the header and footer children must come before the left child in order for them to span all the way across the display.

Listing 21.1   App that uses dockLayout

```
<page>
  <dockLayout>
    <label class="header big" dock="top" text="Header" />
    <label class="footer big" dock="bottom" text="Footer" />
    <label class="nav big" dock="left" text="Nav" />
    <stackLayout>
      <label text="Center child #1" />
      <label text="Center child #2" />
    </stackLayout>
  </dockLayout>
</page>

<style>
  .big {
    color: white;
    font-size: 24;
    padding: 20;
  }

  .footer {
    background-color: purple;
    border-top-width: 3;
  }

  .header {
    background-color: red;
    border-bottom-width: 3;
  }
```

```
.nav {
  background-color: green;
  border-right-width: 3;
}

stackLayout {
  background-color: lightblue;
  padding: 20;
}
</style>
```

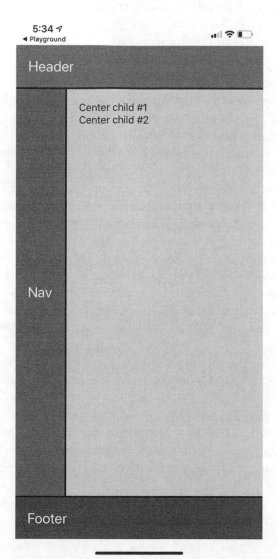

Figure 21.1 A dockLayout example

flexboxLayout implements most of CSS flexbox. Elements that use it can be styled using standard flexbox CSS properties. In addition, it supports the following attributes:

- justifyContent with values stretch (default), flex-start, flex-end, center, and baseline
- alignItems with values stretch (default), flex-start, flex-end, center, space-between, and space-around
- alignContent with the same values as justifyContent only affects containers with more than one line (rarely used)
- flexDirection with values row (default), column, row-reverse, and column-reverse
- flexWrap with values nowrap (default), wrap, and wrap-reverse

Child elements of flexboxLayout can specify the attributes alignSelf, flexGrow, flexShrink, flexWrapBefore, and order.

The gridLayout element organizes its children into cells inside rows and columns. A cell can span more than one row and/or column. This is *not* related to CSS grid layout. The row and column attributes, whose values are comma-separated lists, specify the number of rows and columns, the height of each row, and the width of each column.

There are three options for row and column sizes: an absolute number, auto, or *. Specifying auto makes it as small as possible to accommodate everything in that row or column. Specifying * makes it as large as possible after satisfying the requirements of the other rows or columns. Preceding * with a number acts as a multiplier. For example, columns="100,2*,*" means that the first column is 100 *device-independent pixels* (DIPs) wide, the second column is 2/3 of the remaining space, and the third column is 1/3 of the remaining space.

Child elements of gridLayout specify their grid position with row and column attributes. They can also specify rowSpan and colSpan attributes to span more than one row and/or column.

stackLayout is the most basic of the supported layouts. It simply lays out its children vertically (default) or horizontally. To lay out children horizontally, add the attribute orientation="horizontal".

wrapLayout is similar to stackLayout, but children wrap to the next row or column when space is exhausted. It differs from stackLayout in that its default orientation is horizontal. To lay out children vertically, add the attribute orientation="vertical". To specify a fixed width and/or height for each child, add the itemWidth and/or itemHeight attributes.

While not exactly being a layout, the scrollView component does act as a container for other components. It creates a fixed size area where its child components can be scrolled vertically and horizontally.

21.1.6 Navigation components

Components for creating navigation tabs include `tabs` (displayed at the top of the screen) and `bottomNavigation` (displayed at the bottom). The `tabs` component is more full-featured than `bottomNavigation`. For example, it supports switching tabs by swiping left or right across the content area below the tabs.

Both `tabs` and `bottomNavigation` have children that are `tabStrip` and `tabContentItem` components. The children of `tabStrip` components are `tabStripItem` components, which represent each of the tabs. The `tabContentItem` components hold the components to render when the corresponding tab is selected. The children of `tabContentItem` components are typically layout components containing many children.

`navigationButton` components are buttons for platform-specific functionality, such as the back button.

Another way to support page navigation is to use a side drawer. This is not provided in Native Script. It is an add-on that can be found in the Native Script UI library that is described in section 21.7. See the `RadSideDrawer` component.

21.2 Getting started with Svelte Native

The easiest way to get started with Svelte Native is to use the online REPL at https://svelte-native.technology/repl. This is similar to the Svelte REPL. It allows writing, testing, and saving (as GitHub Gists) Svelte Native apps without installing anything. However, unlike the Svelte REPL, it cannot currently download an app, show a list of saved REPL sessions, or recall them.

Another option is to use the online Playground at https://play.nativescript.org/. This has the same options as the Svelte Native REPL, but it also supports projects using any kind of NativeScript project including Angular, Vue, React, Svelte, plain JavaScript, and plain TypeScript.

Both the Svelte REPL and Playground will prompt you to install the NativeScript Playground and NativeScript Preview apps. Do this on all devices to be used for testing apps. For Android, search the Google Play store. For iOS, search the iOS App Store.

To run your app in NativeScript Playground on a device, click the Preview button in the upper right or click QR Code at the top. Both will display a QR code in a dialog. Scan this using the NativeScript Playground app on the devices. It will launch the NativeScript app inside the NativeScript Preview app.

Like the Svelte and Svelte Native REPLs, NativeScript Playground allows you to create an account, log in, and save projects that can be recalled later. To see and select previously saved projects, click Projects in the top nav bar.

After making code changes, click Save at the top. The app will reload on all the devices that have scanned the QR code of the app.

The left side of the Playground includes a file explorer and a palette of components. Component icons can be dragged into code to add an instance of them.

The bottom area has a Devices tab that lists the devices being used. Any number of devices can be tested simultaneously.

21.3 *Developing Svelte Native apps locally*

For serious development of a Svelte Native app, you will want to create a project where all the required files are available locally and your preferred editor or IDE can be used. To do this, follow these steps:

1 Install the NativeScript command-line interface (CLI) globally on your computer by entering `npm install -g nativescript`.
2 Verify installation by entering `tns`, which outputs help ("tns" stands for Telerik NativeScript).
3 Create a new app by entering `npx degit halfnelson/svelte-native-template` `app-name`.
4 Enter `cd app-name`.
5 Enter `tns preview` to build the app and display a QR code.
6 Open the NativeScript Playground app on a mobile device.
7 Tap Scan QR Code and point the camera at the QR code. The first time this is done, it will ask you to install the NativeScript Preview app if it is not already installed. Press Install to proceed.
8 The NativeScript Preview app will launch and display the app. Before making modifications, this will just display a rocket icon followed by the text "Blank Svelte Native App".
9 On your computer, modify the app. Changes will live reload on the phone.

Live reload is very fast, taking only about three seconds for a small app.

Another option to consider, not covered here, is the Electron app NativeScript Sidekick. For information on this, see the NativeScript blog: http://mng.bz/04pJ.

Here is a basic Hello World Svelte Native app. Simply modify `app/App.svelte` to match the following.

Listing 21.2 Hello World Svelte Native app

```
<script>
  let name = 'World';
</script>

<page>
  <actionBar title="Hello World Demo" />
  <stackLayout class="p-20">                    ⟵  "p-20" is a provided
    <flexboxLayout>                                  CSS class that sets
      <label class="name-label" text="Name:" />     padding to 20.
      <textField class="name-input" bind:text={name} />
    </flexboxLayout>
    <label class="message" text="Hello, {name}!" />
  </stackLayout>
</page>

<style>
  .message {
    color: red;
```

```
    font-size: 50;              ◁──┐  Note that no units
  }                                │  are specified on
                                   │  CSS sizes.
  .name-input {
    font-size: 30;
    flex-grow: 1;
  }

  .name-label {
    font-size: 30;
    margin-right: 10;
  }
</style>
```

Svelte Native apps can be run in an emulator for a specific device. This requires installing a lot of software that is specific to Android and iOS. For details on this, see https://svelte-native.technology/docs#advanced-install.

21.4 *NativeScript styling*

NativeScript supports a large subset of CSS selectors and properties. It also supports some NativeScript-specific CSS properties. All of these are documented at https://docs.nativescript.org/ui/styling.

CSS rules that should affect the entire application are placed in `app/app.css`. By default, this imports `~nativescript-theme-core/css/core.css` and `./font-awesome.css` (for icons).

> **NOTE** `nativescript-theme-core` is deprecated. Svelte Native still uses this by default and it works for now. See https://docs.nativescript.org/ui/theme for details.

Svelte Native component names are treated as custom element names. They can be used as CSS selectors for styling all instances of the component.

For CSS property values that represent a size, when no unit is specified, the value represents *device-independent pixels* (DIPs). This is the recommended unit to use. A "px" suffix can be added to size values for plain pixels that vary across devices, but using this unit is discouraged. Percentages with a "%" suffix are also supported.

Other supported CSS features include

- CSS variables
- The `calc` function
- The generic fonts `serif`, `sans-serif`, and `monospace`
- Custom fonts in TTF or OTF format found in the `app/fonts` directory
- Importing a CSS file from another with `@import url('file-path')`
- Using Sass (with some setup)

Some CSS shorthand properties are not supported. For example, instead of `border: solid red 3px;`, use `border-color: red; border-width: 3px;`. The `border-style` property is not supported. All borders are solid.

The `outline` shorthand property and all CSS properties whose names begin with `outline-` are not supported.

To change the style of text within a block of text, use the `formattedString` element with `span` elements as children. Each `span` can specify different styling. The `formattedString` element must be a child of a component that supports text content such as `button`, `label`, `textField`, and `textView`. The following listing shows an example of using `formattedString`.

Listing 21.3 `formattedString` example

```
<page>
  <stackLayout class="p-20">
    <label class="panagram" textWrap="true">
      <formattedString>
        <span class="fox">The quick brown fox</span>
        <span text=" jumps over " />
        <span class="dog">the lazy dog</span>
        <span text="." />
      </formattedString>
    </label>
  </stackLayout>
</page>

<style>
  .panagram {
    font-size: 30;
  }

  .fox {
    color: red;
    font-weight: bold;
  }

  .dog {
    color: blue;
    font-style: italic;
  }
</style>
```

A panagram is a sentence that contains all the letters of the alphabet.

This text will be red and bold.

This text will be black and normal.

This text will be blue and italic.

21.5 Predefined NativeScript CSS classes

Components can be styled by defining CSS classes that match their name. For example, the following makes all `label` components blue and bold:

```
label {
  color: blue;
  font-weight: bold;
}
```

NativeScript provides a set of predefined CSS classes that can be applied to Native-Script components for common styling needs. These are conveniences that can be used in place of explicitly applying CSS properties.

These predefined classes are appropriate for applying to label components:

- *Headings*—h1, h2, h3, h4, h5, and h6
- *Paragraphs*—body for medium-sized text
- *Footnotes*—footnote for small text
- *Alignment*—text-left, text-center, and text-right
- *Case*—text-lowercase, text-uppercase, and text-capitalize
- *Weight*—font-weight-normal and font-weight-bold
- *Style*—font-italic

The following snippet is an example of using a predefined class.

```
<label class="h1" text="This is BIG!" />
```

There are many provided CSS classes that specify the desired padding and margin (see table 21.5). In these class names, # is a placeholder for a number, which must be one of 0, 2, 5, 10, 15, 20, 25, or 30.

Table 21.5   CSS classes that specify padding and margin

Sides	Padding	Margin
All	p-#	m-#
Top (t)	p-t-#	m-t-#
Right (r)	p-r-#	m-r-#
Bottom (b)	p-b-#	m-b-#
Left (l)	p-l-#	m-l-#
Left and right	p-x-#	m-x-#
Top and bottom	p-y-#	m-y-#

There are several provided CSS classes for styling forms and form elements such as buttons. For details, see the NativeScript documentation for forms (https://docs .nativescript.org/ui/theme#forms) and for buttons (https://docs.nativescript.org/ui/ theme#buttons).

The equivalent of the HTML horizontal rule <hr> element is to use an empty stackLayout with the hr class, as follows:

```
<stackLayout class="hr" />
```

To overlay the default horizontal rule with a thicker, colored rule, add CSS properties to the hr CSS class as follows:

```
.hr {
  --size: 10;
  height: var(--size);
```

```
    border-color: green;
    border-width: calc(var(--size) / 2);
}
```

For more details on NativeScript styling, see https://docs.nativescript.org/ui/styling.

21.6   *NativeScript themes*

NativeScript supports styling themes through a large set of CSS classes. To install a default theme along with 11 more themes, enter `npm install @nativescript/theme`. Additional themes not provided by NativeScript can also be installed. Each theme simply overrides the predefined CSS classes. These support light and dark modes.

To use the default theme, edit `app/app.css` and replace the import of `core.css` with the following:

```
@import '~@nativescript/theme/css/core.css';
@import '~@nativescript/theme/css/default.css';
```

To use one of the other included themes, replace `default` in the second line above with one of `aqua`, `blue`, `brown`, `forest`, `grey`, `lemon`, `lime`, `orange`, `purple`, `ruby`, or `sky`.

21.7   *Comprehensive example*

Up until now, we've been using the Travel Packing app as our example, but we're going to switch gears here in the interest of brevity. The Svelte Native app in this section provides examples of using nearly all of the components included in NativeScript. It provides a good jumping off point for implementing your own Svelte Native applications.

The app has three pages, each presenting examples of components in a given category:

- The first category is components that display information. This includes the `label`, `webView`, `image`, and `progress` components.
- The second category is components that accept user input. This includes `textField`, `textView`, `switch`, `segmentedBar`, `datePicker`, `timePicker`, `listView`, `listPicker`, and `slider`.
- The third category is functions that render dialogs and components used for search queries. This includes the functions `login`, `prompt`, `action`, and `confirm`. It also includes the `searchBar` and `activityIndicator` components.

Page navigation is configured in `App.svelte` (see figure 21.2).

Figure 21.2   Component that
handles page navigation

Listing 21.4 Component that handles page navigation in `app/App.svelte`

```
<script>
  import DisplayComponents from './DisplayComponents.svelte';       ◁┐  These three
  import InputComponents from './InputComponents.svelte';            │  imports are for
  import OtherComponents from './OtherComponents.svelte';            │  the "page"
                                                                     ┘  components.
  function onTapDelete() {
    console.log('App.svelte onTapDelete: entered');
  }

  function onTapShare() {
    console.log('App.svelte onTapShare: entered');
  }
</script>
                                                    The actionBar component
                                                    is rendered at the top of
<page>                                              the screen.
  <actionBar title="Svelte Native Demo">   ◁────────
    <!-- button with upload icon -->
    <actionItem on:tap="{onTapShare}"
      ios.systemIcon="9" ios.position="left"
      android.systemIcon="ic_menu_share" android.position="actionBar" />
    <!-- button with trash can icon -->
    <actionItem on:tap="{onTapDelete}"
      ios.systemIcon="16" ios.position="right"
      android.systemIcon="ic_menu_delete"
      text="delete" android.position="popup" />
  </actionBar>
                              The tabs component is rendered
  <tabs>       ◁──────────────│ below the actionBar. It contains
    <tabStrip>                 │ one tab for each page of the app.
      <tabStripItem>
        <label text="Display" />
        <image src="font://&#xF26C;" class="fas" />   ◁┐  This is a
      </tabStripItem>                                   ┘  monitor icon.
      <tabStripItem>
        <label text="Input" />
        <image src="font://&#xF11C;" class="far" />   ◁    This is a
      </tabStripItem>                                       keyboard icon.
      <tabStripItem>
        <label text="Other" />
        <image src="font://&#xF002;" class="fas" />   ◁┐  This is a magnifying
      </tabStripItem>                                   ┘  glass icon.
    </tabStrip>

    <tabContentItem>            ◁┐  There is one tabContentItem
      <DisplayComponents />       │ for each tabStripItem. Each of
    </tabContentItem>            ┘ these render a page of the app.

    <tabContentItem>
      <InputComponents />
    </tabContentItem>

    <tabContentItem>
      <OtherComponents />
```

```
      </tabContentItem>
    </tabs>
</page>

<style>
  tabStrip {
    --tsi-unselected-color: purple;
    --tsi-selected-color: green;

    background-color: lightblue;
    highlight-color: green;
  }

  tabStripItem {
    color: var(--tsi-unselected-color); /* for icon */
  }

  tabStripItem > label {
    color: var(--tsi-unselected-color); /* for text */
  }

  tabStripItem:active {
    color: var(--tsi-selected-color); /* for icon */
  }

  tabStripItem:active > label {
    color: var(--tsi-selected-color); /* for text */
  }
</style>
```

NOTE   The image elements in listing 21.4, such as the monitor, keyboard, and magnifying glass icons, use FontAwesome icons. To find the hex code for a given icon, search for them at https://fontawesome.com/icons. For example, searching for "house" and clicking the "home" icon shows that its code is f015 and its class is fas. The CSS classes fab, far, and fas are defined in app/fontawesome.css. The CSS class fa-home is not defined by default in Svelte Native.

The following app-wide CSS styling is added to the existing app.css file.

Listing 21.5   Global styling in `app/app.css`

```
button {
  background-color: lightgray;
  border-color: darkgray;
  border-width: 3;
  border-radius: 10;
  font-weight: bold;
  horizontal-align: center; /* to size according to content */
  padding: 10;
}

label {
  color: blue;
```

```
    font-size: 18;
    font-weight: bold;
}

.plain {
  color: black;
  font-size: 12;
  font-weight: normal;
}

.title {
  border-top-color: purple;
  border-top-width: 5px;
  color: purple;
  font-size: 20;
  font-weight: bold;
  font-style: italic;
  margin-top: 10;
  padding-top: 10;
}
```

This app uses several Svelte stores in order to share data across components. They are all defined in stores.js.

Listing 21.6   Stores in `app/stores.js`

```
import {derived, writable} from 'svelte/store';

export const authenticated = writable(false);
export const backgroundColor = writable('pink');
export const favoriteColorIndex = writable(0);
export const firstName = writable('');

// Not a store.
export const colors = ['red', 'orange', 'yellow', 'green', 'blue', 'purple'];

async function evaluateColor(color) {
  if (color === 'yellow') {
    alert({
      title: 'Hey there!',
      message: 'That is my favorite color too!',
      okButtonText: 'Cool'
    });
  } else if (color === 'green') {
    const confirmed = await confirm({
      title: 'Confirm Color',
      message: 'Are you sure you like that color?',
      okButtonText: 'Yes',
      cancelButtonText: 'No'
    });

    if (!confirmed) favoriteColorIndex.set(0);
  }
}
```

This is used as the background color of all the pages. It is pink when the user has not logged in. It is light green when they have.

This function is called by the favoriteColor derived store defined below.

This sets the favorite color to "red" if the user doesn't like "green".

```
export const favoriteColor = derived(
  favoriteColorIndex,
  index => {
    const color = colors[index];
    evaluateColor(color);
    return color;
  }
);
```

This is a derived store based on the favoriteColorIndex store. It updates its value to a color name every time the value of the favoriteColorIndex store changes.

The page defined by the DisplayComponents component provides examples of components that display information (see figure 21.3).

Figure 21.3   DisplayComponents **component**

`htmlView` **and** `webView` **issues**

There are some issues to consider when using the `htmlView` and `webView` components.

The NativeScript docs say "The HtmlView component has limited styling capabilities. For more complex scenarios use the WebView component." Using `htmlView` is fine for simple needs such as rendering rich text using bold and italics. For more advanced styling, use `webView`.

The `webView` component does not calculate its height based on its content, so it needs to be given a height in CSS unless the layout being used gives it a height.

The Svelte Native docs show that the `src` attribute of a `webView` can be set to a path to an HTML file. Webpack must be properly configured to include the HTML file in the bundle. For tips on doing this, see the issue at https://github.com/halfnelson/svelte-native/issues/138.

Listing 21.7 `DisplayComponents` **component in** `app/DisplayComponents`
`.svelte`

```
<script>
  import {backgroundColor} from './stores';

  const myHtml = `                          ⟵——— This is displayed in
    <div>                                          a webView below.
      <span style="color: red">The quick brown fox</span>
      <span>jumps over</span>
      <span style="color: blue">the lazy dog</span>
    </div>
  `;
                                          Tapping the "Start Progress" button
  let progressPercent = 0;                causes this to be called. It animates
                                          the value of the progress bar.
  function startProgress() {   ⟵———
    progressPercent = 0;
    const token = setInterval(() => {
      progressPercent++;
      if (progressPercent === 100) clearInterval(token);
    }, 10);
  }
</script>

<scrollView>
  <stackLayout
    backgroundColor={$backgroundColor}
    class="p-20"
  >
    <label class="title" text="label" />
    <label class="plain" text="some text" />

    <label class="title" text="label with formattedString" />
    <label class="panagram" textWrap="true">                    This renders a string
      <formattedString>                          ⟵———          where runs of text can
        <span class="fox">The quick brown fox</span>            have different styling.
```

```
        <span text=" jumps over " />
        <span class="dog">the lazy dog</span>
        <span text="." />
      </formattedString>
    </label>

    <label class="title" text="image" />
    <wrapLayout class="image-frame">
      <image src="~/svelte-native-logos.png" stretch="aspectFit" />
    </wrapLayout>

    <label class="title" text="webView" />
    <webView src="<h1>I am a webView.</h1>" />
    <webView src={myHtml} />
    <webView style="height: 300" src="https://svelte-native.technology/" />

    <label class="title" text="progress" />
    <button on:tap={startProgress}>Start Progress</button>
    <progress class="progress" maxValue={100} value="{progressPercent}" />
  </stackLayout>
</scrollView>

<style>
  .dog {
    color: blue;
    font-style: italic;
  }

  .fox {
    color: red;
    font-weight: bold;
  }

  .image-frame {
    background-color: white;
    padding: 10;
  }

  .panagram {
    background-color: linen;
    color: black;
    font-size: 26;
    font-weight: normal;
    margin-bottom: 20;
    padding: 20;
  }

  progress {
    color: red;
    margin-bottom: 10;
    scale-y: 5; /* changes height */
  }

  webView {
    border-color: red;
    border-width: 1;
    height: 50;
  }
</style>
```

The CSS padding property doesn't affect image components. This is a workaround to add padding to an image.

The rendered page can be scrolled inside the webView component.

Svelte Native treats ~ at the beginning of a file path as an alias to the app directory. This image can be found at https://github.com/mvolkmann/svelte-native-components/blob/master/app/svelte-native-logos.png.

No webView content will be visible without this.

The page defined by the InputComponents component provides examples of components that gather user input (see figure 21.4).

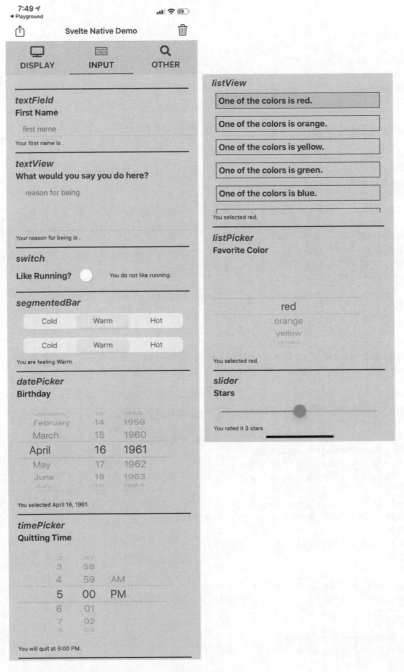

Figure 21.4 InputComponents **component**

Listing 21.8   InputComponents component in app/InputComponents.svelte

```
<script>
  import {Template} from 'svelte-native/components'

  import {
    backgroundColor,
    colors,
    favoriteColor,
    favoriteColorIndex,
    firstName
  } from './stores';

  const temperatures = ['Cold', 'Warm', 'Hot'];

  let birthday = new Date(1961, 3, 16);
  let likeRunning = false;
  let reason = '';
  let stars = 3;
  let temperatureIndex = 1;

  let quittingTime = new Date();
  quittingTime.setHours(17);
  quittingTime.setMinutes(0);
  quittingTime.setSeconds(0);

  function formatDate(date) {
    if (!date) return '';
    let month = date.toLocaleDateString('default', {month: 'long'});
    const index = month.indexOf(' ');
    if (index) month = month.substring(0, index);
    return `${month} ${date.getDate()}, ${date.getFullYear()}`;
  }

  function formatTime(date) {
    if (!date) return '';

    let hours = date.getHours();
    const amPm = hours < 12 ? 'AM' : 'PM';
    if (hours >= 12) hours -= 12;

    let minutes = date.getMinutes();
    if (minutes < 10) minutes = '0' + minutes;

    return `${hours}:${minutes} ${amPm}`;
  }

  function onFavoriteColor(event) {
    $favoriteColorIndex = event.value; // odd that this is an index
  }

  function onTapColor(event) {
    $favoriteColorIndex = event.index;
  }
```

This formats a Date object as a string like "April 16, 1961".

This formats a Date object as a string like "5:00 PM".

```
    function starChange(event) {
      stars = Math.round(event.value);
    }
</script>
```

This is an attempt to get the "stars" slider to snap to an integer value, but it does not work.

```
<scrollView>
  <stackLayout
    backgroundColor={$backgroundColor}
    class="p-20"
  >
    <!-- like HTML <input type="text"> -->
    <label class="title" text="textField" />
    <wrapLayout>
      <label text="First Name" />
      <textField class="first-name" hint="first name" bind:text={$firstName} />
      <label class="plain" text="Your first name is {$firstName}." />
    </wrapLayout>


    <!-- like HTML <textarea> -->
    <label class="title" text="textView" />
    <wrapLayout>
      <label text="What would you say you do here?" />
      <textView class="reason" hint="reason for being" bind:text={reason} />
      <label class="plain" text="Your reason for being is {reason}." textWrap=
      "true" />
    </wrapLayout>


    <!-- like HTML <input type="checkbox"> -->
    <label class="title" text="switch" />
    <wrapLayout>
      <label text="Like Running?" />
      <switch bind:checked={likeRunning} />
      <label
        class="plain"
        text="You{likeRunning ? '' : ' do not'} like running."
      />
    </wrapLayout>


    <!-- like HTML <input type="radio"> -->
    <label class="title" text="segmentedBar" />
    <segmentedBar
      bind:selectedIndex={temperatureIndex}
      selectedBackgroundColor="yellow"
    >
      <segmentedBarItem title="Cold" />
      <segmentedBarItem title="Warm" />
      <segmentedBarItem title="Hot" />
    </segmentedBar>
    <segmentedBar
      bind:selectedIndex={temperatureIndex}
      selectedBackgroundColor="yellow"
    >
      {#each temperatures as temp}
```

This shows another way to provide items to the segmentedBar component. The API docs show passing an array of items using the "items" prop, but that does not work. The children must be segmentedBarItem components.

```
      <segmentedBarItem title={temp} />
   {/each}
</segmentedBar>
<label
  class="plain"
  text="You are feeling {temperatures[temperatureIndex]}."
/>


<!-- like HTML <input type="date"> -->
<label class="title" text="datePicker" />
<wrapLayout>
  <label text="Birthday" />
  <datePicker bind:date={birthday} />
  <label class="plain" text="You selected {formatDate(birthday)}." />
</wrapLayout>


<!-- like HTML <input type="time"> -->
<label class="title" text="timePicker" />
<wrapLayout>
  <label text="Quitting Time" />
  <timePicker bind:time={quittingTime} />
  <label class="plain" text="You will quit at {formatTime(quittingTime)}." />
</wrapLayout>


<!-- like HTML <ul>, <ol>, or <select> -->
<label class="title" text="listView" />
<wrapLayout>
  <listView items={colors} on:itemTap={onTapColor}>
    <Template let:item={color}>
      <label
        class="list"
        class:selected={color === $favoriteColor}
        text="One of the colors is {color}."
      />
    </Template>
  </listView>
</wrapLayout>
<label class="plain" text="You selected {$favoriteColor}." />


<!-- like HTML <select> -->
<label class="title" text="listPicker" />
<wrapLayout>
  <label text="Favorite Color" />
  <listPicker
    items={colors}
    selectedIndex={$favoriteColorIndex}
    on:selectedIndexChange={onFavoriteColor}
  />
  <label class="plain" text="You selected {$favoriteColor}." />
</wrapLayout>


<!-- like HTML <input type="range"> -->
<label class="title" text="slider" />
```

> This acts like an HTML select element when there is an on:itemTap handler.

> This is not reevaluated when the value of the favoriteColor store changes, so the presence of the selected CSS class is not updated.

```
    <wrapLayout>
      <label text="Stars" />
      <slider
        minValue={1}
        maxValue={5}
        value={stars}
        on:valueChange={starChange}
      />
      <label class="plain" text="You rated it {stars} stars" />
    </wrapLayout>
  </stackLayout>
</scrollView>

<style>
  .first-name {
    width: 100%;
  }

  .list {
    border-color: blue;
    border-width: 1;
    margin: 0;
  }

  .reason {
    width: 100%;
  }

  segmentedBar {
    color: red;
    margin-bottom: 10;
    margin-top: 10;
  }

  .selected {
    background-color: lightgreen;
  }
</style>
```

> The slider position doesn't change when the starChange function changes the value of stars. See the issue at https://github.com/halfnelson/svelte-native/issues/128.

The page defined by the OtherComponents component provides examples of components that render a dialog or prompt for a search query (see figure 21.5).

When the Login button is tapped, the dialog in figure 21.6 is displayed.

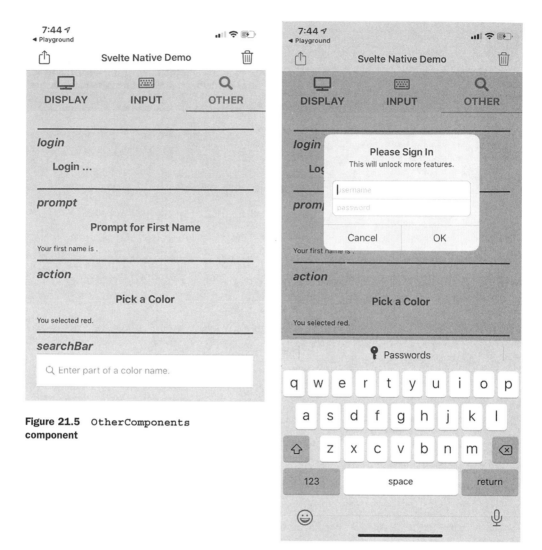

Figure 21.5   `OtherComponents` component

Figure 21.6   Login dialog

If the user enters a correct username and password, the background of all the pages changes from pink to light green to indicate that they have been authenticated (see figure 21.7).

When the Prompt for First Name button is tapped, the dialog in figure 21.8 is displayed.

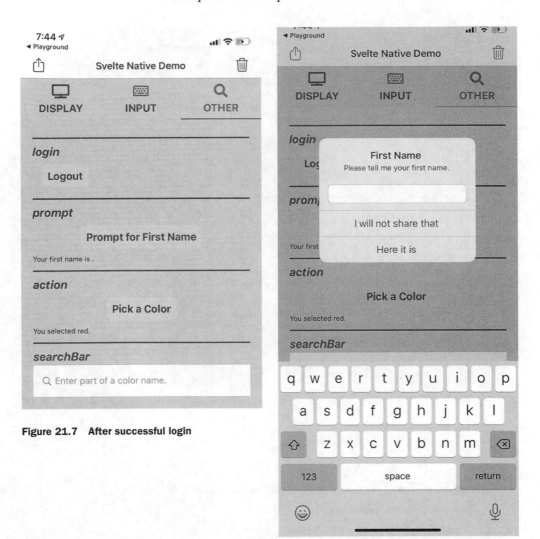

Figure 21.7   After successful login

Figure 21.8   Prompt for first name

When the Pick a Color button is tapped, the dialog in figure 21.9 is displayed.

After entering part of a color name in the search input, a dialog like the one in figure 21.10 is displayed.

Listing 21.9 shows the code for OtherComponents that implements the preceding functionality.

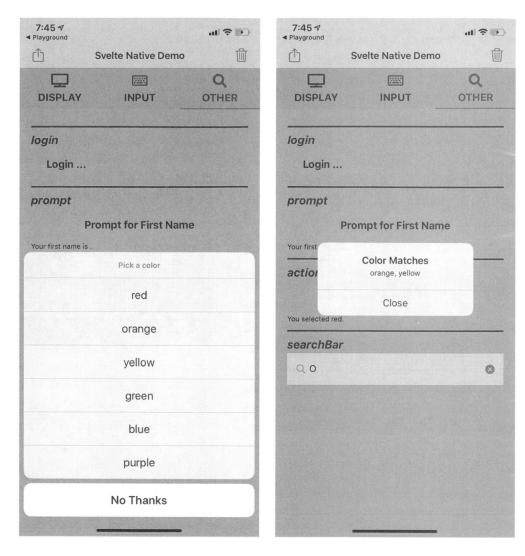

Figure 21.9   Prompt for color   **Figure 21.10   Search results**

Listing 21.9   `OtherComponents` component in `app/OtherComponents.svelte`

```
<script>
  import {login} from 'tns-core-modules/ui/dialogs'
  import {
    authenticated,
    backgroundColor,
    colors,
    favoriteColor,
    favoriteColorIndex,
```

```
    firstName
  } from './stores';

  let busy = false;
  let query = '';

  // Should this be handled in stores.js?
  $: $backgroundColor = $authenticated ? 'lightgreen' : 'pink';

  async function getFirstName() {
    const res = await prompt({
      title: 'First Name',
      message: 'Please tell me your first name.',
      okButtonText: 'Here it is',
      cancelButtonText: 'I will not share that'
    });
    if (res.result) $firstName = res.text;
  }

  function onSearchSubmit() {
    busy = true;
    setTimeout(async () => { // to demonstrate activityIndicator component
      // The event object passed to this does not contain the search text
      // or any interesting properties.
      const q = query.toLowerCase();
      const matches = colors.filter(color => color.includes(q));
      busy = false;
      await alert({
        title: 'Color Matches',
        message: matches.length ? matches.join(', ') : 'no matches',
        okButtonText: 'Close'
      });
      query = ''; // reset
    }, 1000);
  }

  async function pickColor() {
    const NONE = 'No Thanks';
    const choice = await action('Pick a color', NONE, colors);
    if (choice !== NONE) {
      $favoriteColorIndex = colors.findIndex(c => c === choice);
    }
  }

  async function promptForLogin() {
    const res = await login({
      title: 'Please Sign In',
      message: 'This will unlock more features.',
      userNameHint: 'username',
      passwordHint: 'password',
      okButtonText: 'OK',
      cancelButtonText: 'Cancel',
    });
    if (res.result) {
      // Authenticate the user here.
```

```
      $authenticated = res.userName === 'foo' && res.password === 'bar';
      if (!$authenticated) {
        alert({
          title: 'Login Failed',
          message: 'Your username or password was incorrect.',
          okButtonText: 'Bummer'
        });
      }
    }
  }
</script>

<scrollView>
  <stackLayout
    backgroundColor={$backgroundColor}
    class="p-20"
  >
    <label class="title" text="login" />
    <wrapLayout>
      {#if $authenticated}
        <button on:tap={() => $authenticated = false}>Logout</button>
      {:else}
        <button on:tap={promptForLogin}>Login ...</button>
      {/if}
    </wrapLayout>

    <label class="title" text="prompt" />
    <button on:tap={getFirstName}>Prompt for First Name</button>
    <label class="plain" text="Your first name is {$firstName}." />

    <label class="title" text="action" />
    <button on:tap={pickColor}>Pick a Color</button>
    <label class="plain" text="You selected {$favoriteColor}." />

    <label class="title" text="searchBar" />
    <!-- Using gridLayout to position activityIndicator over searchBar. -->
    <gridLayout rows="*">
      <searchBar
        hint="Enter part of a color name."
        bind:text={query}
        on:submit={onSearchSubmit}
        row="0"
      />
      <!-- The activityIndicator height and width attributes
        control the allocated space.
        But the size of the spinner cannot be changed,
        only the color. -->
      <activityIndicator busy={busy} row="0"/>
    </gridLayout>
  </stackLayout>
</scrollView>

<style>
  activityIndicator {
```

```
    color: blue;
  }

  searchBar {
    margin-bottom: 10;
  }
</style>
```

21.8 *NativeScript UI component library*

NativeScript UI is a collection of NativeScript components that are not included by default. They include `RadAutoCompleteTextView`, `RadCalendar`, `RadChart`, `RadData-Form`, `RadGauge`, `RadListView`, and `RadSideDrawer`.

To use these components in a Svelte Native app, first create the app using `npx degit halfnelson/svelte-native-template` *app-name*. Then see the instructions on the NativeScript UI GitHub page at https://github.com/halfnelson/svelte-native-nativescript-ui.

`RadListView` is a particularly popular component. It renders a list of items with animations and support for many gestures including "pull to refresh" and "swipe actions."

Another popular component is `RadSideDrawer`. This provides a drawer-based side nav with a hamburger menu that is used for page navigation. Let's walk through an example that uses this.

To prepare a Svelte Native app for using a `RadSideDrawer` component, do the following:

1 Enter `npm install svelte-native-nativescript-ui`.
2 Enter `tns plugin add nativescript-ui-sidedrawer`.

Our app will have two pages named "About" and "Hello". The About page merely describes the app. The Hello page allows the user to enter a name, and it renders a greeting message.

The side drawer contains the page names. To display the side drawer, click the hamburger icon in the upper left of a page, or drag right from the left edge of the screen. Tap a page name to close the side drawer and navigate to that page. Tap outside of the side drawer to close it without navigating to a different page.

Figures 21.11, 21.12, and 21.13 show the relevant parts of the two pages and the side drawer.

Figure 21.11   About page

Figure 21.12   Hello page

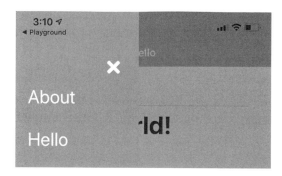

Figure 21.13   Side drawer open

Configuration of the side drawer is specified in `App.svelte`.

Listing 21.10   Topmost component in `app/App.svelte`

```
<script>
  import {onMount} from 'svelte';
  import RadSideDrawerElement from
    'svelte-native-nativescript-ui/sidedrawer';
  import AboutPage from './AboutPage.svelte';
  import HelloPage from './HelloPage.svelte';
  import {goToPage, setDrawer} from './nav';

  RadSideDrawerElement.register();      ◁——  This is required to use the
                                              radSideDrawer element.
  let drawer;

  onMount(() => setDrawer(drawer));     ◁——  This lets nav.js know
</script>                                     about the drawer.

<page>
  <radSideDrawer bind:this={drawer} drawerContentSize="200">    ◁——
    <radSideDrawer.drawerContent>
      <stackLayout>
        <label
          class="fas h2"
          text="&#xF00D;"
          padding="10"
```

This defines the content of the drawer. `⌐▷`

This renders an "X" that can be clicked to close the drawer.

The default drawer width is wider than this app needs, so we set it to 300.

```
        horizontalAlignment="right"
        on:tap={() => drawer.closeDrawer()}
      />
      <label text="About" on:tap={() => goToPage(AboutPage)} />
      <label text="Hello" on:tap={() => goToPage(HelloPage)} />
    </stackLayout>
  </radSideDrawer.drawerContent>
  <radSideDrawer.mainContent>
    <frame id="mainFrame" defaultPage={HelloPage} />
  </radSideDrawer.mainContent>
</radSideDrawer>
</page>
```

← This is where each of the pages will be rendered.

```
<style>
  label {
    color: white;
    font-size: 30;
    padding-bottom: 30;
  }

  stackLayout {
    background-color: cornflowerblue;
    padding: 20;
  }
</style>
```

Functions for navigating to a given page (optionally passing it props) and toggling the drawer between being open and closed are defined in nav.js. The drawer is passed to setDrawer in the preceding listing for App.svelte.

Listing 21.11 Navigation functions in `app/nav.js`

```
import {navigate} from 'svelte-native';

let drawer;

export function setDrawer(d) {
  drawer = d;
}

export function goToPage(page, props) {
  drawer.closeDrawer();
  // Setting clearHistory to true prevents "<Back" button from appearing.
  navigate({page, props, clearHistory: true, frame: 'mainFrame'});
}

export function toggleDrawer() {
  drawer.toggleDrawerState();
}
```

This saves the drawer so it can be used in the goToPage and toggleDrawer functions.

This is currently only called when a page name in the drawer is tapped. However, it could be used from any page to navigate to another page.

This is called when the hamburger icon in the Header component is tapped.

"mainFrame" is the ID of the frame created in App.svelte.

Each page renders a Header component. It contains an actionBar that renders a hamburger icon and a page title. Tapping the hamburger icon opens the side drawer.

Listing 21.12 Header component in `app/Header.svelte`

```
<script>
  import {toggleDrawer} from './nav'
  import {isAndroid} from "tns-core-modules/platform"    <—

  export let title = '';
</script>

<actionBar title={title}>
  {#if isAndroid}    <—
    <navigationButton icon="res://menu" on:tap={toggleDrawer} />
  {:else}
    <actionItem icon="res://menu" ios.position="left" on:tap={toggleDrawer} /
    >
  {/if}
</actionBar>

<style>
  actionBar {
    background-color: cornflowerblue;
    color: white;
  }
</style>
```

> This holds a Boolean value that indicates whether the current device is running Android.

> We want to display the hamburger menu in a platform-specific way.

The AboutPage component used in listing 21.10 is shown in the following listing.

Listing 21.13 AboutPage component in `app/AboutPage.svelte`

```
<script>
  import Header from './Header.svelte';
  import {singleLine} from './util';    <—

  let description = singleLine`
    This is a Svelte Native app that demonstrates
    using side drawer navigation.
  `;
</script>

<page>
  <Header title="About" />
  <stackLayout class="p-20">
    <label text={description} textWrap="true">
    </label>
  </stackLayout>
</page>

<style>
  label {
    color: red;
    font-size: 32;
  }
</style>
```

> This function can be preceded by a tagged template literal to turn a multiline, indented string into a single-line string with no indentation.

The `HelloPage` component used in listing 21.10 is shown in the following listing.

Listing 21.14 `HelloPage` component in `app/HelloPage.svelte`

```
<script>
  import Header from './Header.svelte';

  let name = 'World';
</script>

<page>
  <Header title="Hello" />
  <stackLayout class="p-20">
    <flexboxLayout>
      <label text="Name" />
      <textField bind:text={name} />         ⟵  The user can enter
    </flexboxLayout>                              a name here.

    <label class="greeting" text="Hello, {name}!" textWrap="true" />
  </stackLayout>
</page>

<style>
  .greeting {
    color: blue;
    font-size: 40;
  }

  label {
    font-size: 20;
    font-weight: bold;
  }

  textField {
    flex-grow: 1;
    font-size: 20;
  }
</style>
```

The `singleLine` function used in listing 21.13 is shown in the following listing.

Listing 21.15 `singleLine` function in `app/util.js`

```
// This is a tagged template literal function that
// replaces newline characters with a space
// and then replaces consecutive spaces with one.
export function singleLine(literals) {
  return literals
    .join(' ')
    .replace(/\n/g, ' ')
    .replace(/  +/g, ' ')
    .trim();
}
```

That's it! Copy the techniques from this code into any Svelte Native apps where you want to use drawer-based page navigation.

21.9   *Svelte Native issues*

Svelte Native is a work in progress, and there are still some rough edges.

Some code errors cause the NativeScript Preview app to crash. This requires making code corrections, rerunning the `tns` command, returning to the NativeScript Playground mobile app, and rescanning the QR code. Sometimes after making a valid code change, the app will crash again, and a long stack trace with no references to your code will be output. If there really are no errors in your code, repeating these steps often results in the app running correctly.

You have almost reached the end of your journey, but keep reading. There is plenty of good material in the appendixes!

Summary

- Svelte Native builds on NativeScript to enable developing mobile applications using Svelte.
- NativeScript provides a set of predefined components.
- You can get started learning Svelte Native online using the Svelte Native REPL or the NativeScript Playground. Neither of these options requires installing any software.
- For more serious Svelte Native development, you will want to create a project locally and use your preferred editor or IDE for development.
- The NativeScript UI component library provides more advanced components than those provided by NativeScript.

appendix A
Resources

This appendix lists important resources that are either directly or tangentially related to Svelte.

A.1 Svelte presentations

You have spent a lot of time reading this book. Take a break and watch some great videos!

- *Rethinking Reactivity* (http://mng.bz/OM4w)—This is a talk by Rich Harris given multiple times, most recently at the Shift Dev 2019 conference. It describes the motivations behind Svelte 3 and provides a brief introduction.
- *The Return of 'Write Less, Do More'* (http://mng.bz/YrYz)—This is a talk by Rich Harris given at JSCamp 2019.
- *Svelte 3 with Rich Harris* (http://mng.bz/GVrD)—This is a live stream rebroadcast where Rich Harris teaches John Lindquist about Svelte and Sapper.
- *Simplify Web App Development with Svelte* (http://mng.bz/zjw1)—This is a talk by Mark Volkmann given at Nordic.js 2019.
- *How to Create a Web Component in Svelte* (http://mng.bz/04XJ)—This is from a YouTube channel titled "A shot of code."

A.2 Svelte resources

Check out these official resources on Svelte.

- *Svelte home page*—https://svelte.dev/
- *Svelte tutorial*—https://svelte.dev/tutorial
- *Svelte API*—https://svelte.dev/docs
- *Svelte examples*—https://svelte.dev/examples
- *Svelte REPL (online)*—https://svelte.dev/repl

- *Svelte blog*—https://svelte.dev/blog
- *Svelte GitHub repository*—https://github.com/sveltejs/svelte
- *Svelte changelog*—https://github.com/sveltejs/svelte/blob/master/CHANGELOG.md
- *svelte.preprocess*—https://svelte.dev/docs#svelte_preprocess
- *Discord chat room*—https://discordapp.com/invite/yy75DKs
- *Community resources*—https://svelte-community.netlify.com/resources/

A.3   Framework comparisons

What good is learning something if you can't say it's better than the alternatives? Here are some resources that claim Svelte is better.

- *JS framework benchmarks*—https://krausest.github.io/js-framework-benchmark/current.html
- *A RealWorld Comparison of Front-End Frameworks with Benchmarks*—http://mng.bz/K26X

A.4   Sapper resources

Don't forget about Sapper. Even though it's not out of beta yet, it is still worth learning.

- *Sapper home page*—https://sapper.svelte.dev/

A.5   Svelte Native resources

Ready to move beyond browsers and write native mobile apps? Check out these resources to help you write Android and iOS apps using JavaScript and Svelte.

- *NativeScript*—https://nativescript.org/
- *NativeScript components*—https://docs.nativescript.org/ui/overview
- *NativeScript Playground*—https://play.nativescript.org/
- *NativeScript Sidekick*—https://nativescript.org/blog/welcome-to-a-week-of-native-script-sidekick/
- *NativeScript styling*—https://docs.nativescript.org/ui/styling
- *NativeScript UI*—https://github.com/halfnelson/svelte-native-nativescript-ui
- *Svelte Native home page*—https://svelte-native.technology/
- *Svelte Native API/docs*—https://svelte-native.technology/docs
- *Svelte Native REPL*—https://svelte-native.technology/repl

A.6   Svelte GL resources

How about some 3D graphics using JavaScript and Svelte?

- *@svelte/gl*—https://github.com/sveltejs/gl
- *A Svelte GL demo*—http://mng.bz/90Gj

A.7 Svelte tools

You're going to need some tools to help improve your Svelte code and make you more productive.

- *Ease Visualizer*—https://svelte.dev/examples#easing
- *publish-svelte (pelte) tool*—https://github.com/philter87/publish-svelte
- *Storybook for Svelte*—https://storybook.js.org/docs/guides/guide-svelte/
- *svelte-check*—https://github.com/sveltejs/language-tools/tree/master/packages/svelte-check
- *Svelte devtools*—https://github.com/RedHatter/svelte-devtools
- *svelte-image preprocessor*—https://github.com/matyunya/svelte-image
- *svelte-preprocess*—https://github.com/kaisermann/svelte-preprocess
- *svelte-preprocess-markdown*—https://alexxnb.github.io/svelte-preprocess-markdown/
- *svelte-type-checker*—https://github.com/halfnelson/svelte-type-checker
- *Svelte3 ESLint plugin*—https://github.com/sveltejs/eslint-plugin-svelte3

A.8 Svelte libraries

You don't have to write every line of code yourself. Using libraries like these can simplify your applications.

- *navaid routing library*—https://github.com/lukeed/navaid
- *Routify routing library*—https://routify.dev/
- *svelte-dialog*—https://github.com/mvolkmann/svelte-dialog
- *svelte-fa component that renders FontAwesome icons*—https://cweili.github.io/svelte-fa/
- *Svelte Material UI*—https://sveltematerialui.com/
- *Svelte Testing Library*—https://testing-library.com/docs/svelte-testing-library/intro
- *svelte-moveable*—https://github.com/daybrush/moveable/tree/master/packages/svelte-moveable
- *svelte-routing routing library*—https://github.com/EmilTholin/svelte-routing
- *svelte-spa-router routing library*—https://github.com/ItalyPaleAle/svelte-spa-router
- *sveltestrap Bootstrap implementation in Svelte*—https://bestguy.github.io/sveltestrap/
- *sveltik form library inspired by Formik*—https://github.com/nathancahill/sveltik

A.9 VS Code resources

The majority of JavaScript developers use VS Code to do their editing, and it has great support for Svelte.

- *VS Code editor*—https://code.visualstudio.com/
- *"Svelte" extension for VS Code*—http://mng.bz/jgxa
- *Svelte for VS Code*—https://marketplace.visualstudio.com/items?itemName=svelte.svelte-vscode

- *"Svelte 3 Snippets" extension for VS Code*—http://mng.bz/8pYK
- *"Svelte Intellisense" extension for VS Code*—http://mng.bz/EdBq
- *"Svelte Type Checker" extension for VS Code*—https://github.com/halfnelson/svelte-type-checker-vscode

A.10 Learning resources not specific to Svelte

You're going to need to learn things that are not specific to Svelte in order to write non-trivial applications. Here is a collection of non-Svelte resources that were mentioned in this book.

- *Ajax*—https://developer.mozilla.org/en-US/docs/Web/Guide/AJAX
- *B-tree*—https://en.wikipedia.org/wiki/B-tree
- *CSS media queries*—http://mng.bz/VgeX
- *CSS Modules*—https://github.com/css-modules/css-modules
- *CSS Specificity*—https://css-tricks.com/specifics-on-css-specificity/
- *CSS variables*—http://mng.bz/rrwg
- *Event bubbling and capture*—http://mng.bz/dyDD
- *Fetch API*—https://developer.mozilla.org/en-US/docs/Web/API/Fetch_API
- *Flexbox Froggy*—https://flexboxfroggy.com/
- *Flexbox video course from Wes Bos*—https://flexbox.io/
- *GitHub Actions*—https://github.com/features/actions
- *How to code an SVG pie chart*—https://seesparkbox.com/foundry/how_to_code_an_SVG_pie_chart
- *HTML Drag and Drop API*—http://mng.bz/B2Nv
- *IndexedDB*—http://mng.bz/lGwj
- *JSX*—https://reactjs.org/docs/introducing-jsx.html
- *Markdown syntax*—https://www.markdownguide.org/basic-syntax/
- *Passive listeners*—http://mng.bz/NKvE
- *Service workers*—http://mng.bz/D2ly
- *Web components*—https://www.webcomponents.org/introduction
- *Web Components in Action* by Ben Farrell (Manning, 2019)—https://www.manning.com/books/web-components-in-action
- *Web workers*—http://mng.bz/xWw8

A.11 Tools not specific to Svelte

Earlier you saw some Svelte-specific tools. You'll also want to use tools that are not specific to Svelte.

- *axe accessibility testing*—https://www.deque.com/axe/
- *BrowserStack*—https://www.browserstack.com/
- *Chrome DevTools*—http://mng.bz/AAEp
- *CodeSandbox*—https://codesandbox.io/

- *Color Contrast Checker*—https://webaim.org/resources/contrastchecker/
- *Cypress testing framework*—https://www.cypress.io/
- *ESLint*—https://eslint.org/
- *Firefox DevTools*—http://mng.bz/Z2Gm
- *Gatsby*—https://www.gatsbyjs.org/
- *Homebrew package manager for macOS and Linux*—https://brew.sh/
- *Jest testing framework*—https://jestjs.io
- *Lighthouse audit tool*—https://developers.google.com/web/tools/lighthouse
- *MongoDB*—https://www.mongodb.com/
- *Mustache*—https://mustache.github.io/
- *Netlify*—https://www.netlify.com
- *ngrok tunneling tool*—https://ngrok.com/
- *openssl*—https://www.openssl.org/
- *Parcel*—https://parceljs.org/
- *parcel-plugin-svelte*—https://github.com/DeMoorJasper/parcel-plugin-svelte
- *Pope Tech accessibility testing*—https://pope.tech/
- *Prettier*—https://prettier.io/
- *Rollup*—https://rollupjs.org/
- *Sass*—https://sass-lang.com/
- *sirv HTTP server*—https://www.npmjs.com/package/sirv
- *Snowpack*—https://www.snowpack.dev/
- *Storybook*—https://storybook.js.org
- *TypeScript*—https://www.typescriptlang.org/
- *Vercel*—https://vercel.com/
- *WAVE accessibility testing*—https://wave.webaim.org/
- *Webpack*—https://webpack.js.org/

A.12   Libraries not specific to Svelte

Earlier you saw some Svelte-specific libraries. You'll also want to use libraries that are not specific to Svelte.

- *dialog-polyfill*—https://www.npmjs.com/package/dialog-polyfill
- *DOM Testing Library*—https://testing-library.com/docs/dom-testing-library/intro
- *Express web server*—https://expressjs.com/
- *jsdom*—https://github.com/jsdom/jsdom
- *Marked markdown library*—https://marked.js.org
- *Page.js library*—https://visionmedia.github.io/page.js
- *Polka web server*—https://github.com/lukeed/polka
- *sanitize-html*—https://github.com/apostrophecms/sanitize-html

A.13   Assets not specific to Svelte

Here are links to things mentioned in the book that are not learning resources, tools, or libraries.

- *Chrome web store*—https://chrome.google.com/webstore/category/extensions
- *Firefox Add-ons*—https://addons.mozilla.org/en-US/firefox/
- *Fontawesome icons*—https://fontawesome.com/icons?d=gallery

appendix B
Calling REST services

Calling REST services from Svelte components is as easy as using the Fetch API that is built into modern web browsers.

Most REST services fall into one of the CRUD categories: create, retrieve, update, and delete. These map to the four HTTP verbs: POST, GET, PUT, and DELETE.

Suppose the following REST services have been implemented using any server-side technology stack:

- POST /dog to create a new dog where the request body contains a JSON description
- GET /dog to get all the dogs
- GET /dog/{id} to get a specific dog
- PUT /dog/{id} to update an existing dog where the request body contains a JSON description
- DELETE /dog/{id} to delete an existing dog

Let's walk through client-side functions that call these REST services using the Fetch API. These assume that the constant SERVER_URL is set to the base URL that is common to each of the REST services, such as http://localhost:1234/dog. These functions should be called from a try block so the corresponding catch block can handle any errors that occur.

> **NOTE** Alternatively, the Promise methods then and catch can be chained, but the code looks cleaner when the await keyword is used inside a try block, and errors are caught in a catch block.

The following function calls the REST service to create a dog. The JSON returned matches the JSON passed in, but typically also includes an id assigned to the newly created dog.

Listing B.1   createDog function in dogs.js

```
export async function createDog(dog) {
  const body = JSON.stringify(dog);
  const headers = {
    'Content-Length': body.length,
    'Content-Type': 'application/json'
  };
  const res = await fetch(SERVER_URL, {
    method: 'POST',
    headers,
    body
  });
  if (!res.ok) throw new Error(await res.text());
  return res.json();
}
```
This returns the new dog
with an id property.

This function calls the REST service to retrieve all the dogs.

Listing B.2   getDogs function in dogs.js

```
export async function getDogs() {
  const res = await fetch(SERVER_URL);
  if (!res.ok) throw new Error(await res.text());
  return res.json();
}
```
This returns the dogs.

The next function calls the REST service to retrieve the dog with a given id.

Listing B.3   getDog function in dogs.js

```
export async function getDog(id) {
  const res = await fetch(SERVER_URL + '/' + id);
  if (!res.ok) throw new Error(await res.text());
  return res.json();
}
```
This returns the dog.

The next function calls the REST service to update an existing dog.

Listing B.4   updateDog function in dogs.js

```
export async function updateDog(dog) {
  const body = JSON.stringify(dog);
  const headers = {
    'Content-Length': body.length,
    'Content-Type': 'application/json'
  };
  const res = await fetch(SERVER_URL + '/' + dog.id, {
    method: 'PUT',
    headers,
    body
  });
  if (!res.ok) throw new Error(await res.text());
```

```
    return res.json();
}
```
◁─┐ **This returns the**
    updated dog.

The next function calls the REST service to delete an existing dog with a given `id`.

Listing B.5   `deleteDog` **function in** `dogs.js`

```
export async function deleteDog(id) {
  const res = await fetch(SERVER_URL + '/' + id, {
    method: 'DELETE'
  });
  if (!res.ok) throw new Error(await res.text());
}
```

Note that throwing an `Error` from these functions causes the `Promise` they return to reject.

B.1   *Headers*

Most data provided by HTTP requests is supplied in the form of path parameters, query parameters, or a request body. Another way to supply data is to include headers. There are many header names with predefined meanings. Custom header names can also be specified.

    You saw examples earlier of `POST` and `PUT` requests that include the `Content-Length` header and the `Content-Type` header to specify that a JSON body is included. For REST calls that require authentication, a token obtained from a login process is typically provided in an `Authentication` request header.

appendix C
MongoDB

MongoDB is currently the most popular NoSQL database. Unlike relational databases that use SQL and are organized into tables that contains rows, and rows that contain columns, MongoDB stores *documents* in *collections*. Each collection can have multiple indexes to make queries faster. These indexes are implemented as B-tree data structures (https://en.wikipedia.org/wiki/B-tree). The documents are JSON objects that are stored in a binary JSON format called BSON.

Unlike relational databases that define the structure of a database with a schema, MongoDB does not use a schema to restrict what can be stored in a database. This speeds up development when the structure changes often, since no schema changes are required. It also allows properties present in the objects of a collection to vary.

In practice, all the documents that are added to a given collection typically have the same structure. For example, documents describing a person might all have the following structure:

```
{
  _id: ObjectId("5e4984b33c9533dfdf102ac8")
  firstName: "Mark",
  lastName: "Volkmann",
  address: {
    street: "123 Some Street",
    city: "Somewhere",
    state: "Missouri",
    zip: 12345
  },
  favoriteColors: ["yellow", "orange"]
}
```

Each document has an `_id` property that holds a unique identifier within its collection. Documents in other collections can have properties that refer to these. This can be used to simulate what are called *joins* in relational databases.

This appendix provides enough detail so that you can use MongoDB for implementing CRUD operations on collections of data. It does not cover more advanced topics, such as query optimization, replication, sharding, backups, and security. For detail on these and many other MongoDB topics, see *MongoDB in Action* by Kyle Banker, Peter Bakkum, Shaun Verch, Douglas Garrett, and Tim Hawkins (Manning, 2016).

We'll look at how to perform various actions from JavaScript code. Chapter 17 shows how to do the same using Sapper server routes.

C.1 Installing MongoDB

There are multiple ways to install MongoDB, and they vary based on the operating system of the computer. For details, see the MongoDB documentation (https://docs.mongodb.com/guides/server/install/). We will look at one way of installing for each operating system.

C.1.1 Installing MongoDB on Windows

Follow these steps to install MongoDB on Windows:

1 Browse to https://www.mongodb.com/try/download/community.
2 Click Server at the top to bypass requesting a free trial of MongoDB Atlas.
3 In the Version drop-down, select the version labeled "current release".
4 In the OS drop-down, select "Windows x64".
5 In the Package drop-down, select "msi".
6 Click the Download button.
7 Double-click the downloaded `.msi` file and follow the installer instructions.
8 Open a command prompt window.
9 Create the MongoDB data directory by entering `md \data\db`.

NOTE This will install MongoDB as a Windows service. It will consume resources even when not in use. When it's not needed, the service can be stopped or it can be uninstalled.

C.1.2 Installing MongoDB on Linux

Follow these steps to install MongoDB on Linux:

1 Browse to https://www.mongodb.com/try/download/community.
2 Click Server at the top to bypass requesting a free trial of MongoDB Atlas.
3 In the Version drop-down, select the version labeled "current release".
4 In the OS drop-down, select your version of Linux.
5 In the Package drop-down, select "TGZ".
6 Click the Download button.

7 Open a terminal window.

8 cd to the directory where the .tgz file was downloaded.

9 Enter sudo tar -C /opt -xf {file-name}.tgz.

10 Add the bin subdirectory of this directory to the PATH environment variable. For example, /opt/mongodb-linux-x86_64-ubuntu1604-4.2.3/bin.

11 Create the MongoDB data directory by entering sudo mkdir -p /data/db.

12 Set permissions on this directory by entering sudo chmod +rw /data/db.

C.1.3   *Installing MongoDB on macOS*

One option for installing on macOS is to follow the same basic steps as for Linux. Another approach is as follows:

1 Install Homebrew by entering the command shown at https://brew.sh/.

2 Enter brew tap mongodb/brew.

3 Enter brew install mongodb-community.

C.2   *Starting the database server*

The steps for starting a MongoDB server vary based on the operating system of the computer.

- On Windows, open a command prompt and enter mongod.
- On Linux, open a terminal window and enter mongod.
- On macOS, open a terminal window and enter mongod --config /usr/local/etc/mongod.conf --fork.

C.3   *Using MongoDB shell*

MongoDB shell is a kind of REPL that supports using JavaScript to interact with a MongoDB database.

> **NOTE** There are also many free tools that provide a GUI for performing the same operations. Some to consider can be found at www.guru99.com/top-20-mongodb-tools.html.

To start the MongoDB shell, enter mongo. This displays a prompt where JavaScript-based MongoDB commands can be entered.

Table C.1 is a cheat sheet of commands that can be entered to perform common operations. The following placeholders are used in the commands:

- {db} represents the name of a database.
- {coll} represents the name of a collection.
- {obj} represents a JavaScript object that describes a document.

It is best to use valid JavaScript names for collections. For example, avoid including dashes in their names.

Table C.1

Action	Command
List existing databases	`show dbs`
Create a new database	None; databases are automatically created when a collection is added
Make a given database the current one	`use {db}`
Show the current database	`db.getName()`
Delete the current database	`db.dropDatabase()`
List the collections in the current database	`show collections` or `db.getCollectionNames()`
Create a collection in the current database	`db.createCollection('{coll}')`
Add a document to a collection	`db.{coll}.insert({obj})`
Get the number of documents in a collection	`db.{coll}.find().count()` or `db.{coll}.find().length()`
Output the first 20 documents in a collection	`db.{coll}.find()`
Output the next 20 documents in a collection	`db.{coll}.find().skip(20)`
Output the first 20 documents in a collection that match criteria	`db.{coll}.find({criteria})`
Delete one document from a collection that matches criteria	`db.{coll}.deleteOne({criteria})`
Delete all documents from a collection that match criteria	`db.{coll}.deleteMany({criteria})`
Update one document in a collection that matches criteria	`db.{coll}.updateOne({criteria}, {$set: {updates}})`
Update all documents in a collection that match criteria	`db.{coll}.updateMany({criteria}, {$set: {updates}})`
Add an index to a collection	`db.{coll}.createIndex({ {prop-name}: 1 });` + 1 for ascending order, -1 for descending order
Delete a collection	`db.{coll}.drop()`
Exit from the shell	`exit`

The current database starts as "test," even if no such database exists yet. Here is an example session:

```
show dbs          ←  We don't have an
use animals          "animals" database yet.
db.createCollection('dogs')   ←  A database doesn't have
                                 to exist to "use" it.
```

```
show dbs                                                    ◄──────
db.createCollection('cats')
db.getCollectionNames();                                        ◄──┐
db.dogs.insert({breed: 'Whippet', name: 'Dasher'})
db.dogs.insert({breed: 'TWC', name: 'Maisey'})
db.dogs.insert({breed: 'NAID', name: 'Ramsay'})
db.dogs.insert({breed: 'GSP', name: 'Oscar'})
db.dogs.find()
db.dogs.find({breed: 'Whippet'})
db.dogs.deleteMany({breed: 'Whippet'})   ◄──┐
db.dogs.find()
db.dogs.update({breed: 'GSP'}, {$set: {name: 'Oscar Wilde'}})
db.dogs.update({_id: ObjectId('some-id')}, {$set: {name: 'Oscar Wilder'}}) ◄─┐
db.dogs.drop()                        ◄─┐
db.getCollectionNames()      ◄──┐
db.dropDatabase()      ◄──┐
show dbs               ◄──┐
```

Now we have an "animals" database because we created a collection in it.

The "animals" database now contains the collections "dogs" and "cats".

This deletes all the dogs with a breed of "Whippet".

This changes the name of the one dog with a given ID.

This deletes the "dogs" collection.

This changes the name of all dogs with a breed of "GSP".

This shows that the collection no longer contains Whippets.

This shows that we no longer have a "dogs" collection.

This deletes the "animals" database.

This outputs only the dogs with a breed of "Whippet".

This shows that we no longer have an "animals" database.

This outputs the first 20 documents in the "dogs" collection.

C.4   *Using MongoDB from JavaScript*

Now that you know how to use the MongoDB shell, let's see how to perform the same operations from a JavaScript program. Learning this will allow you to do the same things from server routes in a Sapper app.

There are several open source libraries for using MongoDB from various programming languages. The official library for Node.js is simply called mongodb. To install it, enter npm install mongodb.

The following code performs all the same operations you saw in the previous MongoDB shell session.

```
const MongoClient = require('mongodb').MongoClient;

// MongoDB thinks localhost is a different database instance than 127.0.0.1.
// The mongo shell uses 127.0.0.1, so we use that to hit the same instance.
// I thought maybe this was an issue with my /etc/host file,
// but I commented out all the lines that associated 127.0.0.1
// with something other than localhost and it didn't change anything.
//const url = 'mongodb://localhost:27017';
const url = 'mongodb://127.0.0.1:27017';

// These are recommended MongoDB options to avoid deprecation warnings.
const options = {useNewUrlParser: true, useUnifiedTopology: true};
```

```
async function logCollection(coll) {
  let result = await coll.find().toArray();
  console.log(coll.collectionName, 'contains', result);
}

async function logCollections(db) {
  const items = await db.listCollections().toArray();
  console.log(
    'collections are',
    items.map(item => item.name)
  );
}

async function logDatabases(client) {
  const dbs = await client
    .db()
    .admin()
    .listDatabases();
  console.log(
    'databases are',
    dbs.databases.map(db => db.name)
  );
}

// All uses of the "await" keyword must be in an "async" function.
async function doIt() {
  let client;
  try {
    client = await MongoClient.connect(url, options);
    // Show that we do not yet have an "animals" database.
    await logDatabases(client);

    // Use the "animals" database.
    const db = client.db('animals');

    // Create two collections in the "animals" database.
    const dogs = await db.createCollection('dogs');
    const cats = await db.createCollection('cats');

    // Show that we now have an "animals" database.
    await logDatabases(client);

    // Show that the collections were created.
    await logCollections(db);

    // Add four documents to the "dogs" collection.
    await dogs.insertOne({breed: 'Whippet', name: 'Dasher'});
    await dogs.insertOne({breed: 'TWC', name: 'Maisey'});
    await dogs.insertOne({breed: 'NAID', name: 'Ramsay'});
    await dogs.insertOne({breed: 'GSP', name: 'Oscar'});

    // Show that there are four documents in the "dogs" collection.
    const count = await dogs.countDocuments();
    console.log('dog count =', count);
```

```
    // Show the documents in the "dogs" collection.
    await logCollection(dogs);

    // Find all the Whippets in the "dogs" collection.
    result = await dogs.find({breed: 'Whippet'}).toArray();
    console.log('whippets are', result);

    // Delete all the Whippets from the "dogs" collection.
    console.log('deleting Whippets');
    await dogs.deleteMany({breed: 'Whippet'});

    // Show that the "dogs" collection no longer contains Whippets.
    await logCollection(dogs);

    // Update the name of all GSPs in the "dogs" collection.
    console.log('updating GSP name');
    await dogs.updateMany({breed: 'GSP'}, {$set: {name: 'Oscar Wilde'}});
    await logCollection(dogs);

    // Find a specific dog in the "dogs" collection.
    const dog = await dogs.findOne({name: 'Oscar Wilde'});

    // Update the name of a specific dog in the "dogs" collection.
    await dogs.updateOne({_id: dog._id}, {$set: {name: 'Oscar Wilder'}});
    await logCollection(dogs);

    // Delete the "dogs" collection.
    await dogs.drop();

    // Show that the "animals" database
    // no longer contains a "dogs" collection.
    logCollections(db);

    // Delete the "animals" database.
    await db.dropDatabase();

    // Show that the "animals" database no longer exists.
    await logDatabases(client);
  } catch (e) {
    console.error(e);
  } finally {
    if (client) client.close();
  }
}

doIt();
```

Congratulations! You now know the basics of using MongoDB.

appendix D
ESLint for Svelte

ESLint (https://eslint.org/) is a tool that bills itself as the "pluggable linting utility for JavaScript and JSX." It can report many syntax errors and potential runtime errors. It can also report deviations from specified coding guidelines in order to make the code in an application more consistent.

To install everything needed to use ESLint in a Svelte or Sapper project, enter the following:

```
npm install -D eslint eslint-plugin-import eslint-plugin-svelte3
```

One benefit of the Svelte3 ESLint plugin is that it warns about unused CSS selectors. For more detail, see the eslint-plugin-svelte3 GitHub page (https://github.com/sveltejs/eslint-plugin-svelte3).

To configure the use of ESLint, create the following file in the top directory of each Svelte app.

Listing D.1 The `.eslintrc.json` file

```
{
  "env": {
    "browser": true,
    "es6": true,
    "jest": true,
    "node": true
  },
  "extends": ["eslint:recommended", "plugin:import/recommended"],
  "overrides": [
    {
      "files": ["**/*.svelte"],
      "processor": "svelte3/svelte3"
    }
  ],
```

```
    "parserOptions": {
      "ecmaVersion": 2019,
      "sourceType": "module"
    },
    "plugins": ["import", "svelte3"]
}
```

Add the following npm script to `package.json`:

```
"lint": "eslint --fix --quiet src --ext .js,.svelte",
```

To run ESLint, enter `npm run lint`. Here are examples of messages that can be output by ESLint:

```
/Users/mark/.../svelte-and-sapper-in-action/travel-packing-ch14/src/Baskets.svelte
  18:6    error  'hoveringOverBasket' is assigned a value but never used  no-unused-vars
  20:11   error  'dragStart' is defined but never used                    no-unused-vars
  25:2    error  Mixed spaces and tabs                                    no-mixed-spaces-and-tabs
```

For more information on Svelte-specific ESLint options, see the eslint-plugin-svelte3 GitHub page (https://github.com/sveltejs/eslint-plugin-svelte3).

Many editors and IDEs, including VS Code, have extensions for running ESLint as code is entered or when files are saved.

appendix E
Prettier for Svelte

Prettier (https://prettier.io/) is a code-formatting tool. It can be used from the command line and from inside many code editors. Prettier bills itself as an "opinionated JavaScript formatter," so although the way it formats code can be customized to some extent, there are intentionally only a small number of options.

Most developers prefer to work on software applications with a consistent, widely used coding style. Prettier delivers this for many languages and syntaxes, including JavaScript, TypeScript, JSON, HTML, CSS, SCSS, JSX, Vue, and Markdown.

To install everything needed to use Prettier code formatting in a Svelte or Sapper project, enter the following:

```
npm install -D prettier prettier-plugin-svelte
```

Add the following npm script to package.json in order to run Prettier on all files under the public and src directories that have a file extension of .css, .html, .js, or .svelte:

```
"format": "prettier --write '{public,src}/**/*.{css,html,js,svelte}'",
```

To run Prettier, enter npm run format.

To configure Prettier options, create the file .prettierrc in the top project directory. By default, the Svelte Prettier plugin enforces a .svelte file section order of script elements, style elements, and HTML. This can be changed by adding the svelteSortOrder option in .prettierrc.

To specify options for Prettier that are customized to your preferences, create a file like the following in the top directory of each Svelte app.

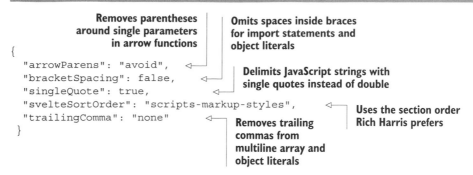

Listing E.1   A `.prettierrc` file

Removes parentheses around single parameters in arrow functions

Omits spaces inside braces for import statements and object literals

```
{
  "arrowParens": "avoid",
  "bracketSpacing": false,
  "singleQuote": true,
  "svelteSortOrder": "scripts-markup-styles",
  "trailingComma": "none"
}
```

Delimits JavaScript strings with single quotes instead of double

Uses the section order Rich Harris prefers

Removes trailing commas from multiline array and object literals

Many editors and IDEs, including VS Code, have extensions for running Prettier as code is entered or when files are saved.

appendix F
VS Code

VS Code (https://code.visualstudio.com/) is a popular, open source code editor from Microsoft that is highly customizable. It supports many programming languages and provides syntax highlighting, error detection, and code formatting. It also has great Git integration, which makes it easy to check out a branch, see at a glance the current branch name, see a list of files that have been modified, see side-by-side diffs, commit changes, and push them. If you are not currently using VS Code for your Svelte and Sapper projects, you really should give it a try!

There are currently three popular Svelte-related VS Code extensions:

- Svelte for VS Code
- Svelte Intellisense
- Svelte 3 Snippets

We will look at how to configure and use each of these. In addition, check out the ESLint and Prettier extensions.

> **NOTE** For information on installing, configuring, and using VS Code extensions, see the VS Code documentation for "Extension Marketplace" (https://code.visualstudio.com/docs/editor/extension-gallery).

F.1   VS Code settings

Before using VS Code to work on Svelte and Sapper applications, there are a few things that should be configured.

For starters, install the ESlint and Prettier extensions. This enables these tools to automatically run inside VS Code after each code change or after every file save.

Also, modify some VS Code settings. To do this, open the Command Palette and enter "settings" (see figure F.1).

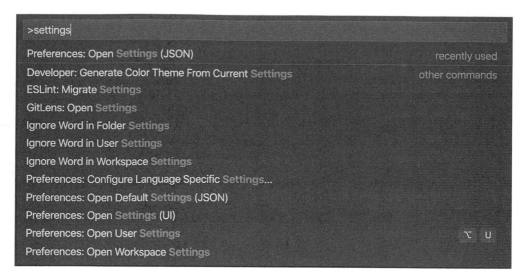

Figure F.1   VS Code Command Palette

NOTE   For information on using the Command Palette in VS Code, see the VS Code documentation (https://code.visualstudio.com/docs/gctstarted/userinterface#_command-palette).

Then select Preferences: Open Settings (JSON) and add the following:

```
"editor.defaultFormatter": "esbenp.prettier-vscode",
"editor.formatOnSave": true,
```

This assumes that the Prettier - Code formatter extension has been installed.

Next, consider installing some of the Svelte-specific extensions described in the following sections.

F.2   *The Svelte for VS Code extension*

The Svelte for VS Code extension is available at http://mng.bz/zrJA. Install it to enable syntax highlighting, code formatting, and intellisense (code completion pop-ups) when editing .svelte files. It also supports the use of Emmet (https://emmet.io/) abbreviations for HTML and CSS.

A major feature of Svelte for VS Code is that it uses the Svelte Language Server at http://mng.bz/0ZYv. This communicates with development tools such as VS Code to provide diagnostic messages, auto-completions (for HTML, CSS, JavaScript, and Type-Script), hover information, code formatting (using Prettier), and more.

Svelte for VS Code also supports using alternative syntaxes in .svelte files such as TypeScript. A preprocessor must be configured for each alternative syntax. See chapter 20 for details on installing and configuring these.

F.3   *The Svelte 3 Snippets extension*

The Svelte 3 Snippets VS Code extension is available at http://mng.bz/mBQ4. Install it to enable the use of many snippets whose names begin with `s-` when editing files with an extension of `.svelte`, `.js`, or `.css`. Snippets enable you to enter a small amount of text that is expanded to more text in order to save typing time.

After typing at least `s-` a snippet can be selected from a popup list. Continue typing to narrow the list. To select a snippet, click it or use the up and down arrow keys to navigate to it, and press the Return key.

For example, selecting the `s-if-else-block` snippet adds the following:

```
{#if condition}
    <!-- content here -->
{:else}
    <!-- else content here -->
{/if}
```

The cursor will be positioned on `condition`. Enter a condition to replace this. Press the Tab key to advance to the comment in the `if` block and enter content to replace it. Press the Tab key again to advance to the comment in the `else` block and enter content to replace it. The other snippets work similarly.

Table F.1 summarizes some of the most useful snippets provided by this extension. A nice feature is that all you need to remember is to type `s-`. After that, you can read the list of available snippets in the popup list and select one.

Table F.1   Useful snippets

Snippet	Description
`s-await-short-block`	Adds an `{#await}` block with no `:then` or `:catch` sections
`s-await-then-block`	Adds an `{#await}` block with a `:then` section
`s-await-catch-block`	Adds an `{#await}` block with `:then` and `:catch` sections
`s-each-block`	Adds an `{#each}` block
`s-each-key-block`	Adds an `{#each}` block with a key
`s-each-index-block`	Adds an `{#each}` block with an index
`s-each-index-key-block`	Adds an `{#each}` block with an index and a key
`s-if-block`	Adds an `{#if}` block
`s-if-else-block`	Adds an `{#if}` block with an `:else` section
`s-on-event`	Adds `on:` event handling to an HTML element that refers to a function
`s-on-event-inline`	Adds `on:` event handling to an HTML element using an inline arrow function

Table F.1 Useful snippets *(continued)*

Snippet	Description
s-script	Adds a `script` element
s-script-context	Adds a `script` element with `context="module"`
s-style	Adds a `style` element

A complete list of the supported snippets can be found on the vscode-svelte-snippets GitHub page (https://github.com/fivethree-team/vscode-svelte-snippets).

F.4   *The Svelte Intellisense extension*

The Svelte Intellisense VS Code extension is available at http://mng.bz/5a0a. Install it to enable the following capabilities when editing `.svelte` files.

- Hover over a component instance, component prop, or function call to see its definition in a popup.
- Hold down the Ctrl key (Cmd key in macOS) and click a name to jump to its definition. This works for component imports, component instances, component props, named slots, functions, and variables.
- Type the beginning of some Svelte syntax to see a pop-up list of potential completions.

Completion for many Svelte-specific props is supplied. This includes the `bind`, `class`, `in`, `out`, `transition`, and `use` props. For example, after entering `<div bind:`, the options `clientHeight`, `clientWidth`, `offsetHeight`, `offsetWidth`, and `this` are offered.

Completion for block structures is also provided. After typing `{#`, the options `if`, `each`, and `await` are offered. Selecting one of these inserts a snippet for completing the block structure. However, the final `}` character on the last line of the snippet is currently omitted (see the issue at https://github.com/ArdenIvanov/svelte-intellisense/issues/24).

appendix G
Snowpack

Snowpack (www.snowpack.dev) is a tool for building web applications, and it is not specific to a particular framework. It supports React, Svelte, Vue, and more. The goal of Snowpack is to speed the development cycle by dramatically reducing build times. It provides an alternative to using a module bundler such as Webpack, Rollup, and Parcel.

Snowpack does not build a single "bundle" containing all the dependency code and app-specific code for the app. Instead, it uses Rollup to bundle each dependency as a separate ECMAScript module. This has the advantage of making build times faster because, after changes to the app code are detected, it only has to bundle the app code. Dependency bundling only occurs again when new dependencies are added or their versions change.

When the app starts, the browser separately downloads code for each bundled dependency rather than downloading a single bundle containing all the code. Browser support for HTTP2 and improved caching makes this efficient.

G.1   Using Snowpack with Svelte

The following steps will create a new Svelte app that uses Snowpack:

1 Create the app using Create Snowpack App (CSA):

```
npx create-snowpack-app snowpack-demo \
  --template @snowpack/apptemplate-svelte
```

2 cd to the new app directory:

```
cd snowpack-demo
```

415

3 Start the development server:

```
npm start
```

This builds app and dependency modules in memory and serves them up to the browser.

4 Browse to localhost:8080.

Additional components can now be defined under the src directory. These will be detected and automatically bundled, and the browser will reload the changes.

The following example app contains nothing that is specific to Snowpack (see figure G.1). It merely demonstrates the use of Snowpack for managing dependencies. Two npm packages are used. To install them, enter npm install date-fns lodash.

Hello, Snowpack!

Name Snowpack
Today is May 26, 2020.

Figure G.1   Snowpack demo

Listing G.1 App that uses the DateDisplay component in src/App.svelte

```
<script>
  import _ from 'lodash';
  import DateDisplay from './DateDisplay';

  let name = 'Snowpack';
</script>

<h1>Hello, {_.startCase(name)}!</h1>

<label>
  Name
  <input bind:value={name}>
</label>

<DateDisplay />

<style>
  h1 {
    color: red;
  }
</style>
```

Listing G.2 `DateDisplay` **component in** `src/DateDisplay.svelte`

```
<script>
  import {format} from 'date-fns';
</script>

<div>
  Today is {format(new Date(), 'MMM dd, yyyy')}.
</div>
```

For tips on modifying an existing Svelte app to use Snowpack, see the Snowpack documentation (www.snowpack.dev/#migrating-an-existing-app).

In development mode (`npm start`), apps built with Snowpack only run in modern browsers. However, the result of a production build does run in older browsers, including IE 11.

To create a production build of an app, enter `npm run build`, which performs the following steps:

1 Creates the `build` directory, if not already present.
2 Creates the `build/web_modules` directory, if not already present.
3 Bundles each dependency into a separate `.js` file in `build/web_modules`.
4 Creates the `build/_dist_` directory, if not already present.
5 Compiles all `.svelte` files to `.js` and `.css` files under `build/_dist_`. These import dependencies from the `web_modules` directory .

For more information on creating production builds, see the Snowpack documentation (www.snowpack.dev/#snowpack-build). It describes an option to create a single bundle containing all the app-specific code and dependencies.

index

A

absoluteLayout Svelte Native 360
accessibility tests 199, 216–225
   axe 220–223
   Lighthouse 217–220
   Svelte compiler 217
   WAVE 223–225
accessors option of svelte:options element 253
action function 227, 359, 368
actions in Storybook 128–129
activate event of service worker 327–328
addons.js file of Jest 226
afterAll function of Jest 199
afterEach function of Jest 199
afterUpdate lifecycle function 147–148, 280
alert function of Svelte Native 359
Amazon Web Services (AWS) 241
Angular, compared to Svelte 17
animate animation directive 88, 177
animation 170–189
   crossfade transition 181–182
   custom transitions 184–186
   draw transition 183–184
   easing functions 171
   fade transition and flip animation
      179–181
   support for 9
   svelte/animate package 172–174
   svelte/motion package 174–177
   svelte/transition package 177–179
   transition events 186–187
   transition vs. in and out props 186
aria-current attribute 267, 276
{#await} block structure 67–70
axe 216, 220–223

B

backInOut easing function 184
beforeAll function of Jest 199
beforeEach function of Jest 199
beforeUpdate lifecycle function 143, 146–147,
   280
bind directive 22, 87–88, 92–95, 108
   bind:this 90–92, 143
   binding child components prop to variables
      92–96
   on form elements 88–90
block structures 64–81
   conditional logic with {#if} 65–66
   iteration with {#each} 66–67
   promises with {#await} 67–70
   Travel Packing app 70–80
      App component 79
      Category component 73–75
      Checklist component 76–78
      Item component 71–72
      running 80
      utility functions 73
blur transition 178–179
body-parser library 293
bottomNavigation component in React Native 363
bounce easing function 171
bounceIn easing function 171
bounceInOut easing function 171
bounceOut easing function 171
build directory 272, 417
build script for Sapper 240
build/bundle.css file 51
bundle.css file 12, 15, 32
bundle.css.map file 13, 32
bundle.js file 12, 15, 32–34

bundle.js.map file 13, 32
bundles 5
ButtonList component 179–180

C

caching strategies for service workers 323–326
capture event modifier 99
CDN (content delivery network) 30
circ easing function 171
class directive 87
clientHeight option 95, 414
client-side routing 152–169
   hash routing 160–162
   manual routing 153–160
   page.js library 162–167
clientWidth option 95, 414
Clock component 24–25
code splitting 15, 264, 272, 284–285
CodeSandbox 30–31
ColorCycle component 145
ColorPicker component 94–95
ColorSlider component 93
component communication 82–105
   contexts 100–101
   events 97–99
     dispatching 97–99
     forwarding 99
     modifiers for 99
   options for 83
   props 83–96
     directives 87–96
     export keyword 84–85
     reacting to changes 86
     types of 86–87
   slots 96–97
   stores 106–123
     custom 117–118
     defining 109
     derived 116–117
     persisting 122–123
     readable 108–109
     using 109–115
     using with classes 118–122
     writable 107–108
component demos with Storybook 225–234
component libraries, creating 254–255
components 43–63
   building custom 59–60
   logic of 53–54
   markup for 45–47
   module context 57–59
   names for 47–48
   reactive statements 55–57
   state of 54–55

   styles for 48–49
     CSS preprocessors 53
     CSS specificity 49–50
     scoped vs. global styles 50–53
     .svelte files 44–45
components subdirectory in Sapper 273
config.js file of Storybook 226
container property of Jest 200
content management system (CMS) 125
Content-Length header 399
Content-Type header 399
contexts 83, 100–101
continuous integration (CI) 199
Counter web component 257
Create Snowpack App (CSA) 415
createEventDispatcher function 59, 287
crossfade transition function 177, 181–183
CRUD (create, retrieve, update, and delete) 14, 292–299
CSS (cascading style sheets)
   libraries 247–250
   predefined NativeScript CSS classes 366–368
   preprocessors 53
   specificity 49–50
css method in custom transitions 184
CSS Output tab in REPL 21
cubic easing function 171
cubicOut easing function 174
cy variable of Cypress 208
Cypress 208–214
   end-to-end tests for Todo app 210–211
   end-to-end tests for Travel Packing app 211–214
cypress directory 209, 273
cypress/examples directory 211
cypress/integration directory 209, 212
cypress/integration/examples directory 211
cypress/videos subdirectory 211
cypress.json file 274

D

damping parameter 176
data-testid attribute 203–204, 209, 212
datePicker Native Script component 368
@debug tag 190–193
debugger statement 193
debugging 190–197
   @debug tag 191–193
   debugger statement 193
   reactive statements 193–194
   Storybook 225–234
   Svelte Devtools 194–196
default slot 96
deferred transition 181
degit command 31

delay animation option 174, 178, 184
DELETE request 298, 397
dependencies property 345
deployment 235–241
    to any HTTP server 236
    using Docker 241
    using Netlify 236–239
        from command line 238–239
        from website 237–238
        plans 239
    using Vercel 239–241
        from command line 240
        from website 240
        tiers 241
derived function 116
describe function of Jest 199, 206
describe.skip function of Jest 206
destroy function 129
detail property of events 98
dev option 273
dev subdirectory of Sapper 272
device-independent pixels (DIPs) in Svelte
    Native 362, 365
Dialog component 133, 150, 232–233, 253
dialog components, implementing 132–135
dialog element 124, 132–133
dialog.close() method 133
DialogPolyfill 206
dialog.show() method 133
dialog.showModal() method 133, 137
directives 87–88
    bind directive on form elements 88–90
    bind:this 90–92
    binding child component prop to variables
    92–96
dispatch function 98, 102–104
Docker 241
Dockerfile file 241
dockLayout of Svelte Native 360
DOM (Document Object Model) 6
DOM interactions 124–140
    actions 128–129
    dialog components 132–135
    drag and drop 135–137
    inserting HTML 125–128
    tick function 129–132
drag and drop 135–139
draw transition 177–178, 183–184
dropDatabase() method of MongoDB 138–139, 305
duration animation option 174, 178, 184

E

{#each} block structure 66–67
easing animation option 171, 174, 178, 184

easing functions 171
elastic easing function 171
Embedded fallback caching strategy 325
empty elements 22, 230
end-to-end tests 15, 208–214, 264
    Todo app 210–211
    Travel Packing app 211–214
Envelope component 96
error handling 272, 279
error.svelte Sapper error page 275
.eslintrc.json file 407
events 83, 97–99
    dispatching 97–99
    forwarding 99
    modifiers for 99
expect function of Jest 200
expo easing function 171
export keyword 25, 35, 55, 58, 84–85
export Sapper subdirectory 273
exporting static sites, with Sapper 320
    example app 309–320
    overview 308
    when to export 308–309
Express 299–300

F

fade transition 37, 178–181
Fetch API wrapper 280
fetch service worker event 326–327
fetchPlus function 337
fieldset element 223
file structure of Sapper 271
fireEvent function of Svelte Testing Library 200
fixtures directory of Cypress 209
flexboxLayout of Svelte Native 362
flip function of svelte/animate 172, 174, 187
fly transition of svelte/transition 177–179, 184,
    250
form element 61, 243
form validation 243–247
format property of Rollup 258
formattedString element of Svelte Native 357, 366

G

get function 110, 300
GET request 269, 297, 327, 397
getByLabelText function of dom-testing-library
    200
getByTestId function of dom-testing-library 200
getByText function of dom-testing-library 200
getCollectionNames() method of MongoDB 403
getContext function 100
getName() method of Mongo DB 403

global attribute of style tag 350
:global(selector) modifier 51
global.css file 13, 34, 115, 326, 349
Google Cloud Platform (GCP) 241
gridLayout element of Svelte Native 362

H

hash routing 153, 160–162
hashchange event 160, 251
helper functions using lifecycle functions 148–150
@html syntax 125–126
HTML, inserting 125–128
htmlView component of Svelte Native 358, 373
HTTP servers, deployment to 236
HTTPS, enabling use in Sapper server 332–334

I

id attributes 50
_id property of MondoDB documents 401
{#if} block structure 65–66, 143
image compression 354–355
immutable option of svelte:options element 253, 273
in animation directive 88, 179
in effect 177
index.svelte file of Sapper 268, 276, 293
innerHeight property 251
innerHTML property 126
innerWidth window property 251
input placeholder attribute 130
install service worker event 326–328
instance context 57
integration directory of Cypress 209
interpolate function 174, 176
interpolation 35
introstart transition event 186
it function of Jest 199

J

JavaScript XML (JSX) 17, 64
Jest 199–208
    unit tests for Todo app 201–203
    unit tests for Travel Packing app 203–208
JS Output tab of REPL 21
JSON files, importing 254
json() function of Rollup plugin 313

L

label component of Svelte Native 357, 367–368
labeled statement 55
LabeledCheckboxes component 87

lang attribute of style element 53, 347
_layout.svelte file of Sapper 276, 278
layout.svelte file of Sapper 275
lifecycle functions 141–151
    afterUpdate 147–148
    beforeUpdate 146–147
    helper functions 148–150
    onDestroy 145–146
    onMount 143–144
        moving focus 143
        retrieving data from API services 144
    setup 142–143
Lighthouse tool 216–220
linear easing function 171, 184, 188
listPicker component of Svelte Native 368
listView component of Svelte Native 358, 368
localStorage 102, 104, 122, 279, 287, 306

M

main.js file 34, 39
manifest-client.mjs of service worker 275
manifest.json file of service worker 326
manifest-server.mjs of Sapper 275
manual routing 153–160
Markdown 352–354
MaskedInput component 129, 131
.md Markdown files 352
memory 7
middleware function 274
modal 132
module context 57–59
MongoDB
    installing 401–402
        on Linux 401–402
        on macOS 402
        on Windows 401
    starting database server 402
    using from JavaScript 404–406
    using MongoDB shell 402–404
monthly loan payments calculator app 35–36
Mozilla Developer Network (MDN) 62, 99

N

namespace option of svelte:options element 254
NativeScript
    Native Script CLI (command line interface) 364
    NativeScript UI component library 385–390
    predefined CSS classes 366–368
    styling 365–366
    themes 368
    See also Svelte Native
nativescript-theme-core 365

navaid library 167
navigationButton component of Svelte Native
    358, 363
navigator.onLine value 325
Nav.svelte file 267, 273
Netlify 236–239
    from command line 238–239
    from website 237–238
    plans 239
netlify command 238–239
.netlify/config.json file 238
Network only geocaching strategy 324
Network or cache caching strategy 324
next middleware function 291
node command 18, 29
NODE_ENV variable 273, 275
node_modules directory 273–274
non-REPL apps 31–36
    important files 33–35
    monthly loan payments calculator app
        35–36
        npx degit 31–33
        package.json 33
npm command 18, 29
npm init –yes command 236
npm install command 29, 32, 36, 40, 63, 247,
    256, 265, 309, 333, 345, 354
npm login command 255
npm packages 29–30
npx command 18, 29
npx degit 31–33

O

Object.entries 67
offline event 326
offline usage 15, 264
offsetHeight element property 95, 414
offsetWidth element property 95, 414
on directive 87, 97, 99, 102, 104, 186
once event modifier 99
onDestroy lifecycle function 145–146
onerror image attribute 126–128
online event 326
online window property 251
onload img attribute 126–128
onMount lifecycle function 128, 143–144, 146,
    206, 280, 282, 288
    moving focus 143
    retrieving data from API services 144
opacity animation option 178
openssl command 333
out animation directive 88, 179
out effect 177
outerHeight property 251

outerWidth property 251
outrostart transition event 186

P

package.json file 33, 163, 168, 201, 206, 236, 240,
    274, 289, 409
page component 359
page layouts 14, 263, 272
page routes 272
page routing 14, 263
page store of Sapper 277
page.js library
    client-side routing 162–164
    using path and query parameters with 164–167
passive event modifier 99
path parameter, with page.js library 164–167
path SVG element 183
Pie component 175
plugins array of Rollup 209, 258, 313, 346, 351
postMessage method of service worker Worker
    object 364
prefetching 15, 264, 272, 277, 282–284
preload function 59, 280, 282–284, 299, 305, 308,
    327, 339
preloading 272, 277, 280–282
preprocess property of Svelte Rollup plugin
    344–346, 354
preprocessors 355
    custom preprocessing 344–346
    image compression 354–355
    svelte-preprocess package 346–352
        auto-preprocessing mode 347
        external files 347–348
        global styles 349
        using Sass 349–350
        using TypeScript 350–352
        VS Code and use of non-JS syntax 352
    using Markdown 352–354
    using multiple preprocessors 354
    using Webpack 345–346
.prettierrc file 409
preventDefault event modifier 99
process.browser property 280
progress component of Svelte Native 368
progressive web apps (PWAs) 274, 321
Promise object 67
prompt function of Svelte Native 359, 368
props 25, 34, 43, 45, 47, 83–96
    directives 87–88
        bind directive on form elements 88–90
        bind:this 90–92
        binding child component props to
            variables 92–96
    export keyword 84–85

props *(continued)*
   in and out vs. transition 186
   reacting to changes 86
   types of 86–87
$$props variable 87
public directory 115, 163, 409
public/build directory 236, 258
public/build/bundle.css file 51
public/build/bundle.js file 258
public/global.css file 8, 30, 51–52, 62, 79, 159, 218, 268
public/index.html file 33, 51, 247
PUT request 298, 397

Q

quad easing function 171
quart easing function 171
query parameter, with page.js library 164–167
querySelector DOM method 200
querySelectorAll DOM method 200
quint easing function 171

R

RadAutoCompleteTextView component of Svelte Native 385
RadCalendar component of Svelte Native 385
RadChart component of Svelte Native 385
RadDataForm component of Svelte Native 385
RadGauge component of Svelte Native 385
RadListView component of Svelte Native 385
RadSideDrawer component of Svelte Native 363, 385
RBAC (role-based access control) 239
React, compared to Svelte 17
reactive declaration 24, 55
reactive statement ($:) 44, 49
reactivity 9–11
   reactive statements 24, 55–57, 193–194
   without using virtual DOM 6
readable store function 108
README.md file of Sapper 274
receive transition 181
render function of Svelte Testing Library 200
REPL (read, evaluate, print, loop) apps 20–31
   CodeSandbox as alternative to 30–31
   exporting 29
   Hello World app 22–25
   limitations of 30
   saving 26–28
   sharing 28
   URLs 28
   using 20–22
   using npm packages 29–30

required attribute of form elements 243
resize window event 251
REST (representational state transfer) 14
REST services, calling 399
Result tab of REPL 21
role-based access control (RBAC) 239
rollup.ce-config.js file 258
rollup.config.js file 31, 254, 258, 273–274, 313, 344, 346, 351, 353–354
rollup-plugin-terser 31
:root syntax 220
routes directory of Sapper 273, 280, 301
routes service worker variable 326
routes/_layout.svelte 276, 282
Routify library 167

S

sanitizeHtml function 126
Sapper 13–16
   apps 263–288
      code splitting 284–285
      creating 265–266
      error handling 279
      Fetch API wrapper 280
      file structure 272–275
      page layouts 276–278
      page routes 275–276
      prefetching 282–284
      preloading 280–282
      running on both server and client 279–280
   exporting static sites with 320
      example app 309–320
      overview 308
      when to export 308–309
   features of 14–15
   how it works 15
   offline support 321–339
      caching strategies 323–326
      enabling use of HTTPS in Sapper server 332–334
      service workers 322–323, 326–331
      verifying offline behavior 334–335
   server routes 289–306
      CRUD operations 292–299
      functions 291
      source files 290–291
      switching to Express 299–300
   tools needed to get started 18
   when not to use 16
   when to use 16
@sapper directory 274
sapper/build directory 308
sapper/build/client directory 15
sapper/export directory 308, 319

Sass 349–350
scale SVG function 183
scale transition 178, 188
screenshots directory of Cypress 209
scrollView component of Svelte Native 362
scrollX window property 251
scrollY window property 251
search engine optimization (SEO) 14, 216
searchBar component of Svelte Native 358, 368
segment prop of Sapper layout components 276
segmentedBar component of Svelte Native 368
Select component 59
send transition 181
server routes 14, 264, 289–306
    CRUD operations 292–299
    functions 291
    source files 290–291
    switching to Express 299–300
server.mjs file of Sapper 274
server-side rendering (SSR) 14, 264
service workers
    configuration 326–327
    events 327–328
    managing in Chrome 328–331
service-worker.js file 274, 327
session parameter of Sapper preload function 280
session store 277
sessionStorage of Sapper 279
set method of writable stories 108, 110, 117–118,
        123, 174
setContext function 100–101
setInterval 108, 145
setTimeout 145
shared.mjs of Sapper 275
shell array of Sapper 275, 326–327
sine easing function 171
single sign-on (SSO) 239
- -single sirv option 168
sirv-cli dependency 33
slide transition 178
slider component of Svelte Native 368
slot element 256, 278, 286
slots 83, 96–97
snapshot tests 199
__snapshots__ directory 204
Snowpack 415–417
special Svelte elements 250–254
speed animation option 178
speed, of Svelte 6
spread operator (...) 46
spring function of svelte/motion 174, 176
stackLayout of Svelte Native 362, 367
start animation option 178
start npm script 163
state management, simplification of 8

state of components 43
static directory of Sapper 274, 326
static site generation 15, 264
static/favicon.png of Sapper 274
static/global.css of Sapper 274
static/images directory of Sapper 311
static/manifest.json of Sapper 274
stiffness animation option 176
StopLight component 85
stopPropagation event 99
stores 106–123
    custom 117–118
    defining 109
    derived 116–117
    persisting 122–123
    readable 108–109
    using 109–115
    using with classes 118–122
    writable 107–108
stores function of Sapper 83, 277
stories directory of Storybook 226–227
.storybook directory 226
storybook-static directory 233
StyleWrapper component for Storybook 229
styling
    for components 48–49
        CSS preprocessors 53
        CSS specificity 49–50
        scoped vs. global styles 50–53
    NativeScript 365–366
    place for specifying global styles 8
    scoped 7
    svelte-preprocess package 349
subscribe method of stores 107, 109, 117
support directory of Cypress 209
Svelte 4–13
    advantages of 4–9
        accessibility 9
        animation support 9
        less code required 6
        less memory required 7
        no JavaScript container required 7
        place for specifying global styles 8
        reactivity without using virtual DOM 6
        scoped styling 7
        smaller bundle sizes 5
        speed 6
        state management simplification 8
        two-way data binding support 8
        web application compiler 4–5
    compared to other web frameworks? 17
        Angular 17
        React 17
        Vue 17
    creating component libraries 254–255

Svelte *(continued)*
  CSS libraries 247–250
  doesn't completely disappear 13
  form validation 243–247
  how it works 11–13
  importing JSON files 254
  issues to consider 11
  reactivity 9–11
  special elements 250–254
  tools needed to get started 18
  Web Components 256–260
  See also animation; client-side routing; compo-
    nent communication; components; debug-
    ging; deployment; DOM interactions;
    lifecycle functions; preprocessors; Svelte
    Native; testing
Svelte 3 Snippets VS Code extension 413–414
Svelte compiler 4–5, 216–217
Svelte Devtools 194–196
Svelte extension 412
.svelte files 5, 7, 11–12, 15, 20, 22, 24, 34–35,
  43–45, 47, 58, 110, 125, 250, 282, 290, 308,
  344, 347, 350, 352, 412
Svelte for VS Code extension 412
Svelte Intellisense VS Code extension 414
Svelte Native 16, 356–390
  dcvcloping apps locally 364–365
  example app 368–381
  getting started with 363
  issues with 390
  NativeScript styling 365–366
  NativeScript themes 368
  NativeScript UI component library 385–390
  predefined NativeScript CSS classes 366–368
  provided components 357–363
    action components 358–359
    dialog components 359
    display components 357–358
    form components 358
    layout components 359–362
    navigation components 363
svelte package 142
svelte plugin for Rollup 346, 353
svelte Rollup plugin function 258, 344–346
svelte:body element 252
svelte:window element 252
svelte/animate package 172–174
svelte/easing package 171
svelte/motion package 174–177
svelte/store package 107–108, 110, 116
svelte/transition package 177–179
sveltc-chcck tool 350
SvelteComponentDev object 91–92
svelte.config.js file 352
svelte-gl 18

svelte-hash CSS class 50
sveltejs/sapper-template 272, 275
sveltePreprocess function 346, 354
svelte.preprocess function 344
svelte-preprocess package 346–352
  auto-preprocessing mode 347
  external files 347–348
  global styles 349
  using Sass 349–350
  using TypeScript 350–352
  VS Code and use of non-JS syntax 352
svelte-routing library 167
svelteSortOrder option of prettier-plugin-svelte
  409
svelte-spa-router library 167
switch component of Svelte Native 368

T

tabContentItem component of Svelte Native
  363
tabs component of Svelte Native 363
tabStrip component of Svelte Native 363
tag option of svelte:options element 254
template element 347, 358
template.html file of Sapper 274
test function of Jest 199–200, 206, 345
testing 198–234
  accessibility tests 216–225
    axe 220–223
    Lighthouse 217–220
    Svelte compiler 217
    WAVE 223–225
  component demos and debugging with
    Storybook 225–234
  end-to-end tests with Cypress 208–214
  unit tests with Jest 199–208
test.only function of Jest 206
__tests__ directory of Jest 199
test.skip function of Jest 206
textField component of Svelte Native 358, 368
textView component of Svelte Native 368
this variable in Sapper preload functions 53
this.fetch in Sapper 339
tick function 129–132
timePicker component of Svelte Native 368
timestamp variable of Sapper service worker
  326–327
title element in svelte:head element 252–253
Toast component 250
Todo app 9, 37–40
  end-to-end tests 210–211
  unit tests 201–203
transition animation directive 88, 179
transition effect 177

transitions
  crossfade transition 181–182
  custom transitions 184–186
  draw transition 183–184
  fade transition 179–181
  flip animation 179–181
  svelte/transition package 177–179
  transition events 186–187
  transition vs. in and out props 186
translate SVG function 183
Travel Packing app
  animation 187–189
  block structures 70–80
    App component 79
    Category component 73–75
    Checklist component 76–78
    Item component 71–72
    running 80
    utility functions 73
  building with Sapper 285–288
    offline support 335–339
    server routes 300–306
  client-side routing 167–168
  component communication 101–105, 123
  component demos 227–234
  components 60–63
  debugging 227–234
  DOM interactions 137–140
  lifecycle functions 150–151
  testing
    end-to-end tests 211–214
    unit tests 203–208
tweened animation function 174–176
two-way data binding, support for 8
TypeScript 350–352, 354
typescript() function of Rollup TypeScript
    plugin 351

U

unit tests 198–208
  Todo app 201–203

unordered list (<ul>) 37
unpacked value 74
unsubscribe method 117
update method 108, 110, 117–118, 123, 129, 174
update(fn) method 107
upper value 24
use directive 88
user-interface (UI) components 3, 11

V

Vercel 239–241
  from command line 240
  from website 240
  tiers 241
vercel projects rm command 240
version property in package.json 255
VS Code 352
  settings 411–412
  Svelte 3 Snippets extension 413–414
  Svelte for VS Code extension 412
  Svelte Intellisense extension 414
Vue, compared to Svelte 17

W

WAVE 216, 223–225
Web Components 256–260
Web workers 322
Webpack 345–346
webpack.config.js file 345
webView component of Svelte Native 358, 368, 373
Window object of DOM 160, 251, 279, 288, 326
workbench.editor.labelFormat option of VS Code 276
wrapLayout of Svelte Native 362
writable store function 107, 122

Z

z-index 132

The Design of Web APIs
by Arnaud Lauret
Foreword by Kin Lane

ISBN 9781617295102
392 pages, $44.99
October 2019

Hugo in Action
by Atishay Jain

ISBN 9781617297007
350 pages, $49.99
Est. publication Spring 2021

Micro Frontends in Action
by Michael Geers

ISBN 9781617296871
296 pages, $49.99
Est. publication September 2020

For ordering information go to www.manning.com

RELATED MANNING TITLES

React Hooks in Action
by John R. Larsen

ISBN 9781617297632
250 pages, $39.99
October 2020

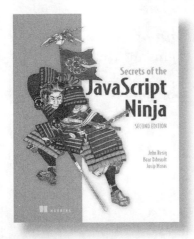

Secrets of the JavaScript Ninja, Second Edition
by John Resig, Bear Bibeault, and Josip Maras

ISBN 9781617292859
464 pages, $44.99
August 2016

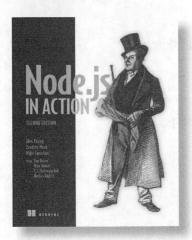

Node.js in Action, Second Edition
by Alex Young, Bradley Meck, and Mike Cantelon
with Tim Oxley, Marc Harter, T.J. Holowaychuk, and
Nathan Rajlic

ISBN 9781617292576
392 pages, $49.99
August 2017

For ordering information go to www.manning.com

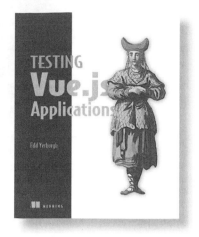
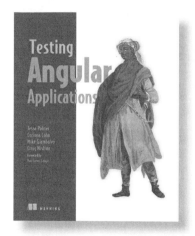
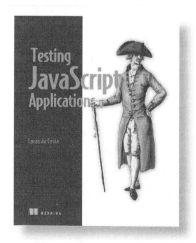